"THE MOVIES ARE"

Carl Sandburg's Film Reviews and Essays, 1920-1928

edited and with historical commentary by
Arnie Bernstein

with an introduction by
Roger Ebert

First Edition

LAKE CLAREMONT PRESS

4650 North Rockwell Street • Chicago, Illinois 60625
www.lakeclaremont.com

"The Movies Are": Carl Sandburg's Film Reviews and Essays, 1920-1928
edited and with historical commentary by Arnie Bernstein

Published October, 2000 by:

4650 N. Rockwell St.
Chicago, IL 60625
773/583-7800; lcp@lakeclaremont.com
www.lakeclaremont.com

Publisher's Cataloging-in-Publication
(Provided by Quality Books, Inc.)

Sandburg, Carl, 1878-1967.
    "The movies are" : Carl Sandburg's film reviews and
essays, 1920-1928 / edited and with historical
commentary by Arnie Bernstein. — 1st ed.
    p. cm.
    Includes bibliographic references (p.) and index.
    ISBN: 1-893121-05-4
    LCCN: 00-104576

    1. Motion pictures—Reviews. 2. Sandburg, Carl,
1878-1967—Knowledge—Performing arts. 3. Film
criticism—United States—Authorship. I. Bernstein,
Arnie. II. Title

PN1995.S36 2000   791.43'75
                 QBI00-901207

**Printed in the United States of America by United Graphics,
an employee-owned company based in Mattoon, Illinois.**

04 03 02 01 00   10 9 8 7 6 5 4 3 2 1

For Gene and Sheila,
who wisely encoded my DNA
with a passion for the written word

Publisher's Credits

Cover Design by Timothy Kocher. Interior Design by Sharon Woodhouse.
Layout by Ken Woodhouse and Sharon Woodhouse. Editing by Bruce Clorfene.
Proofreading by Gabriel Robinson, Sharon Woodhouse, Karen Formanski, Ken Woodhouse,
and Amy Formanski. Photos from the collection of Arnie Bernstein and Scott Tambert
of Public Domain Images. Author photo by Holly Pluard. Index by Ken Woodhouse,
Sharon Woodhouse, Karen Formanski, and Jennifer Smith. The text of *The Movies Are*
was set in California Condensed with heads in Edifice.

Contents

Acknowledgments vi

Preface—"The Movies Are" by Carl Sandburg vii

Introduction by Roger Ebert ix

Carl Sandburg and "The Movies Are"
by Arnie Bernstein 3

Reviews and Essays

1920 15

1921 45

1922 109

1923 155

1924 201

1925 245

1926 293

1927 333

1928 369

Appendix 371

Notes 373

Bibliography 377

Index 381

About the Authors 399

Acknowledgments

First and foremost Cheryl Diddia-Bernstein, whose love and support makes everything possible.

Roger Ebert, a man whose love for film and Chicago journalism is unequaled, for providing this book's introduction.

Steve Jones, Jennifer Karre, and Benjamin Nemenoff, the three hardest working research assistants in publishing, whose tireless dedication helped this project see the light of day.

The resources of the University of Illinois Library at Urbana-Champaign; the Harold Washington Library of Chicago; the Chicago Historical Society; and the Carl Sandburg State Historic Site in Galesburg, Illinois.

Holly Pluard, photographer extraordinaire; Susan Lorenz, my favorite Josef von Sternberg expert; Bob Blinn of Columbia College for all the usual reasons; Charles and Nancy Diddia for their continued faith; Stuart Cleland; and Dann Gire of the Chicago Film Critics Association

The wonderful folks in cyberspace who hang out at alt.movies.silent.

The National Writers Union and Alan Jacobson for professional and legal advice respectively.

My favorite book lovers: Hannah Lynn, Cameron Michael, and Jack Nicholas Peirce; and Meghan Leigh and Lauren Jean Diddia.

Bruce Eldon Clorfene for his yeoman's editorial job.

Sharon Woodhouse of Lake Claremont Press whose wisdom, encouragement, and many other fine qualities made the dream happen again.

And my third grade teacher, the late Suzanne Tanny, who first introduced me to Carl Sandburg. I still remember that report Miss Tanny, and I hope I've done you proud.

Preface

The Movies Are

by Carl Sandburg
Saturday, December 18, 1926

At regular intervals we meet the intelligent and cultivated person of refinement who feels that the movies are not entitled to much observation or consideration from those who are looking forward toward a higher human uplift.

Usually, we find that such persons consider *Black Beauty* quite a horse and the book about *Black Beauty* should be in the list of every young child's reading. Or they believe that *Bob, Son of Battle* or Buck, the dog of Jack London's *Call of the Wild* are important dogs for young people to know about.

Yet such is the swiftness of our motion picture civilization, and so wide the extent of the photoplay area of display, that it is easily safe to say, that there are hundreds of thousands of children, as well as young and old people, who are familiar with certain horses and dogs of the films, but have never heard of these other animals.

A hundred thousand are familiar with Tony, the Tom Mix horse, for a thousand who know Black Beauty.

A hundred thousand and more are close acquaintances with Rin-Tin-Tin as compared with the thousand or less who know Buck or White Fang or Bob, Son of Battle.

And the movie fans know these animals in a way that readers of books of fiction seldom know their animals.

Black Beauty, for instance, is taken as handed on; it does not smite its beholders wit the living glow and shine of Tom Mix's Tony, pawing his hoofs and impatiently waiting for his master or arching his glossy neck as the master pets him after a fast ride dripping with sweat and defeating the enemies of justice.

We recall two men in argument once about Shakespeare, one of them summarizing it with "Shakespeare is."

The movies are.

Men and women of culture may be aloof as they please, or they may try to look at them patronizingly, with no eye for the motives of producers and no ear for the points urged by Elder Will Hays.

The cold, real, upstanding fact holds—the movies are. They come so close to pre-empting some functions hitherto held exclusively by the school and university systems that the philosopher of civilization who doesn't take them into consideration with broad, sympathetic measurement is in danger of being in the place of the drum major of the band who marched up a side street while the band went straight along on the main stem—without leadership.

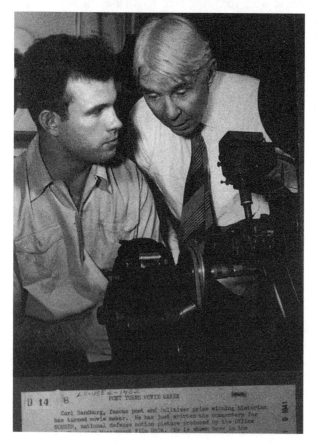

Long after Sandburg's days as a film critic for the *Chicago Daily News*, when he was living in Michigan, Carl Sandburg was briefly involved in another aspect of the movie industry. As the caption (*left*) explains: "POET TURNS MOVIE MAKER. Carl Sandburg, famous poet and Pulitzer prize winning historian has turned movie maker. He has just written the commentary for BOMBER, national defense motion picture produced by the Office for Emergency Management Film Unit."

Introduction

by Roger Ebert

I am writing these words in Michigan, at our summer home. This morning as every morning when the weather permits I walked down wooded lanes that took me to Poet's Path in Birchwood, the road leading past the home where Carl and Lilian Sandburg lived from the late 1920s until 1945, when they moved to North Carolina. Their house still stands, defiantly in violation of later regulations about height and position, its foundations cut into a dune. On the land side it rises five stories, on the Lake Michigan side three, a New England shore house with a widow's walk on the roof.

I have been up there, climbed the ship's ladder to the lookout over the lake to the west and the ravine to the north that carries into the lake a creek that generations of children have redirected with dams of sand. I know this because two of those children, Rob and Rick Edinger, are my neighbors, born on the property they still occupy, and when they were boys they used to dam the creek, and milk Lilian Sandburg's herd of goats, which won blue ribbons at the Berrien County and Michigan State Fairs. A recent owner of the Sandburg house showed me its most unusual feature, a fireproof walk-in bank vault which Sandburg installed to protect his collection of Abraham Lincoln papers and manuscripts. He did not trust the volunteer firemen to arrive in time.

During his residence in the house, Sandburg was writing the third through fifth volumes of his Pulitzer Prize-winning biography of Lincoln. The owner showed me a photograph of the author, bare chested, sitting in the sun on an upended orange crate on a topmost deck overlooking the ravine, writing on an improvised desk. Rick and Rob remember his daily walks on the beach, when he seemed so deep in thought he hardly noticed the world around him. They have both told me, and swear it is true, that one day as a joke they persuaded a tall friend to walk down the beach dressed as Abraham Lincoln in frock coat and top hat. "Good morning, Mr. Sandburg," the figure said. Sandburg glanced up and said, "Good morning, Mr. Lincoln," continuing on his way.

The Michigan years came as Sandburg, by then nearly 50, had enough of an independent income to free himself from daily journalism. The first volumes of the Lincoln biography must have supplied the couple with funds to move to Michigan and buy a substantial house (larger and more imposing than their home in North Carolina, judging by photographs of it).

Commuting to Chicago in those days would have been by the interurban South Shore Line, which came as far as Michigan City, Indiana, before curving down toward South Bend. That would have been an hour's drive to the station in those days; perhaps it was quicker for them to go up to Benton Harbor and take the ferry across—the same ferry that brought Saul Bellow's Augie March to his summer adventures in Michigan. Neither route would have been that quick, and perhaps the Sandburgs were happy to be free of Chicago and daily deadlines.

It has been widely known that Sandburg reviewed movies for the *Chicago Daily News*, but I confess I thought he did it only occasionally. Now here is this huge book of his reviews, which even at some 400 pages provides only a portion of his output. These collected reviews show that Sandburg was not a hobbyist in his film criticism, but a professional who worked hard at it for eight years. Arnie Bernstein says that Sandburg saw the movies on a Sunday and wrote his week's reviews the same day, which, even allowing for the shorter running times of most films in those days, made up a long day's work. (His haste at times is perhaps revealed by the Harold Lloyd picture he praises but neglects to name.)

Many of the programs, especially in the Loop and in the ornate Balaban & Katz neighborhood palaces, would have been supported by stage shows, vaudeville or orchestras, but the live performances were not usually reviewed by Sandburg, perhaps because the *Daily News* had another man assigned to that task.

Chicago in the 1920s and earlier was the hub of several vaudeville wheels, including Radio-Keith-Orpheum (RKO), which sent the Marx Brothers revolving through the small cities of Iowa and Illinois. When I interviewed Groucho Marx in 1972 he recalled going to the movies with Carl Sandburg, adding that the theaters were warmer than the rooming houses where his mother Minnie lodged the brothers. "He would fall asleep and I would wake him up after the movie was over and tell him what it was about," Groucho told me, but he was kidding. Sandburg was an attentive and observant critic, and moreover, his reviews lack the mischief that Groucho no doubt would have supplied.

One thing you notice, reading through this almost daily coverage of the emerging art form, was that Sandburg took film matter-of-factly. Today shelves groan under the weight of analysis of the silent period, the comedies alone occupying dozens of volumes, but to Sandburg they were not timeless art but movies, meant to be enjoyed; one senses he did not think they were as important as the older arts he considers in his *Collected Poems*, where there are many poems about writers, artists, musicians, and all manner of tradesmen and citizens, but hardly any about the movies.

It is interesting that two of the poets most associated with Illinois, Carl Sandburg and Vachel Lindsay, both devoted a great deal of their time to film criticism. Lindsay's book *The Art of the Film* collects longer essays of a theoretical nature, in which he was able to look at the earliest films and detect trends that are still visible today. Sandburg takes the view not of a theorist but of a daily newspaperman whose job is to steer readers toward the good movies and away from the bad ones.

One of his strengths is in seeing the importance of movies as a popular phenomenon. "Is it possible that an extraordinarily good motion picture play can be made from a Harold Bell Wright novel?" he asks, and the answer is yes. He writes:

"Culturally speaking, there are arguments to be made that Hollywood—for real or woe—is more important than Harvard, Yale or Princeton, singly or collectively." He keeps an open mind when going to movies of the broadest possible appeal. He likes Tom Mix's horse, Tony, almost as much as Tom Mix, and then develops an enthusiasm for Tom's dog, Duke. But it is possible to detect a smile, and perhaps a whiff of Mark

Twain, in his writing about a picture like *The Sheik*. "The book had sentences such as 'Kiss me, little piece of ice,' but all lines like that were cut out of the movie and it was so different in that respect from the book that it was a disappointment to all who read the book on account of how wicked it was."

There are also echoes of Twain's uncoiling colloquialisms, with a zing at the end, in this wonderful long sentence from his review of a film of the Dempsey-Firpo fight: "Some think Dempsey is knocked through the ropes, and then comes back through the ropes, there is some guessing about where he has been in the meantime, while he has been gone, who picked him up, what they said to the champion, whether he thanked them kindly, and if the Marquis of Queensbury rules cover the point of who shall help and how much they shall help and in exactly what way they shall help a fighter

knocked through the ropes and off the platform."

Many of Sandburg's lines conceal sly depths. One of my favorites: "The acting of Lillian Gish in *Orphans of the Storm* is believed by some of her friends to be the best she has done."

Sandburg shared the opinion, universally held at the time, that Chaplin was a genius and Lloyd and Keaton only very good clowns. He wrote that each relied on specialties: "Chaplin on his supreme talent as an actor, Lloyd upon novelty and Keaton upon droll 'gags'." That Buster wears better today as an actor might surprise him, but at least he knew how good Keaton was. As Bernstein points out, Sandburg preferred William C. de Mille to his elder brother Cecil B. (he bet on the wrong pony in that race), and shows an ease in moving between genres as he suggests C. B. might profitably study Keaton's *My Wife's Relations* and "learn something." There are a lot of interviews here, as Sandburg talked to luminaries on their way through town. In those days and for decades later, until jet planes replaced train travel, stars and directors took the Sante Fe Super Chief to Chicago, lunched with the press, and the continued to New York on the 20th Century Limited. He spoke with his hero von Sternberg, his favorite William de Mille, and Constantin Stanislavski, the great theater director, who told him in 1923 that the movies "have not even begun to be an art." (This in contrast to Stanislavski's countryman Tolstoy, who before his death in 1910 was already predicting that film would take the place of the novel in the new century.)

Sometimes Sandburg is a schoolmaster, praising *The Hunchback of Notre Dame* for its artistry and its Lon Chaney performance, but flunking its inter-titles: "And why spell forsworn wrong? Why not use some other word you know how to spell rather than bluff?" At other times he is simply a fan, and his greatest enthusiasms stand up to the test of time. He says he has seen Fairbanks Senior's *The Thief of Bagdad* three times, and wants to see it three more, and his praise is Whitmanesque: "Old and young enjoy it and derive new health from it."

Sandburg left the movie beat in 1928, which was the year when silent films died. It was also "the greatest year in the history of the movies," according to the director Peter Bogdanovich, who featured its films in a revival program at the Telluride Film Festival a few years ago. If he is right, 1928 saw the summit of silent art, followed by the cramped compromises of the early years of sound. Sandburg took the transition in stride; he observed in November 1927 of *The Jazz Singer* that "The vitaphone did a great deal to help, reproducing the songs and some of the other sounds in the course of the action." He resists the temptation to quote "You ain't heard nothin' yet."

Arnie Bernstein has performed an extraordinary accomplishment in bringing this book into being. Having tried to track down some of my own relatively recent reviews I know what a scandalously bad job is done of preserving runs of daily newspapers. All of these reviews had to be located, identified, and transcribed. To that enormous task Bernstein adds great knowledge and insight in his introductions to the reviews, providing background, orientation, historical information, helpful footnotes. This is a book that reopens a chapter of journalism and history that might have remained closed forever.

"THE MOVIES ARE"

"Another comic? I am the cinema expert,
the critic of the silent celluloid for the *Daily News*."

—CARL SANDBURG
IN A LETTER TO ALICE CORBIN HENDERSON,
CO-FOUNDER OF THE JOURNAL *POETRY*,
SEPTEMBER 12, 1920

From the collection of Arnie Bernstein.

Charlie Chaplin and Jackie Coogan in a scene from *The Kid*. Sandburg loved Charlie Chaplin's humanitarian comedy, calling the Little Tramp "the world's greatest Charlie." (Perhaps it's coincidental that as a youth Sandburg insisted on being called "Charlie" rather than "Carl," believing the former moniker sounded more "American." At the urging of his wife-to-be, Lillian Steichen, Sandburg switched back to the name given to him by his immigrant Swedish parents.)

Carl Sandburg and "The Movies Are"

by Arnie Bernstein

Over the course of his long and distinguished career Carl Sandburg earned two Pulitzer prizes—one for poetry and one for biography—but it comes as a surprise to many that this great American writer was also a respected film critic. In 1917 Carl Sandburg was hired as a staff reporter for the Chicago *Daily News*. A native of Galesburg, a small town in western Illinois, Sandburg brought a colorful past to the job. His credentials included Army veteran, traveling salesman, aide to the mayor of Milwaukee, Wisconsin, advocate for the American Socialist party, magazine editor, itinerant journalist, and noted author of the 1916 collection *Chicago Poems.* As a *Daily News* reporter, Sandburg initially reported on labor and other issues. In 1918, Sandburg left the broadsheet to serve as a war correspondent for the Newspaper Enterprise Association, a syndicated news service. After the Armistice, he returned to Chicago and the *Daily News* job. Sandburg's coverage of the race riots that swept Chicago's South Side during the violent summer of 1919 proved his mettle as an investigative reporter.

In autumn of 1920 Sandburg was assigned an unlikely role by his employer—that of staff film critic. This was a bold move on the part of the *Daily News*. Despite the emergence of Charlie Chaplin as a popular entertainer, movies were generally not taken seriously as an art form in most critical circles. Even stage thespians often used the term "legitimate theater" to differentiate themselves from lowly movie players. The idea of critiquing and evaluating movies beyond a cursory treatment was in its infancy.

But then, the *Daily News* was no run-of-the-mill newspaper. In Sandburg's era writers were encouraged by publisher Victor E. Lawson to explore new territories overlooked by other papers. Its no accident that other important Chicago writers, including Ben Hecht and Meyer Levin wrote for the *Daily News* around the same time as Sandburg. Founded in 1875, the paper published six days a week (with no Sunday edition) and offered Chicagoans a wide variety of news, sports, criticism, columnists and other features. The *Daily News* remained a Chicago institution until it folded in 1978. With the death of the *Daily News* Sandburg's film reviews slipped quietly into obscurity. Fortunately these columns became public domain, which allowed me the pleasure and honor of compiling Sandburg's forgotten work for this volume.

On Monday, September 27, 1920, while the front page of the paper carried stories about Chicago baseballs "Black Sox" and the 1919 World Series fix, Sandburg made his critical debut with a review of *Hitchin' Posts*, a now-forgotten Western starring Frank Mayo. Though in a letter to a friend he jokingly referred to himself as the new "cinema expert," Sandburg took his new assignment to heart and quickly became a passionate film advocate. True to his other writing Sandburg was no snob, finding value in all kinds of movies. He loved the psychological depth of director Erich von Stroheim and the formula shoot-'em-up adventures of cowboy star Buck Jones. Sandburg felt equally at home extolling the virtues of artistic European movies as he did in recommending novelty films featuring all-canine or all-monkey casts. He once compared the moody cinematography of a Rin-Tin-Tin picture to that of the German Expressionist classic *The Cabinet of Dr. Caligari*. In his seven and one half years as the "cinema expert," Sandburg developed a distinctive critical voice that ultimately complements his better-known work.

The 1920s were a rich period for filmmakers and moviegoers. Though cinema itself was a little over two decades old when Sandburg began his film critic duties, the medium had come a long way both technically and culturally. Audiences were keenly aware of film grammar—establishing shots, close-ups, editing techniques, and other basics of the medium. Though light entertainment was still enjoyed, filmgoers expected and demanded more sophisticated storytelling techniques.

Screen acting was also becoming more complex. Rather than the overwrought gesturing of early films, by 1920 film pantomime (or "mummery" as Sandburg liked to say) had become much more subtle. In the 1910s Theda Bara ruled the screens as a living embodiment of the predatory feminine "vamp" (short for "vampire"). Though the movie vamp hung on for a few more years, by the mid-1920s she had been replaced by a new feminine icon—the fun-loving flapper as personified by Colleen Moore, Louise Brooks, Joan Crawford, and others. Clean-shaven, earnest young men like William Haines, Wallace Reid, and Charles Ray epitomized the flapper's male counterpart. Comedy entered a golden age with the likes of Charlie Chaplin, Buster Keaton, and Harold Lloyd, while scandal tragically thwarted Roscoe "Fatty" Arbuckle and Mabel Normand. Mary Pickford, Douglas Fairbanks, Lillian Gish, and Gloria Swanson were the new American royalty—all because they had box office appeal. Sex was personified by two Hollywood idols: Rudolph Valentino and Clara Bow.

The 1920s were a unique period in American history, full of energetic and maddening contradictions. Jazz had wafted up from New Orleans and trumpeted its way into American culture. So profound was the influence of this music, writer F. Scott Fitzgerald dubbed the 1920s as "The Jazz Age." The vigorous sounds of jazz, unfettered by standard rules for music, blew in a newfound sense of freedom that spilled over into other aspects of daily life like fashion, popular entertainment, and sex. Birth control was more openly discussed and with it the "free love" movement. Women had a new sense of empowerment now that they could vote. Hemlines went up, inhibitions went down.

This cultural freedom was countered by other events. At first the world seemed "safe for democracy" with the Allied victory in the Great War. But with the Bolshevik overthrow of the Czarist reign in Russia, the American government got Red-scared. Attorney General A. Mitchell Palmer demanded Communism be uprooted in America. Smashing the apparent good feelings of post-World War One society, in the early 1920s federal agents were dispatched to find radicals—and it didn't matter that many of these firebrands had committed no crime. More than 5,000 people were arrested in the so-called "Palmer Raids."

Other stories rocked the nation. It was the age of Sacco and Vanzetti, two Italian immigrants executed for murder, though the pair was most likely convicted for their anarchist politics rather than the flimsy evidence used to prosecute them. In Tennessee, public schoolteacher John Scopes ignited a firestorm when he deliberately violated state law by teaching Darwin's theory of evolution rather than the Biblical story of creation. And in Sandburg's Chicago, the world was shocked when Nathan Leopold and Richard Loeb committed the first "Crime of the Century." The duo murdered a local schoolboy just for the thrill of it, then escaped the death penalty when their lawyer, Clarence Darrow, pleaded mental illness as motivation. (Darrow also defended Scopes in court.)

Then there was Prohibition, the biggest checkrein of them all. In 1920 the Volstead Act became law, slapping the 18th Amendment onto the Constitution and supposedly making the United States a booze-free zone. Instead, and to no great surprise, the liquor industry went underground. People were going to drink regardless of the law. Prohibition gave rise to a clandestine commerce of speakeasies, bathtub gin, needle beer, and bootlegging. Al Capone, another famous Chicagoan of the Jazz Age, may have been considered a public enemy by some but Scarface saw himself as an entrepreneur. His clientele eagerly forked over their hard-earned salaries for his products, a prime selection of liquor, women, and political power. Consequently, as a necessary business expense, part of Capone's profits went into the pockets of Chicago officials and police officers. Human life was another expenditure, with Capone's henchmen battling other gangsters in bloody wars throughout the Chicago area. "My rackets are run strictly on American lines and they're going to stay that way," Capone told one interviewer.[1] In the context of the Roaring Twenties, Scarface had a point. After all, the best booze in the country was stocked in the Oval Office of President Warren G. Harding's corruption-riddled White House.

The movies certainly reflected this paradoxical society, amplifying and exaggerating the elements for entertainment and profit. While the spontaneity celebrated by movies delighted some viewers, it terrified others. A growing fear swept certain quarters that motion pictures were leading America down a depraved road of sex, sin, and hedonistic free-for-all. It didn't help matters when popular stars like Wallace Reid and Barbara La Marr succumbed to narcotics addiction. In 1921 bit player Virginia Rappe died in the aftermath of a booze-laden party thrown by screen comic Roscoe "Fatty" Arbuckle. Though his films were perennial favorites, a trumped-up murder charge got Arbuckle's work yanked from theaters across the country. Never mind that he professed innocence at three trials (and was found "Not Guilty" in the last courtroom after two other juries couldn't decide on a verdict). Policing of the movie industry was demanded. Local and state governments sponsored censorship organizations across the country. At the top of this heap was newly-appointed Hollywood morals czar Will H. Hays, the former United States Postmaster General under President Harding. In his capacity as president of the Motion Picture Producers and Distributors of America,

Photos by Arnie Bernstein.

Sandburg's birthplace at 313 E. 3rd Street in Galesburg, Illinois is an Illinois State Historic Site (*above*). Beneath "Remembrance Rock," named after Sandburg's only novel, are buried the ashes of Sandburg and his wife Lilian (*below*). The landscaping comes from a line in the book: "Here stood four pointed cedars he had planted for the four cardinal points from which any and all winds of destiny and history blow. He named the boulder Remembrance Rock, for it could be a place to come and remember."

Photos by Arnie Bernstein.

Surrounding "Remembrance Rock" is "Quotation Walk," a stone pathway engraved with lines from Sandburg's poetry: "When shall we all speak the same language?" (*above*). "Nothing happens unless first a dream" (*below*).

production codes were enforced to make sure film stars would control their libidos both in front of and away from the movie camera. "This industry must have, toward that sacred thing, the mind of a child, toward that clean virgin thing, that unmarked slate, the same responsibility, the same care about the impressions made upon it, that the best clergyman or the most inspired teacher of youth must have," Hays told the Los Angeles Chamber of Commerce.[2] The movie studios, a growing business force in Southern California, responded in kind, concerned more with the bottom line than artistic integrity. A strict "morals clause" became part of any actor's contract. In a foreshadowing of the 1950s McCarthy Era, a blacklist known as the "Doom Book" circulated among studio officials, listing personalities who were suspected of degenerate behavior. The more things change, the more they stay the same; many of the charges leveled at the movies during the 1920s, including accusations that films encourage sex, violence, and other heinous conduct, have been made by countless watchdog groups over the years.

Unlike fan magazines or gossip sheets, Sandburg rarely reported on Hollywood scandals, preferring to concentrate on the matter at hand—the merits of motion pictures. A vigorous advocate against censorship, Sandburg delighted in pointing out the hypocrisy of the Hays office and other censorship boards. "A kiss or a murder may be done any number of ways in a film," he sarcastically wrote on August 6, 1921. "Producer and censor must talk it over and decide under what circumstances and by what methods it is most advisable to present a kiss or a murder for the view of the youth of the country who go to the movie theaters."

Sandburg was impressed by developments in film technology. He duly reported on new cinematic breakthroughs in color, sound, and other innovations, including three-dimensional movies and motion pictures for the blind. Sandburg was also something of a visionary when it came to film aesthetics and theory. In the 1950s French critics (and later filmmakers) Francois Truffaut and Jean-Luc Goddard championed "the auteur (author) theory," which stated a director is to a film what a writer is to a novel. Truffaut and Goddard were predated by Sandburg's more succinct premise, published on November 22, 1922, in a review of the film *For the Land's Sake*. "There is no particular star named as playing in the picture and this perhaps is just as well," Sandburg opined, "because in all pictures the big main star is the director anyhow."

Clearly, as with any film critic, Sandburg had personal predilections that he never hesitated to let show. He constantly exhorted filmmakers to push their creative talents and challenge audiences with intelligent work. Sandburg loved Charlie Chaplin's humanitarian comedy, calling the Little Tramp "the world's greatest Charlie." (Perhaps it's coincidental that as a youth Sandburg insisted on being called "Charlie" rather than "Carl," believing the former moniker sounded more "American." At the urging of his wife-to-be, Lilian Steichen, Sandburg switched back to the name given to him by his immigrant Swedish parents.) William S. Hart and Tom Mix were other Sandburg favorites despite their very different approaches to making Westerns. He often praised the dramatic work of William C. de Mille while damning the sentimental efforts of the director's better-known brother, Cecil B. DeMille. (William and Cecil spelled their surname differently to distinguish each from the other.) Documentaries and newsreel also captured his critical eye. Sandburg loved the natural performances of animal actors, as the essay that serves as this volume's preface shows. He thoroughly enjoyed the thespian abilities of Rin-Tin-Tin and Strongheart, two German shepherds who competed at the box office. Tom Mix's fabled horse Tony was another favorite. And in a seemingly unlikely subject for film criticism, Sandburg devoted an entire column to the natural cinematic talents of fish.

Sandburg had his critical weaknesses, however. He was a tireless champion of D. W. Griffith, the pioneering director who pushed cinematic storytelling to heightened artistic levels with such films as *Intolerance, Broken Blossoms*, and his groundbreaking, though troubling, Civil War tale *The Birth of a Nation*. Griffith reached his pinnacle in the late 1910s. His career went into severe decline in the mid-1920s, and by the end of the decade Griffith's sentimental, Victorian view of the world clearly was out of step with Roaring Twenties mores. Sandburg usually overlooked the once-great director's faults, though he occasionally offered a begrudging comment on Griffith's diminishing talents.

"How can photoplays of today be preserved for future generations?" Sandburg wrote on April 13, 1922. "Will school pupils in 6922, or even 1000 years from now, be able to study early examples of the cinema art as pupils of 1922 study Virgil and Homer?" His words were prophetic. Depending on which source you believe, between 60 and 90 percent of all films made during the silent era have disappeared. The reasons for this are many. Studios, lacking a broad perspective, often tossed out the only existing copies of many films since the reels took up too much storage space. In the sound era, the highly flammable nitrate film on which many silents were photographed served another purpose—they provided wonderful kindling for movie fire sequences. Next time you watch Atlanta burn in *Gone With the Wind*, realize that these flames are probably being stoked by movie history. Other films simply deteriorated with age, transforming movie art to dust-covered reels of celluloid. Thankfully, some films were never returned to the distributor. Consequently long-missing silent films have turned up in some rather amazing places. A complete print of Theodor Dreyer's masterpiece *The Passion of Joan of Arc* was found in a closet of a Norwegian mental hospital. A cache of silent era films was discovered buried beneath a swimming pool in Alaska. Yet for all these wonderful finds, it remains a sad fact that much of the work of so many important film artists, including Charlie Chaplin, Buster Keaton, Mabel Normand, Lon Chaney, and director Josef von Sternberg, will never be seen by latter-day audiences. In this respect, Sandburg's reviews and essays are even more important to contemporary readers. The very act of movie-going has changed dramatically since the 1920s. In an era where movies are watched on cable television, video playback machines, and sterile cineplexes, Sandburg's look at theatrical presentation of silent film is all that more important. Consider Sandburg as a reporter on the frontlines of a world that no longer exists. He was seeing these movies as they were intended to be seen: in large movie theaters, complete with live music and vaudeville entertainment to supplement the on-screen enjoyment. A typical program of the 1920s might include a live performance, a newsreel, a cartoon, a two-reel comedy, perhaps a boxing film, and the main feature. Sandburg considered audiences an important component of the film-going experience and often reported theatergoers' comments.

Sandburg's typical routine was to watch movies on Sundays, write a week's worth of reviews and his Saturday column, then devote the rest of the week to his other work. Lectures, poetry readings, and folk music concerts supplemented Sandburg's income while he began research on what would become his six-book epic on the life of Abraham Lincoln. In 1926, with the publication of *The Prairie Years*, the first two volumes in his Lincoln biography, Sandburg was able to move in new directions. During the 1920-1928 period, Sandburg also published his fourth volume of poetry, *Slabs of the Sunburnt West*, the children's book *Rootabaga Pigeons*, and his documentary study of indigenous music, *The American Songbag*. Though he continued to write film reviews, his Saturday essay was replaced with a twice-a-week column called "From the Notebook of Carl Sandburg." This new editorial venue allowed Sandburg to ponder a variety of topics within the pages of the *Daily News*.

Unlike his *Daily News* colleague Hecht, Sandburg's own forays into film production were unremarkable. In 1929, D. W. Griffith approached Sandburg to consult on the director's upcoming cinematic biography of Abraham Lincoln. Though Sandburg expressed some interest in the project, his salary demands were higher than what Griffith was willing to pay. In the mid-1940s Metro-Goldwyn-Mayer offered Sandburg a unique opportunity. He was asked to write an epic novel about the American spirit, which the studio would then turn into a film. Initially given nine months to complete his book, Sandburg ended up working several years on what became his only novel, *Remembrance Rock*. Ultimately MGM passed on the project. Finally, in the early 1960s, Sandburg was asked by director George Stevens for assistance in writing a screen version of the Gospels. Unfortunately this movie biography of Jesus Christ, *The Greatest Story Ever Told*, was a financial and artistic fiasco. Sandburg's efforts were negligible, lost amidst the cumbersome writing credits which read: "Screenplay by James Lee Barrett and George Stevens, based on the Books of the Old and New Testaments, Other Ancient Writings, the Writings of Fulton Oursler and Henry Denker, and in Creative Association with Carl Sandburg." Ironically, in a 1920s poem, Sandburg suggested a dramatization of Jesus fixing nets with fishermen would be more interesting than the standard Hollywood biblical epic.

In my editing process I have brought some uniformity to Sandburg's film reviews. Between 1920 and 1928, Sandburg wrote more than 2,000 film-related columns. Within this mass of material, there was no one consistent standard of writing. For example, Sandburg might spell out numbers and use numerals within the same piece. To maintain uniformity, I have spelled out the numbers one through nine and used numerals for higher digits. For those unfamiliar with Chicago theater history, I have fully identified movie palaces where Sandburg simply used a truncated name; thus, as example, "Barbee's" becomes "Barbee's Loop Theater." Additionally, some words have changed spelling throughout the years. Sandburg's spelling of the word "okay," for instance, was "okeh." Another example is "to-day" and "to-morrow." In most such cases I have deferred to modern spellings. Typographical errors and misspellings, the bane of the newspaper industry, have also been cleaned up.

In instances where Sandburg clearly was using colloquialisms and personalized spellings (such as "p'tickler" for "particular") the words are untouched. "Slang," as Sandburg liked to say, "is language that rolls up its sleeves, spits on its hands and goes to work." If anything, a few of these pieces are celebrations of that axiom. Some Western film reviews, for example, openly pay homage to "cowpoke" vernacular. Additionally, Sandburg loved to play with language and would sometimes invent words within the context of his column. Generally these "Sandburgisms" make sense, though an occasional word might have readers scratching their heads. For example, combine "vivid" with "audience" and you have Sandburg's unique portmanteau word "vividence." As a critic, Sandburg also had a special accolade for films and filmmakers he particularly admired. Years before Gene Siskel and Roger Ebert applied their thumbs to movie reviewing, Sandburg insisted that good work be "handed a bun."

Because of deadline pressures and the speed Sandburg needed to write his column, there are occasional solecisms in these reviews and essays. His most consistent problem is the run-on sentence. Yet these shouldn't be considered reflections on Sandburg's ability as a writer; rather the grammatical missteps are a historical marker on how quickly Sandburg had to write his column and get it to the editor before the paper was laid out, went to press, and hit the streets. There just wasn't time to be neat.

Readers of *The Movies Are* should also note that some words Sandburg uses have changed meaning over the years. The most notable example in these pages is "gay." A word Sandburg often relied on, a few of these reviews provide unintended double entendres in light of "gay" etymology. Clearly, Sandburg's intent with the word is "merry" rather than sexual preferences.

Reviews and essays are more or less laid out chronologically as published in the *Daily News.* Keep in mind that opening dates for movies during the 1920s were not as uniform as they are today. A film with a November opening in New York might not reach Chicago until the following March. Consequently, you will find several reviews that do not correspond to the "official" release year. Movie reviews are headed by the title of the film; original headlines are used for the essays, unless none was provided. In these latter cases I have written a headline that is in keeping with the subject matter and *Daily News* standards.

Sandburg often wrote multiple pieces on films he passionately cared about. In such cases I have followed the original critique with subsequent reviews in chronological order. For example, Sandburg first wrote about *Nanook of the North* on Saturday, September 2, 1922. Successive pieces were written in September and October; however, all reviews will be found under the September, 1922, *Nanook of the North* entry.

Sandburg was the *Daily News* film critic from the fall of 1920 through mid-1928. I have ended this anthology, however, in January, 1928. There are a few reasons behind this decision. In 1927, Sandburg's byline on the film column was dropped. Though he still remained in the position for another year and a half, Sandburg was turning his attention and talent to new venues. "From the Notebook of Carl Sandburg" was increasingly becoming his main forum at the *Daily News,* and there are some suggestions that the movie column may have been occasionally written by other reporters in the spring of 1928. By February there were subtle changes to some film reviews which indicate either Sandburg was modifying his style or someone else may have been assisting Sandburg with the writing. In June, Clark Rodenbach took over the reviewing tasks. Consequently, rather than risk using non-Sandburg material for this volume I have edited on the side of caution. The last review of *The Movies Are* is appropriately *London After Midnight.* One of the silent era's great "lost films," this Lon Chaney/Tod Browning collaboration has attained the kind of cult status among movie fans normally earned by films still in circulation.

My biggest regret is that I could not include more of Sandburg's reviews; however, space limitations necessitated that I boil down some 2,000-plus pieces to a publishable length. As a result, I have tried to include a broad selection, ranging from obscure and forgotten works to movie classics, so that the reader can have a better overall understanding of Sandburg's scope as film critic.

In adding historical context, my goal was to provide readers with insight on the overall world of movies in the 1920s. Though, as previously stated, Sandburg rarely discussed Hollywood scandal, he sometimes alluded to off-screen headlines, such as in his review of Mabel Normand's *Mickey.* Consequently, in order for the modern reader to completely understand and appreciate Sandburg's work, I have filled in the details. I've also included production, biographical, and historical information when appropriate.

Readers should know a few 1920s cinematic terms. Movies were often referred to as "photoplays" or "photodramas." A "silversheet" was the movie screen. The number of reels in a film usually clocked movie running times. Short subjects were commonly referred to as "two-reelers"; feature-length films could run anywhere from four to eight reels and more. Generally speaking, a silent movie reel was ten minutes long. "Presenters" was another term for producers. Subtitles (or "title cards") were an art form in and of themselves. A necessary element in order to convey dialog or action, a gifted subtitle writer could make a good living in the silent era. As a poet, Sandburg understood the talent necessary to convey a wealth of ideas with just a few carefully chosen words. Consequently, he sometimes critiqued subtitles within the course of a film review.

My original intent with *The Movies Are* was to provide readers with Sandburg's perceptions of the movies; however, the subject matter demanded much more. Happily, the concept of this book has grown from a compilation of little-known work by one of America's great writers into a celebration of both the man and the movies. The title comes from the Sandburg column used as this volume's preface. A deliberate choice on my part, the title *The Movies Are* is something of a tribute to the name of Sandburg's book-length 1936 prose poem *The People, Yes.* Like the American people he loved so dearly, Sandburg was a fervent advocate of silent film. His passion for cinema sings loudly in every sentence of his *Daily News* reviews.

The folksy humor of Will Rogers held great appeal for Carl Sandburg.

1920

September

Hitchin' Posts

Though Sandburg may have written some film reviews in the summer, this was his first byline as the Daily News*'s movie critic. Typically, Sandburg stresses the American aspects of this Western. As he imitates the "cowpoke" slang, Sandburg's critical voice comes through loud and clear.*

Monday, September 27, 1920

The Mississippi River is to America what the Thames is to England and the Seine to France. As the Volga is to Russia and the Rhine to Germany, so is the Father of Waters to the U.S.A. *Hitchin' Posts* takes the Mississippi River just after the Civil War and uses it for the scenery and background of a melodrama. Later the scenery changes to western country, presumably Oklahoma, and a land rush is staged.

Being a melodrama of impossibly good and impossibly bad people, the play works out that old motif of melodrama: a good man and a bad man whose life paths are crossed by the footsteps and voices of a good woman and a bad woman.

If one should draw a keen Harry Hansen distinction, one might say that with the human element removed, this play would have considerable validity as an art project. The Mississippi River and the Oklahoma land rush save it as a drama. A big river and a few good horses will save most any drama. When this film is shipped to Czechoslovakia and there presented for the workmen and peasants, we can well understand how it will stimulate emigration. *Hitchin' Posts* hits off what folks usually mean by the remark that this is a "big country."

Here we have Frank Mayo in the role of a river steamboat gambler, a southern war derelict who collects the wherewithal of life by his skill in poker. He holds four deuces as against the three aces of an almost bankrupt planter and thus wins a bill of sale to four racehorses. The planter kills himself, even though the gambler tells him he doesn't want the four racehorses.

Such is melodrama. It begins with a gambler who offers to give back to his victim what is won from him. Then there is a villain, one real, solid, blown-in-the-bottle melodrama villain. If he orders a cuppa coffee it must be with a sneer. When he shoots at the hero in a close-up he misses. The miraculous bullets that graze heroes and let 'em live on to be more and more heroic!

See this play for the Mississippi River, the Oklahoma land rush and the pathos of characters too good or too bad to be true to life and yet not fantastic enough to carry us away from realities.

October

Ain't Nature Wonderful in New Science Films

Sandburg's discussion of goat-raising in this newsreel foreshadowed events in his own family. In her later years, Sandburg's wife, Lilian Steichen, won numerous awards for her skills in breeding these farm animals. This review is the first of many Sandburg would write in praise of "real life" as movie fodder.

Saturday, October 2, 1920

The Goldwyn-Bray Pictograph recently has brought out educational films that go thoroughly into scientific explanation of things. A cycle of plant life is shown. The seed drops from a plant, rain drives the seed into the soil, the shoots expand, the plant rises above ground and takes form like its ancestor.

Also the subject of goatraising is handled lucidly. A model goat farm is exhibited in action. One is told a first rate goat costs 10 cents a day to keep and it gives five quarts of milk. Moreover, goat milk is declared by the medical fraternity to be free from the tuberculoid germs that may threaten cow's milk.

So far this observer is able to take notice the people like these informational films. As the Goldwyn-Bray pictograph shows a cycle of plant life or a goat farm, it has as much fascination, fun, human interest and general kick of life as the best photoplays. And the after effect is far better and steadier than what follows a feed of melodrama diet. It may be a personal prejudice but we are sure and clear cut in our decision that much of the best science can be ritualized and put on the screen so that audience will enjoy it and will get a taste that calls them back for more.

Tiger's Cub

Pearl White is best remembered as the star of the silent suspense serial, The Perils of Pauline *(1914). Each week White would thrill moviegoers with a new adventure leading up to the inevitable "cliffhanger" ending and the promise of more excitement in the next week's episode. This review, along with its follow-up, highlights Sandburg's role of critic as advocate for realism—albeit a humorous advocate!*

Monday, October 11, 1920

Tiger's Cub, with Pearl White in the leading role, is a Fox production, directed by Charles Giblyn. It's a Klondike picture full of snow, ice, log cabins, macinaws, gamblers and much other scenery and character, but always snow in the foregrounds. Sometimes the people in this film are not like real people, but the snow background is always an honest snow and convinces.

Drammer, solid melodrammer, is what we have here. The old theme of a cold, bitter world of struggle and righteous people eventually triumphant over the wicked, is developed. The girl who ain't got any name except a nickname of "Cub" given her by her gambler father, "Tiger," turns out to be no legitimate daughter of a gambler at all. Instead, she comes from a respectable family—as the plot unfolds. Likewise, the baby they find in her possession is—as the plot unfolds—not her own love child at all, but one which she rescued because of her good heart. Pearl White enacts this role the heroine in true Pearl White Style. And no Pearl White fan should neglect seeing her in her latest.

PEARL WHITE
Starring In Fox Productions

From the collection of Arnie Bernstein.

Pearl White, star of *Tiger's Cub*, is best remembered as the star of the silent suspense serial, *The Perils of Pauline* (1914).

Audiences enjoy this photoplay. It achieves its purpose of delivering thrills—not wild and breath-taking thrills, but good solid melodrama thrills. It does not quite wrench forth tears. But it does lead folks to feel sorry for the character to whom life is cruel and for whom life in the happy end turns out gladness.

Thomas Carrigan is the actor who plays David Summers, newly arrived in the Klondike and immediately flung into a struggle with malefactors for the possession of his father's gold mine and the winning of the heart and hand of the gambler's supposed daughter, Tiger's Cub.

David arrives in the Klondike with a perfect A No. 1 latest model haircut. The barber on the ship bringing him to the Klondike must have cut this hero's hair on the last day aboard ship. Months later, however, as the plot unfolds far in the trackless wilds of Alaska, the hero maintains this same perfect, unquestionable haircut.

If Thomas Carrigan again acts the part of a clean sport and a hard guy in the trackless wilds of Alaska, where the thermometer is remorseless and haircuts come high and seldom, we trust he will see that the thatch of his head bears some resemblance to that of one carving his way to fortune and love, in a hard country on the fringe of the primitive; let the roughnecks appear with their necks rough.

Tuesday, November 22, 1920

Gov. Thomas Rigg of Alaska has written to Edward Sloman, director of the Jack London story, *Burning Daylight*, saying it's a good photoplay but "the wearing of shoes in Alaska is impossible."

"Being an old dog-musher myself, I think I can speak authoritatively," continues the governor. The director makes acknowledgement of the tip.

The observer who writes these commentaries is still waiting for an acknowledgement from the director of *Tiger's Cub*, expressing thanks because of attention was called herein to the fact that the hero of the play travels five months in the wilderness and then appears with a first class metropolitan haircut.

Convict 13

Convict 13 was something of a family reunion for Buster Keaton, who cast his mother and father in supporting roles. During their vaudeville days, Keaton and his parents performed a knockabout comedy act called "The Three Keatons." Unfortunately, only one reel of this two-reel comedy is known to survive. Sandburg's comment regarding Chicago's execution policy was apt. From its first death penalty case in 1840 through the 1920s, hanging was the preferred method of execution in Cook County.

Tuesday, October 12, 1920

To make a hanging comical is not easy. *Convict 13*, a Metro production with Buster Keaton all over the place, does, however, achieve the result of bringing forth rounds of laughter and bursts of merriment from those who look at the trick gallows and the absurd condemned man bouncing up and down from a rubber elastic rope instead of a hemp. One might almost imagine the Metro company wished to meet Chicago's mood and event in its sending of this photocomedy to this locality during the precise week in which this locality and its governmental agencies are about to execute sentence of the law upon seven men who are to meet doomsday.

Buster Keaton is not as yet up to the classic and classy comedy of Charlie Chaplin. It is a safe comment, however, that he is the nearest rival appearing thus far on the heels of Charlie Chaplin as a great comedian.

Convict 13 is at the Rose Theater this week. The Metro ought to be thanked for this preposterous, boisterous fanfarade of horseplay. We are not sure just when before we have heard such successive splits of laughter as the members of the audience threw at the screen while this was running.

Two Anti-Red Films

As the "Red Scare" of the 1920s continued, some Hollywood forces joined with the blazing anti-Communist crusade. These two releases were typical fare, notable largely for the participation of future cowboy star Edmund "Hoot" Gibson. The final sentence nicely sums up Sandburg's reaction to the political hysteria of the period.

Thursday, October 14, 1920

Two new anti-bolshevist motion picture plays are being released this week by the National Association of the Motion Picture Industry, 1520 Broadway, New York, under the auspices of the Americanization committee of the motion picture industry. Harry M. Crandall of Washington D. C., chairman of the exhibitors' branch of the committee, sends the following statement to exhibitors over the country:

"The making of good Americans in this country is a patriotic duty which appeals to all public-spirited men and women who seek to help serve their community and their nation. All that the exhibitors of the country are asked to do is to run the pictures that are now being made by the various producing companies under the direction of the Americanization committee. These pictures are being made by the biggest men in the industry, and not only do they serve their purpose, but they are especially entertaining as well. As good American citizens, it is up to every exhibitor in this country to take it upon himself to do his share in this work. Never mind what your opposition is doing, you show the picture in your theater. The first picture, *This Land of Opportunity*, you all know was a winner. The second picture, *The Land of Lafayette*, was also well received.

"The two pictures that are to be released are *Strangers Beware* and *One Law for All*. The former picture has been made by Metro. The story and production is by Arthur Zallner. The scenario was completed by Julia Burnham and the picture was directed by Addison Smythe. The story deals with the immigrant coming to this country, and failing to get the spirit of the country. He eventually gets so that he begins to criticize the country whenever he gets a chance. He falls in love with a waitress who endeavors to convince the man that he is wrong in his theory. The climax comes when at a mass meeting the man sees the error of his way, and instead of siding with these men disagrees, and a terrible fight takes place.

"The picture is replete with action and interest is sustained right to the finish. During the past week it has been exhibited privately to a number of people who have announced themselves as very enthusiastic over it. The other new picture has just been completed and will be ready for distribution Oct. 16. It is called *One Law for All* and stars Hoot Gibson. The story was written by Ford Beebe, who has taken great pains to incorporate in his spirit the reasons why American laws, ideals and human relationships are better than any other in the world and why this is the best country to live in. The story is typically Western and should prove to be a big box office attraction."

Local photoplay exhibitors have not as yet announced the dates and the places of presentation for these propaganda films.

Everybody's Sweetheart

Though Sandburg rarely touched on Hollywood scandals, in this review he provided readers with a glimpse of star Olive Thomas's tragic demise. At age 16 Thomas was a star on Broadway and a model for Vogue *magazine. Hollywood quickly noticed her beauty and talent. Signed to a lucrative contract, Thomas's popularity only increased when she married popular leading man Jack Pickford, younger brother of Mary Pickford. Thomas's September, 1920, death by drug overdose in a Paris hotel room rocked Hollywood. Lurid tales of her secret life, and Jack Pickford's by association, made for considerable tabloid fodder. Sandburg, on the other hand, chose to take the higher road and concentrated on Thomas's acting abilities.*

Monday, October 18, 1920

Everybody's Sweetheart is a photoplay featuring Olive Thomas, supported by William Collier, Jr. It is a Select picture.

The attendance at photoplays featuring Olive Thomas, since the dramatic and curious incidents connect with her death from poisoning in Paris, and the grief of the husband, Jack Pickford, has been notable. There is a marked increase of attendance reported by exhibitors for the Olive Thomas films. And still more noticeable is the peculiar interest that attaches to a film portrayal of a girl of winsome personality who has passed on to the shadows.

Everybody's Sweetheart concerns two waifs who live at the poor farm, not knowing who they are and very fond of each other, two play and plot together. An old corporal forms number three of this combination. When by a lucky fate there is a change in the head of the poor farm the three make an escape and in the end arrive at happiness. As a play it gives good opportunity for the gifts that belonged to Olive Thomas.

Staking His Life

William S. Hart was a particular favorite of Sandburg's. A veteran of Broadway, where he earned acclaim for his Shakespearean interpretations, Hart also had a deep passion for the American West. Entering the movie business in 1914 at age 49, he set new standards for screen realism with his no-nonsense portrayal of Western life. It was only natural that Sandburg would be drawn to Hart's work. This review, actually written near the end of Hart's film career, epitomizes everything Sandburg loved about the cowboy star. Sandburg's mention of "Dorchester Avenue" refers to the University of Chicago.

Thursday, October 21, 1920

The latest William S. Hart film play, *Staking His Life*, starts with Bill playing saloonkeeper and gambler, ending with a sign on the front door of the old shebang reading, "This saloon is closed forever. I can quit gambling, you can quit drinking. Signed, Bud Randall."

In the words of the continuity writer, the play is all about "how the light of understanding came to Bud Randall and salvation to Bubbles." The bad woman of the play is "Bubbles," while the extra bad man is The Horned Toad from Bitter Creek.

The ingenuity of the studio group surrounding Bill Hart brings fresh admiration with this film. Haven't they been showing him now for years riding horses, gambling, shooting, getting religion, making sacrifices? And wouldn't we almost think soon they would run out of fresh plots and fresh air and the wild west would go a little stale? Yes, naturally we might presume just such circumstances. But it would be presumptuous on our part.

These studio workers around Bill Hart seem to be what on Dorchester Avenue they call indefatigable. They either give new stuff entirely, or if they use old stuff they make it more refreshingly antique.

Take the dance hall scene in *Staking His Life*. It is probably the best wild west dance hall scene that has come along in screen drama. It is from this dance hall

William S. Hart brought his own brand of realism to Westerns.

From the collection of Arnie Bernstein.

Wm. Hart
IN "THE TWO GUN MAN"

crowd that Bud Randall, played by Bill Hart, picks "Bubbles."

And The Horned Toad from Bitter Creek, he rides into town, has a shooting match with Bud Randall, aims at a gambler and kills a minister of the gospel and rides out of town pursued by other riders, all as though this was the first time this p'tickler thing ever was did. Here, as elsewhere, there are the little touches, the numerous evidences of a thorough job.

"The coral gates are open wide and the parson's passin' through," says Bud Randall to his assembled fellow townsmen, ranchers, cowpunchers and gamblers. He says it with lifted hand. The familiar awesome hush of melodrama spreads over the crowd. Closeups of rough men and rough women show tears down the faces. One wonders what the ghost of Bret Harte would murmur over the adaptations and extensions of his short stories of so many years ago.

Bad men and bad women aplenty here. Yet the appeal to persons of reverence who consider religion and morality not only important but essential, is very direct appeal.

The little touches, the numerous evidences of eager craftsmen and thorough workers is here. They know what is wanted in a Bill Hart play. They know the preferences and prejudices of the Bill Hart clientele and they give 'em what is wanted.

The drive, health and gusto of outdoor mountain people must run through a Bill Hart play. Here again, it's put across. It must be this Bill Hart crowd works outdoors so much. That must be the explanation of why there's never in a William S. Hart play the silly fooling with the darker strands of life and sex sometimes met in films from badly ventilated studios.

The new sweethearts they find for Bill Hart in one play after another shows somebody is on the watch for material of the eternal feminine to match off Bill's eternal masculine. A new skirt for every new play is the working rule here, unchangeable as the laws of Medes and the Persians.

Staking His Life is showing at the Castle Theater this week. It is from the W.M. Productions company.

Indian Supers on "Strike"

Well known as a labor reporter, this item allowed Sandburg an opportunity to address worker/management issues in the movie industry.

Friday, October 22, 1920

Blackfoot Indians of Montana recently refused to fight as "supers" for a moving picture for less than union pay. As a result, a California picture company, which wanted the Indians to appear before the camera, moved on to the Crow reservation of eastern Montana where it was thought Indians could be obtained for lower pay.

Sixty principals and a trainload of equipment were brought to Browning, Mont., by the California people and crack riders came from Great Falls, Havre, Fort Benton and other points to dash before the clicking camera as cavalrymen, pioneers, and other characters of the picture, which was to tell a story of Indian fighting in the early days.

Word also was sent to Flatheads, Boy Chippewas, North Pigeans and Bloods of Canada, all Indian tribes, that 1,500 Indians were wanted. When the Indians were told they were to get half the pay the white men received, they refused, almost unanimously to appear.

Madame Peacock

In 1920 Theda Bara, the silent screen's first "vamp," had left the movies for a return to the "legitimate" theater. Sandburg considered Alla Nazimova to be the inheritor of Bara's vamp image. The Russian-born performer had acted in numerous stage productions, including Ibsen's A Doll's House, The Master Builder, *and* Hedda Gabler, *before turning her talents to film. Though known for personal involvement with Rudolph Valentino—she introduced him to future wives and married Valentino herself—Nazimova was a popular film star in her own right.*

Wednesday, October 27, 1920

With Theda Bara in the legitimate and Nazimova thrust forward in a serpentine, sinewy, cinema presentation, this ought to be a most excellent week to size up she-devils and the she-devil business.

The Nazimova lady comes to us in a vehicle that gives full opportunity for she-devil talents and propensities.

It isn't a vamp part, understand. It's a peacock role. The name of the photoplay, as given at Harry C. Moir's Boston Theater, is *Madame Peacock*. And believe us, this is a good exhibit of the proud, stretching, restless, ambulating bird that spreads its tail feathers and subsists on what Henry Thoreau called "spectatordom."

Madame Nazimova has been seen in plays and parts that had more action, fidelity to art and surer motives than in *Madame Peacock*.

And yet it may be said that all who enjoy the temperamental madame should by all means see her in this, probably the most expensive and sumptuous creation of milliners, designers, and the cut, make and trim artists, in which the madame has yet appeared.

To design gowns for a designing woman is a subtle craft. It is a trifle overdone in this production. There are moments when the close fitting garb so evidently interferes with the free play of the knees of the star actress that the audience loses the thread of the drama and sits wondering about the structural stress of the gown and how much it will stand before it gives way. However, she-devils have their own ways and it may be they are privileged.

Getting to the plot, Madame Peacock is an actress, a star, with temperament to burn. Husband, maid, stage manager, property man, playwright, to them all she manifests her pride and insolence. It must be understood she is The Star. No sooner has she a cigarette in her fingers ready for a smoke than men are ready with lighted matches. It is expected as her due. "Laugh when she laughs or you laugh alone," is the motto of the other members of the cast.

The night comes with a new play when another actress gets all the applause and flowers. As it happens, the new rival is her own daughter. And as the plot runs, the daughter in particular, with the help of the father, softens the heart and brings contrition to the soul of the mother. It ends that way.

So, what with Theda in the legitimate and Nazimova on the silver screen, it is quite a week for she-devils.

What the Ocean Hides

> *Compare the following review to Sandburg's "In a Breath," from* Chicago Poems. *The poem reads, in part, "Inside the playhouse are movies from under the sea. From the heat / of the pavements and the dust of sidewalks, passers-by go in a / breath to be witnesses of large cool sponges, large cool fishes, / large cool valleys and ridges of coral spread silent in the soak / of the ocean floor thousands of years."*

Saturday, October 30, 1920

While Mary Pickford is hunting a new way to twist a maidenly lock of hair down her back, and while Dorothy Dalton or Norma Talmadge is working on new boxes of tricks to fascinate working girls into writing for an autographed photograph, excuse us for mentioning the fact that while we have twice watched audiences at the Castle Theater this week absorbing the Ford educational weekly, we have noticed these audiences keeping tensely quiet. Nobody walked out. There were slight breaths of exclamation and surprise occasionally.

What the Ocean Hides is the title of these reels. Four-fifths of the ball of earth we live on is covered with the ocean. And we all eat fish. Therefore, why not take a little trip with some men in a boat who are very wise about this aforesaid ocean? Instead of hearing and reading about sharks, why not see sharks right where they swim, eat and live?

So we ride out on a boat and see the nets thrown out and the sharks one by one hauled up, knocked on the head, dropped on the bottom of the boat. We see a curiously winged shark, all white on the under side and gray with white spots on the upper side. He is the Whip Ray.

The audience liked the Whip Ray. Some laughed, some took a quick breath. It wasn't education they were getting. They were not bothering about zoology. It was live movie stuff and worth the money.

Later we saw our boat head for shore with enough fish to run the largest hotel for a week or two. Then the sharks were swung on hooks to men who took off the hides to be made into aristocratic leather goods.

It may be noticed that many motion picture theaters consider no week's program complete unless it has a news, scenic or educational feature. The general tone and method of these features as they come from the producers, and the reception accorded them by audiences are one of the most significant developments in the movie world.

The girl who simply adores Mary Pickford and simply raves over Norma Talmadge often has a father or a mother or a big brother with a slight natural, decent thirst to know a little more about the world they live in.

November

WALLACE REID.

From the collection of Arnie Bernstein.

A popular and handsome leading man, Wallace Reid's life was cut short by drug addiction.

Always Audacious

Wallace (Wally) Reid, the star of Always. Audacious *was a favorite matinee idol of the late 1910s through early 1920s and ultimately one of the silent era's most tragic figures.*

Tuesday, November 2, 1920

Always Audacious is a photoplay presented by Jesse Lasky and appearing this week at the Randolph Theater. It is a Paramount production, a screen adaptation from a Saturday Evening Post story entitled "Toujours de L'Audace" by Ben Ames Williams. Direction was by James Cruze, scenario by Tom Geraghty.

It's another case of doubles. The doubles sure are running strong in motion picture drama at the present moment. One might imagine that when a producer is in doubt what to produce he says to himself, "Now for a photoplay with two men, one an honest man and one a villain, and they look exactly alike."

However, these are good doubles. There was no mistaking the audience this observer saw at the Randolph. It was enjoying the two doubles doubling on each other's trail, doubling up their fists against each other, each of the doubles trying to show the other as leading a double life.

The identification of the honest man Danton, and the baffling of the crook, Slim, is brought about cleverly in this plot. It seems that Danton, the honest man, is about to lose a lot of property. This is because Slim has got himself identified as Danton. As the hour of 12 approaches the trustee of the estate is nearly ready. Danton, the rightful owner, is about to lose because all the folks around don't believe he is who he is.

And then—a dog runs in. It's his old playfellow. The dog would be sure to smell the right man, the rightful owner of the estate. So when the dog runs to Danton instead of Slim, the trustee of the estate signs it over to Danton. Slim makes a break for liberty, is arrested, put in irons and led to custody, while Danton poses for the newspaper photographers vis-à-vis his fiancée.

And there you are for the latest case of doubles. It's entertaining, photography luminous, action quick, and we'll say there is not of the recent doubles that is slicker and handsomer than this p'tickler pair of doubles, an honest man and a crook, and that daredevil, Wallace Reid, playing both parts naturally.

The Texans

While William S. Hart brought realism to screen Westerns, Tom Mix films were pure escapist entertainment. Mix got in the picture business following a career in the military. After his discharge, Mix worked as horse wrangler, a position that led to a job at the California headquarters of Chicago's Selig Polyscope Studio. Mix appeared in hundreds of Selig Westerns between 1911 and 1917. After moving to Fox Studios, the movie cowboy's fame skyrocketed. Eventually he became America's favorite Western star, surpassing Hart as a box office attraction. Mix's lively pictures instituted a formula copied by countless others in movies, radio, and television. His talented horse, Tony, was another key factor of Mix's popularity. Sandburg was an unabashed Mix fan, championing the Western star throughout the 1920s.

Thursday, November 4, 1920

Sometimes a photoplay can be very positively recommended. One can say pos-i-tive-ly and with no hesitation or regrets, "Go see it."

The Texans with Tom Mix in the leading part at the Boston Theater, is that kind of play. It is especially easy to tell the grown-ups, the fathers and mothers, that this is worth having the children see.

It's a riding and shooting play, from start to finish, all out of doors. There is a so-so love story. About the only special moral to it is where the hero quits drinking for the sake of winning the hand of the girl he is after.

Oh, yes, we might go along and be p'tickler and pick all kinds of faults in this

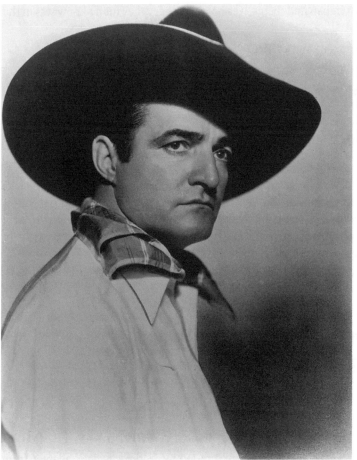

From the collection of Arnie Bernstein.

Tom Mix, the popular 1920s cowboy star and perennial Sandburg favorite.

photodrama. The point is that all its faults are small and amount to little alongside of the big, healthy action to it.

The young folks who want action get it here. The plot is hardly worth telling because it is so much like many other plots. It is the way the plot is worked over into a photoplay. The riding and shooting is heroic, terrifically American, and the desert and mountain backgrounds are superb, nothing less.

The dialogue of the continuity is a little too smart, overdone. But it gets by. Tex, the cowpuncher, played by Tom Mix, has ridden into New Mexico. The barkeep of the first saloon takes away the bottle after Tex pours his drink.

"In Texas when the barkeep removes the bottle, I most generally shoots him," is the way Tex speaks.

"Why didn't you stay in Texas?" thereupon asks the barkeep.

"I ran out of barkeeps," replies Tex, whereupon the whiskey bottle comes back on the bar.

Later Tex and an Indian find themselves holding money they didn't know was in the saddle.

"That money's tainted," muses Tex; " 'Tain't mine and 'taint yours."

Nifty—eh wot? Yet continuity writers must live.

"I'll bet you're afraid to go to bed at night because that's where as many people die," is one offering of Tex to a rival.

The New York girl who wanted a primitive hero and has three swift, breath-taking days of shooting and riding in the deserts and mountains, ends with saying to Winthrop, who came on from New York with her, "I'll be satisfied with life on the Erie Canal, Winthrop." And for that one we hand it to the continuity man.

The way Tom Mix always has his hair combed perfect and nice, even after the most reckless broncho riding, is one point where we protest. However, the New York man from day to day gets a heavier beard and appears in one scene shaving himself. In justice to shaves and hair cuts the play is about a stand-off.

Every boy looking for clean excitement and the wild life will get a good eyeful here. We all want that kind once in a while.

Honest Hutch

The folksy, unpretentious humor of Will Rogers made him a perennial Sandburg favorite.

Friday, November 12, 1920

Honest Hutch is a Goldwyn production, directed by Clarence Badger, adapted from a story by Garrett Smith. It is presented at Barbee's Loop Theater. The star is Will Rogers. Mary Alden is the leading woman.

A great play, one might say of this. No shrieks nor moaning, no special wild whirlings of life—just a quiet play in a quiet neighborhood. Yet a production close to what one might safely call great, in the sense that a story by Mark Twain or a Stephen Foster song is great.

Come to think of it in terms of Chicago personalities and one might say that both John Fitzpatrick, president of the Chicago Federation of Labor, and George Reynolds, president of the Continental and Commercial Bank, would say it is worth seeing for its shrewd wisdom of life and vitality of truth.

Likewise the art of it is so simple and direct, with so few waste motions, one might believe it would be thoroughly acceptable to, and gain the endorsements of, both Lorado Taft and Jack Jones. In the same sense that both Mr. Taft and Mr. Jones approve of Mark Twain's "Huckleberry Finn" and Washington Irving's "Rip Van Winkle," it might be postulated this play, *Honest Hutch*, would gain their approbation.

Ort Hutchins was lazy, a sorry specimen of what may arise on human legs in the bookworm one. Everybody worked but Hutch, who had a crick in his back and a run down farm.

One day, while fishing Hutch digs bait near the foot of a big tree. A gunnysack gets in his way. He digs it out of the ground. A tin box is inside. Fifty bills of the denomination of $1,000 each are in the box.

Hutch runs and digs it down into a new hiding place. Then he scratches his head and does some tall thinking. It occurs to him he can never ask any banker or storekeeper to change a $1,000 bill for him. They wouldn't believe his tangible assets could run as high as $100.

He decides he must work, put up a front, get to a position where it would seem natural for him to spring a $1,000 bill on a banker or storekeeper.

"If it was any less than $50,000, I would never go to work," he muses.

He goes to work the next day, plowing steadily all day. The continuity man observes: "If Hutch's wife could have seen what he was doing he would have been a widower—she would have died of heart disease."

How the certainty of immediate prosperity to result from hard work changed a classic loafer into an industrious citizen—how small events in money, bank robbery, agriculture, domestic science, Sunday school, effect the change in a man if he gets a new straw hat and a hair cut—the manner in which this is handled is quiet, steady and as before noted, quiet, direct and with few waste motions.

The acting of Will Rogers in this piece might have a chapter all by itself. He is an artist, and he does here a genuine portrayal that rings true, gets over, convinces and stays as a good memory.

Movie Location Shortage

The "R.A. Walsh" Sandburg mentions here is Raoul Walsh, a noted director mentored by D. W. Griffith. Walsh appeared in Griffith's The Birth of a Nation *(1915) as John Wilkes Booth. Among Walsh's pictures are* The Thief of Bagdad *(1924),* The Roaring Twenties *(1939), and* High Sierra *(1941), the film that made Humphrey Bogart a star. Ironically, the California location trouble Sandburg writes of has plagued Hollywood for decades.*

Tuesday, November 16, 1920

The motion picture industry, according to leading producers, is threatened with a "location shortage" which may result in hampering production to an alarming extent unless ways and means are devised for meeting this emergency. D.W. Griffith, now operating in the east, says all available photographic points in California have been "shot" from every possible angle. Many other producers, among them R. A. Walsh, producing in conjunction with the Mayflower Photoplay corporation, are setting up the same cry.

Hail! A Coming Star

This is a rare case where the movie publicity machine got it right. Astor enjoyed success well into the sound era, including an unforgettable turn as femme fatale in the classic 1941 mystery, The Maltese Falcon.

Monday, November 15, 1920

A new little auburn haired star, Mary Astor, shortly to be featured by the Famous Players-Lasky corporation, was brought up to be looked at in an Author's League luncheon in New York the other day. Gelett Burgess, introducing the little lady, observed, "Here is a star not yet made. Astronomers tell us it takes 65,000 years to discover a star, but in motion picture circles they are bond in a day." Harry Durant, the promoter, declared She is destined to be one of the greatest motion picture actresses of her day."

The girl was passed along and looked over till it was almost embarrassing. Louella Parsons comments she was almost sorry for the new little star. "She will have to get used to being seen if she goes into the pictures."

Origin of the Custard Pie

A custard pie in the face was a staple of silent comedies. Supposedly, Mabel Normand, a star at Mack Sennett's Keystone studio, in a moment of inspiration, spontaneously grabbed a pie and threw it in the puss of cross-eyed comic Ben Turpin. The gag was a hit, literally and figuratively. In his autobiography, King of Comedy, *Sennett wrote an entire chapter on "How to Throw a Pie." Fascinated by this slapstick practice himself, Sandburg devoted several columns to the subject.*

Tuesday, November 23, 1920

Mack Sennett may or may not be the discoverer of custard pie. Keith Preston, getting over the reminiscences of an Illinoisian for *The Daily News* book page, learned that when Robert G. Ingersoll was a boy in Peoria he went to a picnic where somebody insulted him. His answer was an entire custard pie thrown into the face of the party he wished to so decorate.

There's an Art in Choosing a Pie

Wednesday, December 1, 1920

What kind of pies throw best in the movies? Chester Conklin raises the question.

"In the early days only custard pies were used to smear the face of an enemy," he notes, "but with modern lighting effects, custard didn't make enough shadow. Open face apple pie was then substituted and passed very well till a comedy director discovered that blackberry pies photographed with even more contrast, were more juicy, and ran more comic streaks on the face of the victim target when hit. Blackberries, howsumever, are not always obtainable in winter, so around Thanksgiving season pumpkin pies with their rich brown tints are substituted.

"Squash pie also squashes well on the front of a clean shirt," concludes Conklin.

How Many Pies Make a Hit in the Movies?

Saturday, June 11, 1921

J. L. wishes to have the question answered, "How many custard pies are thrown in order to register a hit in the movies?"

At the Fox studios in Hollywood it is estimated 15 custard pies must be paid for and used up in order to cross a comedian's face with the proper plaster for dramatic effect. At the Mack Sennett studios it is declared, however, there are marksmen who register one hit with only 10 pies.

We heard one crack shot say he always gets more hits and they come easier if he is throwing blackberry pie instead of custard.

The Face at Your Window

Another fine example of Sandburg's feelings about the Red Scare.

Friday, November 26, 1920

The Face at Your Window is supposed to be a bolshevik face, threatening civilization. That is the theme of this William Fox production presented at the Rose Theater. It was directed by Richard Stanton and is from the story by Max Marcin. The cast includes Gina Reilly, Boris Rosenthal, Dina Allen, Alice Reeves.

Even if the William Fox corporation had not set forth distinctly that this photoplay is intended as a "warning," most anybody taking a look at it would feel that somebody intended to warn us against dire possibilities looming black on stormy horizons.

Enlightenment on the meaning and threat of bolshevism and the bolsheviki is important and should be the concern of all who wish to see the advance of civilization. This film produces enlightenment through a mental shake-up similar to the physical results that follow the imbibing of wood alcohol

As art it may be fair melodrama. As propaganda it fails as hysterics always fail. "Keep your shirt on," was not the slogan in making this picture.

Flying Pat

Dorothy Gish is often associated with her better-known sister, Lillian. The siblings' careers began in vaudeville. They made a mutual cinematic debut in D. W. Griffith's An Uneasy Enemy *(1912). While Lillian was noted for her dramatic skills, Dorothy developed into a wonderful comic actress.* Flying Pat *was a typical Dorothy Gish outing.*

Tuesday, November 30, 1920

Flying Pat is a Paramount production featuring Dorothy Gish, presented at outlying houses.

A strictly gish play, plainly intended to be as gishy as possible. All over the place, this Dorothy Gish is, swift of foot and face, a mix of attractions of personality, temperament and tricks. Her popularity is easy to understand. She is a dynamo of expression and movement. Not a large, heavy truck of a dynamo but constructed for the neat and the speedy, once seen not to be forgotten.

Her husband comes back from the war and looks for her. He finds her while she is hiding three or four other men around the house, in library curtains, in kitchen flour bins, under tables. It is a Gish trick to hide a man faster than most any one else in motion pictures. *Flying Pat* is correct—she does almost fly while stowing away one man after another. Of course, it happens she is not off the moral code in her action of hiding the men. There's a good reason and explanation for each man she hides. It does baffle the husband, naturally, and as a whole constitutes a well acted piece of comedy.

Dorothy Gish specialized in comedy roles, though she held her own as a dramatic performer.

From the collection of Arnie Bernstein.

DOROTHY GISH.

December

The Life of the Party

The title of this Roscoe "Fatty" Arbuckle film is painfully ironic. Over Labor Day weekend of 1921, Arbuckle hosted a party in a San Francisco hotel suite. One guest, a minor actress named Virginia Rappe, died under bizarre circumstances. She was found in a bedroom, moaning "I'm dying." Rappe died the next day of peritonitis following bladder rupture. Claims were made that the beloved screen comic had raped the starlet, and Arbuckle was charged with manslaughter. Two trials resulted in hung juries; the third jury acquitted Arbuckle, stating publicly: "We feel a great injustice has been done to him."[1] Yet the damage was done; Arbuckle's career was in shambles. His films, previously audience favorites, were yanked from movie theaters across the country. No studio would hire him to appear on camera. In the wake of the Rappe scandal, Arbuckle reinvented himself as a writer/director/producer, adopting the pseudonym "William Goodrich." (His loyal friend Buster Keaton suggested Arbuckle use the name "Will B. Good.") During the early sound era, Warner Brothers' studios gave Arbuckle a second chance as a screen comic. Despite ill health, the work rejuvenated him. On June 30, 1933, following a day's shooting, he told a friend "This is the happiest day of my life." That night the 46-year-old Arbuckle passed away in his sleep. According to Keaton, he died of a broken heart.[2]

Thursday, December 2, 1920

Naturally Fatty Arbuckle is *The Life of the Party*, now swinging around the circle of Chicago's movie theaters after being exhibited to crowded houses at the Orpheum Theater during the first three days of this week. Fatty is among those present most all the time, and it would be a sad party without him. *The Life of the Party* has cut out his old time slapstick. Instead he furnishes lots of real fun by his inimitable ability as a laugh maker fortified by a series of ludicrous situations. The support is as enthusiastic as if it consisted of all stars.

There is a story that helps make *The Life of the Party* worth seeing. Algernon Leary is Fatty Arbuckle, alias the hero. The milk trust is recognized easily in the fitting role of the villain. Then there is an assistant villain in Judge Villas, before whom Attorney Algernon tries to can the milk trust, but slips on the job because the unworthy judge is milk fed. Algernon and the judge become rival candidates for mayor and during the campaign Algernon risks ridicule by going to a costume dance where all the grownups are dressed like children. Algernon becomes Little Algernon of sweet six.

On the way home, a drunken chauffeur turns Algernon out in a snowstorm and a cruel robber tears Algernon's fur lined overcoat off his back and front. Poor little Algernon is left in his fat and his short panties to freeze to death in a big city. It is

From the collection of Arnie Bernstein.

Roscoe "Fatty" Arbuckle's bright career was destroyed by scandal, though he later worked on many films as an uncredited director.

pathetic. He doesn't.

The judge puts up a job with French Kate, a vamp, to hide in Algernon's room while he is at the dance and disgrace him. She finds a letter there which she rushes over to the judge's room at midnight to show him. Fate turns the tables by fixing it with the aid of the author so that the vamp is caught in the judge's room and he has to withdraw from the race for mayor and let his deadly rival, Algernon, win the blue ribbon. Algernon also wins the judge's best girl. The curtain mercifully hides from further public gaze the embarrassment of young Algernon as a fit of sneezing prevents the pressing of his first chaste kiss upon the girl's well known alabaster brow and her two lips, ripe and ruby red as advertised.

Color Technology

Always fascinated with the technological side of the movie business, this was the first of many pieces Sandburg wrote on the evolving science of cinema.

Saturday, December 4, 1920

Movies in their natural colors are expected to furnish the next big development in the motion picture world, and predictions already are being heard that colored movies may become common before the end of 1921. Most of the large filmmakers are experimenting feverishly in the hope of discovering an inexpensive, feasible process of reproducing, accurately, the original colors in pictures, showing mountains, lakes, countryside, summer foliage, the snows of winter and the vivid decorations of interiors which now usually have to be displayed only in the familiar black and white of the movies. Low cost is what is sought. A few colored scenes are now being shown, but the art is still much too costly and unsuitable for general use.

"A number of color photography systems have been developed in 1920, but none has proved wholly satisfactory," declares John W. McKay, general manager of the Mayflower Photoplay corporation, which has determined to set aside a fund to finance laboratory experiments during 1921." Thus far the methods hit upon have turned out to be either imperfect in results or too expensive to be practicable for commercial purposes. The method sought must produce perfect color pictures at low enough cost to make their marketing feasible on a large scale. The method, too, must permit them to be shown without changing the present equipment of picture theaters all over the country.

The Adventurous Life of a Reel News Reporter

Saturday, December 11, 1920

Some of the stunts which reporters have to do nowadays to take pictures of big news events for the movies are thrilling acts that call for real heroism. Many important news pictures in the movie world cannot be taken unless desperate chances of death are taken.

An inventor claimed to have perfected a glass that couldn't be broken. John Bartone was sent to take pictures of somebody trying to break this unbreakable glass, and he cranked the camera while the inventor emptied a rifle straight into the bull's eye of the camera, which had a square of unbreakable glass in front of it. The reporter took a chance that the inventor actually had made a piece of unbreakable glass. He won.

Jake Coolidge stood on the deck of a fishing boat and took pictures of a Lehigh Valley tug while it burned to the water's edge after being attacked off the Massachusetts coast by a German submarine during the war. Every minute the hidden submarine was expected to rise for another attack.

George Ercole took a wonderful battle picture when he filmed a sea fight between two ships of the czar's navy and a German battleship in the Black Sea.

These are only a few of the incidents recited by the Pathe News publicity man in a story of the thrilling achievements of its staff entitled *The Adventurous Life of a Reel News Reporter.*

What Happened to Rosa

Mabel Normand was a popular screen comedian, as well as a gifted director and producer. Like so many film pioneers, she got her start working in small roles for D. W. Griffith. Eventually she joined Keystone, the comedy studio run by another Griffith veteran, Mack Sennett. After numerous two-reelers, many of which she directed, Sennett (with whom she had an on-again/off-again romance) set Normand up with her own production company. A falling-out with Sennett led Normand to sign with Goldwyn pictures, where What Happened to Rosa *was made. "Mabel was pure emotion," Sennett wrote of her. "All you had to do was say act out this or that emotion, feel this way, or look like you feel this way, and Mabel could instantly do it, throwing herself into the part so thoroughly that she believed it."[3]*

Saturday, December 11, 1920

What Happened to Rosa is the latest tale that Mabel Normand depicts on the screen. Its first Chicago production has been given this week at Barbee's Loop Theater. Mabel Normand's hosts of admirers can watch the little comedy queen to their hearts' content in her newest movie, as she is in the forefront of the picture fully 99 and 44-100ths of all the time. The plot is deliciously simple and can be sketched in a few words.

A fortune teller imparts to Mayme Ladd, a humble little shop girl, the alluring and somewhat quaint "info" that she is going to turn into Rosa Alvaro, a beautiful Spanish maiden, and that she will meet a dark handsome stranger. She does. Everybody is allowed one guess what happens to Rosa. One more guess is permitted as to who plays the twin parts of Mayme, the poor shop girl, and Rosa, the beautiful Spanish maiden.

Way Down East

Way Down East, after The Birth of a Nation *(1915) and* Intolerance *(1916), is considered to be among the best of D. W. Griffith's work. Based on a hoary stage play, the film's star, Lillian Gish, was initially wary of the project. "We all thought privately that Mr. Griffith had lost his mind," she wrote in her autobiography. "Way Down East was a horse-and-buggy melodrama, familiar on the rural circuit for more than twenty years . . . As I read the play I could hardly keep from laughing."[4] Yet Griffith made the story shine, driving his cast and crew to their best in the midst of a brutal East Coast blizzard. Several crew members came down with pneumonia during the shoot. Gish's scene on the river ice floes, where Richard Barthelmess rescues her, is a classic combination of screen acting and direction. Ultimately,* Way Down East *was both an artistic and box office success for Griffith.*

Saturday, December 11, 1920

Color photography has been used with remarkably beautiful effects in David W. Griffith's latest production, *Way Down East*, which had its first Chicago showing at Woods' Theater Monday night. Griffith avails himself of this new movie art to enhance the beauty of Lillian Gish in her transformation from a quiet country mouse to modern Cinderella belle of Society. Griffith himself is here for this stellar production of his masterpiece. He has brought along a special crew of experts to handle the lighting effects. The orchestra, led by Louis Silvers, will furnish specially arranged music and the Chicago orchestra will be larger than the one which accompanied the production of *Way Down East* in New York.

Tuesday, December 14, 1920

The D. W. Griffith version of the old American melodrama, *Way Down East*, was put on last night at Woods' Theater. The plot of the stage play written by Lottie Blair Parker is changed only in a few minor details. The impression while looking at the play is that it is melodrama and the after impression again is that it is melodrama.

As a story this production has none of the originality that marked *The Birth of a Nation* and *Intolerance*, the high spot masterpieces of Griffith hitherto. In wealth of historical incident and big handling of life also this production does not come up to the two former achievements. In point of acting, photography and sustained dramatic interest, however, this is fully up to what Griffith has done before this. In short, then, Griffith began by giving us thrilling entertainment mixed with thought and viewpoint of life that challenged thought, whereas his aim in *Way Down East* is solely and merely to provide thrilling entertainment. This he does put over.

"I love to come to Chicago with my little plays," said Mr. Griffith in a curtain speech called for by the audience after the production was over. "In these days of bolshevism and of tearing down we need to get back to the old fashioned wholesome moralities."

The story of *Way Down East* is about a girl who makes a mistake without knowing it. That is, she gives herself to a man after a marriage ceremony. Afterward she finds out the marriage ceremony was a fake. By this time there is a baby. The baby dies. The young mother goes to work on a farm way down east. Mischievous gossip follows her. Her past is uncovered. She is driven out of the farmhouse by the stern head of the household. A terrible snowstorm is on and she is turned out into this storm.

The son of the stern old man who turns her out into the blizzard follows her and saves her life. In order to save her life he follows her as she runs out on the ice-broken Niagara River and finds herself too weak to take the final plunge. As she lies in a faint on the edge of a cake of ice her love jumps from one floe to another. Just as the ice cake is about to take the plunge over the brink of Niagara, her lover gets to her, gathers her in his arms and brings her to shore, to land, whisky, doctors—and life again. Then they are married.

The part of Anna Moore, the heroine, is taken by Lillian Gish. The hero, David

Bartlett, is done by Richard Barthelmess. Their acting is superb.

The music is superb. There should be congratulations for those who matched off the various musical passages that parallel the action of the play.

The barn dance is too terribly and grandly barney and dancy. Seldom, if ever, have the American farmers gathered in so great and gay a haymow affair as is here staged. No farmers have time or imagination for such splendiferous gayety among the cows and the hay in the wintertime.

The villain, Lennox Sanderson, was done to perfection by Lowell Sherman. Our mitt is extended to him as a paragon of deviltry. They hissed the villain.

Panthea

Norma Talmadge, along with her sister Constance, was a favorite of silent era audiences. Though Norma's talents were not on the same level as those of Lillian Gish or Greta Garbo, she held her own in many melodramatic roles. A third sister, Natalie, had a minor screen career but was better known for her marriage to Buster Keaton.

Monday, December 13, 1920

In *Panthea* Norma Talmadge gives an exhibition of passion at times truly Nazimovesque. *Panthea* is the story of a woman's sacrifice for the man she loves. The unfolding of its sensational plot holds the attention of the audience focused on the absorbing acting of this brilliant star of the movies.

Panthea is a young Russian girl whose beauty and talents attract an unscrupulous baron. With the chief of police this baron arranges to have Panthea arrested on a trumped up charge, whereupon the baron is to rush to her rescue and place the beautiful girl under the weighty obligation of lasting gratitude for saving her from the horrors of a Russian prison. But a former lover spoils the baron's plans by helping her escape from the prison before the baron can stage his rescue act.

Off the English coast the steamer catches fire and Panthea reaches shore to find her temporary refuge in the home of an English nobleman whose estate borders the beach. A son of the nobleman falls in love with Panthea and elopes to Paris with the handsome Russian girl. There the husband composes an opera of merit, but grows sick with despondency over his failure to find a producer who will put his masterpiece on the stage.

In this crucial moment when the happiness of Panthea and her temperamental husband hangs upon a successful presentation of his cherished opera the Russian baron reappears and tells Panthea he will put her husband's opera on the stage if she will sacrifice herself to him. The Russian's girl's adoration for the poor, weak man she has married leads her to consent to the baron's proposal. The opera makes its initial bow with startling success. Panthea's husband discovers the relations between his wife and the baron. The baron drops dead from an attack of heart disease, while Panthea is rewarded for her sacrifice by her husband's tardy understanding of her anguish.

The Mark of Zorro

With The Mark of Zorro, *Douglas Fairbanks transformed from acrobatic comic actor to swashbuckling movie star. After reading "The Curse of Capistrano," a short story in* The Saturday Evening Post, *Fairbanks's wife, Mary Pickford, implored him to look at it with movie rights in mind.[5] "Douglas read without stopping, right through our dinner hour," Pickford recalled. "The film he made . . . started him on an entirely different trend in picture making."[6]* The Mark of Zorro *was an enormous hit, resulting in the 1925 sequel,* Don Q, Son of Zorro.

Wednesday, December 15, 1920

Some of the prettiest exhibitions of swordplay seen since moving pictures first were flashed upon the screen are given by Douglas Fairbanks in *The Mark of Zorro*, now being shown at the Ziegfeld Theater. Doug's latest picture will be considered by thousands to be his best. It is well within the conservative bounds of a critic to pronounce *The Mark of Zorro* one of his best.

The scene is laid in southern California in the romantic days before we wrested that fair province from Mexico. Zorro is a sort of Spanish American Robin Hood. He has conceived the subtle scheme of putting a stop to the abuses of a cruel, corrupt governor by punishing all who maltreat the poor victims. Upon these miscreants he bestows the mark of Zorro. This is a bloody Z cut with a saber on the face or forehead of the unlucky underling who attempts to carry out the governor's cruelties or to do a piece of plundering on his own hook.

Douglas Fairbanks, of course, is Zorro. He is also the son of a wealthy old don who sent him to Spain to be educated. To divert any possible suspicion, he pretends he is an effeminate dandy, much to the disgust of his father, who bewails the fact that the trip to Spain has turned his son's blue blood into colorless water.

In his quick transitions from fire eating Robin Hood to sissified son of a wealthy ranch owner, Fairbanks does some splendid bits of acting.

Ordered by his father, the old don, to pay his addresses to the daughter of an old Spanish neighbor, he declares no girl will marry him for his money. Therefore he proceeds to earn her contempt as a worthless, cowardly dandy, while he wins her admiration and love by his bravery and skillful fighting as Zorro. The windup is thrilling as a melodrama. Single handed, Zorro fights the captain of the governor's soldiers and brands him with the mark of Zorro; he defies the governor and his troops; he rescues his lady love, whom the captain was trying to abduct; and backed by his men who come up just in the nick of time, he forces the evil governor to throw down his commission and flee. Then Zorro sweeps aside his mask.

The Floorwalker

For The Floorwalker, *Chaplin had Mutual Film Corporation build a department store centered by "a running staircase," or escalator. The result was a new twist on the 1910s-1920s comedy standard: the chase sequence. The inspired action both delighted and infuriated Mack Sennett, Chaplin's former boss at Keystone. "When Sennett saw the film he commented: ' Why the hell didn't we ever think of a running staircase?' " Chaplin wrote in his autobiography.[7]*

Monday, December 20, 1920

The world's greatest Charlie, the Charlie whose last name is Chaplin, comes as strong and comical and bewildering as ever in *The Floorwalker.*

Only two reels long is *The Floorwalker.* But easier to remember than many productions that run an hour longer.

When this observer looked it over at the Madison Street Theater the older folks were all bubbling and rippling at the high spots of fun.

And away to the front sat some child—at a guess a six-year-old—a healthy rollicking kid—and this little one kept up a steady stream of laughter—a sort of tickle-me-don't-tickle-me laughter.

It was not the giggles nor a forced laughter heard from this child. It was the fun and the glee of bubbling healthy laughter. The audience heard it and was infected, sometimes joining in.

The Floorwalker is as good as the best comedies in which Chaplin has appeared. And there are folks who consider it the most preposterous array of puppet follies he has yet come along in.

Two familiar mechanisms of modern life are employed to make comedy. The bubbling drinking fountain and the department store moving stairway.

All the wrong ways to squirt water up and out of a drinking bubbler are here tried and tested.

All the wrong ways of walking up and climbing down a moving stairway are shown with the famous Chaplin spread feet.

The plot? Six different persons would probably report six different plots. It is a futurist confusion of plots.

Also, if it had been advertised that Rube Goldberg designed the faces, figures and costumes of the players, that allegation would sound plausible.

Charlie Chaplin still stands as the world's greatest Charlie. There are millions of people over the earth who know him and are for him, like a brother and a family relation and a gay uncle.

The master mummer of the movies, and a great personal tradition of the art of acting in these times, is what we'll say in a world of too much propaganda and not enough fun.

The Forbidden Thing

Harold Bell Wright wrote novels focusing on rural Americans. His best known works are Shepherd of the Hills *and* The Winning of Barbara Worth, *both of which were adapted by Hollywood. Edgar Guest wrote homespun, often religious-themed verses.*

Tuesday, December 21, 1920

The Forbidden Thing is a photoplay produced and directed by Allan Dwan. The star is Helen Jerome Eddy.

This is a drama aimed at the hearts of the numerous readers of the novels of Harold Bell Wright and the poetry of Edgar Guest.

There is nothing problematic or puzzling or under cover about it. It's a plain straightaway oldtimer with two men and two women. One of the women is good. The other woman is bad. The bad woman takes a good man away from the good woman. The good woman marries another good man.

The bad woman—a Portuguese—runs away with a circus, goes around the world, comes home and dies on a sand beach near her husband's fishing shack. The good husband of the good woman has been accidentally killed. The play ends with a happy rearrangement of the good woman and the good man, temporarily gone wrong, who was her first flame of love.

Now—ain't that the kind of action that ought to satisfy the readers of the Harold Bell Wright novels and the Edgar Guest poetry? We'll say it is.

And we'll add that if we had had to make a guess as to who wrote the scenario and handed it into the mitt of the Hon. Allan Dwan we would have said it was a duo and collaboration by Mr. Wright and Mr. Guest.

We expect to meet nice folks who'll say, "I don't care about new fangled highbrow stuff. Let me have something old fashioned with plenty of human courage and the simple love and plain living and old fashioned morality, something like—what's the name of that movie I saw the other night?—oh, yes, the name of it was *The Forbidden Thing.*"

And there we are. Mr. D. Wark Griffith, the other night, at the opening of *Way Down East*, made a crack as though there is such a thing as "old fashioned morality" and somebody or something has robbed us of it. And what is wanted is more motion picture photoplay drama which will help take us back to the "old fashioned morality."

Well, it may be the movies are the cause of crime once in a while, exciting the imaginations of youngsters to become bandits. And there may be pictures that show wrong ways for a young fellow to hug several different best girls he is keeping company with simultaneously. But—there is nothing like that in *The Forbidden Thing*. A whole flock of photoplays let loose the last few months are just brimming over with "old fashioned morality."

The Miracle Man

Though Lon Chaney is not mentioned in this review, The Miracle Man *made the brilliant master of screen makeup a star. Chaney played a down-and-outer nicknamed "The Frog," who faked physical deformities as part of a phony faith-healing scheme. Unfortunately,* The Miracle Man *is a lost film.*

Friday, December 24, 1920

The Miracle Man undoubtedly stands in the minds of many moviegoers and producers as a masterpiece of silent drama art. George Loane Tucker is definitely fixed in the minds of a large number of people as a genius and craftsman, who, if he should produce nothing more worthwhile is to be thanked for what he did with *The Miracle Man.*

This is timely comment now because of the notable tendency to compare this or that picture with *The Miracle Man.*

When *The Penalty* was put on at a downtown theater, it was specifically set forth in the announcements and descriptions to be "as good as *The Miracle Man.*"

We now notice the Mayflower Corporation in its preliminary announcements of Allan Dwan's latest production, *The Scoffer*, alleging that 12,800 film fans have written letters to the New York offices, "classing the picture with *The Miracle Man.*"

Maybe so. We will hope.

Thus far and up to date it may be stated that the productions alleged to be fully as good as *The Miracle Man* have not ridden a similar tide to universal endorsement.

The Penalty, for instance, has stuff to it. It was almost something great. Yet it fell short. It lacked the intangibles that put *The Miracle Man* over.

A while ago this observer saw *The Miracle Man* announced at a South State Street theater. It was a playhouse for mostly casual laborers, here today and in the lumber woods or the railroad bunkhouse tomorrow. The audience was 95 percent men and 10 percent of these did not wear white collars. Admission price was 17 cents. Before *The Miracle Man* went onto the screen a sad and tired octet of burlesquers tried to warm up the place with a little cheer and laughter. But it was no go. There was neither punch nor illumination to their effort.

The Miracle Man, however, brought a tense hush to that audience. If any audience in Chicago ever followed a drama with keener eyes and clutched interest, the producers could take it for themselves as a rare compliment. The George Loane Tucker production sang to them with symphonies of action and clean, strange motifs of life.

We shall hope that when the Hon. Mr. Dwan's latest, *The Scoffer*, comes along, we shall find it is indeed, as alleged, in a class with *The Miracle Man*. Meanwhile it is notable that when an endeavor is made to hit us with a powerful and appealing comparison, it is *The Miracle Man* that is the standard and the pacemaker.

Rudolph Valentino in full regalia for *The Sheik*. The film inspired a 1920s Sheik craze, ranging from screen imitations to "sheik" condoms.

1921

January

Three-Dimensional Photography

*Despite Sandburg's optimism here, P. John Berggren's 3-D camera was a failure.
Essanay Film Company President George K. Spoor ended up spending $4 million
on the process, dubbed "Natural Vision," but 3-D movie technology wouldn't be
perfected for mass audiences until the 1950s. Sandburg may have had more than
a passing interest in the three-dimensional photography process. In his salad days,
he was a traveling salesman of stereoscopic viewers, a device that allowed still
photographs to be perceived in three dimensions.*

Tuesday, January 4, 1921

Within six months the public will have the privilege of seeing motion pictures in
which the objects have three dimensions, pictures in which distance, depth, roundness
and volume are present as they are in real life. For within six months the newly-
invented binocular natural vision camera will be in use.

For seven years, P. John Berggren, physicist, has been working on the invention that
will make three-dimension movies possible. Behind him with money and confidence
has stood George K. Spoor, president of the Essanay Film company.

A disadvantage of the present type of motion picture, according to Blair Coan of the
Essanay company, who made the announcement of the invention, is that it is made for
one-eyed people. The picture is taken with a single lens. It is cast upon the screen
through a single lens. Then people with two eyes, which are constructed to see an
object from two slightly different angles so as to achieve an impression of its
perspective and depth, look at single lens pictures.

"The binocular natural vision camera," said Mr. Coan, "is a mechanical reproduction of the human optical system. There are two lenses in the camera. It was a gigantic mathematical problem to juxtapose those lenses in such a way that a stereoscopic film would be the result. But it has been accomplished at last and 30 of the cameras should be produced and put into use within 6 months."

At a private showing at the Essanay studios, those present were surprised to observe that their own position before the screen had nothing to do with the appearance of the picture. It did not suffer distortion when they sat close to the screen or at one side of it. They lost consciousness of the presence of a screen. The players moved about as if on a stage.

It has cost more than $1 million to perfect the invention. Pictures taken with the new camera can be shown after a slight mechanical change in projecting machines that are now in use in the theaters. Mr. Spoor, who retired from the motion picture business three years ago to give all his time to the development of the invention, is expected to return to the business to produce films with the new camera.

Midsummer Madness

Though his younger brother Cecil is better known, William C. de Mille (1878-1955) was a respected playwright and noted director during the silent era. Sandburg infinitely preferred William's talents over Cecil's, a point continually emphasized in his column. To differentiate from each other, Cecil spelled his last name DeMille, while William used the surname de Mille. William's daughter Agnes de Mille became a noted dancer and choreographer.

Thursday, January 6, 1921

Midsummer Madness is a photoplay produced by Paramount, directed by William de Mille, presented at the Randolph Theater. There are two leading men, Jack Holt and Conrad Nagel, and two leading women, Lois Wilson and Lila Lee.

Not so long ago, William de Mille came to our city, and stopping a day or two, spoke freely about the present and future of motion picture drama. There was one view he had which was more than interesting and almost portentous. He noted that the larger part of photoplays produced in recent years have been derived from books or from stage plays. This condition should not be, he believed.

There ought to be more motion picture plays conceived, written and wrought out first of all as motion picture plays—not cooked over and rehashed from books and stage dramas. The particular and special advantages of motion and light and the rapidity with which scenes and characters can be shifted, are likely to be lost advantages in a photoplay originating from a book written by a writer who has no eye, nor perhaps soul, for the movies.

The present production, *Midsummer Madness*, illustrates Mr. de Mille's thesis. It is a motion picture drama by de Mille secondarily, and a screen version of a novel by Cosmo Hamilton primarily.

The genius of de Mille glows in the scene where one American businessman takes the neglected wife of another American businessman to a lonely mountain lodge somewhat later than half past one in the morning. The arrival of the motor car at the moonlit mountain lodge, the play of the motor light in the suggestive dusks, is a piece of delicate stage craftsmanship, where de Mille says something like poetry. An hour or two later, however, the American businessman has the other American businessman's neglected wife in his arms and his passion is poured out in these words: "I am Pan and you are a Dryad." It is spots like that which swing us away from the illusion that was moving forward and achieving dramatic effects.

The business man who cries his love stress to a woman by saying "I am Pan and you are a Dryad," may get by in an idle hour story book to be read by a quiet reader, such as any of the nice people who read Cosmo Hamilton, but it fails to go over in the swift rush of the movie manner of making love. So much for technique of the photoplay action.

The photoplay, be it said, is a triumph of clean and clear work.

Too Much Sex Stuff in the Movies

Sandburg read the Galesburg Evening-Mail *in his youth and mentions the paper several times in his autobiography,* Always the Young Strangers. *The daily later merged with the Galesburg* Republican-Register *to become the* Register-Mail. *The Arthur Schnitzler-based film discussed here was released later in 1921 under its original title,* The Affairs of Anatol. *Schnitzler was a playwright and novelist who chronicled the underground sexual intrigue among Vienna, Austria's upper classes. Sigmund Freud was among Schnitzler's many fans. Some 79 years after* The Affairs of Anatol *another Schnitzler adaptation provoked a new generation of would-be cinema censors. Stanley Kubrick's* Eyes Wide Shut, *based on Schnitzler's 1926 novella* Traumnovelle *(Dream Story), was threatened with an "NC-17" designation by the ratings board of the Motion Picture Association of America. The "NC-17," which replaced the designation "X," was considered a financial kiss of death by major Hollywood studios. After covering up certain sex scenes with digitally-inserted actors, Kubrick's film was released with a more box-office-friendly "R" rating.*

Friday, January 7, 1921

"Too Much Sex Stuff in the Movies" is the title of a coming *Pictorial Review* magazine article to be published from the pen of Benjamin B. Hampton, former editor and proprietor of the Macomb *By-Stander* and later owner of the Galesburg *Evening Mail*, now president of four motion picture companies in California. There is a decided sentiment in some quarters of the cinema world that the sex stuff has been too strong and gone too far and something must be done about it.

Tuesday, February 15, 1921

In the recent blast on "Too Much Sex Stuff in the Movies," Benjamin B. Hampton, president or otherwise important in four motion picture corporations, wished the public to know that when the armistice came in 1918 the motion picture producers were left with a large output of war films on their hands. Mr. Hampton pointed to the picture going public as voluntarily and with no particular intention of staying away from the war films and thus performing an act of censorship as rigorous in its effects on producers and exhibitors as the decisions of any censorship board.

Both in Mary Pickford's *The Love Light* and in Constance Talmadge's latest vehicle *Dangerous Business*, there is a flare of war drums and a stir of feet moving toward the trenches and the return of boys from the front.

Those who have hitherto enjoyed Constance Talmadge will probably enjoy her in *Dangerous Business* even though this production is remarkably like several others in which she has appeared.

It seems to be quite a week in motion pictures for brides at the altar declaiming they are already the wives of other men and therefore the ceremonial must be come short. This occurs in both *Lying Lips* and *Dangerous Business.*

Arthur Schnitzler wrote a play, "The Affairs of Anatol." Famous Players-Lasky has just finished production of a screen version of it.

At first it was named *Five Kisses.* Then came complaints or doubts or remorse. The choice whether to change the name from *The Affairs of Anatol* to *Five Kisses* was put up to some 2,000 exhibitors with instructions to have

Constance Talmadge, popular for her comic roles, is mentioned in Sandburg's commentary on "Too Much Sex Stuff in the Movies." She retired from the screen at the end of the silent era.

From the collection of Arnie Bernstein.

CONSTANCE TALMADGE

their patrons vote. The tabulated poll as announced gives 161,616 as voting in favor of *The Affairs of Anatol.* The latest advices from Famous Players-Lasky management is that under this title the picture will be sent forth to the public.

In the interval between the announcement of the first title and announcement of the results of the balloting the discussion of "Too Much Sex Stuff in the Movies" reached its highest pitch.

Friday, February 18, 1921

When the war ended many producers had war films on hand. These had been created to supply a rising and unprecedented demand for patriotic films. Two months after the armistice, however, these reels were junk nobody wanted.

Mr. Hampton points to this situation as showing how the public itself exercises a censorship over motion pictures. If the public doesn't want it, then it's junk—with all commercial value censored out of it.

If the public opinion exercises itself with regard to unclean sex pictures, those pictures will disappear from the market as rapidly as the war pictures did, in Mr. Hampton's view.

Nineteen and Phyllis

Friday, January 7, 1921

CHARLES RAY

From the collection of Arnie Bernstein.

As Sandburg humorously notes, Charles Ray had quite a following in the early 1920s.

Nineteen and Phyllis is a photoplay produced by First National, presented at the Rose Theater, starring Charles Ray, with Clara Horton in the support.

Quite a few pictures are being made with Charles Ray as the star. In the statistics of motion picture production for the last year, or the batting and fielding averages and the grand totals of output, it is rather likely young Mr. Ray will be found close to the top. When it comes to quantity he is there. It is not easy to think up any star who is doing more starring in new photoplays than this steady, industrious, sober, always producing another movie Mr. Ray. While Mr. Ray's friends, acquaintances and relations are just coming out of their first thoughts about his last picture, then a new one comes along, and it so happens that the aforesaid friends, acquaintances and family relations have hardly any chance to cultivate deliberate second thoughts about his acting and his plays.

In this one Mr. Ray climbs out on a roof and "rassles" with a burglar. The two of them fall off a roof and hit the grit of the ground below. The burglar was under. The hero is over. So the hero captures the burglar, leads him handcuffed to a house party where prominent citizens pin a medal on him for conspicuous bravery, and he wins the girl.

Three plays starring Charles Ray have come along in the last two months and this reviewer each time has advised all Charles Ray fans to be sure and go because the production was built for and around Charles Ray and those who like his acting would get what they like. For the fourth time now this reviewer suggests this is a nice Charles Ray play and as such and under those circumstances is worth seeing. Sometime, however, we hope to see Charles in a photoplay not done in a hurry and where the lad has a chance to show his best smoke.

Neighbors

The cautionary note at the end of this piece was unusual for a Sandburg review. As it is, Neighbors *is a good two-reeler, packed with sight gags and amazing demonstrations of Keaton's gift for over-the-top physical comedy.*

Friday, January 14, 1921

Buster Keaton is on the map considerable these days. With him life is the making of one knockabout comedy after another.

While Charlie Chaplin is taking it slow and easy and making sure that he is not going to have a public overfed with Chaplin stunts, the managers of Buster Keaton are taking him through many ropes.

No sooner does he fall off one roof than he is called on to fall off another. The latest Buster Keaton comedy is titled *Neighbors*. As B. K. comedies go, this is the goods, a little better than some, not so good as others of the many in which he has appeared in recent months.

There are two or three spots in *Neighbors* which were done in a big hurry. They go a little beyond what is raw and vulgar. They wouldn't classify strictly as indecent, perhaps. But they would go better before an audience of men only.

It will be recalled that this reviewer has spoken several times of photoplays where the sign was up "Adults Only," and it has been noted that there was no necessity for the sign at all because the play dealt with rather inoffensive things that would not bother any ordinary rush hour straphanger.

However, there is stuff pulled in the Buster Keaton comedy *Neighbors* which, it is certain, some theater managers would prefer to have cut out because in the operation of a clean neighborhood theater there are certain queries and objections the manager would rather not have coming to his ears.

One can readily understand how in the high heat of the horseplay that accompanies a Buster Keaton comedy the actors and director might be swept along, thinking anything goes.

The Kid

With The Kid, *a somewhat Dickensian tale, Charlie Chaplin pushed his own creative skills and established himself as a serious artist. The marital trouble that Sandburg alludes to was Chaplin's bitter divorce from Mildred Harris. Married in 1918, Harris filed for divorce two years later, citing mental cruelty. The press eagerly reported the details of this split, a situation Chaplin would face time and again throughout his life. Harris later appeared in several films, sometimes billed as Mildred Harris Chaplin. Ironically, Chaplin's next wife, Lita Grey, had a small part in* The Kid. *This coupling proved to be another marital disaster.*

Saturday, January 15, 1921

The world's greatest Charlie—whose last name is Chaplin—comes to our city next week in the first just off the pan photoplay in which he has been seen in a long while.

The Kid is the name of the play. It begins a run at the Randolph Theater tomorrow. It has taken a year to make the picture.

This *Chicago Daily News* ad promotes Charlie Chaplin's *The Kid* as "Chicago's first big motion picture scoop" (Monday, February 17, 1921).

Ralph Kettering, writing as a representative of Jones, Linick & Schaefer Co., states: "The First National exhibitions' circuit paid over to Mr. Chaplin $800,000 in gold for the purchase of this picture and we have paid an enormous sum to secure the first screening anywhere on earth here in Chicago."

Production of a new Chaplin film starts discussion of the exact sums of money that have fallen into the pockets of the baggy pants of the world's highest paid artist, whose stage is earth wide and whose audience consists of nearly all the people of the earth who have eyes good enough to make out what motion pictures show.

Two years ago Chaplin signed a contract for $1,000,000 for a single year's work. Newspapermen and the public generally were present when the contract was signed. It stipulated he was to appear in twelve different productions during one year and to receive $1,000,000 in monthly payments during the year.

Next year the contract was with Associated First National and stipulated the same money, $1,000,000 but only eight pictures. *A Dog's Life* and *Shoulder Arms*, the first two film comedies under this contract, reached a limit of popularity probably never before touched in the movies. Chaplin withdrew from the filling of this contract after making four pictures.

Then he started work on *The Kid*. While on this job there came the events of his divorce and many stories and much gossip about why he wasn't producing as many new comedies as he used to in the happy days of yore. It seems he wanted to be sure the public wasn't overfed on his stuff. Also, it is said, he wanted to take plenty of time and make a corker of a comedy. Just how much of a corker it is may be seen the forthcoming week. It is in six reels.

Jackie Coogan is the name of the new kid star Chaplin introduces in this production.

Tuesday, January 18, 1921

The Kid is a photoplay written by Charles Chaplin, directed by Chas. Chaplin. The leading role is taken by Charlie Chaplin. It is released by the First National. Presentation is at the Randolph Theater.

Those constant contenders who maintain that Charlie Chaplin is the master mummer of the movies and the world's greatest actor, either in the silent or the spoken drama, now have another exhibit to put forward in behalf of their argument.

After seeing such a large percentage of motion picture plays derived from books and stage dramas, based on this or that story, as originally conceived for a book to be read through printed pages, there is a thrill about watching the masterly work of this cinema production. From the first click of the silver reel, the action is essentially movie action. The soul of its dramatic theory is motion pictures. It is cinema art, the new "eighth art," clear through to where the woman who lost her baby gets the baby back and Charlie Chaplin, the hobo, and his ragtag kid find a new glad home to live in.

Having worked slowly and carefully on this film—taking a whole year to do a picture in the same time that he used to do six and eight pictures—Charlie Chaplin shows he has a wise head. He is centering on quality rather than quantity. It is a habit worth the cultivation of other producers.

There is a further thrill in looking at this film. Consider that it will go to the ends of the earth. It will be shown the world over wherever there is a town having a theater with a projection screen. There will be no foreign translations into all languages, including the Scandinavian, troubling Charlie Chaplin and the artists who achieved *The Kid* with him. Motion pictures don't have to be translated. They tell their own story without the bothersome verbs, nouns and adjectives of labial speech. In other words, then, Mr. Chaplin stands on an art rostrum where he addresses the world. He speaks to all the peoples of the earth. As an artist he is more consequential in extent of audience than any speaking, singing, writing or painting artist today.

Therefore, it is all the more of interest that *The Kid* is easily the full equal of anything Chaplin has done hitherto. And it may be the decision of many movie fans that this surpasses all his previous photoplays.

There is a touch of tragedy, a constant note of pathos, running through *The Kid*. It opens with a woman walking out of a charity hospital with a baby in her arms. She lays the baby in a motor car in front of a rich man's house. The motor car is stolen. The thieves lay the baby next to an ash can in an alley. Along comes Charlie Chaplin. He picks up the baby. A policeman passes. Charlie is afraid to lay the kid down. He takes it home and brings it up. It's a smart, snappy, loveable kid, a juvenile counterpart of its stepfather.

As usual a crack pugilist bullyrags Charlie and knocks him around. And as usual Charlie suddenly finds a brick and gives the pug the blind staggers.

Edna Purviance, as of yore, does the leading lady. And the kid is an achievement in character portrayal by one Jackie Coogan. We can't see it otherwise than that the teeming millions of boys in Charlie Chaplin's audiences will feel a revival of interest in acting. This film is going to quicken the ambitions of all youngsters with a tragedy or comedy streak in their blood.

The Kid is a masterpiece and should satisfy either those who want knock down and dragout or something the whole family will enjoy.

Though the following seems absurd by modern standards, this kind of censorship was typical for the time. In her autobiography, Lillian Gish noted that in the early 1920s Pennsylvania's censor board ". . . did not then permit showing even a picture of a woman knitting little garments."[1]

Saturday, January 29, 1921

Randolph Theater management counts 140,000 people as the number to date who have been to see Charlie Chaplin in *The Kid.*

Censorship has decreed that one little scene, where Charlie shows how expert he is at fastening safety pins and taking care of babies, must be cut out.

Monday, February 28, 1921

All down the line it seems to be well agreed that the incomparable smash of this season is Charlie Chaplin's production *The Kid.* Evidence to support this allegation could be gathered from a thousand different quarters. It is entering its seventh week of showing at the Randolph in Chicago, and its third week at the Strand in New York. Among photoplays *The Kid* stands about where the tin Lizzie does among motor cars, according to Chaplin himself. It doesn't pretend to much class, but it does have the patronage and the crowd. Says Chaplin: "You know that the only man who can afford to be seen driving a tin Lizzie is the one who doesn't have to." So he is going back to short reel plays again, but he wishes it to be noted that he can get by with a six-reel production, such as *The Kid*, when necessary—and when it is the whim of C. Chaplin to do so.

Guile of Women

Having grown up the child of immigrants, Sandburg was well acquainted with the Swedish dialect, which probably explains his ire at the subtitle transliteration in Guile of Women.

Wednesday, January 26, 1921

There is one sure conclusion rises out of *Guile of Women* with Will Rogers starring at Barbee's Loop Theater. And that is the Swedish dialect is no sort of speech to get across in the silent drama.

Much can be done in the silent drama. The dialect, however, of a sailor from Helsingborg who has come to America to live and be Americanized—that broken, hesitant speech is an article too elusive, slow and subtly modulated to be caught effectively in the rapid silversheet.

Just why the Goldwyn corporation should have put upon so excellent a character actor as Will Rogers so dubious a role to play is an affair of the Goldwyn corporation. It is quite possible, however, *Guile of Women* will prove to be a more popular attraction, fetching larger audiences in the theaters than did *Honest Hutch*, in which other recent photoplay there was a rarely plausible plot and first rate characterization.

Clarence Badger directed this production. The story is by Peter Clark MacFarlane, former minister, magazine writer and novelist.

As a Swedish sailor swindled by a woman who keeps a delicatessen store, Rogers is only so-so. Again in other scenes, notably where his sweetheart from the old country turns up as the adopted daughter of a man who owns a steamboat line—the old sweetheart proves true—again Rogers is only so-so. It is good fun, of a sort. The point is that Rogers often has given us this much fun and then something else that took us by the heart.

The surmise may be correct that the Goldwyn corporation believes the Will Rogers public must and should have a certain number of pictures from Will Rogers within stated periods of time and it is better those pictures should be below the best possibilities of Will Rogers as an actor and an artist, then that the Will Rogers public should lose by not having new pictures by their favorite.

It may be some such theory lies behind this production. The hurry of the director, the producers and the photographers has its mark over the various scenes as they flit by. Where *Honest Hutch* had five or six unforgettable scenes, *Guile of Women* doesn't rise to one gripping climax. It is good entertainment, a snappy story, lots of good fun, worth seeing for passing relaxation and all of it is easy to forget.

The Love Light

Directed by Frances Marion and starring Mary Pickford, The Love Light *performed poorly at the box office. The two had worked together since 1916, when Marion wrote Pickford's film* The Foundling. *A prolific screenwriter and sometimes director, Marion ultimately won Academy Awards for her scripts of* The Big House *(1930) and* The Champ *(1931). Legend has it that Marion gave the Academy Award its famous nickname after seeing a prototype sketch of what would become the official statuette. "This looks like my Uncle Oscar!" she exclaimed, thus sealing the trophy's fate. Sandburg refers to Pickford in this review as "Mrs. Fairbanks"; she had recently married Douglas Fairbanks, a pairing enthusiastically cheered by the duo's many fans. Pickford and Fairbanks ultimately divorced in 1936.*

Thursday, January 27, 1921

Mary Pickford is acting on the screen at the Castle Theater this week in a film play named *The Love Light.*

It is a play about the war and things that happened in Italy while the war was going on.

There are times when it looks almost as though the play was written during the war to be shown in Italy to keep alive interest in the war.

Nevertheless, be noted, *The Love Light* is getting an enthusiastic response from the folks who are looking at it on the Castle Theater screen.

Mary—we prefer to call her that rather than Mrs. Fairbanks or Miss Pickford—Mary plays the part of an Italian girl, Angela, on the seacoast, taking care of a lighthouse.

The sea casts ashore a stranger in the uniform of an American naval seaman. Angela helps save his life, marries him, hides him in her home, steals food for him, is discovered by her neighbors, and sees her husband exposed as a German spy.

A German saw tooth bayonet, with the inscription "Gott Mit Uns" forms one of the dramatic properties in several scenes that would have been employed as propaganda during the war. Repeatedly the photoplay gives the impression that its materials were assembled while the war fever was on.

Such are the high spots of Mary Pickford's latest photoplay. Just on form and at a private view one might hazard the judgement the play would not have a successful run. As audiences show their signs to an observer, however, the photoplay is not causing any loss of Mary's popularity. As a vehicle for the best art of this actress, *Suds* was a good deal more of a play.

The support is good. The scenes are Italian and an Italian atmosphere runs through the film. Some of these try for silhouette effects that show promise.

Mary Pickford—we looked it up—is 27 years old now.

February

Brewster's Millions

This was the second version of Brewster's Millions. *The first cinematic rendering was in 1914, with other remakes following in 1935, 1945, and 1985. This latter version featured Richard Pryor in the role Roscoe "Fatty" Arbuckle plays here. A female take on this comedy,* Miss Brewster's Millions, *starring Bebe Daniels as "Polly Brewster," was made in 1926.*

Monday, February 7, 1921

Brewster's Millions is a case where movie producers took a plot out of a book and made a lively photoplay where the action and the actors tie up and move on and put it across.

In its day the novel of the same title, by George Barr McCutcheon, was one of the best sellers. The photoplay has caught the same stuff that made the book go.

It is a case where a young man, Monte, played by Fatty Arbuckle, is trying to spend $2 million inside of a year because if he does spend that much and goes broke, then he gets $10 million, according to the terms of an eccentric relative. He makes many wild plunges at spending. Sometimes his wildest plunges prove to be moneymakers. Where he intended to throw money away it comes back at him in bigger bunches than before.

He hires an ocean-going liner and pays the expenses of all his friends who want a trip to Peru. While they are all having a nice dance in the salon (which is different from a saloon), Monte starts a fire, turns the hose on the fire, soaks all the guests and spoils their clothes. This gives him a chance to pay for all the clothes spoiled.

The director, Joseph Henabery, and the scenario writer, Walter Woods, should have some credit for the way they stage the ship and all the action on it. The roll of the boat is caught in continuity and the titles that toss on the screen and greet the eyes the same as life on the ocean.

The Big Punch

Buck Jones was another cowboy star of the 1920s, appearing in a successful series of low-budget Westerns. He worked well into the sound era, though his popularity had waned by the end of the 1930s. On November 30, 1942, while in Boston on a tour to sell United States bonds, Jones died in the infamous Cocoanut Grove nightclub fire. Sandburg's axiom, "Slang is language that rolls up its sleeves, spits on its hands and goes to work," is certainly demonstrated in this review!

Thursday, February 10, 1921

Buck Jones, a candidate for the nominations already copped off by Bill Hart and Tom Mix, is the star actor in the motion picture play *The Big Punch* at the Alcazar.

Mr. Jones, or Buck, or Old Pal, or howsoever he ought to be called, has a good deal of smoke and there ain't no doubt (nobody feels grammatical coming away from one of them there Western ridin' shootin' plays)—and there ain't no doubt he might a stood a heap better show at being a star if he had started in the game way back when Bill Hart and Tom Mix were in their beginnings.

Howsumever (it is hard to be correct and proper after reading all that Western language the continuity writers sling around so in the Western movies)—how-

From the collection of Arnie Bernstein.

Buck Jones, another popular movie cowboy. He would die in the infamous Coconut Grove nightclub fire.

sumever, it ought be said in *The Big Punch* Mr. Buck Jones gets by as a Western hero with a heavy jaw, a winsome smile, and faking ways.

One time he goes to the penitentiary and we see him among the outcasts. Later he is a circuit rider preaching the gospel in out of the way places where churches have not yet been established. In the end he has religion and a sweetheart, the same articles Bill Hart ends his successful movies with.

Another Myth Goes Down

It's no accident Sandburg published this piece on Lincoln's Birthday. At the time, he was deeply involved in researching and writing The Prairie Years. *In his concluding book,* The War Years, *Sandburg writes that Booth—after shooting Lincoln and leaping from the President's box to the Ford Theater's stage—ran between Laura Keene, star of the play "Our American Cousin," and an actor named W. J. Ferguson. "Some say he ran off as though every second of time counted and his one purpose was escape," Sandburg states. "Others said he faced the audience a moment, brandished a dagger still bloody from slashing (actor Major) Rathbone, and shouted the state motto of Virginia, the slogan of Brutus as he drove the assassin's knife into imperial Caesar:* 'Sic semper tyrannis*'—thus be it ever to tyrants.*"[2]

Saturday, February 12, 1921

School histories and other records assert Abraham Lincoln's assassin, J. Wilkes Booth, called out the words "*Sic semper tyrannis*" at the shooting. W. J. Ferguson, veteran actor and a player in D. W. Griffith's forthcoming production, *Dream Street*, who was a call boy at the Ford's Theater in Washington on the night of the tragedy, declares no such words as the often quoted Latin phrase escaped the lips of the assassin.

"I heard every word Booth said," is Ferguson's recollection. "They were profane words. But I am willing to swear on my oath that he did not say '*Sic semper tyrannis.*' Afterward we saw in the papers he said that, but no one thought of denying it. There was the search for Booth and then the trial. But no one thought '*Sic semper tyrannis*' ever would be heard of again. Though it has become a part of the history of the shooting, I believe firmly that it should be denied. Booth was not thinking of Latin phrases; all he was considering was the quickest way to his horse, which he had wanted me to hold for him in the alley."

Visit with Chaplin

The following was published on Charlie Chaplin's 32ⁿᵈ birthday. This profile was reworked as "Without the Cane and Derby," which was published in Sandburg's

1922 book Slabs of the Sunburnt West. *The poem, which Sandburg dedicated "For C.C.," borrowed heavily from this article and read, in part, "The room is dark. The door opens. It is Charlie playing for his friends / after dinner, the marvelous urchin, the little genius of the screen."*

Saturday, April 16, 1921

Someday Charlie Chaplin is going to show the world a drama of serious acting. The conventional joke to follow this suggestion is the query, "Is he going to play Hamlet?" The answer is, "Nix, brother, he is not—not so anybody notices it—but howsoever, when he does get around to a production of anything approximating the sadness of the *Hamlet* play and a grave digger digging a grave and telling the spectators it is a grave matter—holding up the skull of a man and commenting on the jests that once fell from the lips—when Charlie Chaplin gets around to anything like that in seriousness—it will be a drama with clutches and high speed."

For Charlie, I found on visiting him in his unprofessional and confidential moods, is an artist of beautiful and gentle seriousness. Away back under all the horseplay—the east-and-west feet, the cane, the derby and the dinky mustache—is a large heart and a contemplative mind. He knows what he is doing nearly every minute.

Sometimes he refers to the time he will put before the world a Chaplin film play without the east-and-west feet, the cane, the derby, the dinky mustache. Those who have seen him in his quiet, serious moods understand well that it will be a drama with punch, drive and terrible brooding pauses of high moments.

I have seen four or five renowned actors (most of them admit that they are renowned) play Hamlet, but I have not seen any player better cast for the high and low spots of the life of the Prince of Denmark than this little mocker of a littler mummer out at Hollywood, making farces for the world to laugh at.

Not often is the child joy and play heart of the world to be found in a man shrewd and aware of the hungers and dusts of its big streets and back alleys. Yet Chaplin in his gay moods—and his commonest mood is gayety—is the universal child.

I have heard children four or five years old bubble and ripple with laughter in the course of a Chaplin film. They answer to the child in him. *The Kid* is a masterpiece of expression of love for the child heart—love and understanding.

There is pathos about the rain-beaten dusty walls of the city street where the scenes of *The Kid* were filmed. The walls are still standing about the center of the studio lot. And the thought comes to a looker on, "These are unique walls, different from stage play scenery or exposition art works or any similarly transient creation. These walls and paving stones have already been seen by millions of people and will in future years be known to millions more who shall see *The Kid*.

The home of Chaplin is on a mountain side overlooking Hollywood and Los Angeles. In a night of blue air the city of Los Angeles is indicated by lights that resemble a valley of fireflies.

Charades is a favorite game when there is company in the house. After the Japanese cook and waiters have served "everything there is," the guests go in for pantomimes, sketches, travesties, what they will.

Charlie was paired with a young woman who has done remarkable work in art photography "stills." All lights went out, both in the drawing room where the spectators sat and in the dining room, which was the improvised stage.

A door opened. Here was Charlie in a gray shirt, candle in his right hand, lighting his face and throwing shadows about the room. He stepped to a table with a white sheet over it. He drew back the sheet. A woman's head of hair, than a woman's face appeared. He slipped his hand down under the sheet and drew out his fingers full of pearls of a necklace. He dropped the necklace into his pocket, covered the face and head, picked up the candle and started for the door.

Then came a knocking, louder, lower, a knocking in about the timebeat of the human heartbeat. The man in the gray shirt set down the candle, leaped toward the white sheet, threw back the white sheet, put his fingers at the throat and executed three slow, fierce motions of strangling. Then he started for the door, listening. He stepped out. The door closed. All was dark.

The guests were glad the lights were thrown on, glad to give their applause to the mocking, smiling, friendly host.

At the dinner Charlie mentioned how he once was riding with Douglas Fairbanks in a cab past some crowded street corner. And one of them said in a voice the passing crowds could not hear: "Ah, you do not know who is passing: it is the marvelous urchin, the little genius of the screen."

The ineffable mockery that Charlie Chaplin can throw into this little sentence is worth hearing. He holds clues to the wisdom and humility of his ways.

Every once in a while, at some proper moment, he would ejaculate, "The marvelous urchin, the little genius of the screen," with an up-and-down slide of the voice on the words, "little genius" and "marvelous urchin."

Fame and pride play tricks with men. Charlie Chaplin is one not caught in the webs and the miasma.

With Will Rogers

In the spring of 1921, Sandburg visited Southern California to interview movie practitioners for his column. Consequently, for most of March and April his regular reviewing duties were taken over by other writers. On April 18, Sandburg returned to his beat at the Daily News *with reports from the frontlines of filmmaking.*

Monday, April 18, 1921

"How much time do you put in working day by day," I asked Will Rogers between camera shots at the Goldwyn studio in Culver City. He was working on *Doubles for Romeo.* He answered:

"Saturday I worked fifteen minutes, but I don't know how long we'll be on this dog fight here today."

Five or six old cowboy pals of Rogers were working with him—not actually working—but there they were, rigged out in medieval Venetian noblemen's satin and velvet jackets and knee pants—looking important, healthy and satisfied to be marching along through life with the man who understands them. They keep Rogers company and sometimes do real acting.

The Mighty Cameraman

Monday, April 18, 1921

Cameramen get high pay. Some of them pull down $300 a week.

Such a salary is easily understood. If the cameraman doesn't like the looks of anything in the scene to be shot he says so and it's changed.

Several times I saw everything all ready for a shot. The actors had rehearsed the scene several times. It all looked ready.

"Camera," the director called out and everybody got ready to move, the actresses, ready for their sweetest or haughtiest, the actors screwing their faces to expressions for permanent record to be read by the millions.

"That light ain't right," called the cameraman. And until there was a rearrangement of the light the cameraman didn't click his machine.

He is a boss they all respect, the cameraman.

Chaplin at Close Range

As the following shows, Chaplin was comfortable enough with Sandburg that the beloved screen comic didn't mind being interviewed while stripping off his clothes to change. Sandburg and Chaplin remained lifelong friends, which was duly noted by, among others, the Federal Bureau of Investigation. In the 1950s, amidst the terrors of the McCarthy witch hunts, Chaplin decided to leave the United States. Long suspected of being a Communist sympathizer, Chaplin refused to cooperate with government officials and instead moved to Switzerland. Sandburg, himself a life-long liberal, was also watched by the FBI. Among other items in the Sandburg FBI file was a memorandum noting that in 1942 Chaplin and Sandburg appeared at a Chicago war rally praising "our Russian ally." [3] Of course, in 1942 the United States and the Soviet Union were allies in the fight against Nazi Germany; yet in the post-World War II era this old alliance made Chaplin and Sandburg suspect, at least in the eyes of J. Edgar Hoover's minions.

Saturday, April 23, 1921

The first time I saw Charlie Chaplin was at his studio apartment fronting on the big lot where he and his company do most of their work making pictures. He was slipping out of his underclothes. The friend who brought me introduced us. Before starting for his bath the naked, sinewy, frank, unaffected Charlie Chaplin paused for a short interchange of thought about climate, a warm day's work, and how they had done the same thing over and over 50 times that afternoon. Whether his clothes are on or off, the impression is definite that Chaplin is clean physically and has a body that he can make obedient to many kinds of service.

Legs, arms, torso, he can relax or stiffen. He can be nimble as a cat or stolid as a wooden saw horse, all at a moment's notice.

He came out of the bathroom, rubbing his back with a rough towel, chuckling over how that afternoon he and another actor had rehearsed one little scene and his vis-à-vis had ejaculated 50 times, "Here is your hat—you must have dropped it." Easy and tireless, always working, that is Chaplin. I asked him if he had read *Main Street.*

"I have had time to read only one book the last year, that was Knut Hamsun's *Hunger,*" was the reply.

We got into a limousine, the best make of a famous car.

"I got this for the lady," he said. I didn't ask what he meant. Later I was told the car is for his mother.

"I went into the place where they sell the car and asked, 'What's the best one you've got?' They showed me this. I asked 'How much?' They named the price and I said 'Wrap it up and send it to my home.' "

He speaks in a low musical voice, sometimes with terrible rapidity and then again slow and stuttering. Always his voice sets the tempo and atmosphere of the thing he is telling you about.

"Wrap it up and send it to my home"—this was said with a mild chuckle as though it is only one of a series of inconsequential nonsensical stunts we go through with every day to give life's drab a little color.

"What was this interview or conference between you and Caruso we heard about a while ago?" he was asked.

"The newspapers arranged it. I was to go to Caruso's room and see him while he was making up a performance. I went. At the door we were met by a man who said something like, 'Spaghetti muchacho carissima Charlie Chaplin.' We were passed along from one to another till at last we got to the door of Caruso's room, where the secretary said the same thing, or something like what all the others said, 'Spaghetti, muchacho, carissima Charlie Chaplin.'

"The door to Caruso's room opened and we went in. He was standing in front of the mirror making up. He did not turn to see whether any one had come in—went ahead with his face make-up. The secretary repeated for the last time something like 'Spaghetti, muchacho, carissima Charlie Chaplin.'

"Caruso turned and said, 'O, you come to see the Charlie Chaplin of the opera.' And I answered, 'Yes, and you are shaking hands with the Caruso of the movies.'

"He turned to the mirror and went on with his make-up. 'Make a lotsa money in the movies—eh?' he asked. And with two or three formal exchanges the interview was over."

Of course, it is impossible to reproduce any story Charlie Chaplin tells verbally. He tells more than half the story with his hands, arms, shoulders—with shrugs, smiles, solemnities, insinuations, blandishments, sentences alive with gesture and intonation. As a storyteller for a tremendous audience he delivers his story all with motions and no oral speech. The habit is on him of telling all he can with looks and motions. To meet him and talk with him is to understand better that art of illustrating ordinary talk with an accompaniment of hand and shoulder sign talk.

May

Pictures That Show World War Are a Risk

The Four Horsemen of the Apocalypse made stars out of director Rex Ingram and actor Rudolph Valentino. The film was based on a novel by Vincente Blasco Ibáñez, a Spanish writer whose work was very popular with American readers in the 1910s and 1920s.

Saturday, May 7, 1921

The case of *The Four Horsemen of the Apocalypse*, showing at the LaSalle Theater, is worth considering. As a photoplay it gets away with plot characters, mystery, epic quality about as strong as the novel by Ibáñez.

Now, that particular Ibáñez novel was the deep sensation of the publishing and reading world of its year, the year after the world war armistice. And yet the photoplay is not seizing a public and holding its interest as did the book.

Pictures showing the world war are a risk. During the two months after the signing of the armistice there was a high mortality of war films. Producers fell back on giving the public love, laughter and mystery themes with no complications of how and why the big war was fought with all its angles of race, nationality, religion, economics.

In the book and the photoplay the four horsemen are terrible figures seen in the vision of the seer of the Apocrypha. Their names are Conquest, War, Famine, Death.

The Four Horseman of the Apocalypse made Rudolph Valentino a star.

Sinister mythic figures does Rex Ingram, photoplay director, make of these as four horsemen.

Yet there are four other horsemen invisibly in the background of Mr. Ingram's work. As we see the reels unfold we feel Ingram struggling to send these four horsemen to a film winning. Their names are Race, Nationality, Religion, Economics. Ibáñez in a written book was able to handle them in a way to interest a large audience of readers. Ingram working in the photoplay medium finds it hard work to match Ibáñez in attracting public interest. It may be that as an artist with this theme Ingram does as capable work in projecting photoplay as Ibáñez in writing a book. Only just now the public wants the whole scheme of the war handled somewhat different.

Mary Pickford's *The Love Light* is understood to be one of the least popular of her plays. It came along three months ago with a plot that would have thrilled the Liberty Bond-buying public. Now we have passed on to something else, however. War plays are a risk. That is, films which try to weave in and out of the complicated fabric of race, nationality, religion and economics that baffled the Paris peace conference—such films are a risk. These are four horsemen hard to ride to a winning.

In Los Angeles it is currently reported the bankers have emphatically told the movie producers there are too many unused films and that before the industry is entitled to the kind of support it has had financially, it must see what the public will do about some of the unused stuff. The Mary Pickford play *The Love Light*, with its pre-armistice flavor, is said to be in this class.

Passion

Director Ernst Lubitsch and star Pola Negri were both veterans of the German stage, learning under the tutelage of theatrical visionary Max Reinhardt. Working together in films, Lubitsch and Negri quickly achieved great acclaim. Their German work culminated with the international success of Passion *(also known as* Madame DuBarry*). Lubitsch and Negri both came to Hollywood, where their American colleagues immediately embraced them. With the coming of talking pictures, Negri's fortunes declined with her thick accent. Lubitsch, on the other hand, enjoyed considerable success well into the sound era, bringing what was dubbed "The Lubitsch Touch" to films like* Trouble in Paradise *(1932) and* Ninotchka *(1939). When he discusses the "array of cutouts," Sandburg means material censors demanded cut in order for* Passion *to be exhibited in America.*

Tuesday, May 10, 1921

Passion is having its local opening this week at Orchestra Hall. In New York and other cities it has had a phenomenal run extending over months.

The chief actress is Polish, the scene and characters of the drama are French, while the producers are German. Direction was by Ernst Lubitsch. American releases are by First National.

As history or biography and again as a series of scenes portraying famous and notorious men and women of France at the time of the revolution, *Passion* is one of the notable offerings of the season's photoplays locally.

Pola Negri is easily one of the best birds that have flitted across the screen in recent years. She takes the role of Mme. du Barry and carries it through one and another difficult scene.

She begins as a hat girl, fixing hats in a millinery shop in Paris. Later she is seen as the mistress of King Louis XV. In one boudoir appearance, she puts out her foot and has it kissed by the King of France. Tragedy comes later when she and her love are put to death by mobs.

Such a story lifted from history and biography offers considerable opportunity to the photodramatists to either make a play of it, rising always to higher climaxes of swift action and plot. Or it may resolve itself into a series of short plays, pageants, comedies and tragedies. This is rather the result achieved by *Passion*.

Considering the extent of the weaving of the theme of passion, the play stands remarkably clean as now produced. One wonders what the array of cutouts might look like. Many of these were evidently necessary for American production.

The mobs get by fairly well. They are actually more mobbish than any mobs could be. When a multitude operates in such unison of intense cry and gesture as seen here, one feels organization at work and where there is organization there can be no mob.

To Pola Negri goes the big hand in this photoplay. One may be glad she is seen on this side of the big pond. Whenever the history and biography begin to delay action, she enters and charges the atmosphere with new lights.

The Cabinet of Dr. Caligari

The Cabinet of Dr. Caligari *was a groundbreaking film Sandburg returned to time and again as an example of cinema's artistic and psychological power. Though he doesn't exactly put his finger on the film's aesthetic style,* Caligari *was a classic example of the expressionist art movement which arose in post-World War I Germany. In a nutshell, expressionists emphasized the interior workings of the mind through distortions of physical reality. Sandburg's references to the horror stories of Edgar Allen Poe and the loopy cartoon machinery of artist Rube Goldberg provide a good approximation of the expressionist style. Thomas De Quincey, whom Sandburg also alludes to, was a British writer who focused on the macabre. His best known work is* Confessions of an English Opium Eater. *His fourth reference, Ben Hecht, was Sandburg's colleague at the* Chicago Daily News. *For a year and a half Hecht wrote a* Daily News *column dubbed "1001 Afternoons in Chicago," chronicling the hidden life of the city.*

Tuesday, May 12, 1921

The most important and the most original photoplay that has come to this city of Chicago the last year is being presented at the Ziegfeld Theater this week in *The Cabinet of Dr. Caligari.* That is exactly the way some people say it.

The craziest, wildest, shivery movie that has come wriggling across the silversheet of a cinema house. That is the way other people look at it.

It looks like a collaboration of Rube Goldberg, Ben Hecht, Charlie Chaplin and Edgar Allan Poe—a melting pot of the styles and techniques of all four.

Are you tired of the same old things done the same old way? Do you wish to see murder and retribution, insanity, somnambulism, grotesque puppetry, scenery solemn and stormy, wild as the wildest melodrama and yet as restrained as comic and well-manipulated marionettes? Then it is you for this Caligari and his cabinet.

However, if your sense of humor and your instinct of wonder and your reverence of human mystery is not working well this week, then you should stay away from the

Ziegfeld Theater because you would go away saying Caligari and his cabinet are sick, morbid, loony.

Recall to yourself before going that Mark Twain is only one of numerous mortal philosophers who has declared some one streak of insanity runs in each of us.

Only two American motion picture artists have approached the bold handling, the smash and the getaway, the stride and rapidity of this foreign made film. Those two artists are Charlie Chaplin and D. W. Griffith.

It is a healthy thing for Hollywood, Culver City, Universal City, and all other places where movie film is being produced that this photoplay has come along at this time. It is sure to have healthy hunches and show new possibilities in style and method to our American producers.

This film, *The Cabinet of Dr. Caligari*, is so bold a work of independent artists going it footloose that one can well understand it might affect audiences just as a sea voyage affects a shipload of passengers. Some have to leave the top decks, unable to stand sight or smell of the sea. Others take the air and the spray, the salt and the chill, and call the trip an exhilaration.

There are two murders. They are the creepiest murders this observer has thus far noted in photoplays. Yet the killings are only suggested. They are not told and acted out fully. (No censor could complain in this respect.) As murders they remind one of the darker pages of Shakespeare, of *Hamlet, Macbeth* and again of the De Quincey essay on "Murder as a Fine Art."

Then a sleepwalker is about to kill a woman. He drops the dagger instead and carries her away across house roofs down a street. Oh, this sad sleepwalker and how and why he couldn't help it.

This is one of the few motion picture productions that might make one say, "Here is one Shakespeare would enjoy coming back to have a look at."

However, be cheerful when you go to see this. Or else terribly sad. Its terrors and grotesques will match any sadness you may have and so comfort you. But if you go feeling real cheerful and expecting to be more cheerful, you may feel yourself slipping.

The music is worked out well. The orchestral passages run their tallies of chord and rhythm and silence—they growl or they are elated—with the story running on the silversheet.

When it's a crackerjack of a production and the observer feels good about it he mentions the screen as a silversheet. Whereas if it's otherwise he says celluloid. Personally, in this instance, one says silversheet.

Yes, we heard what a couple of people said going out. One said, "It's the craziest movie I ever went to." The other one said, "I don't know whether I want this for a steady diet, but it's the best picture I've seen in a long while."

Cubist, futurist, post-impressionist, characterize it by any name denoting a certain style; it has its elements of power, knowledge, technique, passion, that make it sure to have an influence toward more easy flowing, joyous, original American movies.

Saturday, May 21, 1921

This is the second week at the Ziegfeld Theater of *The Cabinet of Dr. Caligari*. Two reviewers of motion pictures were talking about the production the other day.

"The name ought to be changed. If this had come from Hollywood they would have done just what they did when they shifted the title of Gertrude Atherton's photodrama from *Noblesse Oblige* to *Don't Nag Your Wife*."

"And what would make a better title to interest the movie-going public?"

"Call it *Who's Loony Now?*"

It does seem as though the audiences who witness the baffling Dr. Caligari and the sinister, sinewy sleepwalker, Cesare, divide broadly into three categories.

First are those who say, "What's it all about? It is interesting but what does it mean? Is it a showing of the workings of insanity? Or am I loony because I don't get it?"

Then there are those who say, "It is some kind of joke but just who the joke is on I don't know. Sometimes it is funny as a comic strip in the newspapers. Then sometimes it makes mysterious motions like a magician when he is going to pull a rabbit out of a hat. It is some kind of a puzzle like the old question on the farm, 'Why does a chicken cross the road?' I am glad I went because I have wanted to see a different movie and this is so different it's a knockout."

Then there is another and smaller group who say, "it is art." They did not make this for the public first of all. A group of designers, players, writers, said to themselves they would produce a photoplay that would be their own idea of a first-rate movie. Then if it happened the public later on liked it they would congratulate the public.

In view of these diverse opinions and outlooks, it might be maintained there would be commercial justice and theatrical propriety in changing the title from *The Cabinet of Dr. Caligari* to *Who's Loony Now?*

Wednesday, July 6, 1921

The one photoplay reviewed by this observer in recent months which brought most frequently the question, "Where can we see it?" is the picture *The Cabinet of Dr. Caligari*. Since its exhibition two weeks ago at the Ziegfeld Theater in May it has been off the screen locally. Dozens of persons said to us, "We notice this movie kicked up more talk than anything in the pictures for a long while." Other inquirers said they had heard about the picture from friends who had seen it in New York, Toledo, Cleveland and Minneapolis. Still others said highbrows in the magazines were spilling considerable ink about *The Cabinet of Dr. Caligari*.

Therefore, it is proper and informative to point out that this particular chilly, creepy, dank, dismal, amazing, terrible and wonderful motion picture is being shown this week at the Bijou Dream Theater, a nifty little hatbox playhouse just across State

Street from the Palmer House Hotel. At the time this photoplay was first shown, we noted it as "the most powerful and original photoplay" that had come under our notice this year. Furthermore we suggested that it would not be out of order for exhibitors to change the title for American exhibition and instead of *The Cabinet of Dr. Caligari*, call it *Who's Loony Now?* It is a queer picture, queer as a haunting ghost story told on a rainy night when the wind whistles up the chimney. In its general characteristics it might seem, as a movie, to be the joint effort of Rube Goldberg, Ben Hecht, Edgar Allen Poe and Charlie Chaplin. It is hoped this information meets the inquiries of those who have written, telephoned and buttonholed us with the query, "Where can we see *The Cabinet of Dr. Caligari?*"

June

Making of Pictures is Industry, Not Art

Saturday, June 4, 1921

The production of motion pictures is first of all an industry and only secondarily an art. Also the exhibition of motion pictures is a business first and an art second.

This is the explanation of why there are so many motion picture productions that look just like a lot of others we have seen before.

The businessmen running the industry have millions invested in it. In amount of capital invested it stands fifth among American industries.

More than 15,000 motion picture theaters receive the output of the industry and give it exhibition. Also thousands of theaters in foreign countries depend on the American output for new photoplays.

Suppose a film is worked out, finished and the director and his staff are doing what they call "the post-mortem," deciding on the final cutouts and subtitles.

An artist might say, "It isn't a finished picture; we ought to throw it away and do a new one; it is not artistic; we can't let it go out."

That is the moment for a businessman to step in and say, "We have spent $200,000—or $400,000—on this picture; already the bankers are saying we throw too much money at the birds in this business; the exhibitors are calling for new stuff; it may or may not be artistic but this picture goes out next week."

So there are good reasons why it is not strictly correct to speak of a place where they produce motion pictures as a "studio." First of all, it is a manufacturing plant where a supply is created to meet a certain demand. On top of that it may be a studio. But as a studio where artists envision, sigh, cry, laugh and launch their conceptions of beauty, it is subsidiary to its other status as a factory where the wants of a public which insists on something new are catered to by business managers and executives.

The plant where Charlie Chaplin works—and he is the owner of it—is in a class by itself. It is a one-man establishment as strictly as the Ford or Edison plants are one-man affairs.

Here is a case where the artist who plays the leading parts and writes the continuity and directs the actors is also the capitalist, the manager, the high business executive.

If Chaplin the artist says, "That's no good: throw it out," it happens that Chaplin, the head businessman of the concern always says, "Yes, yes, that's right, throw it out!"

There will be more caring originality, a younger and bolder striking of stride across new fields—bigger and more finely thrilling photoplays—when there are more directors and players established as Charlie Chaplin is.

The present writer talked with a notable director in the plant of the Famous Players-Lasky company at Hollywood, a man responsible for some big, clean work.

He was asked, "Does it bother you sometimes because you have to work on schedule and have the pictures ready for exhibitors on promised dates?"

He answered, "That is one of the hardest drawbacks; sometime I hope to have enough money laid by so that I can have a studio of my own and not send out anything I can't take some pride in for myself."

And these, in brief, are reasons why sometimes the production of the motion picture plants seems to be extra monotonous.

The newsreels, of course, are on a different basis from the photoplays. They show us the new president and the new president's wife, the new ambassador to France and the wife of the new ambassador to France, the latest strong man who lifts five horses on his back and how he eats ice cream to keep strong, scientists such as Mme. Curie, Steinmetz, Edison.

"Mightiest of all," one newsreel proclaims itself. "Sees all—knows all," says another. And we let 'em pass because they always bring the breath of some fresh event from many miles away.

Riders of the Purple Sage

This Zane Grey Western was remade for the big screen in 1925 with Tom Mix. Other versions were made for the movies in 1931, 1941, and a television telling in 1995.

Friday, June 17, 1921

In *Riders of the Purple Sage*, showing at the Alcazar Theater, the Fox corporation puts over something often attempted but not arrived at once in five times. It has taken a widely successful novel—a best seller of a novel, one of the record breakers in point of sales—and out of this novel has made a photoplay that doesn't look as though it had been made from a book.

Zane Grey as a novelist is the foremost rival of Harold Bell Wright when it comes to sales of works of fiction mounting into the millions of copies. This particular story is one of Zane Grey's leaders. Dustin Farnum, the actor who takes the part of the hero, seems to have been specially made to meet the requirements of a Zane Grey hero. He does noble deeds in the precise way we ought to expect a Zane Grey hero to do noble deeds.

The scenery is laid in Utah. A child is stolen, all the ranch horses stolen and other griefs inflicted on the woman the hero cares most for. The cause of it is a high official of a church in Utah. Time and again the hero—Dustin Farnum can do this stuff—clashes with this high church official, who pulls a gun to shoot the hero and then has his hand or arm nipped by a quick bullet from the quick-shooting hero.

In the windup the hero, his woman and the child, which has been recovered from the kidnapers, head for the mountains followed by 20 men on horseback who wish to capture them. They are forced to cross through a narrow pass high in the mountains. The push of one rock brings an avalanche that kills all the pursuers, closes the pass and leaves the hero, heroine and child to live out their lives in "the great sealed valley" where there is water, sunlight, fishes, birds and where we are sure such people will get along and live happy ever after.

Too Much Speed

Tuesday, June 21, 1921

Too Much Speed is the best all round satisfying motor car photoplay we have seen. It is a Paramount production. The star is supposed to be Wallace Reid, but we hand it to the director, Frank Urson, the writer of the story and scenario, Byron Morgan, to Theodore Roberts and the entire cast, for making a picture they had a good time doing. They enjoyed putting themselves and motor car America into this movie. So much so that their enjoyment gets across to the audience. At least it looked that way in the Randolph Theater where it is showing.

Can men love a motor car with the same kind of abiding affection they used to hold for Kentucky racing horses? This movie, *Too Much Speed*, sort of maintains just that. The film has several heroes and among them is the Pakro car. It wins a motor race in just the nick of time to win revenge for the driver who finishes with the car, to win marriage for the man who manipulated the car's entrance into the race, and a large volume of business for the man who manufactures the car.

Revenge, marriage, business, those are the apparent motives that dominate the theme. The overtone and the highlight, however, come from motor America, speedbug America, the America whose thought is of spark plugs, carburetors, six and eight cylinders, speed and the fastest way of getting some place, even if there is nothing special to be done after we get there. Such is this here movie, *Too Much Speed*.

Again we congratulate Frank Urson, the director of this movie, because he was on the job every minute getting speed into a speed movie for a speed nation of speed people.

Getting the thrills of a big motor racing event into a photoplay is no offhand job. They did that very thing in this movie.

Tom Mix Passes Through Chicago

When Tom Mix came to Chicago in the summer of 1921, Sandburg didn't miss the opportunity to interview one of his favorite film personalities. Sandburg's meeting with Mix at Fox headquarters on Wabash Avenue refers to Chicago's "Film Row" district. From the 1920s through the early 1960s, a mile-long section of south Wabash Avenue was the center for everything from film distributors to movie projector repair services.

Wednesday, June 22, 1921

If Tom Mix had to enter the movie game via an Edisonesque questionnaire he would still be punching cows—but nobody would know it but himself and the cows. At least so he opined yesterday during his short stop in Chicago on his way east to the Carpentier-Dempsey battle to which he has been given ringside seats by his old-time friend, Jack Dempsey.

"Back in the old days when a man had to have a college education to be a success," he drawled in true Western style as he sped along in a car on his way to give the children of the Haven School the treat of seeing him in person, "I used to be pretty worried about my future. What could a rough brute like me do? You don't have to have any education to be a good cowpuncher, you know—just be able to swing a rope, be a good judge of distance and be able to guess where the sheriff is going to be before he decides himself.

"I thought I never would be anything but a cow puncher and cows aren't awfully good company as a permanent thing, you know. They get morose at times and don't seem very talkative. But then the movies came along and I quit sighing for a college education.

"Why, according to Edison, I'm 93 percent ignorant. I could only answer one of his questions. That was the one, 'What are prunes?' I knew all about prunes because I ate so many of them when I was a cowpuncher that I got interested in their origin."

Tom's favorite horse is coming through Chicago today on his way to New York where he and Tom will perform on Broadway for some picture which is as yet a secret. After two days of movie acting, the horse will be sent back west again and the rest of the picture completed there. Tom Mix writes his own scenarios and thinks up his stunts, which are not fakes, as the scars on his face testify. His daredevil tricks keep the Fox studio people on the jump because their efforts to get insurance on Tom have met with no success. They have to watch him closely so that he doesn't do something too foolish.

As yet he has told no one why he is taking pictures with his horse on Broadway and his friends are fearful that he is planning to make a tour of the elevated roads on horseback.

Friday, July 8, 1921

Tom Mix doesn't care. He says so. Sitting in a lobby of the Fox offices on Wabash Avenue, he said it like this:

"What do I care? They say, 'As an actor he's a good horseman.' That don't make any difference to me. I don't care whether they take me for an actor or a horseman. All I want is that they come and see my pictures and they're doing just that."

People were calling him "Mister Mix." The mister stuff sounded off color.

"Would you tell us what you think about making fewer pictures and making them better?"

"Oh, there are fellows with temperament talking about that. As for me, I start work every day at eight in the morning and go on until after five in the afternoon. I've done nine pictures in one year. Done five this year and expect to make three or four more."

"Have you ever done a film where you doubled, where you played yourself and somebody else?"

"No, I've never done any reg'lar doubles. But some fellow got to impersonating me out in Los Angeles. Borrowed $50 in one place and $100 another place, telling the folks he was Tom Mix. Went to some Texas towns, to St. Louis and Washington, playing off he was me. I got hold of him and nearly broke his face for him. He made me lots of trouble. That's the only case of doubles I been mixed up with." So goes Tom Mix, frank, straightaway, radiating the human stuff that gives his pictures a cleaner and more wholesome quality in general than many of the photoplays from the hands of more sophisticated craftsmen who know more about art and hokum.

Fighters in Action in Motion Pictures

Before the advent of radio, close-circuit television, and cable networks, fight fans eagerly lined up at movie box offices to watch their favorite pugilists battle in the "squared circle." Like many reporters, Sandburg enjoyed a good boxing match and often devoted his movie column to fight films.

Saturday, June 25, 1921

Having seen Jack Dempsey in action—in the movies—and having seen Georges Carpentier in action—in the movies—one is able to form an opinion as to which one of the two is the best fighting man and therefore which of the two will be wearing the world's championship belt after the knockout contest of July 2.

Having seen Jack Dempsey train and box—in the Pathe reels—and having seen Georges Carpentier administer a knockout to a rival lover—in the photoplay *A Wonder Man* at the Band Box Theater—one is qualified to say that Jack Dempsey looks hard as nails and Carpentier has speed and can box.

The movies bring before the eyes of the millions figures of destiny and they bring these figures to the common movie fan even more vividly and intimately than to the owners of $50 seats at the New Jersey ringside.

In spite of the fact that actual movies of the real fight will probably not be shown because of the laws which prohibit such exhibition, the fighters, their personalities, tricks, ways of life and methods of battle will be fairly familiar to the millions who follow the silversheet news of current history.

Incidentally, one enterprising fight fan is working on the proposition that the entire Dempsey-Carpentier fight can be filmed in cartoon style. It will not be an actual motion picture of the real thing but it will present all the foot, leg, head and fist work of the fight. Such animated cartoons are not contrary to law, according to this fan, who says he has consulted eminent legal authority and is therefore going to show us who must stay at home just how the final haymaker was swung and what led up to it.

Also, incidentally and as a footnote, we might say we have seen a dull newsreel. Often we have seen audiences all listless through reels of movie conspiracy and weddings and robberies. But thus far, it has always seemed to us that audiences are animated, alive and on their mettle, having a good time and perhaps learning a little, when the silver sheet brings on the President of the Republic, the King of Zamboango, the launching of a battleship or the strongest man in the world eating ice cream after lifting a team of dray truck horses.

Black Roses

An audience favorite in the 1910s and early 1920s, Sessue Hayakawa was a rarity for early Hollywood: an Asian actor who starred in lead roles. After earning a degree in political science at the University of Chicago (which Sandburg duly notes), Hayakawa ended up in Los Angeles and the picture business. Handsome and acrobatic, he played a variety of parts, alternating heroic and villainous roles. For a time Hayakawa even had his own production company. In 1923 he moved to France, where he worked in the French film industry well into the sound era. Hayakawa returned to Hollywood in the 1940s and became an accomplished character actor. His portrayal of Colonel Saito in David Lean's The Bridge on the River Kwai *(1957) earned Hayakawa an Oscar nomination for Best Supporting Actor.*

I20 SESSUE HAYAKAWA
Starring in R-C Productions

From the collection of Arnie Bernstein.

An audience favorite in the 1910s and early 1920s, Sessue Hayakawa was a rarity for early Hollywood: an Asian actor who starred in lead roles.

Thursday, June 30, 1921

Sessue Hayakawa is the star in Black Roses, presented at the Adams Theater. The central theme about which the photoplay revolves is the personality of this Japanese actor, who has forged to the front with a remarkable following in the motion picture world.

It is a murder mystery plot, with the cards all stacked, the stage set and the circumstances riveted, apparently to send the hero to the gallows. But the man and woman, who, in collusion, were responsible for the murder, let their tongues slip in an unguarded moment. Wailing steno-graphers with their notebooks, take the fatal words. The detectives arrive to arrest the hero. He introduces them to the stenographers with the documents and goes free.

The acting of Sessue Hayakawa is a matter that goes back to personality. What is it about his personality that is answerable for the charm and the appeal? Undoubtedly the straight limbed, clean and active manhood of this actor is partly answerable. Also, there is an element of intelligence, suggestiveness of face and eye.

He is "baffling," but baffling in a way that has an appeal to audiences. Then there is the physical suppleness of him, "clean as a hound's tooth." All of which brings us properly to the fact that Sessue Hayakawa, when a student at the University of Chicago, was a tagmate lead in athletics.

He is a wrestler, not only in ju jitsu, but in catch-as-catch-can and Grace-du-man. One of his intimate acquaintances is "Strangler" Lewis, former world's champion wrestler, with whom Hayakawa has appeared in many practice matches. Boxing, baseball and tennis, also swimming, rowing, aviation, riding and dancing are other sports that keep him going.

Swimming springs from 50 to 150 yards are favorite stunts with him, and it was in swimming that he is credited with having hung up several records at the U of C.

Such is Sessue Hayakawa. Much of his success as an actor traces back to his skill in athletics and maintenance of form in that field.

July

Charlie Chaplin's New One

Though Chaplin never made Pouf Pouf, *the embryonic creative ideas that resulted in* Limelight *(1952) are evident in this story outline.*

Wednesday, July 20, 1921

Charlie Chaplin's next big one will show the famous comic tragedian in a role without the hat and the cane, the mustache and derby. In his Hollywood home and studio he is working away on *Pouf Pouf,* a French story in which the hero is a clown who saves the life of a child. It is said that Jackie Coogan may be called in to play the part of the child.

The plot of *Pouf Pouf* has the sort of appeal that sounds like a Chaplin film hit. Pouf Pouf, the clown, has with his bag of tricks brought high laughter to a child in the audience. That night the child is taken sick. It's a bad case. In his delirium he cries for the clown, Pouf Pouf. The child's father is a poor man and the clown is a rich man, starred by the Hippodrome in Paris. In the finish the clown goes to the home of the poor man, puts on his make-up, does his comic stunts for the child, takes the little one in his arms and wins him back to life.

This sounds precisely like the sort of stuff that will put over Chaplin once for all as no comedian at all, essentially, but rather some paradox of a great comic tragedian.

Why Scenarios Go Wrong

Wednesday, July 20, 1921

Dramatic plot is one thing. Narrative is another. The difference between the two is important. Ignorance of the difference is one cause of why so many scenarios go wrong, according to Wycliffe A. Hill, president Photodramatists' League, who says, "Ninety-nine amateur writers out of a hundred write narrative instead of dramatic plots and they do not seem to know the difference between the two."

In using the terms "dramatic plot" and "narrative," there may be some of the same confusion that afflicts a high proportion of films. What Mr. Hill is trying to say to scenario writers may be this:

Don't write stories to be read. Write movie stuff. Write what the director should direct and the actors act. A movie story is not read in a book; it is seen on a screen. Think about it and write it as action and mummery to be played and seen.

August

Nothing "Stuck Up" About Ben

Famous for his permanently crossed eyes, comic actor Ben Turpin granted Sand-burg an interview during a promotional visit to Chicago. The Windy City was old stomping grounds for the screen comedian; in 1907 Turpin entered the movie business for Chicago-based Essanay Studios. Doubling as on-screen talent and off-screen janitor, Turpin rose through the ranks, eventually working as comic foil to Charlie Chaplin, Laurel and Hardy, and many others. He also starred in numerous two-reelers of his own.

Saturday, August 6, 1921

Ben Turpin, who is just finishing a week at McVicker's Theater and who will top the vaudeville program in person at the Rialto Theater during the new week, is letting Chicagoans know something of his past struggles. Just because he is one of the highest salaried comedians in comedies, and just because Mack Sennett wires him three times a day regarding his physical health, is no reason why Ben Turpin should become "stuck up." At least Ben feels that way about it. Someone had told him of a children's hospital over on the West Side. Ben immediately expressed a desire to play "funny" for the kids. It was while motoring over there that Ben looked at a row of brick houses on Washington Boulevard with long rows of stone steps and said, "I used to scrub those steps for 50 cents a pair just 14 years ago." What a confession from a movie idol! And with the same frankness he added: "Yep, I used to be a sort of handy man in this neighborhood. Cut the grass in the summer and shovel the snow in the winter was my task—all for 25 cents. I remember how hard it was for me to save my first hundred dollars. In fact, I never did. Each time I found my bankbook registering about $30 along came a doctor bill and I had to start all over. I was hurt 19 times in two years while working at Essanay. No, I never did save that hundred. The first money I ever put away was when Mack Sennett handed me a thousand dollars upon my signing his contract. That went into the bank quickly. After that saving was not so hard. The little old bankbook whispered in my ear just before I left Los Angeles that my balance had just topped $50,000. Not so bad for a cock-eyed guy of 57 years who was scrubbing stone steps only a few years ago, who was a bell boy at the Sherman Hotel, who eked out a bare living in cheap vaudeville theaters for too many years to remember and who has stayed married to the same woman for almost 16 years."

Broken Blossoms

Originally given a wide release in 1920, D. W. Griffith's Broken Blossoms *remains one of the classics of silent cinema. The story, set in the ghettos of London, revolves around an abused young woman (Lillian Gish), her father, an alcoholic ex-boxer (Donald Crisp), and the peaceful Chinese immigrant (Richard Barthelmess) who changes their lives. Sandburg covered the film as a re-release; yet his comment regarding Griffith's financial stakes and box office profits are apparently misinformed.* Broken Blossoms *was a critical and popular hit; Griffith's monetary difficulties came through a distribution deal which eventually worked itself out. Wrote Lillian Gish, "All Griffith pictures were compared to* The Birth of a Nation *when it came to making money. Whenever his other productions didn't achieve those fantastic profits, the trade deemed them failures. But* Broken Blossoms *was a tremendous success, and proved that a film didn't have to have a chase or a rescue or a happy ending to hold an audience."*[4]

Thursday, August 11, 1921

Broken Blossoms, the D. W. Griffith production, is showing at the Bandbox Theater this week. It is without doubt the most tragic picture, perhaps the most concentrated epic of tragedy, ever put on the screen.

One would call it brutal if it did not contain a sublime romance. In the finish the three principal characters are laid out in death.

One should have no more depression over viewing this masterpiece than over a Shakespearean tragedy, such as *Hamlet, Macbeth* or *Richard the Third.*

It is safe to make the prediction that *Broken Blossoms* is a movie classic that will be revived from time to time for many years to come. Charlie Chaplin says it easily leads all other pictures by Griffith. Griffith lost money on it, according to reports. If that is so, it is a hard commentary on the movie-going public, because *Broken Blossoms* is one of the strong, clean motion-picture triumphs.

How Censors Differ in Thought and Deed

In the summer of 1921, state movie censors from across the nation met at Chicago's Blackstone Hotel. The conclave, organized by Universal Film Manufacturing's president Carl Laemmle, brought together official guardians of public morals with leaders of the film industry. Sandburg, a strong anti-censorship advocate, duly reported on the conference.

Saturday, August 13, 1921

Censors are different from each other. Censors have temperament. Censors may or may not think there are fixed, unchangeable laws, gauges and standards by which products of the human are to be interpreted and stamped "good," "bad."

And yet—after looking over a number of censors collected from various parts of the

United States and Canada—looking them over while they were lunching in the English Room of the Blackstone Hotel—we do not hesitate about saying censors are different from each other, they have temperament just like artists and there is nothing fixed or unchangeable about them unless it is the idea that censorship is a healthy institution for human progress, motion picture producers, city and state governments—and the members of censorship boards.

The Philadelphia censor made a little speech at this meeting last Wednesday and all was droll. The drolleries that may fall from the lips of a Philadelphia censor would surprise those who easily toss him into a fixed Puritan category.

"After a while there will be motion picture plays for children only," said the Philadelphia censor. "That will be a good thing for children. At the same time we may then expect pictures made for adults only. Then it may be censorship boards will be more necessary than ever."

He referred to the expedition the censors are making to California, lending an allusion to California being "dry." There were ironic regrets in his pronunciation of the word "dry." The illusion that all censors favor prohibition, or assume the mask and outward aspect of prohibitionists, was dispelled in the touch of grief put into the comment on a dry California.

The Maryland censor spoke of his job as probably coming to a close one of these days when federal censorship would be established. The Maryland censor was the most softly human of the lot. We are sure he would order any cut film cutout whatsoever only with regret.

The Boston censor, it was evident, enjoys the scissors. He spoke as an official authority and a philosophical authoritarian who regards his work as of high import to human welfare. It was of unique interest that he should challenge the Maryland censor's surmise that eventually all censorship powers would be lodged in federal boards. This would be wrong, as the Boston censor sees it. Each city is an individual case demanding individual treatment at the hands of a censorship authority of that locale and understanding its individual needs.

Mr. Berman and Mr. Hill of the Universal Film Manufacturing company lit up the censorial landscape with happy faces. As the censors continue their journey and pay their visit to the movie production centers in California, holding long powwows with the producers, it is sure that new viewpoints, worthwhile in the relationships of producer and censor, will be developed.

Headin' Home

A popular draw at American baseball parks throughout the 1920s, George Herman "Babe" Ruth also enjoyed box office success in both vaudeville and movies. He appeared in at least three silent films in addition to countless newsreels. Headin'

Home *bears little resemblance to Ruth's real biography; on the other hand, it helped inflate Ruth's folk hero status with the American public.*

Tuesday, August 16, 1921

The two most vastly popular recognized amusements of the American people as a nation are: (1) the movies; (2) baseball.

It is proper, therefore, the movies should present the bimbo high one, the chiefest and foremost, the one and the only known as Babe Ruth.

Previously we have seen the Bambino, the sport, in newsreels, showing how he holds the bat, stands at the plate, maneuvers his eyes and then plugs the pill for the skylights.

Now, however, the one and only, the champion home run hitter who leads all others ever known to the annals of big league and backlot ball, he is now to be seen in a photoplay with a story of his home town, a foiled villain and a sweetheart.

Not unlike some of today's athletes, home run king George Herman "Babe" Ruth parlayed baseball success into a brief movie career.

From the collection of Arnie Bernstein.

Such a poor player he was in his hometown. They wouldn't let him play on the hometown team. So the out-of-town team hired him. And in the ninth inning, with all sacks full, score 14-14, he knocks the ball five blocks away—through the window of a church.

Years later he is seen batting in the big league, while the villain, the man who barred him from playing on the hometown team, sells peanuts in the bleachers.

Then he goes back to the hometown to kiss his mother and eat the pie only she bakes, put a ring on a girl's finger and pay a bill of $13.87 for the church window he broke with his first home run.

The final scenes are long shots at big ball crowds. There is something of sea tides about the swirl of American crowds across the grounds after a big game.

The Yankee Photo Corporation, which conceived and worked out this film play with Babe Ruth in *Headin' Home*, lived up to its name of "Yankee."

The Golem

Writer, director, and star of The Golem, *Paul Wegener, previously served the same roles in his 1915 version of this Jewish myth. This 1920 remake had a profound impact on Sandburg; he constantly held it up as an example of great film-making. Ironically, Wegener became an important part of the Nazi film industry, directing and acting in several propaganda movies, though rumor had it he secretly provided information to the Russians during World War II.[5]*

Thursday, August 18, 1921

The Golem is a masterpiece of motion picture drama. It is a photoplay of colossal proportions. It is so simple in the story it tells and the characters and situations it develops that any child who enjoys fairy stories and legends would enjoy and understand it.

Going farther beyond its simplicity of appeal, it strikes home with haunting challenges for those who ask for art, intellectual conceptions, accomplishment of design and the masterly deliberation of sure artistry.

The Golem is showing at Orchestra Hall this week. It is one of those few original productions of cinema art which rebuke the ignorance and shatter the assumptions of those who like to look down on the movies, who feel that the other arts have nothing to learn from the silver sheet.

The art, the play spirit, the mummery, craft and workmanship which lie back of the production of *The Golem* are of the stuff out of which the future of the movies is to root and establish a cinema art surpassing that of the present hour.

The producers of *The Golem* are the same people who made *The Cabinet of Dr.*

Caligari. Persons who have seen both productions are already disputing which is the better of the two. The dispute is conducted after the manner of two Shakespeareans talking about whether *Hamlet* or *Macbeth* should take first rank.

The story is from an old Jewish legend of The Golem, a mythic figure to be created first in cold clay and then by ways known to the secret books of wizards to have the breath of life blown into him. The King of Bohemia has told the Jews they shall be banished from the city of Prague. A wizard of a rabbi takes down his old books and searches out the secret of making The Golem. He finds it. He shapes a massive clay giant. He calls up circles and sashes of flame and by wizardry gets the breath of life into the clay giant. Then comes one of the most sublime scenes ever put into motion picture film. The rabbi takes The Golem to the court of the King of Bohemia. The King and his women say, "This monster does not interest us. Amuse us, O Jew."

Then the rabbi calls up a vision of Israel, a slow grand set of processionals across a panorama of clouds. The jazzed king and his court ladies laugh as though it's a thing to laugh at. The walls and roofs of the palace begin to tumble on their heads. Silken women jump from the windows for safety. The king calls the rabbi to save him. The rabbi orders The Golem to stand next to the king. Massive stone pillars smash down on the shoulders of the giant, who stands mutely and indifferently doing what he is told.

Later is a time when The Golem refuses to do what he is told. He sets fire to the ghetto, drags the daughter of the rabbi from her room, pushes down the gates of the city—and at the end is defeated by the careless whim of a child he stoops to hold in his arms for a moment.

The music of the symphony orchestra and the chorus synchronizes and matches the dulcets and diapasons of the photodrama.

The Golem is a masterpiece and will stand among the markers of destiny in cinema art for a good long time.

The Blot

Lois Weber, director of The Blot, *specialized in social dramas. Unafraid of controversy, her films addressed such issues as birth control (which she supported), abortion (which she opposed), poverty, child labor laws, and capital punishment. Quite successful in her day, studio boss Carl Laemmle rewarded Weber with her own production company on the Universal lot. She later switched to Paramount, but by the mid-1920s her career was in decline. Poor box office performance led to fewer directing assignments, though she did helm a few films in the early 1930s. Sandburg's reference to Weber's activism on "prohibition of all European films from entry into the United States" reflects the mood of many Hollywood filmmakers at the time. With the importing of foreign actors and directors to southern California, to say nothing of well-received European movies at theaters throughout the country, some Hollywood circles worried that foreign films would hurt the market for homegrown material.*

Friday, August 26, 1921

The Blot, showing at Barbee's Loop Theater, is a photoplay written, produced and directed by Lois Weber. As Miss Weber recently has been an extreme advocate of prohibition of all European films from entry into the United States, *The Blot*, with its reflexes of American life, as Lois Weber sees it, has special interest.

Side by side live the university professor, his wife and family, and a foreign-born shoemaker, his wife and family. One, the university professor, lives in poverty; he and his daughter have holes in the bottoms of their shoes—and these shoe bottoms appear in scene after scene.

So far has their poverty gone that the wife of the professor takes the house cat to the backyard fence, where it can reach over and eat from the garbage can of the foreign-born neighbor, who earns $100 a week and has all the comforts of life. Such is the drift and portent of Miss Weber's latest release.

As a piece of realist portrayal of life, which is what Miss Weber attempts, *The Blot* may be this or that. The college students she tries to depict are out of perspective and off key; the professors in universities, even when underpaid, do not let out the kind of cries for pity which Miss Weber attributes to this professor, and in her sketching of the life of a foreign workman and his family, Miss Weber gives us neither a typical family nor one that breathes individuality.

The Blot, while offered as a piece of realism, is a coarse job of patchwork in its realistic pretensions, attempting to be sensational in its picture of a cross-section of American life.

With the possible exception of the professor's daughter, there is nobody in this movie worth loving, hating, remembering. It seems to have been built out of gossip heard by Miss Weber concerning isolated instances that do not connect with the main fabric of American life.

If the professor's wife must have the cat eat from the neighbor's garbage can, one may prefer that the garbage can belong to somebody else than a foreign-born workman earning $100 a week.

The instance is not typical. Miss Weber hands us cartoons with neither a laugh nor a song nor an honest tragedy in their mummery.

The blot on *The Blot* is its sloven handling of pertinent issues in the American scene of today.

Either a little love or a big hate might have lifted this movie into something worth remembering.

The Three Musketeers

Tuesday, August 30, 1921

The Douglas Fairbanks interpretation of D'Artagnan, the hero of *The Three Musketeers*, is sure to go into the records as one of the more successful Doug Fairbanks movies, whether or not it is to be remembered as a specimen of creative dramatic work.

The literary people who have read Dumas' novel, *The Three Musketeers*, as an instance of the French novel of the romantic school—as well as the people who read *The Three Musketeers* because it is a bully book with a lot of swell fighting and shooting in it—both will be interested in looking over the latest offering of the most strenuous and reckless performer in the films today.

And the chances are that the literary people who want an interpretation with nuances will be disappointed. While the others, those on the lookout for a bully movie that passes the time, with plenty of clean fighting, good humor, touches of the comic, these will be more likely to find what they started for.

As a spectacle photodrama that cost a million dollars, *The Three Musketeers* is not much ahead, if at all, of other million dollar spectacle photodramas which have passed before our eyes in recent months and years.

The scenery in the various sets might have cost a million dollars if they were made of the same kinds of material and then again it wouldn't be quite so much as a million if the materials were something else again. Any contractor could write specifications that would bring the cost up to ten million.

However, leaving aside the point about whether this movie cost a million, a half million or six million, it is the acting, the acrobatics, the antics of Doug Fairbanks that put it over into the clear and keep the audiences rippling.

There are fairly good judges who say it wouldn't make much difference if the scenery had cost only a couple of thousand dollars and dummies had been used instead of supernumeraries, the Douglas Fairbanks crowd wouldn't hold it against him. What they come for is Doug, Doug's ways, tricks and manners.

With all the million dollar scenery, cast, costumes and so on, we don't get the feeling that we are in France and the regions referred to in the George M. Cohan song, "Over There."

Though the Dumas novel says it all happened in France, and the soldiers are in uniforms made up according to research department figures and drawings of what costumes were in the time of Cardinal Richelieu, it also happens that Doug Fairbanks is so decisively Doug and nobody else, that the audience keeps thinking of Doug instead of D'Artagnan, Mary Pickford instead of the Queen of France.

Without a doubt, too, there are Doug Fairbanks fans who believe that as a performer he is the full equal of anything D'Artagnan might have been, and if he had lived in France in the time of Richelieu, King Louis XIII, the Duke of Buckingham and the Queen, Anne of Austria, he would have earned a reputation as a daredevil and a go-getter equal to the leader of the three musketeers made known by Dumas.

The presentation of this exceptionally popular film performance is at the Randolph Theater. It is a production of the Douglas Fairbanks Pictures Corporation. Direction was by Fred Niblo.

September

Vamp of the Movies Replaced by Mothers

Saturday, September 10, 1921

The replacement of the vamp by the mother is one of the noticeable features of the passing films these days.

The woman who raises a brood of clamorous children and takes care of them while they all but kill her with their ups and downs, ins and outs, of the sluices and wine presses of life—the idealized, magnificent, battling she-wolf of a mother—this is now the topnotcher of the movies.

She replaces the lingering, luring, vixenish female desperado known to fiction, drama and movie as the vamp, a creature wild and as impossible, usually, as the marching animals of a dipsomaniac's dreams.

Where a while ago it was *Lying Lips* and *Luring Lips* and the timepieces were striking sex o'clock, we now look on *Over the Hill* and *The Old Nest* where the central theme is a deserted mother and the audiences carry relays of handkerchiefs, and pathos now spurts and now drips from the faucets.

That is one drift. The other noticeable drift is better movies coming along Somehow, the slump that hit Hollywood and other centers of film manufacture and motion picture art, with its resulting reductions in salaries and diminished number of employees, has also witnessed more hard work, more care and deliberation. They're making fewer and making 'em better.

Camille

This Camille, *the fifth film version of the tragic story, is remembered for sparking the off-screen relationship of its star, Nazimova, with rising star Rudolph Valentino. The romantic tale of* Camille *continued to be popular with several generations of moviemakers. Another silent version was made in 1927 with Norma Talmadge. The best known* Camille *is the 1937 version, featuring Greta Garbo and Robert Taylor and directed by George Cukor.*

Monday, September 19, 1921

Nazimova in *Camille* is Nazimova. The lady of the camellias, known to the Dumas story, known to the stage drama and played by Sarah Bernhardt and others, gets portrayed.

But it is Nazimova, her personality, stage ways, stage temperament, that are to the front up stage beckoning.

This is the best motion picture drama in which Nazimova has performed. Whether she can be rated an actress with a genius for character portrayal and the fulfillment of high dramatic moments is a question.

That she is a performer and can dominate stage settings, hold the eye, render poignant instants and rehearse memorable gestures—this must be noted of her ways in *Camille*.

The reminiscences, the silences, the repressionist way of putting across a mixed mystery of an emotion, which was what we saw in the Nazimova of the Ibsen plays on stage, these are not here.

Nevertheless, as entertainment, as popular exhibition of talents and devices, this *Camille* movie is far and away ahead of anything Nazimova was ever seen in when she played the tragedies of the Irreckonable Norse dramatist.

As a movie this is more of a movie than any that Mme. Nazimova has previously shown in. It is more strictly in the peculiar and exclusive technique of the silent drama.

There are more subtitles than there would be if they had put in action to say what words are left to say printed on the screen. But as motion pictures go, this is an improvement, and by long odds, over the previous endeavors of the first rate display of the lean writhing of this now thoroughly Americanized Russian actress.

Camille is worth seeing, very much so. It gets by. The close-ups have some wonderful dissolves. The backgrounds show an order of genius in creation of spiderwebs, draperies and a variety of conceits that hit off the fantastic angles of the life of the lady of the camellias.

It is a sweet death she dies, this lady, as the auctioneers come in and feel of the silk of the bedclothes, making estimates on how much they will bring for payment of her debts—a sweet death and a proper time to die. But it is more Nazimova in a simulation of sweet death of a poignant lady than it is stage mimicry that projects a character.

Rudolph Valentino must be mentioned as the lad who does Armand, while Zeffie Tilbury takes the role of Prudence. Rex Cherryman gives an excellent Gaston and William Oglamond as the father of Armand is surely convincing.

Scenario was by June Mathis. Metro produced it. Ray Smallwood showed form as a director. And if we may be permitted, we would suggest that a vast deal of the appeal and charm in this picture is due to Rudolph J. Berquist, the photographer, and Natacha Rambova, the art director.

The Ziegfeld Theater is showing this Nazimova *Camille* and R. E. Harmeyer, the manager, says its reception thus far indicates at least a four-weeks run. It takes a rarely good picture to do that in these days.

October

Tony Sarg's Aims and Efforts

After developing an international reputation as a puppeteer, Tony Sarg turned his talents to animation. Sarg used cardboard cutouts to create intricate little films that delighted audiences. He also dabbled in screenwriting, penning the script for the 1921 comedy Fireman, Save My Child. *To see a clip of Sarg's* The First Circus *check the Film Preservation website at* www.filmpreservation.com. *"The little theater" Sandburg refers to was a small, independent drama group in Chicago dedicated to staging thought-provoking plays. In many ways, this ensemble was a forerunner of such later Chicago theater companies as Steppenwolf and Organic.*

Saturday, October 1, 1921

When a motion picture theater announces a Tony Sarg feature or presentation, it will be generally found worth looking at. Tony Sarg, it may be odd to relate, comes from among "the little theater" enthusiasts. That is, he knows what the highbrows are talking about in so far as the highbrows themselves know. Puppets and marionettes were Sarg's specialty in "the little theater" fold and among the drama league promoters of "better thinks." Also Sarg became a special student of Chinese shadow and puppet figures used in delivering old mystery plays. Now he has applied his special attainments to the production of one and two-reel movie features. The latest has to do with action about an Egyptian king who had a tooth pulled in the whimsical and rapid movement of photoplay puppets; it is a winner.

Says Foolish Wives Cost a lot of Money; Report Calls Picture a Record Breaker in Amount of Film

After learning his craft as an assistant to D. W. Griffith, Erich von Stroheim became known as "The Man You Love to Hate" in the late 1910s, usually playing a cruel "Hun" in WWI films. While developing an on-screen persona, von Stroheim continued building his behind-the-scenes talents, often working as assistant director and occasional art director for the films he appeared in. After the Armistice, von Stroheim talked his way into directing for Carl Laemmle's Universal studios. He quickly developed a reputation as a detailed filmmaker, sparing no expense in budget or final running time for his richly detailed and psychologically complex extravaganzas. Ultimately, this would lead to von Stroheim's undoing. For Foolish Wives, *von Stroheim had Universal build him a complete recreation of a Monte Carlo casino. The film's final budget was around $735,000, "so close to a million," von Stroheim later said, "(they) decided to call it, for publicity purposes, 'the first million-dollar picture.'"[6] The studio publicity department even built an electric advertising sign on Broadway, spelling the director's name as "von $troheim." "A lot of good that did me!" von Stroheim exclaimed.[7] Between its length and frank subject matter,* Foolish Wives *was a groundbreaking film. Von Stroheim's New York premiere cut ran close to three and a half hours. This version was drastically edited for national release, then cut again at urgings of various censors across the country. "They all came with their scissors," said von Stroheim.[8] Ironically, it turned out, von Stroheim's greatest strengths had ultimately worked against him. Studio executives had final say on the film and, fearing audiences wouldn't sit through a complicated epic, reduced the film even further. It was a situation von Stroheim would face throughout his directing career.*

Saturday, October 15, 1921

The last bulletins from the Universal Film Manufacturing company estimated the cost of producing the film for *Foolish Wives* at $1 million.

A grapevine from the Universal puts that cost at $1.2 million, saying further that under the direction of Erich von Stroheim they have produced 300,000 feet of film which must be cut to 6,000 feet.

This is understood to be a record breaker in amount of film. The final photoplay will represent siftings that gave the director and producers different kinds of headaches.

Picking the best 6,000 feet of film out of 300,000 means work. In the movie business they call that work "the post mortem," which properly slangs it.

Nevertheless, how about this? Does it mean they are going to get a masterpiece of a winning movie because they took a record-breaking amount of film and because they poured umpty umpteen hundreds of thousands of dollars into it? Not necessarily.

We saw Griffith nearly go broke with his lavish expenditures on *Intolerance*. And the public didn't care much about it; when it was broken into three separate movies it had as good patronage as when the three were in one.

Way Down East, a cheaply produced and trashy movie compared with *Intolerance*, has netted another fortune for Griffith. Furthermore, there is the example of *Over the Hill*, a cheaply made movie, with no expensive sets or costly stars, yet a record breaker in box office intake.

These contrasting specimens prove fairly well that money may be thrown at the birds with expensive production that gets no box office results, while on the other hand the cheaply produced film may draw the steady, long run crowds.

Carrying the comparison farther along from the realm of strictly business into the field of aspiring art, we find such instances as Chaplin's *The Kid* paying its author and producer $100,000 at the first jump.

The box office intake from *The Cabinet of Dr. Caligari*, produced in Germany at a cost of $115,000 was more than $400,000 in the United States, while the figures are even more favorable, it is reported, on *The Golem*.

Taking two strictly American examples of great photoplays, there are not so many "great" ones but we can number them on the fingers of our two hands (or less) and we find that *The Miracle Man* made a large fortune for George Loane Tucker and his associates, while Griffith was set way back by *Broken Blossoms*.

And there we are. Von Stroheim has a big leeway and has spent the ransom of 16 Balkan kings on *Foolish Wives*, and it may or may not be what the public wants.

On the other hand some production being wrought out modestly and at low cost in an out-of-the-way producer's lot may prove to be the surprise *The Miracle Man* was. It is this element of chance that gives a sporting phase to the movie world. It is seen in the breath and speech of men.

Saturday, November 26, 1921

Foolish Wives, the Universal million dollar motion picture, which von Stroheim and some 2,000 other people have been working on for the last 20 months, has finally reached the stage where they are endeavoring to refine it to exhibitional dimensions, which means eliminating 790 reels of expensive material. Von Stroheim, who wrote the story, plays the leading role and directed the film, photographed 800 reels—from which 10 reels will be selected to show the public. Editing, cutting and titling *Foolish Wives* is now going forward and at last reports from Universal City, Cal., the picture has been cut down to 25 reels, with at least two months more work to fit it for showing.

Little Lord Fauntleroy

In Little Lord Fauntleroy, *Mary Pickford played the male title role, as well as that of the mother, "Dearest." "People were baffled that I looked nine inches taller as the mother than I did as the boy," Pickford later wrote. "Three of those inches came from an elevated ramp on which I walked whenever Little Lord Fauntleroy was beside me."*[9] *The remaining six inches came from built-up shoes Pickford wore. Then, taking cinematographer Charles Rosher's suggestion of utilizing a stand-in (the first time this now-commonplace device was used in a movie), Pickford played opposite a mannequin decked out in Pickford's trademark golden curls.*[10] *"The scene in which 'Dearest' kisses her son took us 15 hours to accomplish," Pickford recalled. "It lasted exactly three seconds on the screen!"*[11] *The hard work paid off,* Little Lord Fauntleroy *was one of the most popular films of 1921.*

Saturday, October 22, 1921

The appeal of Mary Pickford for a rather wide-flung clan of moviegoers will be strengthened by her acting, her stunts and her portrayal of two characters in *Little Lord Fauntleroy*, a United Artists production having its first run at the Randolph Theater.

The picture is a screen version of the famous and popular children's book by Frances Hodgson Burnett. Those who have read the book and who are also to see the film rendition will have speech among each other about whether the movie is as good as the book or better or worse.

To some fairly good pairs of eyes, which have read the book and have now seen the movie, the verdict is better than the book. Not so often does the comment run that way.

The appeal of Mary Pickford which has cinched for her the hitherto mentioned wide-flung clan of moviegoers is one based on her child angles, the winsome phase, the sweet eyes, the curls, a rapid and whimsical girlishness.

These gifts or qualities have a more free range in *Little Lord Fauntleroy* than in any picture of hers since *Suds* and since several before *Suds*.

In so far as the title of "America's sweetheart" may in justice apply to Mary more strictly than to a dozen other sweethearts in the movie business, the title gains substance through her work in the present instance.

It is a clean picture, exceptionally fine and natural in the flow of its story, splendidly faithful to the spirit of the child's book from which it was derived.

The double exposure is used much, so much that one may hear the audience asking questions and discussing how this or that flash was achieved. For Mary's duty in this movie was to play a fond mother and an equally fond son of that mother.

Therefore, when "Dearest," the mother (played by Mary

A *Chicago Daily News* ad for Mary Pickford in *Little Lord Fauntleroy*, a movie that Sandburg declares is faithful to the spirit of the children's book of the same name (Saturday, October 22, 1921).

Pickford), squeezes to her arms the beloved and curly-locked son, Little Lord Fauntleroy (played by Mary Pickford), the audience sort of loses the thread of the story because of conjectures on how the director, cameramen and actress have manipulated film, camera and printing to arrive at this screen apparition of one person seeming to be two persons in an embrace.

The mother wears a bustle and other pieces of apparel in vogue 40 years ago, when the Fauntleroy story was timed. Clever designing of clothes and hair dress was effected, so that Mary as the mother looks taller than her son.

It will be interesting to see whether this picture with Mrs. Douglas Fairbanks in the leading role will have as long a run as that of her husband in *The Three Musketeers*, which it follows.

November

The Idle Class

"*Tartarin of Tarascon*," whom Sandburg refers to, is a character created by nineteenth century French author Alphonse Daudet. Tartarin was described by many critics as a sort of "Don Quixote from Midi."

Saturday, November 5, 1921

Where Charlie Chaplin's work used to be sketchy and loose, it now ties up into stories.

The Idle Class, his latest movie, a First National picture, is a story. It has a tale to unfold as definitely as anything in the books of O. Henry.

It is a nice story and as such is told nicely—except where it is vulgar, comic and elemental—which it is aplenty.

The tale opens with our hero letting himself out from under a passenger train, dusting his more or less glad rags, which include the large shoes, the baggy pants and the dinky derby.

Our hero then joins up with a bunch of golf players and uses his niblick with skill off and on except for such moments as he is kicked off the grounds.

However, he is also an absent-minded husband of a very good-looking wife (played by Edna Purviance). He reaches for the military hairbrushes, but having covered them with his silk hat he cannot find them.

He inspects his spotless attire before the mirror and then sets out to meet his wife on the incoming train at the railroad station. He finds he has good reason for not going to the depot as planned. The reason is vulgar, comic, elemental.

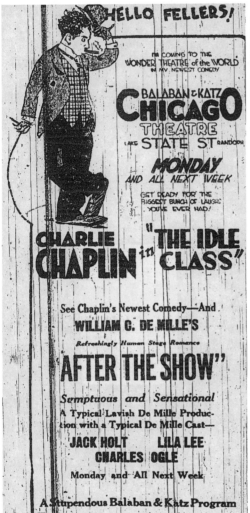

HELLO FELLERS!

I'M COMING TO THE
WONDER THEATRE of the WORLD
IN MY NEWEST COMEDY

BALABAN & KATZ
CHICAGO
THEATRE
LAKE STATE ST RANDOLPH
MONDAY
AND ALL NEXT WEEK

GET READY FOR THE
BIGGEST BUNCH OF LAUGHS
YOU'VE EVER HAD!

CHARLIE
CHAPLIN in "THE IDLE CLASS"

See Chaplin's Newest Comedy—And
WILLIAM C. DE MILLE'S
Refreshingly Human Stage Romance
"AFTER THE SHOW"
Sumptuous and Sensational
A Typical Lavish De Mille Produc-
tion with a Typical De Mille Cast—
JACK HOLT   LILA LEE
CHARLES OGLE
Monday and All Next Week
A Stupendous Balaban & Katz Program

A *Chicago Daily News* ad for Charlie
Chaplin's *The Idle Class*, which according
to Sandburg, "has a tale to unfold as
definitely as anything in the books of
O. Henry" (Monday, October 24, 1921).

Later, on an evening when the husband is due at a masquerade ball, the husband shows up as a knight in armor clad—and the visor of his helmet has snapped shut so no prying will set it loose.

Meantime, our hero, the hobo, whose face is the same as that of the husband, has accidentally wandered into the ballroom and is seized by the wife of the absent-minded husband. The wife very naturally supposes that the man with the face the same as her husband is wearing the hobo make-up as part of the masquerade.

For the hobo, the romance isn't so easy. Only the day before he had stood leaning against a tree by the road when along came this lady on horseback and gave him a glance of her eye.

And while he leaned against the tree he had a daydream and saw the lady's horse run away, her life in danger, while he mounts a short, gray jackass, rides till the jackass throws him, then running a footrace he overtakes the runaway horse, jumps on its back and holds the rescued lady in his arms. Then he comes to—leaning against the same old tree.

Yet it is this same lady that calls him to her at the dance. For a few moments life holds much for the 'bo. Then enters the husband. The hobo takes a tomato can opener and slits the visor loose from the armor.

Exit hobo—sadly—with an earful of thanks from the lady.

That Chaplin is supremely resourceful as a pantomimist is seen in *The Idle Class*, which he wrote before playing and directing.

The absent-minded husband, after a fierce rebuke from his wife, stands at a table with his back and shoulders shaken with what seems to be grief. It is the moment when the grief is to be expected from this tender, yearning man whose worst fault is being absent-minded.

As he turns about and faces the audience, however, it is seen he holds in his two hands a shaker and is seen to be mixing a drink rather than expressing grief.

The Idle Class has its pathos, tells a very human story well, and is vulgar, comic, elemental—along with Don Quixote and Tartarin of Tarascon.

There will be nice people say they see nothing but clever knockabout work in it, while others will say they prefer this to Moliere.

It is a two reeler, about on par with *A Dog's Life*, not so good as *Shoulder Arms*, nor mounting to the size of *The Kid*, which is a six-reeler.

The Dempsey-Carpentier Fight

David Belasco, whom Sandburg points out as a ringside fan, was known as "The Bishop of Broadway." A prolific writer and producer, Belasco is also remembered for telling a young actor to change her stage name from Gladys Smith to Mary Pickford. Another ringside observer, Frances Starr, was a popular stage performer of the time. Tex Rickard, whose looks Sandburg compares to Eugene Debs, was a fight promoter during the Roaring Twenties. As for Debs, he was a strong union supporter and a leader of the Socialist Party. Twice he ran for President of the United States on the Socialist ticket, the second time while in jail for violating the Espionage Act, a dubious conviction that was an attempt to silence Debs's anti-war efforts. Sandburg, an active Socialist in the first decade of the twentieth century, worked with Debs to promote the party. "No one who has heard Sandburg has failed to be impressed by the dignity of his presence, the force of his logic, the eloquence of his speech, and the sincerity of his purpose," Debs once said.[12]

Thursday, November 10, 1921

The Dempsey-Carpentier fight pictures showing at Barbee's Loop Theater are just about everything that could be asked for by any person who wishes to know how that fight looked to those who saw it and how the crowd of 90,000 spectators looked to those who were among the 90,000.

How the fighters trained in the daily regime at their respective camps, how the managers and auxiliaries and aids, even unto the cooks who prepared the beefsteaks of the pugilists, and how at last each of the two boxers acquitted himself in the final exchanges of blows that settled the first world's international championship, it is all here in the films for those who wish whatever advantage may be derived from being an eyewitness of the most notable battle in ring history from the standpoint of aroused interest, the amount of prize money at stake, the number of persons in attendance, and the carrying of the news of the outcome by telegraph and wireless to a wide-flung audience of readers, sports and gamblers.

The brief moments in which the Frenchman had the American staggering, and the far larger number of moments in which the American had it all his own way, executing with friendly ruthlessness a task prerequisite to the receipt of the winner's share of the gate money—it is all here with the fidelity of events seen by the actual eye.

In point of photography these fight pictures more than get by. They are clear, free from blur and fog in the major showings. And the boys who took 'em were a batter that circled the ring from various heights of scaffoldings.

Most of the close-ups are a better view of the ring than was had by perhaps 90,000 of the 90,000 fight fans, if we may so call David Belasco, Frances Starr and many other dignitaries and beauties who occupied ringside seats.

Tex Rickard, the shrewd and the cool, carrying a remarkable physical and facial resemblance to Eugene Debs, is properly staged as the mastermind of the big show, builder of the mammoth lumber coliseum, handler of single checks amounting to $200,000.

The time of the actual fighting was short. The showing of the actual fighting, "the battle of the century," itself, is naturally reserved for the finish of the film exhibit. The preliminaries, therefore, the training and the perfection of arrangements, use most of the film.

Mr. Barbee says he expects these pictures to have at least a 15-week run.

Saturday, November 12, 1921

"I guess perhaps he is a better man than I," is the frank admission made by Georges Carpentier when he witnessed the motion picture of his fight with Dempsey.

Tuesday, November 15, 1921

"Slow" motion photography as applied to the ring has been successfully accomplished in the pictures of the Dempsey-Carpentier fight now on exhibition at Barbee's Loop Theater. This new form of photography has cut down the speed of the contestants to about one-eighth normal and affords the spectators ample opportunity to study the different tactics of the two fighters. Local devotees of boxing are jamming the theater at every performance to witness the films and many an embryo Dempsey is taking advantage of this chance to pick up a few pointers on the art of boxing like a champion.

Tuesday, November 29, 1921

Women and children totaling almost as many as the men have attended during the last week the Tex Rickard official championship pictures which are now playing at Barbee's Loop Theater. "If every American boy would only heed the physical lesson that is taught from the films," said Director Barbee last night, "the future generation would be one that America should be proud of. All mothers and fathers need not hesitate to send their boys to see the pictures, as the scenes are very clean and instructive.

"They show the two fighters going through all their training stunts," he added, "which enabled them to display such wonderful endurance in the ring that eventful day at Jersey City."

The Queen of Sheba

J. Gordon Edwards, who directed The Queen of Sheba, *was the grandfather of film director Blake Edwards. He directed many of Theda Bara's "vamp" photoplays and personally picked this film's star, Betty Blythe, as Bara's successor. Sadly, Edwards's career disintegrated after* The Queen of Sheba. *Though he directed a few more pictures Edwards is largely a forgotten figure in film history. He died on Christmas Day, 1925. None of his films are known to survive.* The Queen of Sheba *was also notable for the technical assistance provided by cowboy star Tom Mix. A tonneau, which Sandburg refers to, was better known as the "rumble seat" in the rear of 1920s-era automobiles. Washington Park was a racetrack located in the south suburbs of Chicago.*

Friday, November 11, 1921

The Queen of Sheba was put on the motion picture screen last night for its first local audience. The showing was at the Woods Theater, where the production is to continue its exhibition for an indefinite period.

New York having watched this film spectacle keep a Broadway theater box office busy for eight months and three weeks, there was local interest in what was to be met up with. William Fox, its producer, is one of the canny guessers in moviedom on what the public wants next and from that viewpoint there was added interest.

The film narrates the tale of the Sheba queen and King Solomon with a declared intention to keep faithfully to the text of the legend as told in the Bible and in other documents. The climax of the first half of the picture gives a view of the new queen just as King Armud is about to clasp her for the first time in his arms, plunging a dagger in the breast of the King and then pushing him over a parapet into the arms of a mob of subjects who had clamored for the dethronement of the sovereign.

The second half of the picture is occupied with the plot of Adonijah, brother of King Solomon, to wrest the throne from his brother. Success would have attended the efforts of Adonijah were it not for the torrent of chariots and short-swordsmen hurled into the breach by the Queen of Sheba.

The fighting amid the towers, bridges, moats and walls roundabout King Solomon is as good as the best spectacle fighting of this type seen in the movies. The chariot race in the first half, however, is the big number. After several ordinary chariot races, quite as horsey and fast as anything pulled off at the old Washington Park track, comes the race between Queen Amrath, wife of King Solomon, and the Queen of Sheba.

It seems that the wife of Solomon challenged the Sheba queen to the race, the stakes being the good favor of King Solomon. There had been a frame-up for the Queen of Sheba to drive some doped horses, but at the last minute she shifted and announced she would not drive her Egyptian nags, but would take her chance on the white Arabian steeds.

The driving is fast and furious. It is such excellently swift driving of the horses and chariots that one is not surprised to hear the grapevine allege Tom Mix and one of his cowboy pals were handling the ribbons that sent the nags around in such fast style.

Betty Blythe plays the Queen of Sheba and Fritz Lieber fills the difficult role of King Solomon.

The cost of the production is stated at upward of $1.8 million. Players and supernumeraries numbered 4,827 persons. The structures built were according to specifications obtained from Assyriologists and archeologists in the University of Pennsylvania. In the chariot races, which were staged by Tom Mix, 150 acrobats were used in battle scenes, 600 Arabs, 350 horses, 14 camels.

Saturday, November 12, 1921

"I ain't never been in Rome or Jerusalem, but in *Queen of Sheba* I done as the Romans done." So says Tom Mix in explaining his special work in the Fox feature now at the Woods.

It is the hand but not the face of the one-time buckaroo, nomad and wild horse wrangler that is recognized in the principal thrill scene of *Queen of Sheba*, the chariot races before the colossal stadium of King Solomon. J. Gordon Edwards directed the picture but it was Tom Mix, the Wild Westerner, who was called upon to stage the races. Whatever Tom does not know about chariots he does know about horses, maintaining the largest stable on the west coast and conducting a really large business in the renting of riding horses and trick horses to film companies.

When the 10 chariots and 40 horses go plunging around the half mile track while thousands of persons rise cheering in their seats that stream upward and outward from the royal box of Solomon it is Mr. Mix of Texas who drives a chariot in the van, and it is his stunts that produce the smash-ups when horses and wheels apparently go recklessly over fallen charioteers and into broken vehicles.

Mix spent a month, it is said, perfecting these racing scenes and drove the automobile which raced about the track just ahead of the noses of the plunging horses while a camera balanced on springs on the tonneau ground off foot after foot of the plunging action.

It was his idea to have the climax of the chariot scenes the race between the rival queens, Sheba and Vashti, who vie for the prize of King Solomon's affections and it was his persuasion and demonstration of "how easy and safe" it was, that prevailed upon Betty Blythe and Nell Craig, the actresses playing those roles, actually to mount the chariots and drive the excited horses.

In this connection, it may be observed that Miss Blythe's face seen over the straining necks and past the snorting noses of the racing horses betrays some trepidation at her position in charge of the reins.

Mix, seriously, is proud of his reputation of never having faked a dangerous scene and does not feel any too comfortable about posing in a flowing Roman robe, even in the "long shots" where he drives his breakneck stallions in the first of the spectacular races. He takes pride in the fact that no one can recognize him.

Fooled the Camels

Tuesday, November 29, 1921

It was easy enough to build Jerusalem again, to put up Solomon's Temple and the Tower of David, but it was another matter to build a series of oases in the burning deserts outside Los Angeles. J. Gordon Edwards, who was building the settings for *Queen of Sheba*, had workmen and archeologists to put up the ancient buildings in restorations, but he was hard put to it to find men who could build a plausible oasis. He had to have oases for the desert scene in which the Queen of Sheba progressed toward Jerusalem on her way to visit King Solomon. The only oases on the desert were gasoline and "free air" stations. From photographs and travel books and at length from an Egyptian student who was studying at the University of California, the Fox organization got sufficient data to build oases. Palm trees were uprooted and carried from the cities and set in the excavations with the result that the final setting was pronounced perfect; at least it fooled the camels and dromedaries in Sheba's caravan, who insisted upon lying down whenever they came to the oases.

The Sheik

Based on a popular romance novel by E. F. Hull, the impact of Rudolph Valentino's The Sheik *on 1920s pop culture cannot be overstated. Valentino, already a popular movie draw after* The Four Horsemen of the Apocalypse, *literally had women swooning at movie theaters across the country over his performance. Valentino's exotic looks smoldered with sexual energy. "A photoplay of tempestuous love between a madcap English beauty and a bronzed Arab chief!" screamed the advertisements. It was no accident that "The Sheik" became a popular brand of prophylactics in the wake of* The Sheik! *Valentino's status as a movie icon was assured. Yet on its initial release, Sandburg couldn't possibly have realized what impact* The Sheik *would have on the American psyche.*

In every motion picture play that has come from the directive hands of George Melford of the Famous Players-Lasky lot and studio, there have been the signs of care and workmanship always, if not art.

Usually, if the plot had a good skeleton of action and character, Melford hangs something worth looking at on it.

This is so with *The Sheik*, a movie based on a story taken from a fast selling novel now reported to be at the height of its popularity.

It is said to be the first time that a novel successful by way of sales reached a screen version at the same hour that its popularity was at a peak in the bookstore records.

The Sheik is showing at Ascher's Roosevelt Theater in its first run this week. Rudolph Valentino carries the heavy role, that of an Arab desert chief.

Through varied storm and calm he seeks the heart of an English girl. In the finish she is apprised that the sheik is the son of an English father and a Spanish mother and they leave the desert to become husband and wife in London.

The pageantry of horsemen and spears on backgrounds of white sand and sloping dune is notable. As spectacle photoplay it should easily have high rank.

Molly O'

With its working class setting, it's no surprise that Sandburg had such high praise for Mabel Normand's Molly O'*. Considered Normand's comeback picture, it was the first film she made upon returning to Mack Sennett's comedy factory following her stint at the Goldwyn studios. Normand had overcome ill health brought on by a high-octane lifestyle, and the dynamic change was obvious in her on-screen energy and radiant looks. Decades after its release,* Molly O' *was believed to be lost. In 1996, however, a single copy was reported found in the Russian film archive, Gosfilmofond. Though missing a reel, as well as title and end credits, the film was otherwise in surprisingly good shape.*[13]

The latest Mack Sennett offering, *Molly O'*, showing at the Chicago Theater in its first local run this week, is a pleasant surprise.

Always there is rough stuff in a Sennett production. Also he is known as the specialist in "bathing beauties" and beach lights of a various order. A sort of acknowledged kingpin of knockabout travesty and up-and-at-'em burlesqueries.

Yet now in *Molly O'* we have something else. This production more nearly rivals Charlie Chaplin's *The Kid* than anything else on the screen this year. On top of the rough stuff and the horseplay and leaving aside certain things put in because they must be there because audiences demand them there, the points that artists call inspiration, taste, subtlety, character, are here.

This *Molly O'* film is one of those rare ones we remember out of a year, so human—so quizzical and quixotic, so playful, having such unexpected turns and blends of what makes the laugh and the tear.

It is spun out a reel or two longer than it ought to go. The end of it should come with the flash of the marriage scene. They didn't know when to stop. But what they give us before the point where they ought to have stopped has such a masterly handling of the elements that go to make a first rate vital photoplay that we forgive 'em and thank 'em.

When this reviewer volunteers to Ben Hecht the above information about what a movie *Molly O'* is, the Thousand Afternoons replied saying, "When I talked with Sennett at the Congress Hotel last summer, he said there is one great subject always successful in stories, stage plays and picture dramas. And that is the story of the poor girl who rises to good luck and meets her hero."

That is the theme worked out in *Molly O'*. It is a little too romantic to be called strictly honest as regards real life. Yet it is so rigorously direct and true in its handling of working class life, people and character, and so large a part of the picture deals in the latter material, that the result is a knitting together of strands making an exceptional and a great production.

Writers like Frank Norris and Jack London would have said that for all its shortcomings it has some finely worthwhile points, and is precisely the type of a picture drama that should command wide attention because of its material and its way of handling that material.

Mabel Normand plays Molly. We wonder if it can be Mack Sennett, the violent, splashy and brash, who is responsible for a love scene by the door where Molly's head, hair, arm, are employed in simple gestures of storytelling. At moments we see only four fingers holding to a door. Well worked out business.

And once Molly, the pipe-fitter's daughter, goes to the home of rich folk. In the kitchen she puts a few dozen cakes fresh from the oven in her umbrella. Later she is ushered out into the street where it is raining. Certain scornful folk are watching her. She raises her umbrella. The cakes from the oven spill on her shoulders. She drifts proudly out into the rain.

To Test a Picture's Worth

Though an innovation in the 1920s, audience test screenings for feature films is now a widespread practice in Hollywood—much to the chagrin of many filmmakers!

Friday, November 18, 1921

Hitting upon a novel method of determining the effectiveness of a motion picture before its release for general exhibition, Thomas H. Ince tested the popular appeal of *Hail a Woman* upon representative audiences in several different theaters at Los Angeles recently.

To insure the genuineness of the test and to obviate the possibility of prejudiced praise from enthusiastic friends, the producer carried the picture to the theater just before it was to be shown between two regular evening shows without advance announcement. While the feature was being shown, the producer and members of his staff scattered throughout the audiences picked up the comment that passed between members of the audience both during and following the performances.

Acting upon the genuine criticism thus secured certain slight changes were made in the picture with the result, it is said, that *Hail the Woman* will meet every audience requirement.

December

White Oak

Sandburg's reference to Zane Grey's "propaganda" undoubtedly was the noted Western writer's 1919 novel The Desert of Wheat. *This unabashedly anti-union novel revolved around violent clashes between wheat farmers and members of the International Workers of the World (the IWW, commonly known as "Wobblies"). Grey portrayed the IWW as corrupt and possible spies for Germany during World War I. Sandburg, on the other hand, was strongly pro-union. During the first two decades of the twentieth century, Sandburg published numerous articles and poems in the leftist magazine (and IWW supporter), the* International Socialist Review. *Sandburg's other political remark in this piece, "the zealotries of the last two or three years," is an allusion to U.S. Attorney General A. Mitchell Palmer's "Red Scare" arrests of 1920.*

Monday, December 5, 1921

The newest Bill Hart film goes by the name of *White Oak*. It employs much of the same material seen in the general run of films that have made the name of Bill Hart spell and signify "the West," "out thar' where a man's a man."

Bill Hart is evidently to the movies what Zane Grey is to books—only Bill Hart does a cleaner job—shoots his stuff and gets away without the suspicions attaching to Zane Grey, particularly suspicions well confirmed as to propaganda.

Undoubtedly during the zealotries of the last two or three years Bill Hart was tempted to tell the world in his films how to go and save itself. But he withstood the temptations and kept himself only to such propaganda as may be found in the oldest melodramas of the stage and both the youngest and oldest of the movies known as "Westerns."

Again in *White Oak*, Bill plays the role of a gambler and a two-gun man, who loves his sister, finds a sweetheart, and toils and shoots his way through various incidents of vengeance and love.

The panoramas put the picture over. For all its overdone pathos—and Bill overworking his facial features struggling with dark emotions—and for all that the plot isn't fresh or original in any special way, those long shots at the desert and the mountains, the battle between the pioneer wagon train white men and the circling band of red Indians has its grip and its thrill.

There is a sense in which some of these Bill Hart Westerns may be called spectacle pictures. They deliver wide panoramas of land, people, wagons and horse, all in action.

It is clean entertainment with certain scenic value, points in stage setting, that as a performance put it past a lot of grand opera scenery we have seen. There is no intention here of indicating that a Bill Hart movie is better than grand opera. The point is registered, however, that as something to look at rather than something to hear, this movie has it over a good deal of grand opera. The contrast is one, perhaps, of no interest either to opera goers or to movie fans. A notation is made of it only because of the big sweep of earth surfaces and pioneer life put on record in this particular film picture. Presentation is at the Castle Theater.

Tol'able David

Tol'able David *portrayed the rural American life dearly loved by Sandburg. D. W. Griffith originally owned movie rights to the story, based on a novel by Joseph Hergesheimer. Certainly the material seemed right for Griffith; yet in the end,* Tol'able David *bore too many similarities to Griffith's* Way Down East.[14] *The property was given to director Henry King, who took cast and crew to West Virginia for location shooting. Today* Tol'able David *is considered by film critics, historians, and fans alike as one of the greatest works of the silent era.*

Wednesday, December 7, 1921

Richard Barthelmess in *Tol'able David* is appearing in a masterpiece of motion picture drama. It is the acting of Barthelmess more than any single factor that shoots it into the high as a masterpiece.

The training under David Wark Griffith, the native genius, aspiration and capacity for work that has nothing to do with Griffith, plus a plot and atmosphere suggested by a great story from the pen of Joseph Hergesheimer, all contribute to what one may

RICHARD BARTHEL-
MESS, as David Dinemon, in
"Tol'able David," First Natl.

From the collection of Arnie Bernstein.

Tol'able David provided 1920s leading man Richard Barthelmess with one of his finest roles.

repeat is a fine thing to run across amid the maze of products from the film manufactories—a masterpiece.

The Inspiration Pictures company presents the photoplay. First National is the distributor—and the Chicago Theater is giving it this week the initial run locally.

Here are outlaws, scum of the country slums of West Virginia. These are about the toughest and sleaziest bad men ever put forth in a movie—these three Hatburn brothers. They are creepy specimens of the rural American Bill Sykes, the hillbilly gone wrong.

Here are homespun folks, as the saying goes, "honest hearts and willing hands," trying to wrest a living from the soil of the hill country and bring up their families in peace as God-fearing folk. But events interfere. Into the peaceful valley comes the scum of the slums, the Hatburn brothers.

It is one of those plots so splendidly told by the screen artists who executed *Tol'able David* that one hesitates about trying to tell the plot because injustice would be done the expectations of those who are to see the picture.

David, the boy, not yet a man nor trusted with a man's tasks, just tol'able David, having seen his brother crippled for life, his father stricken dead and a lovable dog killed by the Hatburns, is in an emergency trusted with driving the hack that carries the United States mail.

A sack of mail gets into the hands of the three Hatburns. David has killed two of the Hatburns and a scene ends with him grappling with the most treacherous and gigantic of the Hatburns for possession of a gun.

The next scenes are of the boy's mother waiting at the post office to witness with pride her boy triumphantly returning with the Untied States mail. Then comes the flash of the front door of the cabin where David was last seen grappling with the giant Hatburn.

The door swings idly. Maybe there is no one in the cabin. The door swings idly. The door hesitates and opens. A wounded, bedraggled, desperate and heroic figure comes out of the door.

It is great story telling we have here—story telling chiefly in the screen medium. The lad, Barthelmess, has served under Griffith. It is no time for a comparison with the best work of Griffith. We may only say this is rarely strong and gripping photodrama.

So much of it is "in key." The parts of it tie up and knit together into a unit, a whole. Gladys Burdette, as Esther Hatburn, is no imitation of anything. She lives her role. The mother, the father, the postmaster, for one weary of the many devices of hokum and slapdash imitative mob appeals, these are worth while.

Joseph Hergesheimer comes off lucky. Seldom does an author see the spirit of his writings caught and built on, so that his own story is all there and in addition all that goes to a silversheet masterpiece.

The Lotus Eaters

Though better known for his roles on stage and in sound films, as well as for an exuberant off-screen life, John Barrymore enjoyed some success as a silent film actor. Generally speaking, his 1920s screen performances were better than the material. Colleen Moore, a supporting player in The Lotus Eaters, *would soon become synonymous with the Roaring Twenties flapper image.*

Wednesday, December 14, 1921

The Lotus Eaters is a whimsical and entertaining production that earns the right to be called a photoplay as distinguished from a plain movie.

There are places in it where the communication of director and actor achieve high moments, the sort of stopovers between stations of stupidity which might be expected from a screen affair wrought out by Marshall Neilan as director and John Barrymore as the leading player.

There are the careless slips, of course. One sees Jacques Lenoi (John Barrymore) land on a desert island after an air voyage and a long swim amid island reefs. And before he has so much as a square meal on the island, his face is seen all clean shaven and talcumed; he looks as though he had just stepped out of a barber shop as he most conveniently meets the heroine.

MARSHALL NEILAN
Leading Motion Pic. Producer

From the collection of Arnie Bernstein.

Three characterizations are achieved by Barrymore, all notable. Young Jacques Lenoi finds his wife faithless to him and in his old days decrees his son, Jacques, shall live on an ocean vessel till he is 25 years of age, and never see a woman till then. The lad at 25 marries the first girl he meets, runs away from her, voyages in a blimp to the South Seas. The blimp is wrecked. He meets the girl he really wants—yet goes back to New York to his wife. She, hearing

An actor in the 1910s, Marshall Neilan became a prolific director in the 1920s. Alcoholism ultimately destroyed his career.

he was dead, had married again. What the wife did about the two husbands, Jacques Lenoi did for a second wife, make a tale of delight nicely worked out. Anna Q. Nilsson and Colleen Moore carry feminine roles with ability. The story was by Albert Payson

Terhune. The first run showing is at the Chicago Theater.

What Do Men Want?

Bert Williams, whom Sandburg refers to in the following review, was a popular entertainer with the Ziegfeld Follies. Sandburg was mistaken when he wrote Lois Weber was "known as the only woman director in the motion picture business." In fact, several women held important roles behind the camera, including directors, writers, and producers. Keep in mind that when What Do Men Want? *was released, the Nineteenth Amendment to the U.S. Constitution, granting women the right to vote, had only been ratified the year before.*

Saturday, December 17, 1921

In the final fadeout of *What Do Men Want?* the husband asks the wife to answer that question.

The wife's answer is that men want "what they haven't got."

The husband then kicks in with his own answer, which is that men want love mixed with "intelligence," the heavy emphasis being on "intelligence."

Such is the wind-up of Lois Weber's latest production, showing at the Senate, Pantheon and Rose Theaters.

Lois Weber, of course, being known as the only woman director in the motion picture business, one looks for the searching feminine intuition, the reputed woman's sixth sense.

Yet there is no more sixth sense, no more sharper intuition in this woman-directed film than in several man-directed pictures having the same plot and situations.

It seems the name of a woman director doesn't mean anything special.

Such comparisons aside, however, this is an excellent program number. Claire Windsor again is the feature player as in previous Weber films. She plays the wife who perhaps wants more than her due and yet perhaps is also neglected by the husband.

Both of them at times force one to remember Bert Williams' ejaculation between two song verses, "I love all mistreated animals."

The husband yields to the fascinations of another woman. The wife almost lets herself go at the entreaties of another man.

There is reconciliation—one saying what men want is "what they haven't got" and the other saying what is wanted is love mixed with "intelligence."

The Sign of the Rose

The Sign of the Rose *was a sort of 1921 version of a "mixed-media" presentation. During the film, leading actor George Beban would come out from the theater wings and interact with the action on screen. The result was a popular, if not critical success, and Chicago moviegoers flocked to see this new wrinkle in entertainment. Beban later toured as an interactive live performer with his films* The Greatest Love of All *(1924) and* Loves of Ricardo *(1926). The Jesse Crawford Sandburg mentions was the house organist of the Chicago Theater for many years.*

Thursday, December 29, 1921

How it feels to be looking at a movie and then have the movie shift all of a sudden into a spoken stage play—and then have the spoken stage play shoot back into the movie or the silent motion photograph drama—just how this feeling goes may be known from the production showing at the Chicago Theater this week, namely, *The Sign of the Rose.*

The picture play, with George Beban in the leading role, as it breaks into the spoken drama is interesting as a novelty. It may be doubted, however, whether there is any art to be developed with a series of shifts from silent to spoken and spoken back to silent.

If the silent is good stuff and audience enjoying it then the break into spoken immediately requires another set of sense organs, those that hear, and the moviegoer who is accustomed to hearing Finston's platoons of violinists or Jesse Crawford's juggling of the cyclopean pipe organ, has a hard time to adjust himself of the jump to the register of the voices of the detective from headquarters, the woman who has lost her kidnapped child and the suspected kidnapper as they slip out of the silent moving pictures and emerge into the spoken stage at State and Lake Streets. A vague lack of something we get when our picture play grinds its keel on the beach sand and we jump into a flivver. Or, it is like all of a sudden having our soup changed to coffee or visa versa. We prefer to finish whatever bowl or cup of narrative we are engaged on before proceeding to the next item of diet.

The close-ups of the last scene—rendered in pictures—where the Italian workman after losing his lone child, selling his furniture, getting his sea bags ready for the trip back from New York to Italy, meets at the door his wife whom he thought lost in a shipwreck at sea—this is high spot melodrama.

Only hard-hearted and indurated sinners would not feel like responding to this elemental Gaelic thing as here given. And with the cinema close-up those in the farthest seats in the last gallery (where this reviewer saw the show) can glimpse the faces clearly.

They put on a shipwreck in this picture. It goes over. It is impressionist. The artist in paint, cartoon and illustration or the old-line stage mechanicians of the Lincoln J. Carter School are backed off the boards.

Reason that Rogers is Leaving Pictures

Though Sandburg writes here that Will Rogers's looks lacked box office appeal, the comedy star actually left the picture business after being refused a pay raise. Rogers attempted independent production in 1922, but the venture broke him financially. Sandburg made a shrewd observation stating Will Rogers would be ideal in an adaptation of Mark Twain's A Connecticut Yankee in King Arthur's Court. *In 1931, Rogers starred in a sound version of the story, titled* A Connecticut Yankee. *Avery Hopwood, whom Sandburg refers to, was a prolific Jazz Age playwright known for his innocuous Broadway comedies. Artemus Ward was a nineteenth century humorist who supposedly influenced Mark Twain.*

Saturday, December 31, 1921

The explanation given for Will Rogers quitting the movies and going back to Broadway and Ziegfeld is that Rogers has a face that failed to make its appeal with a certain stratum of women who are movie fans.

As a moneymaker in the movies the face of Wallace Reid has a value far and away above that of Will Rogers.

As an actor of genius and a personality of tang and power, Will Rogers surpasses Wallace Reid in the way Bernard Shaw has it over Avery Hopwood or the Lincoln tradition outshines Artemus Ward.

The homely man who doesn't give himself 100 percent horseplay and knockabout work is liable to arrive in the movies where Will Rogers has. He commands a public, but it is one limited by its discriminations, its understanding of an artist who mixes intelligence and his own direct personality into his presentations.

It's the type known as handsome that's wanted in the pictures. Wallie Reid is a hundred percenter when it comes to the looks that are popular. His acting is the same, the effect is the same in practically every picture he is in—that is, he doesn't achieve any character portrayals or project new designs and atmospheres. But they go to see the lad. He has the looks. He is the standard model.

See what was done in Rex Beach's *The Iron Trail* instead of a two-fisted, gaunt, quizzical fighting man of the type that might be expected to build a railroad bridge against great odds in the Alaska wilderness, they cast for the part the pleasant and gentlemanly Wyndham Standing. He has the handsome looks wanted by a certain stratum of movie fans.

The same point goes for Harry Myers in *A Connecticut Yankee*. It is precisely the kind of a role into which an actor like Will Rogers would shoot gleams of expression to thrill the ghost of Mark Twain. But the Fox casting directors knew what they were doing, probably. The call is for handsome men, as handsome goes these days.

What's the particular difficulty in this layout? Do the women of America see so many homely, gawky men at home and on the streets that they go to the movies to be refreshed with a look at the type pictured always in the books, magazines and advertisements as the handsome type—the standard model of which Wallie Reid is the perfect and punctilious paragon? Is this it?

Sheet music for Mabel Normand's 1918 feature *Mickey*, which was re-released in Chicago in February, 1922, just as the William Desmond Taylor scandal threatened her career.

1922

January

Rent Free

Once again, Sandburg's Swedish heritage causes him ire with subtitle writers! On a more serious note, his comments regarding Wallace Reid's productivity are eerie in retrospect. A popular box office draw, Reid was physically burned out by his seemingly non-stop production schedule. As a "cure" for exhaustion, a studio hanger-on introduced the handsome star to morphine. The cure quickly became an addiction that required a daily fix. Eventually Reid could no longer function. Within a month of Rent Free's release, his wife Florence Reid (who performed under the name "Dorothy Davenport") sent him to a private hospital. It was too late; Reid was a full-blown junkie unable to live without a fix. His ravaged body and mind quickly deteriorated. Reid would die in January 1923.

Thursday, January 5, 1922

In *Rent Free*, the privilege is offered us of seeing young Mr. Wallace Reid in a photoplay.

The same privilege was offered us a couple of weeks ago in another release of another photoplay.

And about a month before that it was also and again our privilege to witness young Mr. Reid playing a photoplay role in which he was the star with the electric sign spelling.

In *Rent Free*, showing at the Chicago Theater, Mr. Reid is observed in the role of a hero in a snappy hero story plot.

The story is different from the other two stories in the two most immediately current recent releases.

But though the story is different, Mr. Reid's smile, his characterizations, his stunts and gestures are in effect the same as in the other two most recent releases.

Lila Lee, who is the heroine in *Rent Free*, for instance, delivers a character. She portrays a person enters into a life and puts across something not to be seen in the other photodramas in which she has played.

A painter, Buell Arnister, Jr. (W. Reid) is ousted by his landlady about the same time Barbara Teller (Lila Lee) and Justine Tate (Gertrude Short) are thrown out by their landlady. A kind-hearted janitor gives them a tent to sleep in on the roof. The painter likewise is making his new home on the roof. There are complications, "heart affairs," reconciliations.

The story holds the audience. Direction was by Howard Higgin, and considering his material he did well.

The smart title writer, who wrote the texts in this movie is ignorant of Swede dialect, knows neither Swedish janitors nor Swedish sailors, and as a subtitle writer in that respect is traveling on his nerve.

The Boat

At the time of The Boat*'s production, Buster Keaton was married to Natalie Talmadge, sister of Norma and Constance Talmadge. Norma Talmadge was married to Keaton's producer, Joseph Schenck, hence Sandburg's reference to the multi-layered familial/film relations. Dr. George Washington Crile, whom Sandburg cites here, performed both the first successful thyroid operation and direct blood transfusion. Considering Keaton's legacy as a mechanically adaptive comic filmmaker, the quote Sandburg chose is particularly apropos.*

Monday, January 9, 1922

Buster Keaton has done his best comedy in *The Boat*. It is a bird of a film taken from various angles.

It is so excellent a comedy one need not hesitate about saying if Joseph Schenck and the promoters and counselors of young Keaton would allow the lad to take his own time at making comedies, and not be always making them against a set release date, then young Keaton might have a chance to pass over the line that divides the mountebank knockabout entertainer on the one hand and the big artist doing his best work leisurely and deliberately on the other hand.

The suggestion is entirely valid because of the facts that America has plenty of enterprising, sagacious managerial talent on the order of Joseph Schenck while there is all too little in the screen world containing the possibilities of Buster Keaton.

The boat in *The Boat* is impossible in its building and launching. But there comes a time when the boat is being churned on the high seas, when it rolls over, fills with water, and the comic bath tub life boats have to be let down, rising to that moment of comedy when the laughter subsides because the story interest, the ingenuity and quick surprises lift the piece into first-rate comedy.

The Boat is the first to come from Buster since he married Natalie Talmadge.

Up to date the marriage is justified by the Keaton output. And we shall await Natalie's next, wondering whether double-barness has given her a similar impetus.

And we hope, inasmuch as this is a family affair, Joseph Schenck being the husband of Norma Talmadge, that Mr. Schenck will not rush young Keaton so much on his releases.

However, if Mr. Schenck can't do that much for Mrs. Schenck herself, it is not likely he will do it for Mrs. Schenck's sister's husband. Moreover, as the scientist Crile has it, "Man is an adaptive mechanism," and Mr. Schenck is offered this earful for what it is worth.

Galleries are Again Holding Their Own

Are movies a bad influence on the public? Or is sophisticated content a sign of better, more challenging filmmaking? These eternal questions are posed in a column from Sandburg's Saturday musings.

Saturday, January 14, 1922

We are told that the galleries of the legitimate theaters are beginning to fill up again and we are told furthermore that this may be due to the fact that the patrons of the swift and lurid spoken drama quit the galleries of the legitimate to sit in the audiences that witness the silent drama, the photoplay, which was delivering action more swift and lurid than the spoken word drama could.

This drift of drama patrons from spoken to silent and back to spoken, it may be. If so, does it mean that some uplift has hit the movies and they are delivering a renovated and inspired product that attracts a superior element of the population, while the melodrama fans are quitting the films to go back to the galleries? We cannot say. There are no statistics nor tabulations.

The movies of this hour do make an appeal to human intelligence and to emotions less directly of the jungles than was the case four years or 10 years ago. The changes in the deeper trends of the spoken drama have amounted to little or nothing in recent years, while in the silent drama those changes have been incessant and go deep. The motion picture producers found themselves with a vaster, much farther-reaching market than they at first counted on. It made them anxious and careful. The selection of Will Hays and the hitching of his talents and experience into the picture industry is only one incident of many.

Grand Larceny

Anatole France, whom Sandburg refers to, was the 1921 winner of the Nobel Prize for Literature. France, whose real name was Jacques Anatole Thibault, was a strong proponent of using marionettes to perform Shakespeare and other classics. Grand Larceny *is a fine example of how feminist ideas, strengthened by the 1920 passage of a woman's right to vote, were making a social and cultural impact.*

Tuesday, January 17, 1922

Grand Larceny is a remarkable photoplay. It is far out of the ordinary, first of all because it doesn't bother with a happy ending, and secondly, because practically the important action and expression is by three players only.

It is so sincere and straightaway a piece of silent drama, leaving so much to the intelligence of the American audiences fed on happy endings, that we wonder just how far it will get as a box office success.

The ending, however, while not happy, is smart, with a grand, defiant gayety. It is an ending something like that of Ibsen's *The Doll House* with an added fling of humor.

Ibsen has Nora leave one husband, telling him she's tired of being a doll, and without blaming anybody, is going out by herself to learn life anew. In *Grand Larceny* the woman leaves two men, her first and second husbands.

Each of the husbands, one former and the other latter, want her back. And when she says she is going to quit the life of a puppet tossed back and forth between two temperamental, jealous men, one asks if she will come back. She says, "Yes."

"And will you come back to him or to me?"

Her answer: "Who knows?"

Elliott Dexter plays the first husband, John Annixter, while Lowell Sherman has the role of the second husband, Barry Cleve. Claire Windsor mounts into the difficult task of portraying the wife and carries it through to a great finish.

All three of these players give an accounting of themselves here, set up a standard of what can be done by a few sincere, capable players in silent drama, taking a hackneyed theme and putting the twists on it that almost reach the Anatole France ideals of marionette plays—"I wish to see masterpieces played in slapdash style in barns by strolling players."

The presentation is at Ascher's Roosevelt Theater. It is a Goldwyn picture.

"The woman who can be stolen from one man can be stolen from another," declares the first husband to his wife, while to the man he accuses of stealing his wife he ventures the prophecy, "A man who steals one man's wife will steal another."

"Grand larceny must be punished," is his doctrine, "and the wife-thief is the lowest breed of all."

The two husbands try to get at the woman's heart and learn who she blames for their array of mutual follies.

"I don't blame either of you—I blame myself," is her passionately bitter answer.

Is Ibsen reaching Hollywood? We never heard the question asked except with a horselaugh—until *Grand Larceny* came along.

February

The Wise Kid

Director Tod Browning would develop into one of Hollywood's great stylists, specializing in atmospheric horror films like The Unholy Three *(1925);* London After Midnight *(1927);* Dracula *(1931), making a star of Bela Lugosi; and the disturbing, yet compassionate* Freaks *(1932). On the day this review appeared, the* Daily News, *like many newspapers across the country, published lurid head-lines regarding the murder of Hollywood director William Desmond Taylor.*

Thursday, February 2, 1922

The humanly winsome quality of an O. Henry story is wrapped up in *The Wise Kid*, a Universal picture directed by Tod Browning, with Gladys Walton and Norman Hammond in the leading parts.

"I'll kiss the calendar the day you get the lockjaw," is what "the wise kid" tells her sweetheart in one of their numerous quarrels where they try to slang each other off the map.

She is a restaurant cashier and he runs a truck delivering pies to the restaurant where she works. Their slang quarrels reach a point where they give each other back their presents, even to the ring she wore. And she has taken up with a handsome thief who talks about his rich father and borrows a hundred dollars from her. However, in the finish she and her sweetheart capture the thief, recover diamonds for a rich broker, get a check for $1,000 and get married.

A richly American sketch this *The Wise Kid*. It could be sent over to Europe and Asia as representative of the life of the young working people of America. There should go a warning to the English, however, and to the Australians that the slang defies translation.

Mickey

In the opening paragraphs of this review, Sandburg displayed a critical integrity that few of his peers could match. Newspapers of the day were filled with reports regarding the murder of film director William Desmond Taylor. Taylor had been found dead February 2 in his Hollywood bungalow with a single bullet hole in his back. Mabel Normand, the star of Mickey, *had been one of the last people to see Taylor alive, having visited him the night of February 1. Normand came to pick up a Sigmund Freud book Taylor had bought for her.*

Though the two were not romantically involved, Normand's name was attached to many rumors surrounding the crime. Ingenue Mary Miles Minter, who had appeared in several Taylor films, was also linked to the shooting when a nightgown with her initials and a love letter she had written were found in Taylor's home.

Despite a police investigation and lurid reporting, Taylor's murder remained a mystery. Gossip swirled around Hollywood, linking Taylor to illegal narcotics and possible blackmail plots. There were also whispers that perhaps the virile director was secretly a homosexual. Over the years Los Angeles police as well as armchair detectives bandied about various theories. Film director King Vidor, a contemporary of Taylor's, attempted to solve the crime with his own investigation, a search detailed in the 1986 book A Cast of Killers. *The murder even inspired a Web site, known as "Taylorology." In the wake of the Arbuckle scandal, the Reid death, and then the Taylor killing, U.S. Postmaster General Will Hays was brought in to "clean up" Hollywood and the potentially damaging impact movies could have on the public.*

Though Normand's name was initially linked to the scandal, police quickly ruled her out as a suspect. The damage to her career, however, was done and got worse.

Mickey *was originally shot in 1917, and released the following year. Normand had almost complete control over the film, choosing her director and participating closely in the editing process. She also picked the cast, which included her future husband, Lew Cody. Production of* Mickey *was delayed when Normand developed lung problems; it is now believed this was an early symptom of the tuberculosis that ultimately killed her in 1930.*

Wednesday, February 22, 1922

In picking this hour and moment for a revival of the picture play, *Mickey*, with Mabel Normand playing the chief role, Mr. Weil of the Castle Theater has shown courage.

Inasmuch as Miss Normand in various actions of truth, rumor and gossip meets us daily on Page One of the newspapers, the State Street playhouse is going on the theory we might also wish to meet her as artist and player.

She is worth meeting as artist and player. *Mickey* is an honest and a quaint picture play that earned upward of $1 million for its producer, Mack Sennett. There was much fine collaboration in the making of it, in story, direction, photography. And then after those considerations are reckoned, it is Mabel Normand who puts it over.

In quizzical and swift surprise, in facial flash of mummery, she is the nearest approach the motion pictures have to a feminine equivalent of Charlie Chaplin. A still picture of her in ordinary apparel conveys hardly a hint of the drolleries rough and fine of which she is capable.

If this reviewer should try to name women of the motion picture stage who use intelligence in their work, possessing some definite theory of pantomimic art, with a great and tantalizing ideal of that pantomimic art, this reviewer would name Mabel Normand among the first. She is among the fine and irreckonable artists, a personality and a worker whose art is to be put among memorable things.

March

A Sailor-Made Man

> *Though only four reels long,* A Sailor-Made Man *is considered to be comedian Harold Lloyd's first feature-length film. Leading lady Mildred Davis, whom Sandburg refers to as Lloyd's "partner in the peregrinations," became the bespectacled comic's real-life romantic interest; the two were married on February 10, 1923.*

Monday, March 6, 1922

Rather than the tough beefsteak of tragic events where people go for a good cry over the way life uses us all, this *A Sailor-Made Man*, with Harold Lloyd stepping and slipping and sliding in the stellar role, is a piece of film goods we might call a bun and a cream puff.

The only intention is to prove that man is the improbable, preposterous, laughing animal of the universe.

He gets enlisted in the Navy, does the hero, and his first cruise is to Java, where certain ameers and kabashes attempt to take his life and that of an American girl, but in numerous and repeated instances he foils, baffles and waylays them till it's time to go home.

There seems to be a plot with a sequence of events. That is, while the film moves and the eyes take it in there seems to be a plot. But afterward in trying to make a concrete and lucid statement of this plot we find it collapses.

Definitely, however, we may say this five-reel chunk is probably a livelier thing than any of the short ones in which Harold Lloyd stars, steps and slips on the banana peelings of hard fate. Mildred Davis is his partner in the peregrinations.

It is showing at neighborhood houses.

New Color Process

The early color process Sandburg describes is most likely either the Super Speed Cine Negative Film-Orthochromatic or Panachromatic Cine Film, two 1922 processes Kodak used for motion pictures. Hope Hampton was a leading lady in several early to mid-1920s features.

Saturday, March 11, 1922

The day when it can be proved on the screen that "the rose is red, the violet's blue"—or the other way 'round, if desirable—is at hand, thanks to the busy experimenters with color photography. For a long time it has been the fashion to introduce a few color pictures on the screen showing flowers, sunsets and the like, said to be actually photographed in nature's colors. Now it is asserted that by a new process known as the Kodak process for motion pictures, finally perfected after years of effort, the real tints of moving objects can be caught and reproduced.

By way of demonstration a private view was given this week in the Chicago Theater's projection room of Miss Hope Hampton photographed in various activities. The claim made for this color process by its promoters is that it is softer and more delicate than others and therefore ideal for "close-ups" as it reveals the delicate flesh tints and reproduces the exact colors of hair, complexion and costume.

The pictures of Miss Hampton were remarkably life-like and beautiful.

MILDRED DAVIS
Starring In Pathe Comedies

232—HOPE HAMPTON, as
The Opera Star, in "Star
Dust," First Natl. Attraction

From the collection of Arnie Bernstein.

Harold Lloyd's leading lady, Mildred Davis, became his spouse in real life (*left*). Hope Hampton, who was a featured player in many silent films, lent her talents to an early experiment in color technology (*right*).

April

Pay Day

Pay Day was Chaplin's last two-reel comedy, shot over the course of 30 days. Sandburg's mention of the cinematography is noteworthy; at the time, Chaplin's regular cameraman, Roland E. Totheroh, was among many members of his profession learning the intricacies of artificial lighting.

Monday, April 3, 1922

The latest offering from the studio of Charlie Chaplin, a movie named *Pay Day*, showing at the Chicago Theater, McVicker's Theater and the Rialto Theater, can be looked at from two angles.

First, it has some hoary and classic human jokes, old stuff, such as the wife sleeping with a rolling pin all ready to beat up her husband coming home late on pay day night.

Second, it has some of the pleasantly original situations ever worked out in a motion picture, along with flashes that show Chaplin as the restless artist, creative, sleuthing for new ways of handling cinema themes.

A barber shop quartet singing under a window through which water is thrown onto the quartet, working to a climax where a porcelain china washbowl is broken on the heads of the singers—this is one of the oldest things in journals of the comic.

The quartet, assembled by Chaplin, however, is something to look at. They are something beyond human or less than human. A breed of puppet clay figures they seem to be, loosely and ironically modeled hoodlums with jaws and mustaches suggesting responsibilities which they hope to sing away on the night air.

All the street car riders in the United States will thank Charlie for his treatment of the rush-hour traction problem. Here we have the comedian standing in the rain with a leaky umbrella over him. Suddenly he dashes. Next he is seen as part of a scrambling mob trying to get on a car. They fill the car. Charlie, being little and being last, is left behind and goes back to the sidewalk to stand and wait with his leaky umbrella over his head.

Three times he fails to get the car—in the scrimmage he is squeezed out. The fourth time, however, he leaps to the top of the mob in football halfback style, walks on their heads and is first into the car. The squeeze along the aisle sends him to the front. He is seen dangling in jeopardy, about to fall through the front door of the car. A fat man gets on behind, bumps and pushes his way onto the rear platform. And this final pressure shoots Charlie out onto the pavement—a child of grief—a lost one of the legions of hard luck.

The photography of these street car scenes is a bold job. It is kin to some of the

A Charlie Chaplin publicity shot. In Sandburg's review of *Pay Day*, Chaplin's last two-reel comedy, he says, "All the street car riders in the United States will thank Charlie for his treatment of the rush-hour traction problem.

scenes in *The Cabinet of Dr. Caligari.*

As usual in a Chaplin film, there is no time wasted. There are pauses, but they are like the hesitations in good dancing.

There is old stuff, so old it was probably known among the Cro-Magnons. But it is frankly such and in the manner of Shakespeare picking the pockets of Plutarch for plots.

And, on the other hand, the latest editions of the newspapers have no fresher nor more original contribution to the traction problem than the scenes where Charlie is trying to catch a car, and when he at last does catch it is shoved out the front door by the rush hour jam getting on behind.

Be Reasonable

In his autobiography, King of Comedy, *Sennett wrote: "My boys and girls would . . . go to work in dead earnest. The result was always the same: pandemonium and chaos. Restraint, logic, and inhibition took flight and roosted on Cloud Seven with their sides aching."* [1] *The "sweetness" Sandburg refers to in the Mabel Normand comedies* Mickey *and* Molly O' *reflected Normand's unique comic sensibilities, which were in sharp contrast to the usual Keystone slapstick formula.*

Wednesday, April 5, 1922

The Mack Sennett comedy, *Be Reasonable*, is one more film that has audiences rippling over a succession of mishaps, accidents, breakdowns and stumbles.

There is a formula for the Sennett film. Something must be happening every few feet of reel. And when it happens it should be something not expected as a result of what happened before. Sometimes, of course, what happens is exactly what the audience guesses would happen. But if this comes too often then Sennett knows he has failed.

Sennett even believes that the public is vulgar and wants vulgarity. There is, however, a difference between vulgarity and smut—and the smut is not there in this one, *Be Reasonable*.

Sennett even believes that people who call themselves nice have a streak of the vulgar that requires exercise and the relief of laughter. So he gives them vulgarity and they take it as what they pay for and look for further announcements of Sennett films.

Just why Sennett is afraid to put into his two reel comedies some of the quaint sweetnesses and fine character touches in such six reel productions as *Mickey* and *Molly O'* is not as yet known or understood. The two reelers keep coming as the horseplay of "cut-ups."

The Silent Call

Wednesday, April 12, 1922

When they made *The Silent Call* they made a movie. It is the best dog story ever told in the films, and probably better than any dog story ever told in printed books. The action, romance, plot, fidelity to the main facts of life, while roaming wide, imaginative ranges, these and a hundred nameless qualities put it over as one of the best productions of the year.

John Bowers and Kathryn McGuire take the leading human roles. But the star player is Strongheart, a wolf dog. Born of a "lobo," a buffalo gray wolf for a mother and a wolf dog from the ranches for a father, he is the pet of Clark Moran, a naturalist who writes books for a New York publishing house. Moran goes away one winter to see about a new book. Some "lobo" that winter is leaving killed cattle around the hills and valleys. A kangaroo court at the ranch decides the pet of the ranch is guilty. They try to shoot him but he gets away, back to the wild, where he meets a partner. There are cubs. The nest is blown up by a dynamite stick, thrown by a cattle rustler.

What the dog does to that cattle rustler in the finish of the picture is a big intense piece of story telling through the screen medium. There is a romance of a man and a woman, there are battles between sheriffs' posses and cattle thieves—but all these events weave in and out and cling around the life and ways of a wonderful dog that surely had adoration and understanding from those who made the film.

The first run showing is at the Chicago Theater. We repeat, when they made *The Silent Call*, they made a movie. It will go on the lists of the good, better and best picture dramas.

The Age Limit of a Film

Thursday, April 13, 1922

How can photoplays of today be preserved for future generations? Will school pupils in 6922, or even 1000 years from now, be able to study early examples of the cinema art as pupils of 1922 study Virgil and Homer? Or are film classics such as *The Kid* doomed to fade from posterity's page?

What is the life of a motion picture? The answer to this question is being sought by the technical staff of Watterson R. Rothacker, whose film laboratories do developing and printing for such stars as Chaplin, Coogan, Ray, the Talmadges, Fairbanks and Miss Pickford. Have the little figures on a strip of film an age limit at which they will fade away? How long will the celluloid base under the figures endure?

The problem is a hard one. There is so little to go by: the oldest piece of film in the world is still so "young." The scientists must first find a method of stimulating aging in film and then seek a rejuvenating or preservative process.

May

Dr. Jekyll and Mr. Hyde

The Barrymore version of Dr. Jekyll and Mr. Hyde *was originally released in 1920. The production was updated from Robert Louis Stevenson's Victorian London to modern-day New York City. A perennial movie favorite, as well as the subject of numerous parodies and reworkings,* Dr. Jekyll and Mr. Hyde *first hit the screen in 1908. Other silent versions were made in 1910, 1912, and 1913. 1918 brought the animated short,* Dr. Jekyll and Mr. Zip. *In addition to the Barrymore rendition, Sheldon Lewis played the title part in a second 1920 version of* Jekyll.

Friday, May 5, 1922

Among photoplays that take high rank, that rate as superb attempts if not achievements as masterpieces, there must be a place for *Dr. Jekyll and Mr. Hyde* with John Barrymore in the leading dual role of deep difficulties.

This photoplay stands as something equal to—probably surpassing—the narrative delivered as a novel by Robert Louis Stevenson.

Not many screen actors can make comparison with the stage actor, John Barrymore, in depicting two characters struggling within one man.

The facial contortion at times goes to terrible extremes. The danger on the part of the actor is excess. And Barrymore keeps just safely this side of excess in this production.

There is no other instance of a stage actor making a sortie into the films and going back to the legitimate, who gets away with it as completely as Barrymore does in *Jekyll and Hyde*. In another photoplay Barrymore was not so lucky nor competent. But this stage *Jekyll and Hyde* is intense and surpassing to a degree that puts it over rarely and wonderfully in the silent drama.

Scenario and direction, too, represent ability and care. At a moment when Dr. Jekyll has a dream horror, and the transformation into the repulsive Mr. Hyde is underway, a man-sized scorpion crawls along the floor, leisurely climbs on the bed and merges with the sleeper's bodily form.

The Roosevelt Theater one-day revival of this picture this week was worthwhile. Let the neighborhood houses follow.

Will Rogers Lassos Motion Picture Fans

The Ropin' Fool *was the first film Will Rogers released in his ill-fated attempt to become a producer. He made several personal appearances on behalf of the picture, including this one in Chicago reviewed by Sandburg. Rogers's Valentino joke refers to bigamy charges faced by the screen idol at the time. In 1922 Valentino married his second wife, Natasha Rambova, before the divorce from his first wife, Jean Acker, was finalized. Noted for his political comedy as well as his lariat abilities, Rogers's satirical observations on Washington D.C. shenanigans remain fresh, timely and incredibly funny years after the cowboy humorist first uttered them.*

Saturday, May 20, 1922

A film sketch, *A Ropin' Fool*, with its leading player, Will Rogers, making a personal appearance in connection therewith at the Ascher Theater this week, has in it the suggestion of a type of picture playhouse performance that may be heard of more often in the future.

The picture itself shows Rogers as the cowboy always twirling his lasso. It is his habit to be roping something every few minutes. He ropes steers and goats. He goes to bed at night to be awakened by a rat running from a hole in the wall. He knots a string and lassoes the rat and hitches it to a bedpost.

A cat bothers his sleep. He fixes a lariat of twine, leans out of the window, lassos the cat and brings it in.

A patent-medicine man is barking his wares on the main street of the little town in the cattle country. "The ropin' fool" runs a rival show. He lassos a rider on a horse, then the horse. He throws a rope so it lands in a figure eight, tying first the rider, then the horse.

For a windup of his show he throws three lariats at one and the same time completely tying horse and rider with rope. It spoils the show of the medicine man, who keeps going with remarks about his brother who could do each stunt better.

The hour comes when they are going to hang "the ropin' fool." The halter is around his neck. A sheriff, warned by the sweetheart of "the ropin' fool" rides up and commands the hanging to be stopped. The leader of the seeming lynchers then explains they are only taking a movie and the camera is hidden in a covered wagon near by.

About this time "the ropin' fool" has taken the halter off his neck, mounted his pony, lassoed the director of the movie and is away. The sketch closes with the movie director being hauled downtown downhill by "the ropin' fool" riding under fast headway.

After the film is run, Rogers comes out, twirling a rope. While he executes circles and planes with a skill born of natural knack and perfected in a thousand stage performances, he reels off a patter of jokes, commentary and philosophy, that keeps the house rippling.

"The Republicans promised us prosperity. But so far as I can see the only man that got prosperity from the Republicans was Will Hays. It's sure some job he's got. It's his business now to straighten out that boy Valentino. He's got to tell Valentino whether that boy's married or not.

"I'm the only moving picture star that's got the same wife he started out with. Still, I don't want to claim any special credit for myself. Maybe I never had the chance—they never asked me to a party in Hollywood the whole year and a half I was working in the pictures.

"I know all those people out there. I ride horses and I meet them at the barns.

"My act will last as long as the government lasts—because as long as there's a government there'll be funny things to talk about and make gags."

A showman, an actor, humorist, projector of rhythms and pauses—with qualities akin to Abe Lincoln and Mark Twain—this is Will Rogers. The aftermath of him is good and clean.

Darkest Hollywood in Short Travesty

Robert E. Sherwood, a contemporary of Sandburg's, was film critic for the old

Life *magazine (a humorous journal that predates the photojournalism periodical)*
and the New York Herald *newspaper. He later became a Pulitzer Prize winning play-*
wright as well as a screenwriter. Sherwood's script for The Best Years of Our Lives
(1946) earned an Oscar for Best Adapted Screenplay. Like Sandburg, Sherwood
despised the hypocrisy of self-appointed and official moral guardians. Through
Darkest Hollywood with Gun and Camera, *an early effort from the writer, aptly*
illustrates Sherwood's belief: "Who invented hokum? Think how much money he'd
have made from the film producers if he'd sold his invention on a royalty basis."

Saturday, May 27, 1922

Through Darkest Hollywood with Gun and Camera is the title of a film which had
its scenario written by Robert Sherwood, motion picture editor of *Life.*

It is a travesty in two reels, having to do with people and places in the motion
picture capital of the world, with a special intention of making the reported vice,
crime, wickedness and perversion of that locality something to laugh about.

Coincident with the appearance of this film may be noted the production of a stage
revue to show in Chicago this summer entitled *Hollywood Follies.*

As time goes on there will probably be considerable spotlighting of the community
in southern California named Hollywood.

Culturally speaking, there are arguments to be made that Hollywood—for real or
woe—is more important than Harvard, Yale or Princeton, singly or collectively. That
is, what Hollywood says on the screen reaches an audience of tens of millions at a time
when that audience wants to see.

The amount of gossip about Hollywood is going to increase along with the increased
responsibilities of Hollywood. What is very evident is that Hollywood is becoming
aware of the fact that responsibility goes with power.

June

Sheiks as They Ride Through the Movies

In the wake of Valentino's success with the turgid melodrama The Sheik, *Roaring*
Twenties culture was swept up by a kind of "sheik-mania." Eager to jump on this
gravy train, producers cranked out variations of "sheik" films. The horde included
The Fable of the Sheik *(1923), Ben Turpin's parody* The Shriek of Araby *(1923),*
The Desert Sheik *(1924),* She's a Sheik *(1927),* The White Sheik *(1928), and the*
animated short Felix the Cat Shatters the Sheik *(1926). The best of the lot, of*
course, was Valentino's sequel to the original, The Son of the Sheik *(1926).*
Sandburg cared little for the genre, as this sarcastically comic essay shows.

Saturday, June 3, 1922

"What's the low down in all these pictures about sheiks?" a young man writes to ask. And here's the low down.

The American rights to the novel called *The Sheik* were bought by the Paramount corporation. A picture was produced titled *The Sheik*, under the direction of George Melford. The book had sentences such as "Kiss me, little piece of ice," but all lines like that were cut out of the movie and it was so different in that respect from the book that it was a disappointment to all who read the book on account of how wicked it was.

Then there is a French made film entitled *The Sheik's Wife*. In this one the plot is a good deal like the Paramount film. The Arabian hero had an education at Oxford University and is acquainted with many of the best people in England. The heroine is an English girl who wants to have a romance out "in the vast stillness of the desert." Because she brings her husband a girl child instead of a boy he tells her he has to leave her. In its handling of the desert, the camels and the Arabians, this is the best of the sheik films.

Then there is *The Shriek of Araby*, produced by the Fox corporation. It is different in some respects from the other sheik films. But it does have a sheik and it does have an English girl falling for him. And there are British offices and a garrison near by. In riding and shooting it is the best of the sheik films. We have a suspicion Tom Mix was giving advice on it.

Ask us for the low down on sheiks again in a couple of months. If there are more sheiks we will try to tell you what they are and how they get by.

The Trap

Though ultimately a minor film in his body of work, The Trap *is notable as the first film to bill Lon Chaney as "The Man of a Thousand Faces." Chaney's ability to change his look from film to film remains legendary. Throughout the 1920s he was a genuine artist of transformation, designing and applying incredible visages to his own face.*

Tuesday, June 6, 1922

Lon Chaney in *The Trap*, showing at neighborhood houses, plays the part of a French Canadian, who is wronged in love and money matters, and achieves a vengeance.

Gaspard has a mine his father left him. Benson (Alan Hale), by legal methods in land registration, takes the mine away from Gaspard. But later when Benson also gets Thalie (Dagmar Rodwsky) in marriage, Gaspard swears revenge, waits seven years, sees Thalie die of neglect and overwork, incites "The Gorilla" to an attempt at killing Benson, who in self-defense shoots and nearly kills "The Gorilla." This leaves Gaspard the leading witness in the trial of Benson and he sends the man he hates to prison. The child of Benson, now being left with Gaspard, wins the heart of the man so that he resolves when Benson, the father, comes out of prison, he shall not have the child.

In the climax of the play, the child walks into a trap arranged for its father, Benson. There is a large wolf in the trap. Gaspard saves the baby.

It may be that Lon Chaney is shown to best advantage in this film. The director, Robert Thornby, may have got the best slants at Lon Chaney and his possibilities. But some of us doubt it.

It is a better than average movie. Some of its moments attain high spot film drama. Then it halts. At that, the director may have known a strong knit story could have been made—but the time limit for the making of the movie was up.

Gay and Devilish

Sandburg's feelings on Will Hays and the morality crusade against Hollywood come through loud and clear in this review.

Monday, June 26, 1922

Gay and Devilish, showing at neighborhood houses, is a flapper picture with Doris May as the leading feminine feature.

The story, the action, the hair bob, the persiflage, is flapper from start to finish.

The producers, Robertson-Cole, publish the piece as "packed with pep and a riot of jazz." Of course, the "pep" is there, if by "pep" it is meant nobody ever stands still and somebody is always handing out a slam in the slats or taking one.

And it is a "riot of jazz" if a series of events such as might take place under the eyes of any average honest chaperone constitutes a "riot of jazz."

The flapper, played by Doris May, is persuaded by her parents to marry one Peter Armitage, to retrieve family finances. It's a little point this particular movie just slides over with perfect ease. The father and mother merely tell the girl she ought to marry a gezink she has never had her eyes on in her life, never heard of before. But she says "Yes" when the old folks put the proposition to her.

This is precisely one of those slovenly done pieces of dramatic business that might be taken as a sample of what puts Hollywood in bad with many people; a portentous and terrible problem of life to any girl who has had to face it—yet this movie has her saying "Yes" all in a jiffy. It makes neither drama nor farce nor incident worth the rehash of gossip.

We can point to producers who would have insisted either the incident of the girl consenting to marry a bank account merely as such should be made either true and tragic or preposterous and comic.

Here it's neither. For things like this they had to hire Will Hays. And he has his job cut out for him.

Otis Harlan, as a comedian has his points. Cullen Landis as the young handsome man can work. But with a story titled *Gay and Devilish* when it's only simpering and so-so—what's to do? "I prithee, my lords, what's to do?"

July

My Wife's Relations

Made just a year after his marriage to Natalie Talmadge, there has been speculation over the years that My Wife's Relations *was a none-too-subtle commentary on Keaton's home life.*

Monday, July 2, 1922

In *My Wife's Relations*, Buster Keaton has achieved comedy, pungent, vulgar comedy, wherein the vulgarity has vital power, the nutriment of first-rate Roquefort cheese.

Somehow it recalls for us the remark of Robert Frost that he knows a young man who regards the moment where *Hamlet* pronounces the word "Rats!" as the most portentous and effective moment in that particular play of Shakespeare.

We hope Cecil DeMille will take a few minutes off and see this achievement of Buster Keaton and his helpers.

The elder DeMille, the flashy DeMille, might learn something. He might learn the mistakes of his picture, *Saturday Night*.

Here is vulgarity, working-class vulgarity, people of bad manners, as the phrase goes, people whose behavior is far from such, beyond words, without pedigree, except among the animals of the barns and the health that goes with what Ezra Pound calls "the unkillable infants of the poor."

A little like Frank Norris' *McTeague*, people are the dummies, mummies and rummies that shamble, scramble and slide on their bottom ends across the flickers of this picture.

This is the nearest approach this reviewer has witnessed to the master handling of Charles Chaplin in presentation of human comics, with massive overtones and rapid implications.

There will be those saying Charlie is a little schoolmaster showing them how to better find themselves in the pantomimic art science of the cinema. And there will be others who say otherwise.

The main point is that Buster Keaton's *My Wife's Relations* is a hummer of a comic two reeler.

Once in a blue moon there is the positive and unmodified advice in this column, "Go see it." About the film *My Wife's Relations*, the recommendation is positive, "Go see it."

Orphans of the Storm

Considered the last great film of D. W. Griffith, Orphans of the Storm *was adapted from a popular melodrama, "The Two Orphans." Struck with the relationship between the two sisters of this play, Griffith cast the two siblings of his stock company, Lillian and Dorothy Gish, as the leads. To give the story more passion, he reset the original story against the backdrop of the French revolution. A Gallic setting, including replicas of Notre Dame, the Palais Royale, Versailles, and the Bastille, was built in Griffith's Mamaroneck, Long Island studio. Griffith went so far as to consult a Harvard University expert to ensure accuracy. For his part, Griffith conceived* Orphans of the Storm *as "great anti-Bolshevik propaganda. It shows more vividly than any book of history can tell, that the tyranny of kings and nobles is hard to bear but that the tyranny of the maddened mob under the blood of lusting rulers is intolerable."[2] In his first paragraph, Sandburg notes the new ownership of the Roosevelt Theater by the famed Balaban & Katz theater chain. What he refers to as "methods familiar to the patrons of the Chicago, Riviera and Tivoli" are Balaban & Katz's trademark white-gloved ushers and overall grand presentation of cinematic entertainment.*

Wednesday, July 5, 1922

The Roosevelt Theater under the Balaban & Katz regime has had a reopening. The electric signs shine with new and different color arrangements. The methods familiar to the patrons of the Chicago, Riviera and Tivoli are in evidence.

Orphans of the Storm, the picture representing the most recent efforts of David Wark Griffith, is the feature of the reopening week.

The picture interests. Griffith in all he has done since the masterly *Broken Blossoms* has aimed first of all at being interesting.

He took Lottie Blair's *Way Down East* and made it metropolitan and Niagara rather than rural and of the hay meadows. Now he has taken the French revolution for a background of the melodrama tale of "The Two Orphans."

In fidelity to history, it may be the equal of Carlyle and Edmund Burke. But the Kentuckian Griffith knows much less about the French revolution than his fellow southerner, Thomas Watson. In handling history, Griffith is about as painstakingly accurate as Thomas Dixon, author of *The Clansman*, which furnished the plot for *The Birth of a Nation*.

We may dwell incidentally on three points now because of the seriousness with which Mr. Griffith has spoken of the possibility that he may show us a screen history of the world told through a series of love stories beginning with tadpoles and fishes and carrying the narrative through Adam and Eve, Solomon and Sheba and so on until some up-to-the-minute story of modern times would end the history.

The acting of Lillian Gish in *Orphans of the Storm* is believed by some of her friends to be the best she has done. Her sister, Dorothy, appears. And Joseph Schildkraut, who has the role of "Liliom" in that stage play, has the leading male role.

The synchronizing music and the orchestra delivering it are worthwhile.

If the love story were woven through imagined events of an imaginary country in an updated era, we might give *Orphans of the Storm* a higher percentage.

And if Griffith had lived a longer time with even a few basic acts of the French revolution, he would have shot out a film with more living and convincing scenes.

Some prefer to take their views of the French revolution from the Frenchmen Guizot, Hugo, Balzac, rather than the Kentuckian, D. W. Griffith.

Tell Me Why

After radical birth control pioneer Margaret Sanger produced and starred in a 1917 film about family planning (aptly titled Birth Control*), the topic was featured in several 1910s-1920s photoplays. In the age of the Volstead Act, though, public discussion of birth control still had the power to shock. Consequently, official participation by the Chicago Department of Health in the screening of* Tell Me Why *gave this film some social significance, as Sandburg notes.*

Monday, July 10, 1922

A physiological and anatomical exhibition of various phases of birth control, a photoplay which is meant to carry a lesson and which is a better acted and directed picture than many which have no intentions of carrying a lesson, are the main features of a program Barbee's Loop Theater is putting on as this year's equivalent of the production *Wild Oats*, which had so long a run last year.

The questions, "What should a young man know?" and "What should a young woman know?" are to the forefront in this generation as they have been in previous generations. A somewhat official visa and sanction attaches to the program at Barbee's through the presence in picture and person of the city commissioner of health and other officials.

"Consequences are unpitying" is a line from George Eliot that might pass as a subtext for the pathological exhibit.

As for the picture, which is titled *Tell Me Why*, it romanticizes the businessman seriously anxious to be a father, and his wife anxious to have nothing to do with motherhood, who changes her mind about the matter.

It is a surprisingly well told screen story, considering that it is aimed to point a moral and distribute important knowledge.

Studio

Al St. John, Studio's lead, was generally second banana in silent comedies though he did star in some two-reelers. During the sound era he grew a beard and switched genres, playing supporting comic roles in "B" Westerns under the name "Fuzzy" St. John. Incidentally, St. John was the nephew of Roscoe "Fatty" Arbuckle. Note in this review how Sandburg takes the opportunity to champion the working class.

Tuesday, July 11, 1922

In the work of Al St. John, who projects two-reel comedies there seems to be a cleaner, steadier and surer handling all the time.

His latest two-reeler, entitled *Studio* is about the best he has done. It is cut down to the point where its movement is swift and there is the succession of preposterous events that make worthwhile film comedy.

Some of the things that might happen around an impossible motion picture studio are shown. We have often seen, for instance, the film comedian held prisoner in a house to be blown up with dynamite. The emergence of the prisoner from the blow-up has been staged various ways. This springs a new one.

In all St. John films he aims at being an interesting acrobat at all moments when interest may not be sustained by his ability in dramatic art. Sometimes the juncture of these gifts for acrobatics and dramatics gets an excellent result as when he practices with bombs as though they might be baseballs. One explodes and he issues from the explosion looking like a large deformed ape needing a bath. He goes aquesting and finds he has a double, which is an apparition in a mirror. Yes, these are more or less old devices of a sort. But the acrobat, St. John, and the acting comedian, St. John, hit this off in a way that sends audiences rippling.

We noticed two window washers watching this film and it made them forget the day's work. And they didn't have to think about tomorrow and the windows to be washed tomorrow. Maybe St. John was thinking about window washers when he composed his thoughts to make this film *Studio.*

Ohio Censor Board Sets Up Standards

Always keeping his eyes on the vagaries of censorship, Sandburg let the following speak for itself.

Saturday, July 22, 1922

The makers and sellers of motion pictures are watching with interest the action of the censor board of Ohio. Issuance of the Riegel Code, setting forth the standards, which are to govern acceptance in the state of Ohio, is the signal for fresh discussion of whether standards of cultural measurements and values can be set up and put to effective service.

What goes before and what comes after a certain piece of action in a film should be a governing factor, according to the picture industry men. That is, standards vary with the context. This theory, it is claimed, is violated by the code of the Ohio censor board.

Vernon Riegel, director of that board, has announced that all scenes must be eliminated which are obscene, salacious, indecent, immoral or teaching false ethics. This statement is illustrated by the following list of scenes ordered to be cut out:

Those based on white slavery or commercialized vice.

Those making prominent illicit love affairs.

Those exhibiting nakedness or persons scantily attired; suggestive bedroom or bathroom scenes.

Scenes depicting unnecessarily prolonged expressions or demonstrations of passionate love.

Stories with improper, vulgar gestures and postures.

Scenes which tend to give the idea that sexual vice accompanied by luxury makes vice excusable.

Themes and scenes dealing with the underworld.

Stories that make crime, gambling and drunkenness attractive.

Stories which may interest the immature and susceptible in methods of committing crime.

Scenes which tend to produce approval of business institutions or conditions that naturally tend to deprave or degrade mankind.

Productions that tend to incite sympathy for those engaged in criminal activity.

Scenes which make crime attractive.

Scenes ridiculing or deprecating public officials, officers of the law, the United States army, the United States navy, or other governmental authority or which tend to weaken the authority of the law.

Scenes which offend the religious belief, ridicule ministers, priests, rabbis.

Deceptive subtitles.

Salacious advertising matter.

Besides the foregoing objectionable film subject matter, Director Riegel has ordered all pictures barred "which exhibit motion picture stars who have committed crimes or whose names are in question, judged by generally accepted moral standards."

Sawing a Woman in Half

Saturday, July 29, 1922

There is going the rounds a little two-reeler titled *Sawing a Woman in Half.* It is something by itself.

The first half of the film is taken up with showing how this act has been presented in vaudeville performances. The necromancer is the man of baffling skill and mystery, which same is played by John E. Coutts the same as he has played it in vaudeville and probably before the crowned heads of Europe, such as they are if there are any—the master mind directs a committee which volunteered from the audience.

They put the little lady, with her hands tied, inside of a box. Fasteners and padlocks are put on the box. The locks on the box are locked with further locks. She looks fastened in for fair.

A cross-cut saw is operated. The box is sawed in two in the middle. So far as optical vision and human logic is concerned it might seem the little lady locked in the box is sawed in two and the next thing in order is to telephone Pete Hoffman.

And yet, however, nevertheless, when the box comes apart there is the little lady all smiling. The saw never touched her. It is baffling.

The second half of the film shows how and why it ought not to be baffling at all, that the little lady was well taken care of and they would have to saw somewhere else than where they sawed if they expected to saw a woman in half.

A film guaranteed to attract the attention of lowbrows who wish to see a mystery— in the first half—and of highbrows who wish to understand the rationale, the why and the wherewith of the mystery. It's a film to be recommended. It's "something to think about" in the way that Cecil DeMille couldn't savvy, because he would think it was over the heads of the people.

Sawing a Woman in Half has a decided thrill for all who hate women and all who don't.

August

Grandma's Boy

With Grandma's Boy, *Harold Lloyd came into his own as a filmmaker. His second feature (after the four-reel* A Sailor-Made Man*), this was Lloyd's first real character-driven comedy.* Grandma's Boy *took five months to shoot, a lengthy period by 1920s standards. The effort paid off;* Grandma's Boy *was a box office hit. Charlie Chaplin considered this film to be a model for comic ingenuity. "The boy (Harold Lloyd) has a fine understanding of light and shape," Chaplin said at the time.*
*"(*Grandma's Boy*) has given me a real artistic thrill and stimulated me to go ahead."* [3]

In *Grandma's Boy*, Harold Lloyd appears for the second time in a vehicle of major size or six reels.

There has been a tendency in some quarters to rate Lloyd as a "cutup," a young man with a talent for practical jokes rather than ability in comedy.

In *Grandma's Boy*, however, he has a plot and story better than ordinary to work in. The combination of the story, the direction and the acting put this film play out of the ordinary.

Not that the story is particularly original. But the setting and the handling of it are exceptional.

It is a case of "mamma's boy," the lad tied to his mother's apron strings, getting grownup—and his grandmother infuses courage into him by telling him how his grandfather in the Civil War triumphed against many and sinister enemies by carrying a token, an image of a Zuni god.

The boy takes the token, carries it, and by that token startles the village by his bravery in capturing a murderer feared by the whole posse that failed to capture the murderer.

Later, the mother-grandma shows him that the token, so-called, was only an umbrella handle.

The showing is at the Roosevelt Theater.

Is "Love Interest" End and Aim of All?

Another strong Sandburg criticism of Will Hays and censorship.

Saturday, August 5, 1922

Among the people who make motion picture plays there is a saying or phrase, "the love interest."

Often when Hollywood is under attack for its employment of what is called "the sex motive," the reply of Hollywood has been "We can't have a picture unless we have the love interest."

It seems, however, that since Hollywood has been under attack so fiercely from so many different quarters—and particularly since the specter of a censorship has come to haunt the cinema business and art—there has been an increasing percentage of pictures where "the love interest" is toned down, is subordinate.

The clinch and the kiss are there—but they are not all over the place, not trailed across the film from beginning to end, as in so many of the pictures that called forth the fierce criticism from many quarters.

Whether this represents some of the fine Machiavellian effort of Will Hays is not known. It might be Hays on the job. Or it might be the word sent out by the producers who, with the horse sense of good businessmen, have come to understand what it is that has caused the hue and cry for censorship.

There were two pictures, *Out of the Dust* and *Out of the Snows* showing across the street from each other on Madison Street this week.

In the first the dominant theme was "the winning of the West," with the Frederick Remington sketches and paintings of the far West as the background. The "love interest" was there—but not all over the place.

In *Out of the Snows* there was likewise the "love interest" but the snow and the wrestle of man with the wilderness was the chief thread of interest.

Bushes of white salt, snowshoes, lithographs of icicles and other suggestions of bitter cold weather were drawing patrons in from the hot July sidewalks. The doorman said, "It's a kind of psychology; they want to keep cool."

Furthermore, one may note that in such current productions as *Grandma's Boy* and *The Dictator* there is "the love interest," but it is incidental.

We may look with pleasure and interest to see what William Fox is to achieve in his forthcoming film of *A Fool There Was*. This same title is attached to one of the earliest Fox productions with Theda Bara as the woman who snared men to her deadly pitfalls.

The love interest, so called, will be played down and handled different in the days, days, days to come.

Inventor in Chicago at Work on Motion Pictures for the Blind

The Chicago Rothacker studio was an important center for technological developments, as well as a hub for industrial and educational filmmakers. Despite their good intentions, Rothacker's films for the blind never achieved any real distinction.

Wednesday, August 9, 1922

An inventor is now working at the Chicago Rothacker film laboratories on a play whereby the blind could at least approximate the sensation of "seeing" motion pictures. This inventor already had several important scientific discoveries to his credit and his new cause was such a worthy one that the manager assigned him a corner of the laboratory as a workshop and instructed the laboratory technical staff to be of any assistance possible.

The fundamental principle of the sought for invention is a new material which would be super-sensitive to light. The inventor says he is making progress toward perfecting this new material. The blind person would sit in a darkened room with a strip of this material drawn tightly over the palm of his hand. By means of a miniature projection machine motion pictures would be projected on this material, just as on a theater screen at present. This material, being so ultrasensitive to light, would have the effect of accentuating the light and shadows, as it were, to the point where the blind person could feel the movements, or play, of the lights and shadows.

The inventor, of course, does not claim that blind persons ever will be able to experience the full beauty of a motion picture but that they will be able to follow the action of a photodrama. He says that the invention he is striving for should seem no more impossible than movies themselves or the phonograph would have been considered 100 years ago.

Producers Too Scared?

For an interesting response to the issues raised here, see Sandburg's review for South of Suva *just a week later.*

Tuesday, August 15, 1922

The producers of most motion picture plays nowadays are too scared of putting out pictures "over the heads of the public," according to John Barrymore.

Scenes are often cut out because "they wouldn't get that in the west, the middle west or the south."

Applying the point to his own career on the stage Barrymore says, "If I have not always had uniform success it is not because the plays were above the heads of the audiences that came to see them.

"As a matter of fact, any girl in a ten-cent store in a small western town can 'psyche' a movie from seeing a third of it. She has seen so many pictures that she can tell you that Myrtle, in spite of the most insistent, varied and acrobatic inducement, is going to retain her virtue and win over Luke's stern old father with the high hat."

Is it lack of imagination the movies suffer from? Are stories that ought to go two reels spread out over six? Barrymore says, "There is relatively no imagination." William Allen White puts the case likewise, only not so softly.

Or is there good reason to the argument of picture producers who say—not for publication—that censorship and fear of censorship stifle imagination and the creative spirit?

Or is it, after all, the fact that the movies are a business, colossal commercial and industrial enterprise, with imperative order to fill every week from theater managers, demanding new pictures?

Or is it that the picture industry is so young, is such a cub, has been so few years learning?

On the answers to these questions might be found explanations due people who complain of pictures, plots and players repeating themselves and getting monotonous with action lacking imagination from month to month.

Out of the Inkwell

Using a combination of live action and cartoon figures, Max Fleischer developed a new method of animation, called rotoscoping. Essentially, rotoscoping involves tracing a live figure, then turning these sketches into animation. Finding clowns energetic and easy figures to rotoscope, Fleischer used them to develop his Out of the Inkwell *series. Each episode began with a live-action shot of Fleischer's hands drawing a clown. The figure would suddenly turn animated and leap off the drawing board into a new adventure. This popular series lasted well into the sound era. In 1922 the clown was nameless; Fleischer eventually dubbed him "Koko." Betty Boop and Popeye were among Fleischer's later cartoon creations.*

Wednesday, August 16, 1922

Some words should be spoken about Max Fleischer and his series of two-reelers called *Out of the Inkwell.*

The only one this reviewer has seen was at the Roosevelt Theater and was titled *Bubbles.*

It is a sketchy and mixed action Fleischer gives. Fun and fantasy, mystery, surprise and grace—these come out of his inkwell.

The artist sits at his drawing board with an inkwell—and soap suds and a pipe. Clowns get into the bubbles and fall out and spill over the place. The bubbles go out of the window and get into motor cars and on wash lines and make trouble. Sometimes the bubbles swell to enormous proportions. Sometimes they come blowing back through the same window whereof they went out.

It is a fantasy of nonsense clean and keen. Children particularly and all grownups with a little child zest of life, will enjoy every flicker of Max Fleischer's *Bubbles.* We hope his series, *Out of the Inkwell,* keeps up the flying start it begins with.

South of Suva

Tuesday, August 22, 1922

John Barrymore made the point a while ago that the average young woman working in a 10 cent store in a small town in the middle west is able to guess nine times out of ten just what is coming next after she has seen one-third of the flickers of an average movie.

We are reminded of this on seeing a film of the type of *South of Suva.* The young heroine, played by Mary Miles Minter, is on her way to the South Sea Islands. Into the ear of an elderly woman on shipboard she whispers the confidence that she is going to join her husband, who doesn't expect her.

She finds Mr. Latimer, her husband, carrying loads of intoxicants while various native women in spare apparel make advances to him and he meets 'em half way.

Marooned with a husband she doesn't care for and without money to pay her fare elsewhere, she impersonates the ward of a man she has begun to care for. It would be a tight pickle for the elements of a happy-end romance—unless the story could have the husband killed off—which is neatly and quietly done.

And we believe John Barrymore's average young woman working in a 10 cent store in a small town would have "figgered" out the dispatch of the husband before it was shown on the celluloid.

Presentation of *South of Suva* is at neighborhood houses.

Blood and Sand

Valentino's stardom was assured with Blood and Sand, *a sizzling drama of passion, bullfighting, and doomed romance. The story was remade several times, including a 1941 version with Tyrone Power and Rita Hayworth and a 1989 Spanish telling featuring an unknown Sharon Stone in the temptress role originated by Nita Naldi.*

Thursday, August 24, 1922

Blood and Sand, the photoplay version of the Ibáñez novel, having its first run at the Roosevelt Theater this week, gets by as a starring vehicle for Rudolph Valentino, and a fair bid as a successor to *The Four Horsemen*, which as an Ibáñez story it is expected to do.

Valentino, guised forth in velvet and plush garments, legging hither and yon in silk stockings, assuming the lover tempted and in dire straits through several reels, sighing, bullfighting, answering multitudinous applause with a flourish of his cape, watching two women each with a lover's eyes, and at last dying the death of a hero—the part is one up to the Valentino tradition as such.

Those who rate Valentino an actor of high degree rather than a matinee hero first of all will, after seeing *Blood and Sand*, continue to give him a topnotch place, while those who count him a quiet, exotic personality of appeal rather than a young man of rare gifts in the art of mummery, will ask to see him in more photoplays before conceding he has the smoke of genius on top of talent and looks.

Lila Lee is seen as the wife of the famous matador, Gallardo (Valentino), and gives a portrayal of the Spanish gentlewoman. Nita Naldi plays Donna Sol, the lure, the sinning angle of the triangle, who gets the heroic matador in tow, "gives him the air" and sends him to desperation.

He kills the bulls, the hero does, with his sword, fearlessly—and a little woman gently pushes him off the cliffs.

Fred Niblo directed the picture. June Mathis made the very faithful translation of the novel into scenario script.

Colossal Effort Devoted to Picture Production

The set for Douglas Fairbanks in Robin Hood *was tremendous, covering ten acres of land in Southern California. The castle was specially designed, encompassing needs for historical realism, filming conditions, and Fairbanks's many stunts. Fairbanks took great pride in the structure. Upon seeing the castle, Charlie Chaplin declared, "What a wonderful opening for one of my comedies: the drawbridge comes down, and I put out the cat and take in the milk."[4] Though Fairbanks loved Chaplin's gag, the castle was only used for* Robin Hood. *Fairbanks insisted on copyrighting his film as* Douglas Fairbanks in Robin Hood *to make sure his audience wouldn't be taken in by fly-by-night producers releasing a hurried imitation.[5] See also Sandburg's review of the film, Monday, October 16, 1922.*

Friday, August 25, 1922

Motion pictures as an "arrived factor" are scarcely more than 20 years old, but today they are so big a part of industrial and artistic life as to amount to a modern miracle.

Along with its progress the film has taken a place paralleling such lines of endeavor as the building of the Eads jetties or Brooklyn Bridge.

Producing a picture of consequence no longer means a few days' session with a camera in a shack, as in the old days of the game. Even an ordinary picture now means an indefinite preparation, an extreme range of technical accessories, an outlay comparable to an average man's life earnings, and a regiment of mechanics and actors. And for exceptional pictures—there must be always a few exceptional pictures even as there are other exceptional specimens of man's handiwork—engineering on a magnificent scale is employed. In its own field the cinema has its Roosevelt dams, its pyramids and its Woolworth buildings.

The conspicuous example at this time of huge doings in film production is the elaborate reproduction of old world 12th century atmosphere and story for the modern eye by an industrious swarm of studio wizards at Los Angeles. Out beyond Hollywood is the show place of the season, the bulking medieval castle erected for *Douglas Fairbanks in Robin Hood*, which has set not only the tourist agasp with its overpowering size, but amazed the movie colony itself.

Simply because it is the most ambitious photoplay undertaking so far carried out in this country, This *Douglas Fairbanks in Robin Hood* work is worth looking into aside from outlay, which, as one writer has deftly expressed it, is "so great that you wouldn't believe it was half that much if we told you what it actually is."

Fairbanks, it seems, after deciding to put on the screen the fascinating legendary bandit of Sherwood Forest, decided that the spirit of the era to be pictured would be faint unless visualized in its entirety—that the social and physical aspect of the 12th century—Robin Hood's background—must be present, else the force of Robin Hood's intensely romantic insurgency be lost. For this reason medieval life must be reproduced with its princes, its knights, its peasants, its castles, its walled towns, its hovels, its oppression and its license, its customs, its moods and its urge. And this required engineering from a hundred different angles—from story idea through costume sketches, casting and so forth to actual architecture on the scale of cathedrals.

Honor First

John Gilbert was a rising star when Honor First *was released. Along with Valentino, Gilbert was one of the1920s' most popular romantic leads. By the early 1930s Gilbert's career came to a crashing end. Though some claimed his voice was too high-pitched for sound, the truth was Gilbert's turgid romantic style was better suited to silent films. Like Valentino, Gilbert died young, felled at age 41 by a heart attack in 1936.*

Wednesday, August 30, 1922

Honor First is a film showing at the Rose Theater, in which we get acquainted with John Gilbert, a handsome young player executing a dual role.

There are two brothers, one a hero of large, clean proportions, the other a dire dastard whom many people would call a fiend in human form and there would be none to murmur, "Says which?"

Not only does the villain have an unclean military record. Not only does he impersonate his brother so as to tarnish the reputation of that brother.

On top of those villainies he marries the girl the hero wants and instigates a conspiracy to take away money from that girl by foul means—not to mention his twice employing a murderer to kill his brother.

Yet in the end it goes hard with the villain. He dies as this kind of a screen villain should die, stabbed in the back by a man he himself paid to kills his brother.

Rather slow in spots is this film melodrama. But it certainly picks up at the end where they bring in sections of the Fox newsreel to show platoons of French soldiers marching in review before Marshal Foch.

And the movie fadeout of the hero and heroine clasping each other to their bosoms here has a twist of a new version. The pair of them holding hands walk slowly and dreamily down an avenue of horse chestnut trees.

After seeing this picture one has thoughts about what dramatic uses may be made of sections lifted out of the newsreels.

September

Nanook of the North

Already enamored with documentaries and newsreels, Sandburg was completely taken by Nanook of the North, *devoting several columns to the film. The documentary itself was an enormous hit; when its heroic "star" passed away two years later, his obituary was reported in newspapers worldwide. In one* Nanook *piece Sandburg mentions Fridtjof Nansen, Williamur Steffanson, Roald Amundsen, and Sir Ernest Shackleton, four men who explored the Polar regions.*

Saturday, September 2, 1922

How would you like to make a trip into the frozen arctic regions and toil there for two years in the effort to secure an out-of-the-ordinary picture drama of life? Then, having completed the picture, how would you like to pack up the 20,000 feet of precious negative, ride with it over 800 miles of ice and snow on a dog sled back to the first point of civilization, board a train for Montreal and having arrived there, take the film to the laboratory to be developed—only to see a short time later, the negative that had cost so much in time and labor go up in smoke? No doubt you would feel somewhat discouraged. The majority of us would give up the job and turn our minds and energies to the working out of other endeavors. But Robert J. Flaherty, fellow of the Royal Geographical Society, was not so easily discouraged. He turned around and went right back again.

Why did he do this? Because he knew that the thing he found the first time he traveled to Ungava Bay, 800 miles north of civilization's most northerly outpost, was worth going after again. It must have been such a man as this that Kipling had in mind when he wrote the "Explorer." Perhaps Robert Flaherty heard the same whisper, as did the Explorer:

"Something hidden. Go and find it. Go and look behind the Ranges—Something lost behind the Ranges. Lost and waiting for you—Go!"

At least he found a "something" on his first trip. That "something" was Nanook, "the mighty hunter," chief of the small band of Ivitimuit Eskimos.

The picture opens at Orchestra Hall today.

Monday, September 4, 1922

The *Nanook* picture showing at Orchestra Hall must be placed on all-round points among the great motion picture achievements.

Nothing in books or pictures showing the life of the Eskimo people, with character, action, love, fighting, philosophy—nothing has surpassed this. It is hard to think of anything its equal.

Nanook is an Eskimo up in the Hudson Bay country. He lives with some 300 of his tribe scattered over an area of snow, ice and water of about the extent of the land of England.

He is a great and a shrewd, wise hunter. We watch him dip down headfirst into a snow level where he set a fox trap—and brings up the white fox—alive.

We see him spear the seal underneath the hole where the seal comes up for air. And the capture of the walrus, weighting two tons, a massive animal, one of a small herd that escaped into the sea—one of them holding the harpoon of Nanook in his insides.

And Nyla. She is the wife of Nanook, carrying the baby in a fur sack on her shoulders, chewing the sealskin leather boots of her husband in the morning to soften them that the mighty hunter may go forth for their food.

We see an igloo, a snow house, built in an hour, and a windowpane of ice put in. We note the malamute dogs, the huskies, snarling, running, hauling the family sled.

The photography is first rate, better than ordinary. The English concern that gave us this picture has our thanks. For entertainment as a drama, as well as for the knowledge, instruction and "savvy" to it, it is a great picture.

Thursday, September 7, 1922

The picture opens with a laugh. Nanook in his frail kayak comes ashore. He slowly extracts his bulky figure from the only part of the craft that is unhooded, picks up a youngster that is stretched across the forward "deck" and puts him ashore. Then, from the "hold" he extracts Nyla, followed by several others, and finally by a tiny husky. It resembles legerdemain.

Among the incidents that stand out are the capture of the walrus, in spite of the aid given the two-ton brute by his mate; the battle of strength between Nanook and the great seal, speared through the ice; the trapping of the white fox under the snow; the fight between the master dog and one of his companions who disputes his leadership—an animated leave out of the *Call of the Wild* ; spearing salmon through the open ice; trekking over piled-up ice and snow where two miles may be a day's journey; the scenes in the gathering dusk of the swirling blinding snow—with no airplane motor to accelerate it.

Nanook, chief of the 300 Itivimuits who inhabit a territory nearly as large as England, is a real screen hero and apparently a happy one.

Saturday, September 9, 1922

That picture, *Nanook of the North*, is not merely a picture to learn something from, not only a brilliantly conceived travelogue, with facts of geography and points of science worth attention from all those who are for the Darwinism theory and all who are against it.

Besides showing how people live where there is no land to raise crop for food, no timber to cut wood and build houses, that is, besides geographic facts, *Nanook of the North* is a story.

It is as clean and big and strong a story as *Robinson Crusoe*. It is as mysterious, sinister and gripping as *Treasure Island*. Its characters are fewer than in *David Copperfield*, but they are more memorable.

Neither Jack London nor Rudyard Kipling ever did a story that surpasses *Nanook*. It is up to the best handling Jack London ever gave to his proposition, "Man is a creature of the thermometer." And the love life of Nanook and Nyla stands comparison for the tenderness, struggle and mystic hope with the weave of passion and motive in *Without Benefit of Clergy*.

The story of Robinson Crusoe, however, is probably the best one to compare the story of *Nanook* with. The *Nanook* film lacks the nice and goody-good stuff of *The Swiss Family Robinson*. But it does have the dramatic loneliness, the battling with primitive elements seen in *Robinson Crusoe*; and then what Crusoe didn't have, a beautiful wife and a bunch of children that soften and light up the sinister white silences of the arctic.

Friday, September 22, 1922

Civilization, of a sort, has produced some curious reactions, according to comments overheard in Loop movie houses. At one theater, the dramatic scene in a triangle play showed various forms of temptation with pitiless clearness. The scene was accepted calmly as part of the ordinary course of life.

Later, on the same afternoon, at a performance of *Nanook of the North* at Orchestra Hall, Nanook, the hunter, lying on the ice beside an air hole, speared a seal wherewith to feed his hungry family and their equally hungry sledge dogs. After much hard work, Nanook hauled the seal out on the ice, cut it into convenient sections, threw chunks to the dogs and gave the baby a piece of fat meat to suck on the way home. Whereat two flat dwellers remarked that it was "disgusting."

Saturday, October 21, 1922

That photoplay *Nanook of the North*, is one of the few films that has come along the past year which is worth going to see once, twice, three times and more if you feel like it.

It is a classic that takes its place in the film world as a sort of parallel of *Robinson Crusoe* in the book world.

Every child that enjoys books and pictures about travel, and every grown person who would like to travel, should see the picture for the way it sweeps one out and away from the things just around the corner, carrying you to a cold, wild, white corner of the earth.

The film is the product of the Revillon Freres corporation. They are a big fur selling concern with headquarters in Paris, France. They have stations and outposts at several points in the far north where the fur-bearing animals live.

An Englishman who seems to have an Irish name, Robert Flaherty, a fellow of the Royal Geographical Society, went up into the Hudson Bay district under auspices of the Revillon Freres corporation.

The idea of Flaherty was to make a picture that would be a first-rate travel picture and at the same time tell a story, weave through as a drama. This he has done, thoughtfully, amazingly well.

If there ever was a fellow of the Royal Geographical Society who ought to have a medal and a string of medals, besides his own satisfaction and joy as an artist and a scientist, Flaherty is the man.

Nanook of the North is a novel and a poem and a biography and an epic. It takes the curse off motion pictures to the extent that those who anathematize the movies without making an exception of *Nanook of the North* thereby display merely their own pathetic ignorance of one picture product that stands comparison with the things of highest excellence produced by other arts.

Nanook is a magnetic and loveable character. His wife, Nyla, their children, their dogs, their pups, their snow houses, they too are magnetic and loveable.

Jack London wrote of the "white silence" of the north. Nansen, Steffanson, Amundsen and Shackleton have conveyed to us some of the airs of the region where the people make no wood nor iron, plant no crops, eat no vegetables nor fruit.

But the classic that excels them all in its delivery of the character and atmosphere of that region is *Nanook of the North*, a movie.

It is a work of genius to throw this informative material into the shape of a living, tingling drama. One may hear the children ripple with laughter at various places in this picture play.

Nanook comes in a seal hide canoe. He is landing. He seems to be alone. He goes to the canoe, dips down through the one big hole in the top of the canoe and brings out his wife, with a fine naked baby in a pouch on her back, goes back again for two husky boys one by one, and last of all the pup they are raising. Of course, the children laugh. It has magic and surprise.

The final scene shows the family sleeping in a snow house while outside the wolf dogs howl as the snow piles on their hair. We see the wind sweeping long levels of snow. We flash inside the snow house and the last of the film is the sleeping face of Nanook, peaceful, masterly, ready with his brood around him, ready for anything.

We have seen him trap a live fox and bring the live fox up out of the snow with his bare hands. We have seen him harpoon a walrus and drag forth a seal from under the ice. We have seen him driving the snarling dogs through a fierce blizzard with his Nyla and the little ones. It was a stroke of dramatic art to show him last of all sleeping with peace and understanding on his face.

Just Tony

Cowboy star Tom Mix readily credited part of his success to the popularity of his horse, Tony. Just Tony *was designed to showcase the talents of Mix's equine partner.*

Friday, September 8, 1922

Tom Mix makes so many pictures, nearly as many as Charlie Ray, that whenever we go to see a new one, we expect to see him slipping.

And while we are sure Charlie Ray makes more pictures than he ought to for his own good and the good of his friends, we don't feel the same way about Tom Mix.

Except for the film a few months ago, where Tom went to Czechoslovakia and got out of his own country, his batting average had held up.

His latest, *Just Tony*, showing at the Rose Theater, is a pippin of a picture. It may be Tom Mix should have only half the credit.

It's a horse that's the star, strictly. A wild horse roaming the desert valleys was Tony. The ranchers did him wrong. And he stole into their corrals at night and sneaked out their best horses.

Jim Perris (Tom Mix) is hired to come on and catch the wild horse. He does the job. And thereby hangs the thread of love, murder, fighting.

Again there is that peculiar sincerity that goes with the Tom Mix pictures. It is no stage of love of horses and understanding of the whims and ways of horses that runs through this picture.

The picture reminds one a little of *The Silent Call*, where the dog, Strongheart, was the main player. However, it is no direct kin as a story. The plot is an adaptation from the Max Brand novel, *Alcatraze*.

Claire Adams has the leading feminine role and makes good support for T. Mix and Tony. Lynn Reynolds was the director and deserves a bun.

Claims Movies are Rest Cure

Monday, September 25, 1922

How would you feel tomorrow if your doctor were to order you to throw away your medicine and prescribed instead two hours a week at the movies?

That is no figment of imagination. Doctors in Chicago today are doing precisely that. They are curing nerve-worn people by ordering them inside a picture theater.

Anna Dwyer, M. D., physician of the Municipal Court, says:

"In sending patients to the theaters, I am doing nothing unusual. Such action is based on the soundest medical practice. Good music is a tonic. It brings nerves back to normal, tones up the whole system. A very easily observed sense of stimulation and elation is to be seen in crowds leaving and particularly on individuals who have been nerve-fagged, near exhaustion when entering."

Sinclair Lewis and Film

Sandburg and Sinclair Lewis shared common interests as writers, social advocates, and friends. Both also had books released by Alfred Harcourt's fledgling publishing company. Lewis once described Sandburg's writing to Harcourt as "Rough but real."[6]

Tuesday, September 26, 1922

The report that *Babbitt*, the latest Sinclair Lewis novel, would be seen in a film version this season is put straight by a statement of Lewis in New York.

He says there will be no *Babbitt* picture until the screen translation of *Main Street* has gone the rounds of all the picture theaters that want to show it.

Main Street is now approaching a finish in the films and will be seen in Chicago locally before winter.

Meanwhile, for any such Sinclair Lewis fans as require a film by him, there is *Free Air*, a screen story from his novel which preceded *Main Street*. It was shown at the State-Lake Theater recently and is now showing in neighborhood houses.

Free Air is an exceptionally good movie. Sinclair Lewis will be lucky if *Main Street* and *Babbitt* turn out to have as good direction and playing as *Free Air*.

When in Chicago a few weeks ago, Lewis visited friends at *The Daily News*, and was handed a telegram informing him that a story of his published in a local fiction periodical had been sold—as to film rights—for $4,000. The sum received for the film rights was nearly six times the amount received from the magazine.

Lewis was asked about *Babbitt*, his latest novel, whether he believed it had good screen material. He said he didn't dare to make a guess, that he set out to write a novel to be read from a printed book, with no film ideas in the background.

"I'll be glad if *Babbitt* makes a good movie," he said. "A lot of people who never read books go to the movies, and they would get as much of my novel as the movie could tell."

October

The Wildness of Youth

These two pieces are a good example of how Sandburg used his column to debate the social and artistic merits of movies.

Thursday, October 5, 1922

Are the movies changing? Are there any universally recognized new trends in the motion picture art?

It can't be proved by *The Wildness of Youth*, showing at the Castle Theater and at Barbee's Loop Theater.

An Ivan Abramson production, distributed by Graphic, it is perfectly moral, all right, of course. There is nothing in it likely to lead young men and women to lives of crime and careers of vice.

Yet it is silly so often, it is so far from honest realism or grand burlesque that we can understand people saying, "What can we do about the movies so that our children won't be lured into wasting time with such trash as this?"

This is the sort of picture that brings into creation the "Better Films Committee" of those organizations which try to select and guide their friends to—films different from *The Wildness of Youth*.

There is a place for lurid melodrama and catastrophies connected with a sequence never seen in real life. There are likeable heroes and villains amid the travesties of classic melodrama.

But when a melodrama falls into the hands of such workers as made *The Wildness of Youth*, there is no chance for catastrophies, heroes, villains, to win their way into the hearts of those who see the picture.

There is a genius for the lurid and a gift for the clumsy whereby art may shine through. But when a job is silly—and from beginning to end with hardly a lapse is silly—what is there to say?

Two Current Films Up for Comparison

Saturday, October 7, 1922

Two pictures of current showing are worth comparison and contrast.

The Wildness of Youth, for instance, is a good specimen of the jumble of jazz and melodrama common five and six years ago, the kind that helps "put the movies on the blink."

The silly, the trashy, the obvious, the slipshod, the shoddy, it is here. Most any sophomore class in any college in America, most any group of amateur players putting on a night of play and fun at a neighborhood club could improve on the acting, the plot, the points possible, in this picture.

It is the kind of picture that makes certain young people say, "Is this life? Do we want to take this in and keep it and remember it?"

And on the other hand, the silly satisfied stupidity of it is precisely the element in the movies that inspires the people who cry for censorship, control, regulation.

These people say, "We don't want this kind of trash beckoning to our children."

Charlie Chaplin once told a Chicago friend, "I like a murderer—if he's got character."

The trouble with a film like *The Wildness of Youth* is that it has no character. It doesn't class with the maniacs who must be controlled with a straitjacket; it has no power nor flashes.

It belongs with the drooling and the aimless of the wards for the feeble minded. It is the type of picture that leads to the comment, "Movies are made for morons."

On the other hand there is character to such a picture as *The Girl Who Ran Wild*, a production based on the Bret Harte story "M'Liss." The concern that made this picture has in its time, especially a few years ago, put out pictures of about the grade of *The Wildness of Youth* mentioned above. Gladys Walton, the leading player, has been seen in considerable trash. One may notice, however, that the same players and directors are evolving new theories about the movies. They are learning possibilities of the human face in portraying character and telling a story.

Gladys Walton, having been seen in some of the worst trash ever filmed, may also be seen here in a remarkably vivid and intense piece of character work. One might believe that Bret Harte himself would have enjoyed this screen rendition of his famous story.

The movies? They are making them better than ever and as bad as ever.

Douglas Fairbanks in Robin Hood

"Elton Thomas," who is credited with the screen story on Douglas Fairbanks in Robin Hood, *is actually Fairbanks himself. Fairbanks often used this pseudonym; his birth name was Douglas Elton Ulman. See also Sandburg's essay* Colossal Effort Devoted to Picture Production, Friday, August 25, 1922.

Monday, October 16, 1922

The first public showing of *Robin Hood*, the latest Douglas Fairbanks picture, on which he has been working ten months, came off last night at Cohan's Grand Theater. Fairbanks himself was there, seated with Mary Pickford in a box.

The audience called for speeches. Mary Pickford threw kisses and Doug stood up and made this speech. "I'm so nervous and excited I don't know what to do with myself—I hope you'll like my picture." In an intermission speech of about equal length, he concluded by saying, "If you like the picture I'll be tickled to death."

His hopes were realized. They liked the picture. They were, in that way of speaking tickled to death.

The story of Robin Hood, the English outlaw, that legendary character who becomes known to all school children who read their books, is told in this silver sheet rendition with a skill and a graphic power that will put it across to any boy or girl more keenly, vividly and humanly than any of the storybooks. It will be a screen classic, very likely.

It is not a child story, simply and merely. It has punch and go, a passing of puppets and a grand balance of the comic, so that it is a picture for grownups as well as the kiddies.

The story as given in some versions in the books is departed from yet not in any way so as to mar the main point of the Robin Hood tradition. The production is gigantic. It is evident that a faithful research department worked hard and the costumes and the builders of sets had a big leeway in an expense account.

This is Douglas Fairbanks' masterpiece. It will win him new friends and hold all his old ones. The outpouring of people who couldn't get into the theater but waited around for a look at him was probably the largest crowd of its kind that the local theater district has seen. It was a testimony to a unique personal popularity.

Besides Fairbanks' strong work as Robin Hood, there is the characterization of Richard the Lion Hearted by Wallace Beery. It is exceptionally strong. Enid Bennett first appears as Lady Marian Fitzwalter—and takes her place among the women of grace in the screen world.

Elton Thomas, who is responsible for the story, should be given praise. To hold a movie audience two hours and weave all the strands together like a compact novel, is a task—and here well done. The direction was by Allan Dwan, the photography by Arthur Edeson, and both are to be congratulated.

Good luck and a long run to the new Doug Fairbanks picture. It will make friends and set new standards for the movies.

Charlie Chaplin sent a floral piece, a large target of white roses and carnations, inscribed, "Sure to hit the bull's eye." Of course, Charlie knows what he meant by "bull's eye." The job has its percentage of hokum. But as art goes, its percentage of honesty and sincerity is high.

Oliver Twist

The Charles Dickens tale of Oliver Twist *has been the inspiration for many filmmakers. This was the fourth silent version. At a 1983 tribute to his Fagin co-star,*

Lon Chaney, an adult Jackie Coogan recalled: ". . . I've worked with only two people in the years I was in the business, Mr. Chaplin (in The Kid*) and Mr. Chaney that . . . were everything."* [7]

Tuesday, October 31, 1922

Oliver Twist, a photoplay version of the Charles Dickens novel of that name, which is this week's offering at the Chicago Theater, has for its leading player young Jackie Coogan.

And because it is a Jackie Coogan affair with notable photography, with a Lon Chaney character portrayal of Fagin, and with other capable character interpretations, it is a better than ordinary picture—and probably stands as the best screen translation yet made of the work of the premier English humanist in fiction.

Jackie Coogan is inching higher as a boy. The boy grows older or grew older, whichever it is, this boy of boys whose boyhood is under the eye of the movie millions and minions. Yes, the boy grew older since he was "the kid" in *The Kid.* But he isn't slipping. He is coming along and under faithful handling. His own genius is often matched by strokes that keep him good company. When he is starving, asleep, they have little skeleton toothpick dancers dancing on his stomach. There are *Caligari* flashes of dark and reckless photography, of which there should have been more to rightly gather that world of Fagin and of Bill and Nancy Sikes, and of Monks, the high-class crook who tried to use those lower down.

Except for the direction of Lon Chaney in *The Miracle Man*, it seems he hasn't had a chance to show form until here in *Oliver Twist*. He plays Fagin, the old crook who teaches Oliver the pickpocket technique. As he progresses in this role it becomes more fantastic till at the finish it is macabre, ghastly.

Both Lon Chaney and Lionel Belmore, who plays Mr. Brownlow, are so lost in their parts that picture goers familiar with them in many other films, are not reminded of the actors. This is saying much for their acting for the story for costumes and sets. Not as much can be said for Jackie Coogan. The impression is that we are seeing the phenomenal kid of the movies rather than the boy of the Dickensian buffets of fate.

They made a good picture of *Oliver Twist* and many boys, girls, men and women who don't care a hoot about reading books will enjoy the movie and get as much from the movie as most readers of the book got from the book.

November

The Ghost Breaker

Sandburg's mention of Wallace Reid as being "under critical examination by the surgeons in a Minnesota sanitarium" is foreboding; the star was in the throes of withdrawal from drug addiction and would be dead in a few months.

Tuesday, November 7, 1922

The difference between being in the silent drama or photoplays and the spoken drama or stage plays is illustrated in the case of Wallace Reid, the young man whose face is reproduced so often in hat ads and announcements of new shaving soap.

While Mr. Reid is under critical examination by the surgeons in a Minnesota sanitarium, according to Associated Press dispatches, the film actor in the silent drama or photoplay is being seen by those who like his style of acting as exhibited in *The Ghost Breaker*, which is this week's offering of the new McVicker's Theater.

By way of personality, good looks and acting, it is sure there are some people who will place Lila Lee, the leading woman, as the real star of the sketch.

Lila Lee is a good example of the caprices of destiny. Of chiefly Teutonic strain in ancestry, with her father the proprietor of the North Side Turner hall, she is nevertheless constantly cast in Spanish parts. When Valentino was picked for that Spanish picture, *Blood and Sand*, he insisted Lila Lee must be the dark lady of his sonnets, so to speak.

The hero, as played by Mr. Reid, is due to fall heir to a baronial estate and its treasures. A villain with a plot interferes. The ghosts seem serious until they are revealed as crapshooters, with the hero's valet, played by Walter Hiers, as leader in the game.

The hero breaks the ghosts and wins his baronial estate. Mr. Reid is unheard of except as a winner, of course. The fadeout has the Spanish dark lady of the sonnets in his arms.

It is a typical snappy Paramount picture story.

Against Censorship in Massachusetts

The following two essays are good examples of how Sandburg covered the issue of film censorship, reporting the facts while injecting a sarcastic comment on would-be guardians of public morality.

Saturday, November 25, 1922

The motion picture industry is feeling jubilant over the package handed censorship in the state election returns in Massachusetts.

Picture producers and exhibitors cooperated in the use of films and screens for reaching the Massachusetts voters with the arguments against censorship.

It is claimed this was partly responsible for the majority of 340,000 votes by which the proposed censorship law got a fatal knockout.

Of course, it is also claimed the intelligence of the voters and their rightness of sentiment had influence in the tidal wave.

The big vote for Al Smith for governor of New York, on a pledge to support a platform with a plank against censorship and in favor of repealing the present censorship law in New York state, is also held by the picture producers and exhibitors to be a little job in which they had a modest share.

Will Hays, the Indiana psychologist sometimes called "the czar of the movies," issued a statement declaring the ballots were a warning to politicians heckling the movies and were a challenge to the picture producers to take the pictures seriously. Hays said:

"Censorship of motion pictures has been defeated in Massachusetts in a direct vote of the people by a majority of 240,000. This overwhelming vote against censorship is a splendid response to the appeal of the press and citizens of that state that the commonwealth of Massachusetts stand against this undue political aggression. Just as certainly is it a definite and unmistakable challenge to the motion picture industry to carry out its program for its own continual improvement in the full discharge of its duty to the public. This responsibility is accepted by the industry in the spirit of highest service and it will in grateful earnestness fully discharge this duty."

The field is one in which producers and exhibitors are keenly interested. They predict that the present motion picture audience of 20 million moviegoers a day will be increased within the next 10 years to 30 million.

Vagaries of Censorship
Saturday, November 25, 1922

Those keeping tab on vagaries of censorship may observe that in London, England, the British Board of Film Censors, of which T. P. O'Conner is the president, approved the film *Foolish Wives*, and it is on exhibition at the New Oxford Theater, while at the same time the Council of the Cinematograph Exhibitors' Association has definitely gone on record with disapproval of the film as not being clean in morals.

December

Distinction Made Between Photoplay and Merely a Picture
Saturday, December 2, 1922

Just what is a photoplay? When is a film production entitled to be called a photoplay and when should it be put in that big classification of merely a "picture," the safest name always to call any piece from the studios and factories of a movie corporation?

For instance, that excellent picture, *The Headless Horseman*, in which Will Rogers plays Ichabod Crane, has a good feel of photoplay technique, along with the best picture acting Will Rogers has done. Yet one feels after viewing the picture that what they have achieved is a first rate piece of storytelling. They did not try to make a photoplay, a film drama, so much as they tried to tell the famous American story by Washington Irving, "The Legend of Sleepy Hollow." It clings to the purpose of telling that story. The personality of Will Rogers and one or two of the subtitles have a modern touch. But in general it seems to get and hold the atmosphere of those days in New York state when the stories of the Revolutionary War were becoming a little stale and the yarn of the headless horseman offered a change.

Certainly *The Young Rajah*, the latest Valentino shine, is not strictly a photoplay. It is a long, rambling, sensational novel told through the medium of the screen. Most any intelligent person could piece together the whole story if given only the subtitles. There are constant departures into the spectacular, the sensational and bizarre, attempts at mystery for mystery's sake and without any particular relation to the story.

Also we are aware the director had in mind the Valentino vogue and cult of the hour, so the hero's face and eyes are staged to the extent of many feet of film not strictly necessary for the movement of the drama. *The Young Rajah* is rather a spectacle picture built for a star rather than a photoplay.

Taking another current instance, however, *The Dangerous Age* is a photoplay. Through a large part of it, it employs strictly motion picture technique. The subtitles alone wouldn't tell the story at all. We learn what manner of man and woman John Emerson and his wife are by what we see on the screen. The scenario and continuity writers, the director, were enamoured of motion picture technique and how to tell a simple story by that technique.

And though, without a doubt there will be a wider popularity in the immediate future for *The Dangerous Age* and *The Young Rajah* than for *The Headless Horseman*, and though the latter will command a much lower rental from exhibitors, it will probably outlast the two former pictures. And there will be those who viewing these three pictures of release this week, will say that *The Headless Horseman* has a measure of art, sincerity and intelligence that puts it among the vital creations of the silversheet world. They loved that old chimney corner legend which Washington Irving got from the grandfathers of his time and they put much of the wild, driving fantasy of it into the picture. That Will Rogers, homely, gay, whimsical was on the job with his tricksy suggestions is evident.

Among pictures we are sure will not add force to the saying "silly as a movie," may be placed *The Headless Horseman*.

Clarence

This is one of many William de Mille film reviews in which Sandburg bashed the work of de Mille's brother Cecil B. DeMille

Tuesday, December 5, 1922

William de Mille's photoplay translation of the Booth Tarkington stage play, *Clarence*, is this week's picture at the new McVicker's Theater.

The story is in comedy vein with the Tarkington edge of satire well captured by William de Mille, with the accent on the William to distinguish him from his blind, blundering, hokum-soaked brother Cecil.

The William de Mille pictures all seem to open with a representation of a stage, with curtains rising as if a stage play is to be presented. It befits what follows and sort of hints, "Here come our puppets—they shall play for us a story."

Able and vigilant direction the puppets in *Clarence* have. Wallace Reid comes nearer a first rate characterization than in any picture he has shown in. We feel Wallie Reid being handled, sobered, held down, toned to the part of the disabled soldier, who finds a job in a home where many things need fixing and he in a droll, quiet way, does the fixing.

AGNES AYRES, as Diana Mayo, in "The Sheik," A Paramount Picture

From the collection of Arnie Bernstein.

Agnes Ayres, a co-star in William de Mille's *Clarence*, seen here in *The Sheik*.

The plot is an intricate Tarkington weave, kept to its paternity by the W. de Mille handling. So intricate is the rush of cross weaver that a reviewer would prefer to say that it mixes a bunch of characters in rapid shifts of motives; hardly having any real heroes or villains, after the manner of that notable Irish play, "The White Headed Boy."

One can understand some studios would not have consented to let this picture go out with a non-committal and simple title such as *Clarence*, when it could truthfully else be called *The Marriage Troubles of a Rich Family*.

It mixes people and intentions as fierce as the Tiernan case. A city editor might say, "This is where the family scandals of Page One get from the movies—it is good reporting of life." It is so mixed that one moviegoer trying to tell another the plot may get tongue-tied. Yet it all sinuates to a fairly logical climax.

Tarkington is in luck that William de Mille handled this. And W. de M may have the consolation of knowing that it is directorial skill and quiet intelligence of the kind manifest here that help save the movies from being unreservedly branded as unrestrained, over-emotionalized and in ancient English, pathological English, "silly."

Agnes Ayres, May McAvoy and Kathlyn Williams are among the capable players in the cast.

The Man from Hell's River

The Man from Hell's River *marked the cinematic debut of one of Sandburg's favorite performers—and an enduring Hollywood legend—canine star Rin-Tin-Tin.*

Tuesday, December 19, 1922

The Man from Hell's River is an Irving Lesser presentation of a picture adapted from a James Oliver Curwood novel, showing in neighborhood houses. Irving Cummings and Eva Novak are the leading players.

Of course, there is snow, there are sled dogs, there is the forest, the wilderness, the Northwest Mounted police, this being a story from a Curwood novel.

"When will Pierre be back?" asks one subtitle, which is answered in the following subtitle, "When he gets his man—maybe tomorrow—maybe a year."

Pierre naturally is of the Northwest Mounted. In this case his role is carried by Irving Cummings. He is known as "the man from Hell's River."

It is, as we expect from a Curwood novel, an instance of two men wanting a girl, one of the men a fiend incarnate, so to speak, and the other a hero endowed and blessed with all the ways and traits that go to make a flawless man.

The girl is Mahalia, played by Eva Novak. Also per Curwood, her past is a misty, moisty past; she seems to have come from nowhere, and only toward the end of the story do we learn she is of people otherwise than we suspected at first.

Her father, it seems, was a murderer, escaped penalty for his crime, and came to the wilderness as a fugitive, only to find that he was known to one man, and this one man demanded the daughter's hand in marriage as the price of silence. In all Curwood pictures there is someone who must pay the bitter price of silence. Yet, ere the final reels of the film flicker, the hero learns the truth and takes her from the bad man's clutches.

In this film a police dog helps the hero. Rin-Tin-Tin is the dog and he flashes streaks of sincerity across the picture.

Subtitle for man driving sled and dogs: "Comrades of cold and hunger, fighting through the trackless snows and the unmapped wastes," and so on.

From the collection of Arnie Bernstein.

A magazine advertisement for 1923's star-studded *Souls for Sale*, part of a satirically proud tradition that explores the dark side of Hollywood and includes such classics as *Sunset Blvd.* (1950), *Whatever Happened to Baby Jane?* (1962), and *The Player* (1992).

1923

January

Night Life in Hollywood

Night Life in Hollywood *was an attempt by producers to show the supposedly "clean" image of Hollywood. Sandburg's note that ". . . the audience takes special interest in being shown the home of Wallace Reid, his wife and children" has certain poignancy; Reid would die just eight days after this review was printed.*

Monday, January 8, 1923

Night Life in Hollywood sounds like the title of a picture in which we might expect a good deal of humor in its view of Hollywood.

As the picture is handled, however, the ignorance of life, the "boobs" and the "boob" way of looking at things, also the wicked and salacious motive in life—it is outside of Hollywood, while that suburb of Los Angeles is not only conscientious, clean, moral, upright, scrupulous, but also religious.

One view shows us 60,000 people on a Sunday morning worshipping in the big Hollywood Bowl.

That Hollywood has a bowl and that 60,000 people go there and worship at one time might be challenged unless one saw the evidence of the camera before one's eyes.

To begin with a family in Arkansas is shown, a "hick" family, reading the newspapers all about Hollywood. The young man believes this is the place to go to see and join in with human wickedness. He packs his suitcase and goes. Arriving, he finds the motion picture capital a place that refuses his vulgar and indecent advances.

The model homes and families of various players are shown. At this juncture of time and events, considering what has happened, the audience takes special interest in being shown the home of Wallace Reid, his wife and children.

Eventually the young man from Arkansas marries a Hollywood movie queen. But only after they have taught him to behave.

J. Frank Glendon does good playing of a cheaply conceived character, that of the Arkansas "hick" who got the notion from the newspapers that Hollywood was different from Arkansas.

"Story's the Thing" Says One in the Work

The more things change, the more they stay the same. Sandburg's 1923 argument that Hollywood neglects good stories in favor of hot personalities continues to ring true.

Saturday, January 13, 1923

The one thing to go after first of all in making a good movie is a story.

The writer who writes the scenario in the beginning, and then the writer who writes the continuity, telling the director, the cameramen, the actors, what scenes best to do—these two writers make or break the picture right in the beginning.

This is the way Richard A. Rowland looks at it. And he is the general manager of the Associated First National Pictures, Inc.

He watches umty-ump millions of dollars thrown at the birds in the making of film every year. And he tells us, "The story's the thing."

And he goes on to say that 65 percent of a photoplay ought to be made by the scenario writer and the continuity writer before ever the camera begins to grind or the players put on their costumes or the director picks up his megaphone.

Haven't we all seen movies where we had the feeling the story was sort of mixed up at the start and the director and the players were not sure just what they were going to do but they were saying to themselves, "We are working, the camera is grinding, we hope the film will look like a reg'lar picture when we get through with it!"—haven't we all seen 'em?

"Photoplays offer a tremendous diversity of entertainment," says Rowland. "And this very quality has developed in the public a discriminating sense which the producer finds more difficult each day to impress.

"The industry is peopled with clever talented artists, but the demands upon them are appalling. The making of a film is as arduous a task as the producing of a stage play, but if only five out of 60 stage plays are successful, the theater-going public is satisfied. In pictures, however, audiences demand a hit every week. The scenario writer is in Babe Ruth's quandary. Babe is great as long as he makes home runs. He may be a hero Monday but he is apt to be a lub on Tuesday. Scenario writers are subject to the same fluctuations of popular flavor.

"Many of these writers have genius. But there are not enough to supply the demand for story material. I look forward to the day when our universities will offer training in scenario writing just as fully as today they prepare students for legal and medical professions."

This, of course, is laying a blame or responsibility outside of the motion picture industry itself, outside of the material film production field.

The most important angle of Mr. Rowland's statement is that which says 65 percent of a picture should be made by the author and continuity writer before the camera beings to grind.

The heads of the industry, may, if this should be found true, act accordingly and pay more attention to those units of production rather than the playing stars and the directors.

February

Thirty Days

Thirty Days *was the last film of Wallace Reid. His death from narcotics addiction would have repercussions throughout Hollywood for the next several years.*

Thursday, February 1, 1923

Wallace Reid's farewell picture, entitled *Thirty Days*, is this week's feature at Barbee's Loop Theater. For the benefit of those who have always enjoyed his work, it may be said that this production probably groups among his good pictures. It does not classify with his best work, but it is distinctly among the better of his screen achievements.

The story is from a stage farce comedy, which was written by A. E. Thomas and Clayton Hamilton. It deals with the troubles of a young man with an open heart and a willingness to help other people. His fiancée accuses him of flirting when she finds him trying to cheer up a weeping Italian woman who seemed to be in distress. The jealous husband of the woman arrives on the scene at the wrong time.

While trying to avoid an encounter with the irate husband, the young man learns he has a warlike foeman to deal with, one who is wanted by the police for stabbing another man who tried to make free with his wife. Therefore John Floyd (Wallace Reid) gets himself sent to jail for 30 days, the theory being that there he will be safe from attack by his enemy. In jail, however, he again comes face to face with the irate and jealous husband. Therefore he operates so as to get out of jail. But on that same day his enemy too is released.

These farcical reverses continue till the time when the Italian takes himself away to

Italy.

The heroine is played by Wanda Hawley. Herschel Mayall has the role of the irate Italian husband. Carmen Phillips is the flirtatious wife. Charles Ogle is the hero's friend and Cyril Chadwick his rival in the main heart affair.

Direction of the picture was by James Cruze.

March

The Shriek of Araby

Tuesday, March 13, 1923

Some of us have long had a hankering to see Ben Turpin, the man with the trick wabbly eyes, handled by producers with something more than a slapstick sense of humor.

A little of this is realized in *The Shriek of Araby*, a Mack Sennett production showing this week at Barbee's Loop Theater.

It is the best picture in which Ben Turpin has ever worked his wiggly optics.

And it has some of the slyest satire of Mack Sennett—along with a well arranged parade of girls so clothed that the photographing of the film had to be done in at least a temperate zone.

There has been so much sheiking in books and in the films that we are pleased to see this take-off, this travesty, come along and kid the sheik business good and proper.

Kathryn McGuire, with looks that are stately and dignified, sits at her easel in the desert painting a picture, with an artist's cape and the fixing of a studio girl wishing to paint the sandy wastes of Araby.

Ben Turpin, on a horse, steals her, takes her to his sheik tent, cows, conquers and subdues her, and she eats out of his hand in the style one becomes accustomed to in the sheik books and plays.

"Beneath the desert stars, love staggered," runs a subtitle. "I'll knock your block off in the name of Allah," goes another.

A nice, healthy movie, considering how the sheik business has been going on the last couple of years.

The Filmless Movies: How They Are Made

Sandburg notes three 1920s figures in this piece: Franklin P. Adams, a popular New York newspaper columnist; Lloyd Lewis, a colleague and friend of Sandburg's; and Jesse Crawford, the talented house organist at the Chicago Theater. His refer-

ence to the Ruhr occupation concerns a hot news item of January, 1923, as French and Belgian forces took over the German Ruhr district.

Saturday, March 17, 1923

At a Sunday night benefit performance recently the newspaper columnist, Franklin P. Adams, offered a stunt he called "A Filmless Movie."

He read off a row of moving picture subtitles. Anyone with a little imagination who knows the movies could just sit back with eyes shut and fill in the picture reels.

This columnist's experiment sort of ties up with a trick they did at the Columbia University, where they have a department teaching the teachable things of the picture business. University students were sent to movies with instructions to copy all the subtitles. They came back with notebooks out of which anyone—with a little imagination—could have the "filmless movie" just by reading the notebook of subtitles.

Of course, if this scheme is carried too far and encouraged too much, so that our young people learn to work their imaginations and run off their own "filmless movies" from pages of subtitles, there is no telling where it may end.

It might reach the time when the straphangers on the street cars will stand up hanging their left hands in leather and their right hands in pages of subtitles which they will be reading. Some will be seeing the filmless movie full of pathetic scenes and they will be crying, letting go of the strap to take out their handkerchiefs, while others will be enjoying the comedy filmless movie. And those would be strange scenes to look at in our rush hour streetcars.

There would be sure to be some people reading the murder trials, the Ruhr occupation and the market reports in the newspapers, and they as practical people would feel sorry for the filmless movie fans, cursed with such handy imaginations.

The fiction magazines, of course, could use the same idea for the benefit of their readers who don't have time to read all the stories. Little thumbnail summaries and sketches of the plots and characters could be published. It would all fit in with the tabloid trend of the time, tabloid histories of the world and mankind, tabloid outlines of science, and so on.

We were just getting serious about this thing when Lloyd Lewis came in and when we put up the matter to him, he said he can sit in the Chicago Theater and by closing his eyes and listening to the pipe organ play of Jesse Crawford he knows whether the silversheet is flickering off kisses, tears, fights, funerals or humpty dumpty horseplay.

Hollywood's Sympathies are with Wallace Reid's Widow

Following Wallace Reid's death, his widow, Dorothy Davenport, decided to wage a personal crusade against drugs, alcohol, and other forms of debauchery. Despite the objections of her late husband's family, Davenport succeeded in producing (and sometimes starring in) a series of anti-vice exploitation films.

Monday, March 19, 1923

Hollywood's sympathies are all with Dorothy Davenport, Wallace Reid's widow, in her feud with the late star's mother and sisters over the advisability of starring in a "dope" picture, the proceeds of which are to be used for founding the Wallace Reid Anti-Narcotic Memorial Sanitarium in Los Angeles. Reid's relatives say the fact that he died because of his fight against the drug habit was merely an incident of his career and should be soon forgotten. Dorothy Davenport replies that Wallace Reid died a national hero because of his brave fight, that if he could express a wish today he would want his untimely taking off to serve always as a warning against drugs and that he would think no memorial could be as fitting as a sanitarium where other unfortunates will be nursed back to health, strength and usefulness.

April

Bella Donna

Thursday, April 5, 1923

Pola Negri's first picture of American manufacture, titled *Bella Donna* is this week's feature at McVicker's Theater.

The story is evidently one that was written, devised and arranged so that it would have an interest, if not a compelling and overwhelming attraction for the same people who got hit with high enthusiasms over *The Sheik* and all things sheikish in the wake of the original, the first and only of the sheiks.

Well, Pola Negri can act. She has looks, temperament, personality, the invisible elements.

And in this, her first American picture, there are scenes, single sketchy spots, where she shows what she can do.

Y'see, there was a rich man and she was his wife and they lived in Venice and she was so beautiful that he was jealous of what other men might do to her and so one night when she was telling another man to keep his hands off her what does her husband do but come in, throw the other man off the balcony, killing him, so while the wife goes free, the husband is hanged for murder, though the murder is kept out of the picture.

That for a beginning, a starter. Next the little lady is in London, skating on thin ice, what with no money and having to pawn her wedding ring. Along comes an engineer, just as she was trying to shoot her head off, only the revolver missed and the engineer saves her from shooting herself, leaves his fiancée, marries this little new lady he's

Pola Negri, a talented beauty from Poland. According to Sandburg: "Pola Negri can act. She has looks, temperament, personality, the invisible elements." *Bella Donna* was her first American movie.

picked up and they go to Egypt, where more terrible things happen and there is a grand crash.

Early in her life a fortuneteller said she would bring bad luck on all who loved her, which the picture tries to prove and does prove.

It is one of those pictures that makes out to be sad and is not sad at all, except in spots where Pola Negri's work holds it together.

It would have been a great picture if they could have had time to love it a little, but it had to be finished by the release date set by the manufacturers and distributors.

Stanislavsky Tells About Motion Pictures and Their Faults

When Constantin Stanislavsky and a troupe of actors from the Moscow Art Theatre came to Chicago, Sandburg interviewed the renowned acting teacher/ theater director. Stanislavsky's contempt for movies was legendary; he once stopped speaking to two of his favorite thespians for six months after learning they had moonlighted as film actors.

Friday, April 6, 1923

The Russian players at the Great Northern Theater have shown us acting of such emotional lucidity that it penetrates the barriers of an alien speech. There is this odd relationship between the Moscow Art Theater and the movies that both have aimed for a universal idiom of acting that both address themselves to audiences of any language and that both have measurably achieved it. But their development of this springs from different impulses, they are really antagonistic in their attitudes toward each other, and the superficial similarity only accentuates their estrangement.

It is natural enough that Constantin Stanislavsky, the founder of the theater, should not succumb easily to the movies. The animate theater is a passion with him—its living, instantaneous actuality, which the screen captures only as a reflection, is the very meaning and justification of the theater to him.

What does he think of the movies as an art?

"So far films are not an art—they have not even begun to be an art. They have not yet come to any consciousness of the significance of their own presentation of life, which is the beginning of art. They are at present a mechanism for reproducing— sometimes beautifully, nearly always casually—the phenomena around them. The recreative imagination is not yet born in them.

"You must remember first of all that in Moscow in the last eight years we have seen very little of the pictures made in recent years. I speak as one who has seen pictures in their more rudimentary stages. Still when I was in Germany I saw some of the more pretentious new pictures, and I found them finer in their mechanics but no more sophisticated in their intellectual development. All the pictures I have seen concern themselves with things happening to people—with sentimental or violent affairs, with robberies or murders, incidents of love or jealousy. They are as indiscriminate as newspaper items, in which everything happens but nothing is of any importance. Those stories they tell do not interest me. I do not even understand them.

"Each art must create, before all, the life of the human soul. If the people who make pictures wish to create an art they must set their goal as high as any other. They must desire, no less than Shakespeare or Michaelangelo, to know the secret of man's existence—they must use the materials of their craft with the deepest conscience to show as beautifully and significantly as they can what they glimpse of man's postures before the universe."

"If you are asked to make a picture," he was asked, "in what manner would you produce it?"

"I do not know. But I should not even dream of starting to make a picture until I had learned all I could of the resources of pictures. I should not think of making a play to show at first. For a long time I should wish to make pictures for my own study and use in a laboratory. I would like to take pictures of motion everywhere—of a man walking, of a horse running, of water under the wind, of trees, of animals, of effects of sunlight, of all the moving quick aspects of life and nature—and I should like to have time to sort out this body of experimental material, to study it over until I could come to some understanding of it and could select what is significant in motion. It would be expensive and take a great deal of time—and perhaps as pictures are made I suppose this labor would not pay. But it will have to be done some time if some one is to arrive at a visual chronic scale."

Three Jumps Ahead

Under his given name "John," Jack Ford, director of Three Jumps Ahead, *became renowned in Hollywood as the leading filmmaker of Westerns.*

Friday, April 6, 1923

It must be three months since we saw a Tom Mix picture, having missed one and maybe two, because Tom is working so fast we don't have time to see all he makes.

At the Pastime Theater, however, we took a look at *Three Jumps Ahead*, the latest Tom Mix release, with Jack Ford as director.

And we wish all people who desire to see a rousing, swift-moving hummer of a melodrama to see this one. It has nearly all the best features of a Nick Carter or Old Cap Collier detective story.

The "Will o' the Wisps" are a gang of cutthroats and thieves who have their hangout in a cave under a waterfall. Riding their horses along the stream and then through the waterfall, they leave no trail that either dog or man can follow. Thus they are baffling to honest men, sheriffs, detectives and agents of law and justice.

Steve, who is played by Tom Mix, and his uncle, get captured and jailed in a private cooler kept by the robbers in their cave under the waterfall. They are beaten with a blacksnake whip, taunted, jeered at. And finally Steve is offered a chance to get his horses back and save the life of his uncle, provided he will do a certain dirty deed required by the "Will o' the Wisps." He is willing. Time comes when he must decide, however, whether he will do what the bandits bid him or whether he will follow the way of his heart with a maid.

It seems as though there is more reckless horseback riding in this picture than any Tom Mix has made.

The slick, sure-fire humor of Jack Ford, the director, is recognized. The Fox corporation, in hitching up these two children of the sun, has made a good combination.

Suzanna

Though weary from scandal and gossip, as well as some banning of her films in the wake of William Desmond Taylor's murder, Mabel Normand pressed on doing what she knew best. "We needed to toss (her) right back into the teeth of the fools and harpies who had damned her," wrote Mack Sennett, "and at the same time back into the laps of people who liked her. Suzanna was a big one."[1]

Wednesday, April 11, 1923

Suzanna, the Mack Sennett production in which Mabel Normand is the leading player, is having its first run at Barbee's Loop Theater this week.

The picture tells a story of a girl, Suzanna, who is a sort of roustabout in the hacienda of Don Fernando. And though Ramon, the handsome son of Don Fernando, has chosen Suzanna as the fairest of the fair the stern father has decreed that he must marry Dolores, the daughter of Don Diego. And Suzanna is ordered to leave and take up her abode in an Indian mission. Thither she is wending her way when she meets the carriage of Don Diego on the way to the wedding of his daughter, Dolores, to Ramon. Don Diego asks her to ride with him to the wedding. At the fiesta Suzanna dances with wild grace and when the men throw their sombreros about her dancing feet she kicks each one out of the circle until Ramon's hat enters. Him she chooses. All of this, naturally, makes it harder for Ramon to think calmly about his father's decree that he must marry Dolores. Everything is ready for the wedding, the ceremony is about to be performed, when Ramon dashes away, lifts Suzanna onto a horse and they ride for the cactus and sage desert. In the hour they are captured and Ramon's father, Don Fernando is about to wreak vengeance on his son it is revealed that Suzanna is the rightful daughter of the rich Don Diego and thus fully competent to assume the place of wife to Ramon.

There is more of the wistful and less of the comic element than in previous Mabel Normand pictures.

Suzanna classes among the first-rate pictures now worth seeing.

From the collection of Arnie Bernstein.

Suzanna was Mabel Normand's comeback picture with Mack Sennett. This publicity card was released in conjunction with a candy manufacturer.

64. Suzanna tells Pancho that she will marry him even tho she is the rightful daughter of Don Diego.

Movie Stars Differ About the Subtitles

Saturday, April 14, 1923

The motion picture play is often called the silent drama to emphasize the fact that it is not spoken drama.

Of course, there is some dispute as to whether the printed subtitles, in quotation marks, are not a sort of substitute for the human voice—and from that angle the photoplay is not voiceless.

A few producers, Charlie Chaplin notably, get along with as few subtitles as possible, hardly any at all. Their theory is that the moving pictures should tell the story, the actions, movements, gestures of the actors, keeping the story alive and holding it together.

Chaplin often refers to himself as a student of the art of pantomime. He is interested in the business of telling stories by action, without words. He understands this art so well that he can make motion pictures that interest the people of foreign countries; in that respect he surpasses all other picture producers. The Chinese, Russians, Tasmanians and Senegambians call Charlie one of their own. Among Mohammedans, Shintoists and non-Christian peoples who know nothing about the story of David and Goliath there will nevertheless be an attraction in the way Charlie tells that story, all by action in *The Pilgrim*.

The art of pantomime comes to one's thoughts on seeing the fine work of the Russians from the Moscow Art Theater. Their voices count, naturally, a good deal in the total impression they achieve. Yet a large part of their playing is in silences, when silent faces, shoulders and feet project character.

Among the women in the movies Mabel Normand may be named as one who understands pantomime down to fine points. While her latest picture, *Suzanna*, is not up to her previous ones, *Mickey* and *Molly O'*, in getting the range of her genius, it is an outstanding picture, one of the best in the current output.

There are subtitle writers who can make the screen sparkle with their comment on the passing play. George Ade, Rupert Hughes, that recent combine of Tom Mix and Jack Ford, keep their audience rippling with a swift, careless patter. So it is probable that while pantomime art as an element of the movies will come to be better understood, we shall always have a line of entertaining chatter from certain born specialists in that line.

Prodigal Daughters

Sandburg's mention of "Dill Picklers" in this review is a reference to the Dill Pickle Club, a group of avant-garde writers and artists Sandburg associated with in Chicago. Along with Sandburg, the membership included Ben Hecht, Charles MacArthur, Sherwood Anderson, and what the group's president, auto mechanic

Jack Jones, categorized as "Irish revolutionists, labor leaders, artists, sculptors, poets, writers, and assorted nuts."[2] Playing a newsboy in Prodigal Daughters *is future director (and cousin of producer Jesse Lasky) Mervyn LeRoy. LeRoy later directed Swanson in the 1931 film* Tonight or Never.

Thursday, April 19, 1923

The famous emotional film actress, Gloria Swanson, is to be seen in this week's feature picture, *Prodigal Daughters*, at McVicker's Theater.

In the role of "Swiftie" Forbes, Miss Swanson, as usual, assumes the character of a woman who understands her own fascinating powers over men, and is always doing things dashing, reckless, full of pep, pepper and pepperino.

Anyone doubting Miss Swanson is loaded to the guards and filled with tip, tabasco sauce and hot chili beans may be convinced otherwise in witnessing her in this performance.

There are two daughters. Their father is in Europe. For three years they do what they wish to do and learn such things as that each of us "must live her own life." When the father comes home and tells them he knows how they ought to live their lives and they'll have to listen to him, they get huffy, blow the works, and set up a lavish, scrumptious, elegant studio in Greenwich Village.

And we may say here that what Hollywood tries to make us think Greenwich Village is like, will only win the scorn and derision of the Dill Picklers everywhere.

A day comes when the father refuses to pay for the blowouts and dances at "Swiftie's" studio. She drifts down and down. We see her slap the face of a department store manager who asks her with a smirk to have dinner. She drifts to dinner with a gambler, the place is pinched by the sponge squad, the daughter slides down a fire escape and runs home all mussed up to put her arms around her father's knees and beg a Christmas Eve forgiveness. (Just why they didn't have snow falling on this Christmas Eve is anybody's guess.)

Ralph Graves has the role of a young man who faithfully sticks to "Swiftie" through all her detours. Theodore Roberts is the father.

All moviegoers who enjoy the famous emotional actress, Gloria Swanson, may again enjoy their heroine in this film at McVicker's.

May

The Covered Wagon

A landmark Western, The Covered Wagon *was an American epic. Approaching his subject with documentary-like realism, director James Cruze created a moving portrait of daily life on a wagon train. Though the film has its faults,* The Covered Wagon *proved to be a trendsetter for the genre. Sandburg, a lifelong student of Americana, was quite taken with* The Covered Wagon, *penning several pieces on various aspects of the film.*

Thursday, May 3, 1923

The Covered Wagon is a notable production based on one of the most dramatic themes, an epic in American history.

Life as it was lived in the trains of covered wagons that crossed the Great Plains, the Rockies, the great desert, on the way to California and Oregon is shown in the picture with wealth of detail, and apparently with rare matching up of drama with historical fact.

The picture is showing at Woods' Theater, where it takes two hours to run. A large orchestra organization synchronizes, sometimes making too much noise to go with the silences of prairie and mountain. And soloists contribute with their voices, as though there were fear that the silent drama by itself needed vocal help, the audience requiring this extra stimulus of imagination. However, those are asides. It seems that under the direction of James Cruze an Emerson Hough novel has been cast into film form, the result being a creation that will take a little of the curse off the name of the movies.

We are shown a wagon train of perhaps 100 wagons under the captaincy of Mr. Wingate, Oregon bound. They are joined by another wagon train, "The Liberty Boys," under Will Banion (J. Warren Kerrigan). His eyes fall on Molly Wingate (Lois Wilson). But she becomes pledged to Sam Woodhull (Alan Hale), though in the end the best man wins. The fording of the Platte River, the buffalo hunt, the attack of the Indians on the wagon train and their repulse—it all seems to be done with remarkable fidelity.

Thursday, May 10, 1923

The lure of the open road is, and has always been, the strongest appeal to venturous men of every race, and even the most stolid of city dwellers thrills at the thought of free highway, with its promise of adventure. Every poet has sung of the joy of faring forth upon the open road. Robert Louis Stevenson not only wrote of the romance of roads, but in his latter years his greatest interest lay in the building of a memorial highway in Samoa. Imaginative men of finance have found outlet for the poetic side of their natures in the planning and construction of highways, and the great railway lines in every land grew from the romantic dreams of a Cecil Rhodes or a James J. Hill.

America, by reason of its vast distances, is necessarily a land of the greatest romance in road building, and it is this spirit that was caught by Emerson Hough and set forth in his fine novel, *The Covered Wagon.* The screen version of that novel, now being shown at Woods Theater, amplifies and glorifies the vivid descriptions of the printed pages and is, on that account, a legitimate and a perfect complement to the author's work. The theme is so well suited to the art of the camera that *The Covered Wagon* has already taken its place among the four or five wholly admirable pictures, artistically, that have ever been made.

Nothing could well be more fascinating in fiction or in the motion pictures than a record of the development of the trails of America, that gradually became highways, and that eventually marked the routes of the great railway lines. Mr. Hough's narrative deals with the most important and picturesque period of this development—the moving of the vast wagon trains which bore to the West not only the stout-hearted pioneers but as well the peaceful weapons of agriculture and the material adjuncts of civilization. No greater heroism has been shown by any group of people before or since, than was displayed by those pioneers who voluntarily braved the perils of storm, flood, fire and the attacks of hostile savages to found an empire in the American wilderness.

This piece re-examines the film after it opened at second-run theaters.

Saturday, May 8, 1923

While *The Covered Wagon* is being exhibited at a number of the large neighborhood theaters, it may be that certain moviegoers are asking themselves whether it is a picture worth seeing.

It is a question easy for a reviewer to answer, because the picture is decidedly one of the worthy productions.

The story or idea which it tackles and holds for more than two hours is one of the big ones of American history, the nerve and audacity, the pluck and the vision of the men, women and children who first crossed the great plains west of the Mississippi, then the Rocky Mountains, the great desert and the Sierra Mountains, for the purpose of settling the Pacific coast country.

Of course the picture is intended as entertainment and as such could not tell all the hardships, could not show accurately the atrocities of Indians on the whites and the punishment inflicted by the whites on the Indians.

Neither does the picture show the filth of a good deal of the life in the covered wagons, when lack of laundry facilities, often amid terrible dust storms, made cleanliness impossible for cleanly people. There were "cooties" of the same sort as in army life. And there were horse flies that bled the animals to blind rage.

Likewise, there were trains of covered wagons that ran out of food and left their skeletons of people and horses along the trail.

These things, of course, in a picture intended first of all to entertain, to make photoplay audiences forget their troubles would be impossible.

It is a case where actually history has to be softened down and smoothed over, or else the makers of the picture would never get back the $100,000 or so that they put into it.

And yet the picture stands up among the most interesting since the movies started winning their large daily audiences.

The love story is told in a way that holds attention. The star players include Lois Wilson, Ernest Torrence, J. Warren Kerrigan, and the panorama of the long train of wagons winding over vast stretches of prairie and then amid mountain passes is a recurring theme that holds audiences in an extraordinary way.

Friday, May 18, 1923

Among the motion picture offerings which have come to this city within the recent times *The Covered Wagon* is one of the few having notable and lasting values.

It is a two-hour film, covering the story of two wagon trains heading for Oregon and California just before the time of the finding of the gold in California.

On the two wagon trains were two persons who cared much for each other—one a young man, the other a young woman.

At a point in Utah where the one trail forks into two trails they part. The woman goes to Oregon, the man to California.

The end of the story has to do with their meeting, how the man came to her in Oregon, he having got his fortune out of the California gold rush.

From that angle, the picture is a romance.

But aside from its love story, the picture is filled with the fighting and shooting, fording rivers with wagon trains, Indians ambuscading wagon trains, scouts who drink whisky and fight and ride magnificently.

And above all, the picture repeats at regular intervals the panorama of the moving wagon train across the plains and valleys, always going west.

The one picture to compare this one with is *Nanook of the North*. It may not be quite up to the stern, spare stuff of the latter picture. Yet it must be counted among the memorable silversheet productions. Credit must be given to James Cruze, the director, who seems to have been interfered with hardly at all by the Famous Players-Lasky company in the making of *The Covered Wagon*.

Musical Score for Covered Wagon Includes Classical Airs

The following is an excellent example of Sandburg as reporter, documenting what ultimately would become a lost art—the musical scoring of silent film for live orchestra.

Wednesday, August 1, 1923

The musical score of *The Covered Wagon* at the Woods Theater was arranged by

Hugo Risenfeld, who directs musically and managerially the Criterion-Rialto-Rivoli houses in New York. Dr. Risenfeld wrote an original march for the great scene of the towing horses and oxen swimming the Platte, and he contributed his melody "My Heart is There" for the love theme of Molly Wingate and Will Banion. Some popular and some well-known classical works appear in the range of selections.

After the dedication to the late Theodore Roosevelt to the patriotic tune of "Daughters of the Revolution," Massenet's "Suites Alsacienne" times with the first view of 500 covered wagons in their camp, which is followed in the subsequent more intimate scenes by "Folk Melody in G." Saint-Saen's "March Heroique" appropriately introduces the Liberty Boys from Missouri, on whose arrival the expedition waits. Soon with the grandly swelling notes of Elgar's "Pomp and Circumstance" and the 2,000-mile way to Oregon is begun.

Another theme that suits the difficult and often pathetic crawl across the wilderness is Rachmaninoff's "Prelude in G Minor." Livelier and more violent strains are provided by selections from Dvorak's "Bartered Bride." Of course "Oh, Susanna"—Stephen Foster's pioneer ditty—is an oft utilized air, particularly with the banjo-playing "kid," Jed Wingate, and the other camp merrymakers. Also, not readily to be forgotten are Kampinski's "Aphrodite Suite" in the quarrels of the rival suitors for Molly's hand; the orchestration of the hymn, "Lead, Kindly Light," for the aged settler's burial and Mlle. Chaminade's joyous "Autumn" to emphasize the caravan doctor's informal but breezy announcement of an increase to the caravan, "It's a boy!"

Souls for Sale

Movies about the dark side of Hollywood have formed their own sub-genre, and stars have gladly participated in these biting insiders' looks. Souls for Sale *is part of a satirically proud tradition that includes* Sunset Blvd. *(1950),* Whatever Happened to Baby Jane? *(1962), and* The Player *(1992). The cameo appearances by 1920s Hollywood names in* Souls for Sale *include: Hugo Ballin, Mabel Ballin, T. Roy Barnes, Barbara Bedford, Charles Chaplin, Chester Conklin, William H. Crane, Elliott Dexter, Robert Edeson, Claude Gillingwater, Dagmar Godowsky, Raymond Griffith, Elaine Hammerstein, Jean Haskell, Alice Lake, Bessie Love, June Mathis, Patsy Ruth Miller, Marshall Neilan, Fred Niblo, Anna Q. Nilsson, Zasu Pitts, Blanche Sweet, Florence Vidor, King Vidor, Johnny Walker, George Walsh, Kathlyn Williams, Claire Windsor, and Erich von Stroheim.*

Tuesday, May 15, 1923

In *Souls for Sale*, a Goldwyn production written and directed by Rupert Hughes, is set forth an eloquent advocacy of the viewpoint of Hollywood and the heart of moviedom by one who believes in it.

The production is this week's feature at the Chicago Theater and holds its own strongly with the film fans of that unimpeachable emporium.

The girl, Mem, came to Hollywood and by work, by what she called "slavery," so hard were its hours and unflagging labor, she arose to stardom.

The man to whom she thought she was married comes to her house, to her room, knocks around among her precious trifles, musses up the place, takes her by the throat and says, "I love you," her answer being, "I loathe you."

The climax is one wild storm scene, a hurricane that wrecks a circus tent in which cameramen are filming a picture. Lightning cracks down from the storm, sets the tent and seats on fire, a madman starts the "wind machine" with its murderously whirling propeller going toward a crowd of "extras."

But the girl, Mem, finds the one man she cares for. And the man she thought was her husband gets struck by lightning.

Eleanore Boardman plays Mem, Richard Dix has the role of the heroic motion picture director with an irreproachable code of honor, Lew Cody is the shady husband, Barbara La Marr and Frank Mayo are other well known players.

Among extra stars are Marshall Neilan, Hobart Bosworth, Charlie Chaplin, Kathlyn Williams, Mabel Ballin, Milton Sills, Anna Q. Nilsson, T. Roy Barnes, Claire Windsor, Fred Niblo, Johnny Walker, Blanche Sweet, Bessie Love, Claude Gillingwater, and enough stars to make a moviegoers' holiday.

June

Safety Last

One of the best-known comedies of the silent era, Safety Last *is best remembered for the image of Harold Lloyd hanging off the hands of a skyscraper clock. Lloyd's creative inspiration came after seeing a "human fly" scale the side of a downtown Los Angeles building. Realizing there was comedy to be had in such a situation, Lloyd structured a story that culminated with his climb up L.A.'s International Bank Building at Temple and Spring Streets.* Safety Last *has remained a classic over the years, continuing to thrill new generations of audiences decades after the film's original release.*

Friday, June 1, 1923

Harold Lloyd's latest release, *Safety Last*, has opened with an eye on summer prospects at Orchestra Hall. It is a six-reel picture, presented with accompanying films from the most fascinating in the Pathe kitbag.

The large and growing number of Harold Lloyd fans will enjoy *Safety Last*. It is full of the tricks which have earned him his friends, and in some scenes he is probably

From the collection of Arnie Bernstein.

Harold Lloyd hanging on for dear life in the most famous scene of *Safety Last*, one of the best-known comedies of the silent era.

funnier than in any previous pictures.

He is seen working in a department store as a clerk. Bargain counter rushers are tearing his coat and necktie off, so the floorwalker reports him and he is warned to make a more presentable appearance. About this time a girl enters—from his hometown—the girl he is engaged to marry. He has written her about the important position he holds and how much money he is putting by so they can soon marry. She congratulates him on his rapid advancement. He carries on a bluff that he is a floorwalker and still later that he is the general manager of the store. He sends her to her hotel in a wealthy customer's limousine.

A bad end he would have come to only he made an arrangement with the general manager of the store to bring hundreds of people to the store, prospective customers. He was trying his hand at what the general manager called "exploitation." But it happened the "human fly" he contracted with to climb the outside of the store walls couldn't come so he had to be this "human fly" himself.

Mildred Davis, Bill Strothers and Walcott D. Clark are in the supporting cast. The picture was directed by Fred Newmeyer and Sam Taylor.

Einstein's Theory of Relativity

During the 1950s McCarthy era, Sandburg publicly defended Einstein against political smears raised against the scientist by anti-Communist zealots. In 1956, Sandburg became the first recipient of the Albert Einstein Commemorative Award in Humanities at Yeshiva University's Albert Einstein College of Medicine in New York.

Friday, June 15, 1923

One of the best films in Chicago at the present hour is the motion picture explaining Einstein, which is having its first run at McVicker's Theater this week.

The *Scientific American* a few months ago announced that this picture had been made and that from a technical and educational standpoint the editors said it was extraordinary.

Of course we understand a thing might please the editors of *Scientific American* and be a fine thing from their way of looking at it—and then not count for very much as a regular picture in a place where they have been showing Gloria Swanson in all her glory or Elliott Dexter in all his dexterousness.

However that may be, they did a mighty good job on this Einstein film. They make it clear that Einstein has a grand old skypiece—a high-speed think tank—and we get a little look at what is going on inside of the works.

That Einstein said maybe only a dozen men in the world would understand his book on "Relativity" ought not to scare anybody away from the picture.

There is a lot of entertainment in it—even a little laugh or a smile here and there.

Of course, the boys and girls who are out to be "stepping high" or those who must have a story with a plot and somebody getting killed or falling in love or falling into a pile of money or falling down a coal hole—well, they won't get so very much out of this film—they will have to pass it up and try something else, such as *Only 38*, the main feature film on the same program at McVicker's Theater.

But there are people who will enjoy this Einstein picture, because everybody already knows something about relativity only they don't know how much they already know until they see a picture like this.

It will be interesting to hear what the McVicker's management has to say about how the Einstein picture goes over or goes under with its customers.

July

The Barnyard

One of the lesser silent film comics, Larry Semon enjoyed some audience popularity in the 1920s, particularly in Europe. However Semon, who also directed, gradually fell out of favor with studios when his later films faltered at the box office. He attempted to become a serious actor in Josef von Sternberg's gangster drama Underworld *(1927), but it was too late. Bankrupt and in poor health, Semon died in 1928 following a nervous breakdown.*

Monday, July 2, 1923

Larry Semon's latest release, *The Barnyard*, has its points—though there isn't much kick, surprise nor novelty to some of its old-time hokum.

An egg rolling off a shelf and falling into the face of a sleeping person, the shell breaking so that the white and yellow smear of the egg flow with broad currents over the face of the sleeper—this has been done at least once every six weeks in the two reelers from Hollywood in the last 10 years.

It probably classifies as old stuff that is known as sure fire. They do it not because it interests them as artists in the cinema domain, but rather because they believe it cannot fail to win laughter and that is the high aim.

The best feature of this picture—a well worked out, original scheme—is the use of the farm animals. The scene of the sketch is a barn loft where the hired hands sleep and get up and comb their hair in the morning. Pouring water out of a pitcher into a wash basin, four young ducks issue forth. The door of the wash stand comes open and first a line of small ducks come out and gradually we have large ducks and geese. A suitcase is opened for a fresh bandanna and the suitcase is full of the kittens of black cats. And so on. They did it good while the going was what it was.

Day Dreams

With Day Dreams, *Buster Keaton continued to push the darker edges of his comic outlook on life, a creative effort Sandburg duly notes.*

Tuesday, July 3, 1923

The latest release showing Buster Keaton, the comedian, is a two-reeler titled *Day Dreams*.

There are touches of poetry and imagination to it, also gleams of democracy as distinguished from aristocracy.

And it is a film that may be recommended for clean humor, comic action and a little philosophic background of life.

As such we may hazard saying it is among the topnotchers of the season's output.

The hero goes to New York and writes back to the heroine he is employed in a hospital working on operations requiring the highest of skill. We see what the romantic girl imagines he is doing—and after that the cat and dog hospital where he has a job.

There is masterly handling of what the girl imagines he is doing when she gets a letter saying he is now in Wall Street and has made a big clean-up there.

Buster Keaton is to be numbered among those of the film industry and art who seem to be learners, not satisfied with past films, aiming to make each new reel say more with less cull celluloid than the previous one.

We wish the same might be said of more of the makers of the two-reelers described as comic and labeled as comedies.

Hollywood

Turning the camera on itself, Hollywood *was the story of a Midwestern girl's adventures in Tinsel Town. It portrayed the film community with all its ups and downs, the star wannabes, the glamorous social life, the hard work and—in one poignant moment—the human face of movie colony scandal. Director James Cruze cast unknowns as the Midwestern girl and her family so their story would appear more "authentic" to film fans. The cameo appearances by real movie personalities were a who's who of 1920s Hollywood: Gertrude Astor, Mary Astor, Agnes Ayres, Baby Peggy, T. Roy Barnes, Noah Beery, William Boyd, Clarence Burton, Robert Cain, Charlie Chaplin, Edythe Chapman, Betty Compson, Ricardo Cortez, Viola Dana, Bebe Daniels, William C. de Mille, Charles De Roche, Cecil B. DeMille, Helen Dunbar, Snitz Edwards, Douglas Fairbanks, George Fawcett, Julia Faye, James Finlayson, Alec B. Francis, Jack Gardner, Alfred E. Green, Alan Hale, Lloyd Hamilton, Hope Hampton, William S. Hart, Gale Henry, Walter Hiers, Stuart Holmes, Sigrid Holmquist, Jack Holt, Leatrice Joy, Mayme Kelso, J. Warren Kerrigan, Theodore Kosloff, Lila Lee, Lillian Leighton, Jacqueline Logan, Jeanie MacPherson, Hank Mann, May McAvoy, Robert McKim, Thomas Meighan, Bull Montana, Owen Moore, Nita Naldi, Pola Negri, Anna Q. Nilsson, Charles Ogle,   Guy Oliver, Kalla Pasha, Eileen Percy, Carmen Phillips, Jack Pickford, Mary Pickford, Zasu Pitts, Charles Reisner, Fritzi Ridgeway, Dean Riesner, Will Rogers, Ford Sterling, Anita*

Stewart, George Stewart, Gloria Swanson, Estelle Taylor, Ben Turpin, Bryant Washburn, Maude Wayne, Claire West, Larry Wheat, and Lois Wilson. Sid Grauman, owner of the famed Chinese Theater, also made an appearance.

Yet the most touching moment must have been a scene that took place in a casting office. As would-be stars came and went a sad figure sat in the background, waiting for work he knew would not come. The pathetic character was Roscoe "Fatty" Arbuckle, still struggling emotionally and financially in the wake of the Virginia Rappe scandal. His unbilled cameo added an ironically honest moment to this fictional tale. Unfortunately, we may never know just how good or bad Hollywood really was. No copy of the film is known to exist.

Thursday, July 26, 1923

The new Orpheum Theater, with its dove gray interior embellished with hints of maroon, is having for its first run one of the best pictures which has ever hit the city.

Hollywood is a finely genuine picture, a James Cruze production, and the best piece of reporting, storytelling or defensive propaganda which has as yet come forth from the world's motion picture capital.

It tells a rattling live story; it projects some real characters; it depicts the people, ways, manners, methods and atmosphere of Hollywood. And as a piece of reporting on the solid, established Hollywood—the sober organization which must deliver fresh pictures every so often to the 20,000 movie theaters of the country—the business which classifies financially as the fifth largest among the capitalized industries of the nation—it is about as valuable and reliable a document as anything that has come along.

We see Angela going to the pictures in her Midwest small town. She knows she is cut out for a movie star. The family goes to Hollywood; also, the young man who wants to marry her sells his pants-pressing establishment and goes along to Hollywood. And, as it happens, Angela doesn't catch on in the pictures. Her father has a nose, a "beezer," wanted as a "type." Her large-footed, upstanding sister and her mother are wanted as types. The erstwhile pants presser, too, becomes an actor in the Westerns. The whole family become movie stars except Angela. In working out this story James Cruze brings in a long string of movie stars. This reviewer enjoyed particularly the acting of Cecil DeMille and his brother William.

One may see fine collaborative effort in this picture. They had a good time doing it. They made it as they wanted it, setting forth the most appealing human angles of their hometown. It will make friends for the motion picture crowd of the present hour, and will be a pleasant eye-opener for some who have taken too fantastic a slant at Hollywood.

Down to the Sea in Ships

This low-budget whaling adventure is notable as the cinematic debut of 1920s icon Clara Bow. As a Brooklyn teenager, Bow submitted her photo to a "Fame and Fortune" beauty contest in the fan magazine Motion Picture Classic. *She won and had her picture printed in the magazine, which led to a part in the 1922 film* Beyond the Rainbow. *Unfortunately Bow's scenes in* Beyond the Rainbow *ended up on the cutting room floor. However, Elmer Clifton, the director of* Down to the Sea in Ships, *saw Bow's photograph in* Motion Picture Classic *and decided to take a chance on the beautiful 16-year-old. Though it would take a few more years before Bow would become a Hollywood legend, the young film actor was on her way.*

Tuesday, July 31, 1923

Down to the Sea in Ships is one of those pictures which shows that the movies are coming stronger.

It is a bang-up story of the sea. Besides that, it is a rehearsal of history and the people of past times, the days of the whaling industry, and the lives of Quaker folk in a seaside village. And it is scattered through with little cinema poems.

The things of the sea which we read about in books, which we hear about in sailor songs of the old days of schooners and clippers—they are here.

The harpooning of a whale, the turning of the big animal and its move outward to sea dragging a small boat along with it—the sailor lad on the home-going ship on watch up in the halyards (any landsman would guess they were halyards), sighting the black storm coming—the wedding party in the Quaker church and the sad and glad end of that party—these are all scenes well worked out—touched with that elusive thing called romance. Elmer Clifton produced and directed the picture. And who is Elmer Clifton? Why—he is the fellow who made *Down to the Sea in Ships.*

The pink sport sheet crowd that demands "punch" in its picture will say this is the gravy.

And the educational committees of the public schools as well as the better films committees of the women's clubs—they will say it's worth seeing, and showing to the children.

And that is going some in the making of a movie. It is having its first run in Chicago this week at the Roosevelt Theater.

August

"The Movies are Getting Decidedly Better"

This is a good example of how Sandburg entwined his love for movies as an art form with his admiration for the American people. Additionally, his side-by-side comparison of noted New York journalists Broun and Farrar with the writers of a small Midwestern weekly is typical of Sandburg's unpretentious outlook on the world.

Saturday, August 4, 1923

Along with occasional reading of the New York reviewers of the movies—such as Heywood Broun and John Farrar—we take a look regularly at *Capper's Weekly*, the Kansas farm paper which is read from end to end of the corn belt.

And we noticed this week the opinion hot off the hat in that paper: "The movies are getting decidedly better."

The easy sneer at the movies is passing away. The refined snort of cavalier contempt for the film drama is not quite like it used to be. A change has come.

This has different causes, reasons, explanations and facts behind the happening of it.

First of all the picture industry has been centered in a few large organizations. They saw tremendous future for the film if handled right. And they saw that a censorship and a handling as stiff as that of the Volstead prohibition law would come along if the percentage of trash and hokum were not cut down. That is part of the change.

Then, too, the producers, directors, players, photographers, scenario writers, have all been working in an infant industry and art. They have learned more about telling stories on the screen; if a man is to take his coat off he can be shown starting to take it off and the next showing has him with it all the way off; the process of wriggling out of the sleeves needn't be shown unless that action has some feature of character. And so on.

The makers of the movies have been collaborating. They have watched pioneers such as Charlie Chaplin, D. W. Griffith, and later, James Cruze.

It is such current pictures as *Down to the Sea in Ships, The Covered Wagon, The Spoilers, Out of Luck, Salomy Jane, Penrod and Sam* that are responsible for the changing opinion and viewpoint about the movies.

When Heywood Broun and John Farrar in New York think so on one hand and *Capper's Weekly*, the Kansas farm paper, which is read from end to end of the corn belt, says so, on the other hand, it is a sign of change.

A Questionnaire

Saturday, August 25, 1923

A magazine editor is sending out a form letter asking straight and pertinent questions about the short subject reels.

And as though we didn't hear him the first time he has sent us three copies of this letter, each about two weeks apart.

He asks, "Why is it that exhibitors pay little attention to the short subject on their program?" Answer—The exhibitor, whether he runs a downtown house or a neighborhood theater, naturally can't have his whole program made of short subjects; he must have one big feature; the one big feature takes about an hour or more. Generally then, he has one or two short reel subjects, most often a two-reel comedy and a newsreel. This usually eats up about an hour and a half or more of time, which seems to be considered about enough time for pictures. If the show runs longer it is filled with music or vaudeville specialties, or, in some cases, grand opera numbers. It seems to be the case that the big feature pictures are planned to take an hour or more, going six to ten reels, seldom less than six, which takes an hour. There seem to be few or no producers with the whims of a Charlie Chaplin. He found, for instance, that what he wanted to tell in *The Pilgrim* could be told in four reels; he could have stretched it to six reels and made a "one hour program picture," but he doesn't work that way. So, when theaters were showing this Chaplin four-reeler they had more room on their programs for two reel subjects. It seems that there may be more room for short subjects if the producers can be persuaded to make their longest pictures shorter. But we should remember there is a sort of theory or tradition that to make the longer pictures shorter makes the higher price lower to the exhibitor. And there we are.

Question—"Do you think the exhibitors in your locality are accurately gauging the psychology of their audiences by ignoring the short subjects in building their programs?" Answer—The exhibitors know a lot about gauging the psychology of their audiences. Some exhibitors have made large fortunes and built chains of theaters because of their expert ability in gauging the psychology of their audiences. It may be that they have not given the short subjects a fair test; this reviewer believes that there is more science, history, poetry and valuable exciting knowledge in the general mass of short reel subjects than there is in the general mass of "big feature pictures." Just why more of these are not shown, the exact reason why more two-reel educational subjects are not exhibited, is not clear as yet, outside of the big main reason that the feature program of six reels and more takes most of the time. For one thing, we must understand that the exhibitor has to run a theater, tend to its furniture, heating and ventilation, music, tickets, front lobby displays and so on, so that he doesn't have much time to go through the extensive lists of short subjects, view them personally and pick what might please his line of customers. If the exhibitors had more time they might be able to make a wise choice of short reel subjects in which case the children wouldn't have to go to school and study geography or science because they would learn a-plenty at the movies.

Question—"How important do you regard the short subject, comedies, educationals, newsreels, in building up programs?" Answer—On this point we might testify that there is something of a curse resting on the two-reel comedy. A high percentage of the two-reelers are rot and silly slapstick with no imagination nor healthy fun. As to the newsreels, they are decidedly popular and are being used by many exhibitors. Just why more sciences and educationals are not used is not clearly known. Of course, if people like prizefights and dancing and jazz parties better than books or science, history and poetry, it is going to be hard to make them like the beautiful two-reeler on the Einstein theory of relativity better than flashes of Cecil B. DeMille's screen version of *The Admirable Crichton*, which he titled *Male and Female*.

September

Dempsey-Gibbons Fight Pictures

In advertisements for this popular fight film, the Rose Theater informed patrons: "To accommodate the crowds, theater will be open 24 hours daily, showing every hour." They also promised that this was "not a training camp picture."

Wednesday, September 5, 1923

The fight pictures showing the recent contest between Jack Dempsey and Tom Gibbons are released for first exhibition locally in the Rose Theater.

This fight picture is not savage, brutal, bloody, gory and primitive—not from any way we look at it.

It goes 15 rounds and that is, of course, a good deal of time in which savage and bloody actions might happen.

Two men, well trained and set up physically, both of them good boxers and one of them a marvelous and brilliant boxer, stand up and box and clinch and break away and go to it again, for 15 rounds. That is what we see in this film.

We notice as we look at the boxers that Gibbons looks sort of undernourished, a little neglected in his muscular structure, and somewhat frazzled when put in comparison with Dempsey.

We sort of suspect Gibbons to make up for what he lacks in looks by what he can put across to surprise us. Yet the fight he puts up sort of goes with his looks. To begin with, he seems to lack smoke and at the end the world knows he hasn't got it.

Sometimes there are bursts of laughter, snorts of amusement from fight fans in the audience, when it happens that Gibbons hotfoots like a good foot racer away from the fierce mitts of Dempsey.

As a boxing show it is worth looking at. So far as the world's champion heavyweight, Mr. Dempsey, is concerned, we get a clearer notion of what he is as a boxer in this picture than from the Carpentier or Willard pictures. In those he was a fighter rather than a boxer.

Just what he will look like in the Firpo-Dempsey fight pictures is anybody's guess.

Alice Adams

In 1935, director George Stevens remade Alice Adams *with Katherine Hepburn and Fred MacMurray as the romantic pair.*

Monday, September 24, 1923

The picture called *Alice Adams*, which is showing at neighborhood theaters, has its story taken from Booth Tarkington's novel of the same name.

Florence Vidor is the film actress who was chosen to take the title role, while Claude Gillingwater has the part of her father, Virgil Adams.

The best acting in the piece is done by Margaret McWade, who is the worrying mother trying to bring up her family decent and respectable, scolding the father on to

Florence Vidor, a popular leading lady of the 1920s and director King Vidor's first wife.

From the collection of Arnie Bernstein.

money making in order that the daughter can have a chance to play around and put up a front as something which is when it isn't.

It is a case where the verandah tries to get along without mentioning the ash can. As it turns out the verandah can't and the ash can can.

The story as screened comes close to the believable in spots, particularly where the young man who is sparking Alice Adams comes to their house invited to dinner, and they try to make out they are of the people who belong, but after the gravy is spilled and a lot of other things happen it seems they don't belong and the young man calling, coming from a house where they do belong, witnesses for himself that he was mistaken and so far as he and Alice Adams are concerned there is nothing more doing.

He sees her as a bluffer and a faker. She sees herself as such. And the next notice of her she is at the door of the local business college where she is going to prepare herself for a career as a working girl, and when she meets other people she is going to tell them before they have a chance to quiz her that she works for her living and she doesn't want anybody to have any mistaken understandings about that particular part.

The picture is a Metro production, which was directed by Rowland C. Lee. The book from which the story was taken won the Pulitzer Prize the year that it was published.

Merry Go Round

The making of Merry Go Round *caused new battles between director Erich von Stroheim and Universal producer Irving Thalberg. Both men, considered geniuses by their peers, had stubborn ideas about what constituted great filmmaking. With von Stroheim, realistic detail and a fully-told story were vital to artistic success. Thalberg on the other hand disdained what he considered von Stroheim's financial excesses. As with his previous film,* Foolish Wives, *von Stroheim demanded that no cost be spared on* Merry Go Round. *Thalberg, tired of the director's unbending will, finally had von Stroheim fired from* Merry Go Round, *replacing him with Rupert Julian. Von Stroheim's star, Wallace Beery, quit the film in protest. Beery's role ultimately went to George Seigman. Von Stroheim demanded his name be removed from* Merry Go Round, *a request Thalberg happily granted. The director's name never appeared in the credits, though von Stroheim's script was shot largely as intended. Most reviewers acknowledged Julian as the film's director; Sandburg, recognizing von Stroheim's contributions, commended the director without mentioning Julian.*

Tuesday, September 25, 1923

Merry Go Round is a picture much out of the ordinary, with a story and characters set forth with a good deal of the skill which is of the cinema world only.

Or to put it another way, this is one of the exceptional pictures that tells a good deal of what it has to tell in motion picture language strictly and exclusively, a universal and untranslatable language.

There is a Chicago girl named Mary Philbin who is entitled to flowers and compliments—if those could amount to anything in a case like this—for the acting she does in this picture. She has pantomimic ability.

And that is the ability which the director of this picture, Erich von Stroheim, seems to have struggled to bring to the front, often accomplishing his purpose.

The story is of a peasant girl's love for a man who rejected her to marry a countess.

The father of the peasant girl is a clown who is almost murdered and has his injury avenged by a gorilla who escapes from his cage and climbs to the sleeping room of the assailant.

In this scene Mr. von Stroheim showed considerable restraint. It is so customary to leave as little as possible to the imagination in the case of a movie murder.

Here we see the gorilla enter the window of the room, approach the bed where the victim lies sleeping. And later we see the gorilla issue forth from the window and climb down and get back into his cage.

But—does the peasant girl in the end win back her love, the man who left her and married the countess? That is the question on which events hinge toward the end of the story.

The cast includes besides the enjoyable Mary Philbin other capable ones such as Norman Kerry, George Hackathorne, Cesare Gravina and George Seigman.

Zaza

In her autobiography, Gloria Swanson called Zaza *". . . the fastest, easiest, most enjoyable picture I had ever made."[3] Her co-star in* Zaza, *H. B. Warner, was later cast as one of Swanson's card-playing "wax works" partners in the 1950 version of* Sunset Blvd.

Thursday, September 27, 1923

The photoplay titled *Zaza*, which is this week's feature at McVicker's Theater, is taken chiefly from the stage play of the same name, though such theatergoers as saw Mrs. Leslie Carter in the stage play must not expect to see that story played to very closely.

Y'see, this is modern and brought up to date. They put the Great War in it. Very often these days they are putting the Great War in. We may well expect that when *Romeo and Juliet* comes to us in film form they will have Romeo somehow wearing a tin hat in the trenches or being soothed in hospitals by the Red Cross girls.

It is Gloria Swanson, the famous emotional film actress, who has the part of Zaza in this photoplay. She works fast, at high-speed and high pitch, all over the place. There is hardly an instant in the flickering of the reels but what she is rushing hither and yonder.

The leading man is H. B. Warner. He plays Bernard, the man who puts up Zaza at a bird of a country cottage and they live as though life is just for and between those two. That is, Zaza does not know nor have any suspicion there is anybody else in Bernard's life—until one day he goes away and she follows and what she finds is a home and a wife and a child all belonging to him. And Zaza had intended to tear up the place, but after she sees the child playing at the piano she hasn't the heart.

However, it should be noted that Zaza fights with another woman and tears nearly all the clothes off the other woman. It is the first fight we have seen in the pictures where two women beat each other up nearly as bad as men do.

And Bernard went with his family to America, the great war broke out, he came through Paris with his children, it is told to Zaza that his wife died several years before. And the final fadeout follows shortly thereafter.

We shall look for Romeo in a tin hat saluting the captain and asking: "When do we eat?"

October

Six Days

A forerunner of Jacqueline Susann, Jackie Collins, Danielle Steele, and numerous others, Elinor Glyn was a novelist who specialized in lurid romances. She enjoyed immense popularity with readers in the early twentieth century, which naturally made film producers interested in Glyn's delicious plots and character. Glyn adapted her writing style to the picture business and quickly became a behind-the-scenes player herself, occasionally serving as producer and director as well as scenarist.

Friday, October 5, 1923

Elinor Glyn's story, *Six Days*, is being presented in its picture setting at the Chicago Theater this week.

Charles Brabin, the director of this picture, should be handed a bun or a blue ribbon or a decoration, if it would please him, for the keen, spare narrative quality of this screen-told story.

There are plenty of us who couldn't read an Elinor Glyn novel who can enjoy this picture from start to finish.

The story starts with a Wall Street banker shooting himself because his bank is to be closed, leaving his widow and daughter penniless. The scheming mother arranges for her daughter to marry an English baronet of wealth, but before the marriage takes place the baronet has to go to Egypt on a government mission. His fiancée falls in love with a sculptor, who is the son of a cast-off woman of the baronet.

While exploring intricate trenches and dugouts of the war fortifications around Rheims, the young couple are trapped underground for a period of six days. A priest who is trapped with the young couple in the underground labyrinth marries them before the six days are up.

A definitely named space of time seems to be necessary for most of the productions of Elinor Glyn. Previous to *Six Days*, she produced *Three Weeks* and *One Day* and since *Six Days* she has been heard from with *The Great Moment*.

Corinne Griffith will be much loved by many picture-goers for the showing she makes in this production. There will be those mentioning her as the most sweetly and winningly melancholy heroine that has come forth on the silversheet. She will be mentioned in superlatives.

Frank Mayo, whom we used to see so often as a Western two-gun man, is here as the sculptor, and carries his role well. Myrtle Stedman, as the ambitiously designing mother, and Claude King as the English baronet, give capable character interpretations.

It is a Goldwyn-Cosmopolitan production and Charles Brabin, the director, did some exceptionally good work.

The White Rose

Though a minor film in Griffith's body of work, The White Rose *had its moments and did relatively well at the box office. Ivor Novello, whom Sandburg singles out here, was a relative newcomer to movies. However, the Welsh-born actor had already developed a strong reputation as playwright and songwriter. "Keep the Home Fires Burning" is probably Novello's best known tune. Novello later wrote a string of successful stage musicals, though he supplemented his theatrical passions with an occasional film role or screenwriting job.*

Tuesday, October 9, 1923

The newest and latest picture from the studio of David Wark Griffith, entitled *The White Rose*, and opening a run at the Orpheum Theater, is a characteristic Griffith picture.

Those who know other Griffith pictures, his ways, style, manners, and mannerisms, would know this was a Griffith picture even if they had not read any announcements in the newspapers, or if they had missed seeing the Griffith name on the electric sign in front; or if they were careless about reading the initials "D. G." and the name

"Griffith" which are spelled between reels.

One original thing is achieved by Griffith in this picture. He saw that the far south, the Louisiana country, had possibilities for landscapes. And he shoots these landscapes in moonlit dissolves among Spanish oaks draped with their dreamy mosses, and their associate features of magnolia and massive drifts of water lilies down the drowsy rivers of the land the Creole calls home.

It was an original thing for Griffith to do this. Many a million-dollar picture with its attempts at the spectacular fails to get the moving effect achieved by the Griffith cameras in these southern landscapes.

The story itself concerns two young couples who all four go wrongly or unwisely down life's pathways. And if the film should break off at a certain point about 10 minutes before the finish we would have the kind of grim all-round tragedy that the Chinese or the Russians enjoy at their theaters. It would be as poignant as *Broken Blossoms*.

But Griffith found out in the presentation of that tragedy *Broken Blossoms* that the movie going public of America does not like the kind of sad endings he makes. So he is through with sad endings. And the two young couples instead of dying or marrying where they ought not to marry, all get pet up and connected and harnessed up just the way that makes all the endings happy endings.

Those who go to see this picture should aim to see the beginning first. It is that kind of a picture.

Mae Marsh has the leading heavy role, while Carol Dempster is a good second. Both are worth looking at.

Ivor Novello is the name of the newest male lead discovered by Griffith. Some say he is as handsome as Rudolph Valentino, while others will say that isn't possible. Others will say he compares favorably with Conway Tearle or with John Gilbert.

November

Flaming Youth

Once relegated to anonymous parts in minor dramas and Tom Mix movies, Colleen Moore's career took off with Flaming Youth. *With her energetic spirit, to say nothing of her bob haircut, Moore's character personified the Roaring Twenties flapper. "Sweet young thing I was not. Pat, the heroine of* Flaming Youth, *I was," she wrote in her autobiography,* Silent Star. *"Never had I been so happy in a movie role before. I loved every scene. After six years of treacle, it was heaven to be given a little spice."* [+] *An enormous popular success (and having the distinction of being banned in Boston!),* Flaming Youth *had young women across the country bobbing their hair and dressing up like Moore's offbeat character. The flapper had arrived.*

Monday, November 5, 1923

Flaming Youth, which is shown this week in neighborhood theaters, is one of the best-told screen novels which has come along. It takes a rather long and involved story, rather complex with human motives, and it delivers it with remarkable simplicity. We recommend the picture *Flaming Youth* as being one of those in the current output which has no trash, which has a high aim and realizes far.

It may stand as a type of storytelling or novel narrative on the screen, which is to be seen more and more in the motion pictures as the ability develops that can handle it. This is a First National picture, which was directed by John Francis Dillon, and he should have credit for excellent work; and there should be credit for Colleen Moore and Milton Sills, but particularly for Colleen Moore, who has so many scenes and such difficult ones.

She is called on for many shadings of expression, and it is evident she and the director co-operated effectively, efficiently and with belief in what they were doing. They cared. Though a large part of the theme concerns youth, high life, jazz and such, the picture maintains a high level of sincerity and seriousness. It is just the kind of picture that ought to be looked over by some of the directors at Hollywood who so often put out careless work.

It might be said that the story takes a mother who goes in for fast social life and doesn't care much how far her daughters go. And two men have given their hearts to this mother. She dies, and one of the men keeps her memory and writes letters to her ghost, while another comes back and becomes acquainted with her daughter. What happens to this older lover and the youngest daughter as they meet and are drawn along is interestingly developed.

Myrtle Stedman, Elliott Dexter, Phillippe Smalley, Walter McGrail are players who render excellent support.

The Hunchback of Notre Dame

Lon Chaney's genius at facial transformation was never better displayed than in his role of Quasimodo in The Hunchback of Notre Dame. *Taking his lead from Victor Hugo's description of the tortured bell ringer in the novel* Notre Dame de Paris, *Chaney designed makeup so horrifying that reportedly some members of the cast and crew averted their eyes whenever Chaney was in sight. Chaney spent three hours every day altering his face and body into that of Quasimodo. Hugo's classic story has been remade on various occasions: in 1939 with Charles Laughton in the lead, a 1956 French-Italian co-production featuring Anthony Quinn, and a 1996 animated version with Thomas Hulce as the voice of Quasimodo. Anthony Hopkins also played the role in a 1982 television version, followed by Mandy Patinkin in a*

1997 television production titled The Hunchback.

Friday, November 9, 1923

In *The Hunchback of Notre Dame* may be seen what is surely Lon Chaney's masterpiece, the best piece of character work he has done in his interesting life in the movies.

For one familiar with the famous novel by Victor Hugo, one of the warmest and grandest writers of the French language, there might be the feeling that it would be the strong, unshapely hunchback himself who would be the hardest part of the book to put on in a screen drama.

As it happens, however, the hunchback is the best figure of all the puppets, and the outstanding thing of the production.

It is a picture worth seeing; it is evident that Wallace Worsley, the director, and others cared, and were painstaking; and lots of money was spent to make a big smash of a picture.

Yet the production falls short of being a masterpiece; somehow, with the exception of the hunchback, the characters and the masses of people and their action don't have the funny, crazy, ragged, massive, loveable human stuff that goes with the novel of Victor Hugo.

The beggars don't seem to have any secrets. So fine a character portrayalist as Ernest Torrence, doing the king of the beggars, only rarely gets into the proud, wild, isolated quality of a leader of tatterdemalions by natural right.

Patsy Ruth Miller as Esmerelda, the dancer and mascot of the beggars, does excellent work; there was capable direction of her; and she added her own charm and intelligence. Tully Marshall does a good quizzical King Louis XI.

But why should the subtitles be written by somebody who does not know how to spell, and who is ignorant of grammar? Victor Hugo, for instance, had a contempt for grammatical and correct speech, was an adept in slang. But Hugo did know grammar. If he used the expression "from whence" he did it on purpose, knowing he was ungrammatical, which is not the case in one subtitle of this picture.

And why spell forsworn wrong? Why not use some other word you know how to spell rather than bluff?

And among thieves and murderers they don't say, "I'll slit your throat"; they say, "I'll slit your windpipe." They use the word windpipe instead of the word throat on such an occasion.

There were other slips indicating pretences to culture that is full of holes and apertures similar to well-known cheeses.

The director, the scenario writer of this picture didn't love his people and understand them in quite the way that Victor Hugo did.

Rosita

With Rosita, *Mary Pickford changed her on-screen image from the innocent girl known as "America's Sweetheart" to a woman of some sophistication. Working with director Ernst Lubitsch, Pickford went into the project with high hopes. Despite their differences on the set, Lubitsch and Pickford worked well together and the film was released to positive reviews.* Rosita *did well in Chicago, New York, and other major metropolitan areas. The film failed miserably, however, with Pickford's core audiences throughout rural America. Dismayed by the experience, Pickford denounced* Rosita *on numerous occasions, dismissing the picture as the worst of her career. She finally had it pulled from release and continued to criticize the movie decades later. "So much for* Rosita,*" she wrote in her autobiography, "my first punishment for wanting to grow up on the screen."*[5]

Saturday, November 10, 1923

In the growing up of Mary Pickford, the late news is that she has produced *Rosita*.

In making this one she has gone farther and done better than in any previous picture.

It may be said without fear or favor and with no expectation of successful contradiction.

More than that, we may add that this is a movie that has some thought and feeling back of it, some real intimate understanding of history and past times, and a projection of that real intimacy and understanding.

In other words, this is that rare thing, an intelligent movie, where the players and the director seem to know that motion photography drama depends more than anything else on pantomime, and pantomime is a thing requiring for its success both deliberate science and reckless art.

Something like that.

As Mary and Doug toasted their feet one evening when the fruit farmers were covering the orange blossoms because it looked like frost, they decided to bring over from Berlin one Ernst Lubitsch, because of what they had seen of his work in some imported pictures.

And Lubitsch came over and directed Mary as a Spanish dancer, and Holbrook Blinn as King Louis of Spain, and Irene Rich as the queen, and George Walsh as Don Diego, and Bett Sprotte and Snitz Edwards as the big and little jailer—and there isn't really a star in the piece.

It is one of those dramas so well done that nobody is bothered with a star and his or her stardom.

Suffice it to say as chronicle of fact or registration of opinion that Holbrook Blinn is beginning to stand out as a silversheet actor, that rare phenomenon, a first rate spoken state player who can get across much first rate acting in the silent screen drama.

The story here is the same as in another current picture, *The Spanish Lancer*. And the two movies probably cost about the same outlay of cash. But the Mary Pickford picture is the one that will last longer and please more people—it is our guess—because somehow they cared more and took more time.

The opening run of *Rosita* is at the Orpheum Theater.

The Three Ages

Buster Keaton's first feature-length picture was actually three two-reelers linked by the common theme of love through the ages. Loosely structured after D. W. Griffith's Intolerance *(1916), a four-part exploration of intolerance in history, Keaton and Wallace Beery played romantic rivals in all three segments of* The Three Ages. *The film is notable as one of the first features to incorporate live action with animation. Keaton's entrance in the first segment, as a caveman riding on a dinosaur, was created as an in-camera special effect. First the comic actor was photographed against a white background on the upper portion of the film frame. The film was then rewound in the camera and an animated dinosaur was added beneath Keaton.[6]*

Wednesday, November 14, 1923

In the history of the world there are three ages of importance, the stone age, the Roman age and the modern age.

So we are told in the newest Buster Keaton release entitled *The Three Ages*, at McVicker's Theater this week, in which the frozen-faced comedian is to be seen for the first time in a six-reel, regular one hour picture.

In his six-reel pictures it seems that Buster Keaton is going to stick to the game rule and principle he has ever employed in the two and three-reel pictures, namely that he will continue to refuse to let his face reveal any semblance of a smile or mirth of any sort or ilk.

Taking his cue from the more serious pictures, on which this is a burlesque, the opening reel has a book with a title shown, and the cover is opened as though we are all anxious to read the book, and then two or three pages of reading come along, as though we were going to settle down to a lesson in history and instruction with regard to how civilization rose out of the dark days of savagery.

Well, when the picture starts we are in the stone age; stones are piled all around; stone mountains and boulders.

A young woman attired in wildcat skins is combing her hair and flaunting her tresses to the breezes, though we observe that she has a permanent marcel wave that must have set her back a day's pay at the Hotel Alexandria.

Suitors appear for the hand of the maiden. The father tests them with a club. The one who goes under can't have her. In this notable scene Wallace Beery and Buster Keaton are the competitors. Buster loses.

In Rome again we see the same struggle for a woman wearing a permanent wave. And again in the modern age it is the same. Two men want the same woman. And the strongest gets her—but in the modern age strength is not the same kind of strength as in the stone and the Roman ages.

The star players, as some people will figure it, are the mammoth and the dinosaur.

The White Sister

The White Sister *was the first American-produced film to be shot on location in Italy. Concerned about how the Catholic church was to be portrayed, the Vatican provided director Henry King with its head ceremonial director as a technical advisor.*[7]

Thursday, November 15, 1923

The White Sister is a large-sized production directed by Henry King, with Lillian Gish as the star, having its opening runs this week at the Great Northern Theater.

This picture is a screen dramatization of the famous tragic story in F. Marion Crawford's novel of the same title. The production of it took place in Italy, with a few of the leading players exported from America, and the remaining of a considerable cast being employed from Italian talent.

In its faces, houses, scenic backgrounds, its tone color is Italian, while it should be remarked that the picture seriously and reverently treats a religious theme and evokes religious atmosphere.

The dominant mood of it is serious, with a somberness that mounts into the tragic. The chief dramatic appeal is based on a nun's "marriage to the church," and the attempts and treats of one formerly betrothed to her, on his return after reports of his death, to induce her to break her vows. The symbolism of the different phases of the ceremony is given extended treatment.

The direction was by Henry King, whose narrative skill on the screen was so notably demonstrated in *Tol'able David*. The excellently serious and capable acting of Lillian Gish as Angela Chiaromonte, in this, her first large serious work out of the hands of David Wark Griffith, testifies that she has had talent beyond the simpler parts she has hitherto essayed. Ronald Coleman, as the lover of Angela, J. Barney Sherry as the priest, and Juliette La Violette as the governess of Angela, render good support.

Fish Films

Sandburg's love for animals in the movies reached a whole new level with this quirky essay.

Saturday, November 17, 1923

Speaking of fish, there are no more picturesque and fascinating players in the movies than some of the fish in the animal kingdom pictures.

If it should happen that you see the fish series of the animal kingdom pictures announced for exhibition, you will enjoy as pleasant a quarter of an hour as you might at the zoo or at an aquarium.

They are superior, spontaneous, unique, free and easy and natural performers, are these fish, all from deep sea waters, and each of them having his habits explained in the subtitles.

The coffer fish, for instance, is spotted. The cowfish has ways of its own.

And the silver moon fish is not only one with a poem of a name, but one whose swimming style and pantomimic act are worth seeing.

The same may be said for the sea breamer.

There are types of the shark that are harmless; they wouldn't eat either man, woman or child; they are peaceable, law-abiding sharks.

The burrfish is found in the salt waters from Cape Cod down to Florida and is not worth trying to eat, if you catch one.

The jewfish weighs 500 pounds, just an ordinary specimen, while the clear-nosed skatefish has—so we are told and we agree it is correct—"a face that is almost human."

The spadefish is the zebra of the sea; he is striped for fair.

All these are rather serious fish.

For comedy we may look on the globefish; it can blow itself up like a balloon; if it fears capture it blows up till it is so light it floats on the top of the water out of reach of any large fish that might want it for a dinner.

And there is the sucking fish; if the sucking fish wants to go anywhere it steals a ride by fastening itself on the underjaw of a shark, where it cannot be shaken loose; instead of car fare it carries a disk with suckers on it that cling to the big fish it wishes to ride.

We may hope and trust that more fish pictures come along in the movies.

December

Dempsey-Firpo Fight

The Dempsey-Firpo fight was short, bloody, and controversial. Dempsey knocked down Argentine boxer Luis Firpo, known as "The Wild Bull of the Pampas," seven times in the first round. Yet Firpo hung on, blasting Dempsey with a strong right that sent the American flying out of the boxing ring into the press box. Journalists pushed Dempsey back through the ropes, an illegal act ignored by the referee and fight judges. In the second round the two heavyweights went at each other with a vengeance. This time Dempsey floored Firpo twice, the second time with a winning knockout.

From the collection of Arnie Bernstein.

Jack Dempsey's fight films were huge box office draws throughout the 1920s.

Thursday, December 6, 1923

The famous prizefight between Jack Dempsey, the North American who holds the world's heavyweight championship belt, and Luis Angel Firpo, the South American who holds the championship belt for all territory south of Panama in this western hemisphere, is now to be seen in motion pictures in the Alcazar Theater.

As pictures, which tell what the fight was like, and which give us the same feelings we would have had if we had bought railroad tickets and rode on the cars a whole day and then scrambled and scrimmaged another day to get a $50 or $100 seat for the purpose of seeing a fight that lasted six minutes, from start to finish—these pictures are the goods.

They are important, nifty, excellent, crackerjack pictures, either for the fight fans or for people who wish honestly to see what it is that fight fans travel far and scramble and scrimmage to have a look at.

This is where we see Dempsey in training at Saratoga Springs and a line of fight fans laying down dollar bills to watch Jack fight his shadow, punch the bag and punch the living punching bags in the shape of old-time prizefighters.

Also we see the wild bull of the Pampas down at his training quarters in Atlantic

City.

Also we have a look at Tex Rickard, the undisputed champion promoter and entrepreneur of prizefights.

Finally, and in conclusion, we see Dempsey and Firpo step out with their mitts up ready for the fastest walloping match in the world's recorded fistic history—nothing else.

All the fight fans watch close where the referee counts nine, and Firpo gets up and is handed another knockdown.

Some think Dempsey is knocked through the ropes, and then comes back through the ropes, there is some guessing about where he has been in the meantime, while he has been gone, who picked him up, what they said to the champion, whether he thanked them kindly, and if the Marquis of Queensbury rules cover the point of who shall help and how much they shall help and in exactly what way they shall help a fighter knocked through the ropes and off the platform.

Then come the slowed-down pictures, which show more clearly how they took punishment and handed it to each other.

These are the best fight pictures that have ever come along.

It was not a boxing match nor a pugilistic show nor a fistic panorama.

It was a fight from the first tap of the gong.

Those who usually get sick at seeing fights may find that this one is over and ended so quick that there isn't time to get sick.

The two fighters take their punishment so wonderfully, get to their feet so quick after a knockdown, that the fight fans all go out and take life more gaily than ever.

It looks as though the motion pictures are going to enable us all to know just about what happened, without our having to bother with riding to the ringside and scrambling for a seat, and if we're a little late then having to sit two blocks away from the fight, so that even if we use any field glasses we are not sure which fighter is getting the worst of it.

The motion pictures give us the same close-up as if we had our heads where the movie camera stood. Such is progress.

Why Worry?

John Aasen, Harold Lloyd's co-star in Why Worry?, *was perfectly cast as the giant "Colosso." Standing eight feet, nine inches tall and weighing more than 500 pounds, Aasen had a formidable screen presence that worked well against Lloyd's smaller stature. Despite Sandburg's predictions, Aasen's film career was brief; he had minor roles in a few more comedies, including films with W. C. Fields and Laurel and Hardy, then retired from the screen.*

Tuesday, December 11, 1923

Why Worry?, Harold Lloyd's newest picture, which is on for two weeks more at the Roosevelt Theater, is out of the ordinary, original in respect to plots and tricks, and original in its use of a giant character who does stunts like those in Grimm's Fairy Tales.

The plot, such as it is, centers around a Mexican revolution in which Harold Van Pelham, with a bad case of heart disease, suddenly finds himself.

Harold is under orders to take a pill every so often.

And he must beware of excitement.

And there is so much excitement that often he doesn't have time to take pills.

Harold wins for a friend, a giant about eight feet tall, named Colosso.

In the course of their lives in a few brief days they not only overcome squads and battalions of soldiers, foil renegades and adventurers, but they conquer a whole army and put it to flight with coconuts.

It sounds impossible, but as played it is a mixture of the plausible and the preposterous.

They said they would produce a laugh maker in this picture, and they have done just that.

The organization with which Harold Lloyd has surrounded himself understands him and how to play him, what kind of story he needs and how to use it.

Fred Newmayer, who directed this one, shows skill.

The part of the giant Colosso is played by John Aasen, and he will be heard from again in the screen world. He is too good to lose.

Jobyna Ralston plays the nurse to Harold and she, too, will win friends with her work in this picture.

On Sydney Chaplin

Charlie Chaplin's older half-brother, Sydney, was perhaps the most important person in Chaplin's life. Together the two had survived a Dickensian childhood in the slums of London. The siblings found work in theater and English music halls, the British equivalent of American vaudeville. After Chaplin's Hollywood success as a director/producer/writer/performer he often relied on Sydney's creative advice and frequently cast his sibling in supporting roles. Though Sydney never reached the comic heights of Charlie's "Little Tramp," he did enjoy some success as a featured player during the 1920s.

Saturday, December 22, 1923

Ever since Sydney Chaplin lost his hat in *The Pilgrim* it has been certain that he had found eventual stardom. His hat went and fame came. Funny as was his brother Charlie, whom he supported in that comedy (which reliable information has it still holds the box office record for a popular priced week in Chicago), funny as was Charlie, he never rocketed a house any higher than did Syd searching for the missing derby.

You remember Syd's terror-stricken face, when as a smug and parishioner in a small town he called upon the visiting dominie and, on turning to go, finds his hat completely gone? He hunts, he loses his temper, he snaps at his wife and little boy, he loses his head. It was perfect pantomime, illustrating exactly the ridiculous confusion that overspreads a 100 percent American when he can't find his hat.

A man without his hat is undressed; his dignity is gone; he is terribly ashamed. He can stand the loss of anything better—money, home, wife, reputation. This is one of the trivial monstrosities of life. Sydney Chaplin understood this.

For years Sydney Chaplin has been helping his brother direct and act comedies. Sydney has usually been the boob and blundering companion of the vagrant heroes played by Charlie.

From the collection of Arnie Bernstein.

Sydney Chaplin not only worked with his half-brother Charlie, but also enjoyed an on-screen comedy career of his own.

He has acted the unnamed associate of that poetic vagabond who holds the center of the screen. Often Syd plays two or three lay parts in Chaplin films. He was the Kaiser, and two different soldiers in *Shoulder Arms*. He was the officious brakeman, the cheated bridegroom and the hatless parishioner in *The Pilgrim*. Only people on the inner circle of pictures know how good he has been.

Now comes word that he is to have a big part, a chance of his own in *Her Temporary Husband*, a feature length comedy-romance wherein he is a drunken valet who says to Owen Moore, the master who is always firing him, "We will never get anywhere this way, sir. You know I will never leave you."

He is to have big names with his. Mr. Moore, Sylvia Breamer, Charles Gerrard, Tully Marshall, Chuck Reisner (Charlie's "gag" man, and the actor who played the "tough" in *The Kid*), but these names will come after his, and their pantomime will be tuned and keyed to his storytelling gestures.

The Extra Girl

*Despite Sandburg's pronouncement here that Mabel Normand's ". . . greater work is ahead of her,"*The Extra Girl *was the gifted comic actor's last good film. On January 1, 1924, just a few days after Sandburg's review was published, Normand was again involved in a scandal. Her career had just about recovered from the Wiliam Desmond Taylor murder, but on that fateful New Year's Day Normand was party to another shooting incident. Joe Kelly, Normand's chauffeur, fired a pistol owned by Normand at Courtland Dines, the wealthy son of an oil baron. At the time, Dines was dating Edna Purviance, Charlie Chaplin's one-time leading lady and a good friend of Normand's. Though Dines was only wounded, the press leaped all over the story. It got worse; "Joe Kelly" turned out to be Horace Greer, an escaped convict from an Oklahoma chain gang. Rumors of alcohol and drugs also swirled around the growing scandal. Normand left Hollywood for an ill-fated attempt to tread Broadway stages, though she eventually returned to California. In the late 1920s Normand made a few short comedies of little substance for producer Hal Roach. She also married a former co-star, Lew Cody, in what was a bad joke carried too far by the duo. Her health and spirit faded as the great screen comic's life came to a somber conclusion. On February 23, 1930, Normand died of tuberculosis. She was only 38 years old.*

*Regardless of Normand's tragic off-screen life,*The Extra Girl *is full of comic charms. The most famous sequence has Normand nonchalantly leading what she thinks is a dog on a leash; in reality she is being followed by a very real lion. "Mabel Normand was the only actress in the world who could look unconcerned while a lion breathed down her neck," Mack Sennett later wrote.*[8]

Wednesday, December 26, 1923

The new Mabel Normand picture, *The Extra Girl*, which is opening its run at the Orpheum Theater, has one recommendation to start with; and that is that they took their time with it. Miss Normand is not one of those who comes in a new release every two or three months.

The story of *The Extra Girl* is a good deal like those of Miss Normand's previous pictures. There is a harum-scarum girl around whose life centers a lot of money lost and won, and a bright young man.everybody knows is the one who ought to marry her, and a lot of puzzling as to whether in the windup he will win her.

Mack Sennett, the producer, names himself as the author of the story. He aimed at writing what he calls "sure fire stuff." It is all there in this regard. The plain, honest home folks, the good looking daughter, the quarrel as to whether she shall marry a successful businessman or a handsome, industrious young man whose prospects are not all that they might be, the ladder up the side of the house to her room, the escapes and pursuits up and down that ladder, the flight, the forgiveness, the loss of the hard-earned savings and earnings of the plain, honest home folks, the detection and pursuit of the dastard robber.

As to this robber, we must pause. He is a Sennett masterstroke. He seems for all the world to be the bright, energetic, enterprising, sagacious, straightforward young American. His face is his fortune. Anybody would hand him the money on his showing the maps of the places where the oil wells are gushing. Yet, after all, he is what he is. We are surprised. It tricks us as life does. And Mr. Sennett knows it and intended it so.

As for Mabel Normand, this is the best acting she has done. There are moments in it when she rises to great pantomimic art, and the revelation of a personality that has tone color, ranges, shadings. No other woman in the movies has so vivid a feeling for the comic mixed with a serious and striking personal loveliness. Her greater work is ahead of her. The important thing is that her work constantly hits a wider gamut.

George Nichols and Anna Hernandez play pa and ma. Ralph Graves has the role of the young man who should marry the heroine. William Desmond and Carl Stockdale are other members of a well-chosen cast. Direction was by F. Richard Jones.

Uncensored Movies

In this parody, Will Rogers poked fun at fellow stars Tom Mix, William S. Hart, and Rudolph Valentino.

Monday, December 31, 1923

The case of Will Rogers and the movies is a case by which one might prove a good deal about American art and American culture of the present time.

The big main reason Rogers left the movies was because he was too homely and horsey and plain and unvarnished.

He can ride the toughest broncos in the going; he is a past master of the lasso; horses love him and go wild about him, but most of the women going to the movies don't.

He has rich humor; he is a salty American wit, and friends of his have said: "Will, you would be all right in the pictures only you know too much—you're too smart."

Well, all this sort of leads up to Will Rogers' latest release in the movies. It is a little 10 minute affair titled *Uncensored Movies.*

Mainly it consists of parodies or burlesques on some of the famous stars. The one of Tom Mix is a masterpiece of humor. We can see Tom Mix himself laughing at it.

He rides the horse, Tony, and the pursuers in motor cars with speedometers registering 90 miles an hour can't catch the man on horseback.

A jackrabbit running alongside is losing breath so the horseman leans down and picks up the rabbit and gives it a rest.

Coming to a crossroad he changes a sign so it reads wrong and the four pursuing motor cars eventually one by one topple over the edge of a precipice and turn somersaults before they hit bottom.

Then back he goes to where his sweetheart has been kidnapped; he jumps his horse across several wide chasms and arrives at the cabin where the kidnapper has the girl. A whole gang engages him there in a hand-to-hand encounter. He conquers them all with his swift and adroit boxing and wrestling.

One of the hot buns amidst the movies—a sort of cream puff of human intelligence—is this *Uncensored Movies* by Will Rogers.

We hope Rogers will live long and have health, doing what he pleases to do, because he is one of our worthwhile national possessions.

Douglas Fairbanks worked out daily to get his already athletic
physique in top condition for his role in *The Thief of Bagdad*,
the first time he appeared in the movies without a shirt.

1924

January

A Woman of Paris

Frustrated by the way their films were distributed, Charlie Chaplin, Douglas Fairbanks, Mary Pickford, and D. W. Griffith joined forces in 1919 to create United Artists. The quartet's idea was to continue independent production and control how their movies were released. Chaplin's first production for UA was A Woman of Paris. *It was also his first dramatic film, a risky venture for the internationally loved comedian. After finishing* The Pilgrim, *Chaplin contemplated making a film of the life of Napoleon. He then encountered Peggy Hopkins Joyce, a celebrated Jazz Age figure renowned for her multiple romantic liaisons, including several marriages and divorces with millionaires. "Peggy told me numerous anecdotes about her association with a well-known French publisher," Chaplin wrote in his autobiography. "These inspired me to write the story of* A Woman of Paris *for Edna Purviance to star in. I had no intention of appearing in the film but I directed it."[1] Chaplin actually had an uncredited role, playing a clumsy railroad porter.*

Saturday, January 12, 1924

The first picture of which Charlie Chaplin is the author and the director—but in which he does not act—is starting its run at the Orpheum Theater.

It is nine reels long, has the scope and extent of a novel, and is the most important photoplay since *The Cabinet of Dr. Caligari* and *The Golem*.

The outstanding point about this production is that the people in it come out of shadows and go back into shadows a good deal the same way that characters do for us in life.

Before any people are shown there is an old French stone house, which seems to say, "I am a house; all houses have human mysteries; I am still puzzling over the births, deaths, marriages, crimes and benedictions that have been known across my doorways."

The story is simple. A boy and a girl in a French provincial town are betrothed. Her father doesn't want the marriage. Fate sends the girl to Paris alone. Two men contend for her there. She goes back to a changed life.

As a story it is told on the screen in the same way that a man might tell about things that happened to the people who lived next door neighbor to him many years ago; the years have passed so the story has had time to happen; and in his heart and mind there is charity and understanding; they were all people; what happened just happened; it hurts to tell it, yet they were all loveable people and the story must be told because they all had ways that were loveable, notwithstanding hard or mean things they did.

This picture is so big hearted and simple, so fine and sure in its handling of people and laying the blame on nobody, that there will be some moviegoers a little mixed up about it; they are those who want either straight melodrama or straight comedy.

And *The Woman of Paris* is neither; it is as dark and mixed as life, or the Book of Ruth or the Book of Esther in the Old Testament.

Edna Purviance has the leading role. The leading men are Charles French and Adolphe Menjou. Other players are Carl Miller and Lydia Knott.

Chaplin's Dramatic Creed

Thursday, January 24, 1924

In his undertaking to express his dramatic instincts in a picture that is not one of his traditional comedies, Charles Spencer Chaplin has stirred the movie world with the production of *A Woman of Paris*, now at the Orpheum Theater. He turned out a piece of work that reveals a generally unsuspected side of his nature, a serious attitude not only toward life but also toward the representation of life upon the screen. *A Woman of Paris* tells a not unfamiliar story in decidedly unfamiliar terms. Chaplin admits that he has striven for novelty not in material but in treatment. "I have tried to get away from the old systems of doing things," is his simple explanation of the unusual angles found in his one straight dramatic photoplay.

February

Victor Seastrom in Hollywood

Victor Sjöström was already an established director in his native Sweden when he arrived in Hollywood. Intending to study American film techniques, Sjöström (who used the name "Seastrom" while in the United States) was hired by the Goldwyn Company to direct several pictures. Sjöström's films were notable for their moody use of light and shadow, as well as his psychologically tortured characters. He returned to Sweden at the close of the silent era. Though Sjöström remained largely behind the scenes in the Swedish film industry for the next 40 years, he gave a memorable lead performance as the aging professor in Ingmar Bergman's Wild Strawberries *(1957).*

Saturday, February 2, 1924

In movie circles around town they are chuckling about the way Victor Seastrom, a Swedish director, came to Hollywood and spoiled a pet idea out there.

A pet idea of a lot of American directors was to have fancy, pretty and illogical lights shining on the actors from places where lights in life never are. Many directors throw bright cross lights on a man sitting under a lamp reading a book or a girl in her dressing room with only one window in it. They have thought it didn't matter where the lights came from if the picture was pretty.

Seastrom, who has done strong, realistic pictures in Sweden, came to Hollywood to do *Name the Man* for Goldwyn. He came in silent, kindly, and did things his own way. American directors gave him advice as became the tetrarchs of the camera and showed him how to light his sets.

Seastrom smiled and went on doing things his own way. He had an idea. This was that everything in a picture must be reasonable; that if a girl sat in a room where there was only one window all the light would naturally come through that window. There were to be no tricks with the camera and kliegs just to make things pretty.

He made his picture that way. He talked to the actors that way. Film men who have seen the picture say the actors must have got his idea; that they show in their acting that there is a reason for what they do; that their hands and feet and eyes show you what their heads are thinking.

Seastrom, the whisper is, gets a queer feeling into his people with his heavy, kindly voice, talking, talking, talking—something the way Griffith works.

Seastrom doesn't like the megaphones or caps turned backward or leather puttees. He was an actor once, rated as Sweden's best, and his voice leads his actors now into slow, certain moods. He made Mae Busch cry real tears in the murder trial scene where she hears her fate dooming down from the bench, they say.

These are things one hears from movie men who saw him work. Whatever there is of this in the picture will be seen when it unreels at the Chicago Theater next week. At any rate Seastrom has made a stir in Hollywood, where it takes something nowadays to make a stir.

Going Up

Note Sandburg's review of the accompanying stage show in the last paragraph of this piece.

Wednesday, February 13, 1924

What you would do and feel if you were alone with an airplane a thousand feet in the air is what *Going Up* shows you.

It is a comedy that tortures you with laughter and fear. By means of cameras in neighboring planes they show you the hero, a man who had written much of aviation but who had previously succeeded from ever going up, trying to fly so that a big-eyed girl below will love and admire him.

He is in an agony of ignorance and helplessness. He pulls levers and it goes up, he pushes them and it falls a mile. He yanks and hauls and it somersaults and dives, climbs or maybe drifts end over end like a leaf coming down from an autumn tree with a drowsy, easy, good-by motion.

A French "ace," hero of cloud fights in the war, is trying to rival the terrorized author-flyer, and he pulls his plane down out of the sky, rolls his eyes and says that he can't fly against a madman, a daredevil like that. The French ace shakes hands with the big-eyed girl and tells her a better man has won her.

Everybody below thinks the blunders and awful accidents of the aviation-ignoramus up there are amazing stunts and that every helpless mishap is a brilliant and gallant feat of skill.

Luckily the young man is not killed when the crazy machine crashes at last and luckily he can smile and accept without confession the kisses of the worshipful young lady.

Going Up is just as funny as when George M. Cohan had it on the stage and immeasurably more exciting. In fact, the excitement outruns the humor on the screen. Douglas McLean is the man who goes up, Marjorie Daw the girl who looks up and Francis MacDonald (a very good actor when the world wakes up to his worth) the Frenchman who gives up.

Presentation is at the Chicago Theater, where a stage prologue of much imagination and mechanical cleverness takes girls, singers, dancers, many people up into the wings singing.

The Birth of a Nation

Perhaps the most controversial, as well as influential, film of the silent era, D. W. Griffith's The Birth of a Nation *garnered both great acclaim and derision. Certainly*

Griffith's cinematic and storytelling techniques were groundbreaking. Yet his portrayal of African-Americans in the post-Civil War South, contrasted with a heroic Ku Klux Klan, was historical revisionism at its very worst. The social, historical, and cultural impact of The Birth of a Nation *has been debated for generations.*

One thing Griffith could not be faulted for was his depiction of the Civil War. The war had ended just five decades previous to 1915, the original year of The Birth of a Nation's *release. Veterans and their descendents were an audience that Griffith, himself the son of a Confederate lieutenant colonel, could not let down. The film's battle recreations still retain great power. Part of the realism in these sequences is due to Griffith's special effects technology; movie incendiary devices at the time were practically non-existent, forcing the director to use real cannons and live ammunition.*

In his review, written for the film's 1924 re-release, Sandburg directly addressed the thorny issues raised by the film. Interestingly, in her autobiography, The Movies, Mr. Griffith, and Me, *Lillian Gish, the star of* The Birth of a Nation, *wrote: "Many years later, when Carl Sandburg brought me his four volumes on Lincoln, he said, 'I think you will find the first two volumes especially interesting, because I tried to put into them the same American flavor and spirit that Griffith got in* The Birth of a Nation.' *When I repeated that remark to D. W., he was flattered and delighted."[2]*

A *Chicago Daily News* ad for *The Birth of a Nation*, perhaps the most controversial and influential film of the silent era (Monday, February 11, 1924).

Wednesday, February 20, 1924

The Birth of a Nation has a peculiar standing among motion picture plays. There is probably no other photoplay that rates so highly as an artistic production which at the same time has so low a rating as history.

If a boy or girl or a young man or woman should ask this reviewer if *The Birth of a Nation* is good reliable American history, this reviewer would answer that it is about the same kind of good, reliable American history as *Uncle Tom's Cabin*.

Just as the author of *Uncle Tom's Cabin* was a sensitive Connecticut woman, who saw slavery as a terrible wrong and presented her viewpoint in a terribly exciting book, so the author of *The Birth of a Nation* is a sensitive Kentuckian who saw the reconstruction period after the war as full of terrible wrongs and he has presented his viewpoint in a terribly exciting photoplay.

David Wark Griffith puts on the screen the wrongs of the south as he heard them from the lips of his home people as a boy—just as Harriet Beecher Stowe put into *Uncle Tom's Cabin* the wrongs of Christian America as she heard about them from the lips of brothers and kinsmen as she built a home and gave birth to seven children and felt a sacredness attaching to all human flesh.

Thus far, we have seen no screen version of *Uncle Tom's Cabin*. But we can almost imagine that if a child or young man or woman should be shown a good photoplay of *Uncle Tom's Cabin* after seeing *The Birth of a Nation* it might be the case that the student would say, "The history of the United States seems kind of mixed when we get it this way."

And we may as well admit that putting the history of the United States on the motion pictures is a hard and a mixed job.

We wish all luck to Griffith in the film *America*, which he is now working on. We hope it will be more strictly accurate than *The Birth of a Nation*, though we doubt if it is strictly accurate that it will be the hummer of a melodrama which is to be seen in *The Birth of a Nation*.

The Call of the Wild

Jack London's tale The Call of the Wild *has been put to film on several occasions. Two silent versions, in 1908 and 1921, preceded this production. The story was re-made in 1935 with Clark Gable and in 1972 with Charlton Heston. There have also been numerous foreign and television versions. Producer Hal Roach, singled out by Sandburg in this review, was better known for his comedy films, including work with Stan Laurel and Oliver Hardy, Harold Lloyd, and the "Our Gang" kid films.*

Wednesday, February 27, 1924

Jack London's famous novel, *The Call of the Wild*, is now to be seen in a motion picture play which is showing in neighborhood houses.

One can easily understand how there will be argument among dog enthusiasts about this picture.

The hero—which is a dog—is a full-blooded St. Bernard.

Now, of course, the St. Bernard breed of dogs have their points, and in some particulars the St. Bernard is among the best dogs that ever struggled through snowdrifts with food and wine for benighted and famished travelers.

In other particulars, however, police dogs, sheepdogs, malamutes, and so on, have their superior points.

For a dog that flits back and forth between civilization and wilderness, with consummate devotion for a human master in civilization, and yet hearing the call of the wild teasing at his ears we have seen other photoplays which really captured Jack London's meaning as effectively as this picture.

A good dog story and a good tale of life far in the northland, as such tales go, is this film version of London's famous story.

This reviewer admits a prejudice against the St. Bernard dog for the role of Buck, the dog that goes back to the wild. His face is too kind, he is too sober, of too steady a gravity, not enough of a plunger and speculator. Yet maybe a St. Bernard is, under the mask of serious expression, not so respectable a home guard as we think.

Hal Roach is the producer of this picture, with Fred Jackman as director.

March

Our Hospitality

As Sandburg notes, Our Hospitality *was another family affair for Buster Keaton. His wife, Natalie Talmadge, was the love interest; his father Joseph and his son Joe were also in the cast. (Incidentally, Keaton's real first name was also Joseph.) The highlight of* Our Hospitality, *which Sandburg doesn't mention, is a harrowing rescue sequence that required Keaton to swing out over a waterfall. Insisting on doing his own stunt, Keaton's wire lifeline broke in the water and he was nearly killed. The cameras captured it all and this hair-raising footage went into the final cut.*

Monday, March 17, 1924

In a piece of pleasantry to pass the time away and to ease the rib muscles by which laughter is exercised, there is justice in recommending *Our Hospitality*, a Metro production featuring Buster Keaton and Natalie Talmadge. It is being presented at neighborhood theaters.

Not often do we have a chance to see a Hollywood married couple performing in the same film drama. It seems that more often the producers or directors or important men who do not appear on the screen are married to the film actresses.

But this is a case where we see one of the Talmadge sisters yoked with her husband in a photoplay cast. Not only that, but their first and only child and heir, Buster Keaton II, is also in the cast, playing a part designated as "The Baby." Also, there is Joseph Keaton playing a railroad engineer.

It is a family picture, with a copper-riveted guarantee that no theater manager will put up a sign "For Adults Only," unless as a joke.

What's it about? The scenes are mostly in Kentucky, where two clans are feuding against each other with pistols and knives. And the son of one clan is in love with the daughter of another clan. The time is the year 1830. A railroad train of that time, running eight miles or so an hour, makes a trip from New York to Kentucky.

The "frozen faced comedian" seems to have left the two-reel comic field for the six-reel farce realm. And he and his family shall not suffer so long as they can put out pieces of this kind.

We can see families going to see this picture and coming away saying, "What a family!"

Incidentally, Buster Keaton directed the picture, assisted by Jack Blackstone.

April

A Society Sensation

Wednesday, April 2, 1924

The revival by the Universal company at the Randolph Theater of one of the earliest of the Rudolph Valentino pictures is worth while as a little piece of film history.

The Valentino fans are likely to enjoy it because in *A Society Sensation* the boy appears as a young struggler.

The scenario writers and the directors had not yet found out just how to tog him out, how to arrange his hair, and present him as the box office winner he proved later to be.

Then, too, we notice the advance of photography, and realize that for the Valentino shadings of comeliness, a film is wanted that has sharp contrasts of light and shade.

The black hair of the hero is not brought out at all in its completely decisive blackness. Nor is it slicked down in the slickness seen in the later pictures.

Also the sideburns are lacking.

This early Valentino film is a document in personal history and as such will afford laughter for those who have seen him in later photoplays as one of the breath-taking stellar attractions.

Powder River

Friday, April 4, 1924

Among pictures now showing locally one of the best to be recommended is *Powder River*.

This reviewer has been to see *Powder River* once at the Monroe Theater and expects to go at least twice more and see the whole picture from beginning to end.

It is not often a picture takes hold of us so that we are not satisfied till we have gone once, twice and again to see it from start to finish.

Yet such is *Powder River.*

The opening reels show a submarine boat leaving its base of supplies, moving through stormy weather out into the wide ocean and there sending a shell through two large steamboats and one large sailing vessel.

In the case of one steamboat the crew is warned that the craft is to be shot through; the crew takes to boats on the open sea; the captain is taken onto the submarine as a prisoner; the crew are seen drifting on the wide ocean—as the big vessel slowly turns over and goes to the sea bottom.

Sad and majestic is the final downgoing of the sailing vessel with its yards of sail full bulging as she takes her plunge to the bottom of the briny deep.

Then come official pictures of the United States Signal Corps, showing American troops at Cantigny, in the Argonne and elsewhere, stretcher men picking up the wounded—the plain, grim, terrific pageantry of war.

The words of writers telling us what war is are rather weak compared with this simple and straightforward movie of the thing.

Tuesday, May 13, 1924

As the war movie, *Powder River,* goes the rounds of neighborhood theaters it should be known and understood that this is an important, authentic and fascinating motion picture.

The first part is film which was employed by the German government during the war to illustrate to its people certain operations of the undersea boats. The swift operation of a submarine, leaving its base of supplies, and proceeding to the high seas, is shown. Three different large vessels are shown making headway on the ocean, when each is stopped by the submarine, the crew taken off and the boat shelled and sent to the bottom. One big steamship heaves slowly and as she goes under her boilers explode and she executes a monster splash.

Then comes the showing of the transports, which carried the American expeditionary forces across the convoys of battleships, destroyers and boats laying dense smoke screens. Actual fighting scenes from the Argonne, Chateau, Tinerry and Cantigny are put on the screen. We have vivid glimpses of doughboys under fire running forward and throwing hand grenades.

An observation balloon is sent up, and as an enemy airplane approaches to attack the balloon we are shown the aircraft gunners throwing a barrage around the balloon. In the end the enemy plane sets fire to the balloon, but is itself wrecked, spins to the ground, and we look into the quizzical face of the aviator who lived through the fall without a hurt.

This reviewer has gone twice to see this picture from beginning to end and has noticed that the audiences consist largely of young men, a high percentage of men who were in war service. They watch the screen with a curious and solemn attention. A picture to be recommended as interesting and informational is *Powder River.*

Saturday, May 31, 1924

One of the pictures worth seeing and worth telling others they ought to see it is one titled *Powder River.* Twice before we have flashed that signal from this corner, and so long as the picture goes on showing at neighborhood houses we shall keep on hinting that *Powder River* is a piece of powerful film drama, combined with accurate historical material. It is exciting to look at, and it wraps up more sure history than any book as yet written about the war, so far as we know now.

Our point that men who were in overseas service take a special interest in this film drew an interesting letter, among others, from J. Mitchell, 2114 West North Avenue. He writes:

"In reading your write-up on the film *Powder River,* it occurred to me that you might be interested in the thoughts of an ex-soldier as he viewed this picture. I served nearly three years (half the time in France) with an English infantry regiment, so I assume that you might find something of interest in what I have to say.

"The scenes shown in this picture were mostly long shots taken from a distance. Under these circumstances, it is impossible for the uninitiated to get the feel of the thing. The ex-soldier, however, can distinctly recall similar situations when, for instance, he was crouched in a trench under a heavy shellfire, and sweated blood. He probably remembers the look on the face of the man next to him, and the suppressed terror . . . of these little affairs. He also will probably recall the occasions when word was passed around that 'we are going over in a few minutes,' the feeling of being condemned to death, and the thoughts of tomorrow.

"The layman, through this film, gets a better idea of war than he could do otherwise, but the ex-soldier comes out with a feeling that he has lived through it all over again. He swears he'll never go near another war picture, but probably goes to the next one they show."

Private Mitchell ends his letter, "I hope I haven't bored you," (we should say not) and "I felt I had to get this letter out of my system"—which is just the feeling we all have about the *Powder River* picture—and it interests us that a man who saw trench service says it's the real thing.

Icebound

Wednesday, April 9, 1924

As we came out of McVicker's Theater after having seen William de Mille's last picture, *Icebound,* we heard two women talking.

They were enthusiastic in their talk and sort of didn't care who heard what they were telling each other.

One said "It's—it's great."

And the other said "Yes—different."

Not once a year do we hear so fine and sure a tribute to a picture.

We have been waiting for this picture from William de Mille. It out-classes by a long way everything he has done hitherto. It lives up to the promises he gave us in patches here and there, in former pictures.

He takes the New England family, the Jordans, and has us now crying, now laughing and now solemnly considering. The quick shifts of tragedy and comedy are masterly. The people are almost like everyday people.

"How can a fellow work where everybody is mean—and the land is icebound!" exclaims the son, Ben Jordan.

He is leaving home. The mother has given him money. But she won't give him a parting kiss.

He says, "You're a real Jordan, ma—icebound."

And when he is gone she tells Jane Crosby, the adopted girl in the house, "If any boy is ever going to be happy it's going to be through some woman who isn't icebound."

When the mother died the relatives were all there waiting.

The family doctor told Jane Crosby, "She said, 'The Jordans are waiting around me like crow buzzards around a sick cow.' "

A boy is sniffling. His aunt tells him, "The idea! Ain't you got no handkerchief when you come to see your grandma die."

In little details such as a woman hitching around and fussing with a rocking chair the picture is finely human. Those who have read Robert Frost's poetry and books like those of J. T. Trowbridge will see cross sections of life resembling parts of those books.

But no matter who wrote the story and the continuity, it is William de Mille's picture more than anybody else's. He put more of his inmost thoughts in this one than in any he has hitherto offered us. As an artist his work resembles that of his brother, Cecil, in about the same way a living, breathing body resembles an automaton.

Lois Wilson and Richard Dix are the two leading players. Miss Wilson gets into her part more believably than Mr. Dix. In characterization, some of the minor players, so to speak, surpass the major. As Ma Jordan, Alice Chapin is superb—she and the director collaborated in a marvelous portrait. Helen Dubois, Edna May Oliver, Vera Reynold, Frank Shannon, all have fine creative moments.

The picture is highbrow and it isn't. It is that rare and fine thing, a photoplay with high spots for both highbrow and lowbrow.

We hope it goes big and shall list it among those that have a niche among the movie classics.

Icebound, the William de Mille picture which is shown at neighborhood theaters, is proof that a competent photoplay can be made of simple materials.

We have seen the burning of Rome, the volcanic destruction of Pompeii, the wrath of mad kings and jealous queens who ordered massacres and conflagrations.

But none of them throws the real scare hidden in the simple scene of some boys playing cards and gambling in a barn when a lantern is kicked over, fire starts and the barn goes up in smoke as the farm boys lead the horses out.

It doesn't always require a million dollars worth of chariot races and spectacles of mobs, nabobs and jewelry to interest a movie audience.

Some of the million dollar pictures remind us of the man who came from an elegant party where it was said of an overdressed woman, "She looked like a pawnbroker's dream."

Singer Jim McKee

The "turbulence" of Hart's life that Sandburg refers to in Singer Jim McKee *was the growing troubles between the cowboy star and studio chieftains. Tom Mix, Buck Jones, and Hoot Gibson were the big Western heroes of the screen, with fast-paced adventures movie fans found easy to digest. On the other hand Hart's slow-paced, old-fashioned Westerns had fallen out of favor with audiences. Hart stubbornly refused to change his style and the results were disastrous.* Singer Jim McKee *flopped at the box office, leading to the end of Hart's association with the Famous-Players Lasky studio.*

In *Singer Jim McKee*, the latest Bill Hart picture, we may notice the first interpretation that has come from that film star with regard to how it feels to be a father. That is, Bill has put on the screen some of his emotions out of the turbulence of life during the last couple of years. While strange and new events were happening to him he was, between whiles writing the scenario for a picture, the first script for which he takes the sole responsibility.

We are shown a cabin where two prospectors live, who have been failing to find pay dirt. One of them is Singer Jim McKee, who has a little Spanish in him, and always must be singing, no matter what happens. Also there is his partner and the lone child.

It is for the child's sake they commit the crime of highway robbery. And the paint horse on which McKee is riding is shot and falls over a precipice.

On the arrival of the sheriff's posse, McKee gets away, while the father of the child stays and is shot and killed. Fifteen years are then passed over, the child has grown up, and cries because she cannot have a dress as good as the other girls at the Saturday night dance. The way the affectionate father gets the dress and what happens afterward will probably interest all Bill Hart fans, if only as a showing of how Bill personally thinks a story ought to go along on the screen.

Phyllis Haver and George Russell are also members of the cast. The direction was by Clifford S. Smith. Presentation of the picture is at neighborhood theaters.

May

America

Though Sandburg danced around the issue, D. W. Griffith's America *was a dismal attempt to recreate the drama and action of* The Birth of a Nation. *Made at the behest of Will Hays and the Daughters of the American Revolution, Griffith attempted to transplant the success of* Birth *into a Revolutionary War setting. Like most critics, Sandburg notes Griffith's masterful staging of Paul Revere's ride. However,* America *made it clear that the once-great director's talents were clearly in decline. Ultimately the film did poorly at the box office.* America's *young star, Neil Hamilton, became a popular leading man during the silent era. When sound came to Hollywood, he switched to supporting character roles. Modern audiences best remember Hamilton as the straight-laced Commissioner Gordon on the 1960s* Batman *television series.*

Monday, May 5, 1924

America, which is having its first showing at the Auditorium Theater this week, is a patriotic picture depicting scenes from the Revolutionary War period of American history.

Just a year ago the Daughters of the American Revolution addressed a letter to the motion picture industry inquiring why a film of the Revolutionary War had not been undertaken, and suggested that it should not be delayed. On receipt of the letter Will Hays, director general of the industry, asked David Wark Griffith to lend his genius to the task.

In the opening subtitles we are told that the picture is not an endeavor to deliver history, as such, but has for its aim the presentation of the scenes of valor, struggle and sacrifice by which the separation of the 13 colonies was won from England and the independent republic of the United States of America established.

Paul Revere, George Washington, Patrick Henry, Samuel Adams, John Hancock, Thomas Jefferson, Gen. Gage and other celebrities of early American history are characterized. The chief romantic figure is Nathan Holden, an express rider who carried messages from Massachusetts to Virginia, took part in the battles of Lexington, Concord and Bunker Hill, was in the winter camp at Valley Forge and then was with

Arthur Dewey as George
Washington in a scene from
D. W. Griffith's *America.*

FROM D. W. GRIFFITH'S "AMERICA".

WASHINGTON AT PRAYER, VALLEY FORGE, PA. 1777—1778.

the Morgan expedition. But between times he saw Miss Nancy Montague of Virginia, and against fearful odds won his way to her favor. Neil Hamilton, who will remind many fans of Richard Barthelmess, has the role of Holden, while Carol Dempster plays Nancy Montague.

The ride of Paul Revere is the outstanding and important piece of motion picture art in this production. David Wark Griffith came from that incomparable stamping ground of fast horses, the state of Kentucky, and he has put into his production his personal sense of glory about good horseflesh. The poet Longfellow is surpassed and out-done in the swiftness and breathtaking quality of the scene of the Paul Revere ride.

Girl Shy

Wednesday, May 14, 1924

Among the young men film acting for fame and fortune, the one whose name is Harold Lloyd keeps coming along, and no mistake.

In *Girl Shy*, which is opening a run at the Orpheum Theater, Harold is seen in his best picture.

He is learning the tailor's trade—and writing a book on how young men in love should so act that they will capture what they want.

As he writes on his typewriter how to take the vamp captive by "indifference" there is a farcical scene enacted in which he subdues and overwhelms a vamp.

Next there is the flapper, who is to be conquered by caveman tactics; as he writes his chapter on the typewriter the scene is filmed for us.

Yet, though he is submitting a book to a publisher on how to win girls, he himself is as shy as a woodland fawn.

He meets a girl who takes him captive.

Then he loses her—throws her away ruthlessly—in a scene that compares finely with some of the stage scenes of George Cohan, where the aim is that the onlookers shall not know whether to laugh or cry.

We put *Girl Shy* among the pictures far better than ordinary, with much first-rate action and many rapid surprises.

In support of the star are Jobyna Ralston, Carlton Griffin and Richard Daniels. It is a Pathe production, ably directed by Fred Newmeyer and Sam Taylor, from a snappy story by Sam Taylor, Fred Wild and Tim Whelan

June

Rex—King of the Wild Horses

Tuesday, June 10, 1924

The first film play staging a horse as its chief hero is to be seen in *Rex—King of the Wild Horses*.

He is seen roaming the wide open spaces of the West, untamed and seemingly untamable.

He finds a rival, and it is the wild black horse in a fight with the wild white horse. Black wins.

But a man comes. He tames the black horse.

And it is the black horse who is called on to help when a king of cattle thieves must be chased and captured.

Will the wild black horse jump the rocky chasm, carrying a rider, as he used to jump that same chasm when he was a free wild horse?

That is the question near the end of the picture.

A big scene they worked out in the fight between the two wild horses.

For those who like horses better than dogs Rex is a better movie actor than Strongheart, the dog.

150 EDNA MURPHY
With Fox Film Corporation

From the collection of Arnie Bernstein.

And for those who like animals and don't make any choice as between horses and dogs, this will be a bully film play to go and see.

Edna Murphy, one of the human co-stars in *Rex— King of the Wild Horses.*

Among human beings who as players support Rex, the king of the wild horses, are Edna Murphy, Charles Parrot, Sidney De Grey, Leon Barry and Pat Hartigan. The picture is of Pathe imprint.

The Perfect Flapper

Friday, June 13, 1924

Those interested in the gradual process by which a young woman may get drunk, and the expressions on her face from time to time as she gets more and more drunk, are permitted to see this depicted by Colleen Moore in *The Perfect Flapper*, at the Chicago Theater.

The role is one of a young woman brought up in a very prim household, and when at last she goes to a party where there are wet goods flowing freely, she goes farther than she intended or knew, and has suddenly left the party with a respectable married man, and they have tried to climb a vine-hung ladder at a country roadhouse when they are photographed by a newspaper man, and it happens their pictures are on the front page of a newspaper the next morning as they wake up in their respective homes with headaches.

That, of course, is a hard plot to swing in these days, and have it carried through so that it does not rouse hostile sentiment on the part of those who are watching the morals of the movies. Yet with the capable direction of John Francis Dillon, and the playing of Colleen Moore, Sydney Chaplin, Phyllis Haver, Lydia Knott, Frank Mayo and Charles Wellesley, the film comes through right end up.

The steady laughter of the audience at the Chicago indicated enjoyment of humor and vivacity. This is the type of plot often and usually mishandled in the movies.

"Ride 'Em Cowboy" Always Goes

Saturday, June 21, 1924

The Western pictures keep going. The riding and shooting hero, with a background of Rocky Mountains or the Sierras, is always wanted.

Styles come and go in vampires and working girls, in sheiks and Romeos, in villains who look the part and she-devils who don't.

But "Ride 'Em, Cowboy" always goes.

It is as American as the American dog.

And there is one noticeable thing among these Westerns. That is some of the actors are terrific and steady workers.

Take Tom Mix, Buck Jones and Hoot Gibson—three riders who do their own riding and never need a double for a rodeo.

They are among the most tireless workers in our country.

It seems as though they are no sooner done with one picture than they have begun the next.

They take their vacations making pictures.

If they let up on riding before the camera, and climbing hand over hand up a rope till they reach the top of the mountain butte, they simply lose appetite, suffer from loss of sleep and cry for the camera, the horse and the director calling through the megaphone, "We're ready now—get into that."

Their work is not what a critic would class in the output of first-rate genius.

But they are producing first-rate entertainment—and always clean—and what with their audiences of millions—and especially the young and impressionable—they have an importance as artists, these smiling and wholesome young bucks, Tom Mix, Buck Jones and Hoot Gibson.

For they are bucks—bucks that ride bucking horses and sawbucks—and they are young and will all three die young, no matter how long they live. It's the riding, the horses, the mountains that does it—and the kids that enjoy their pictures.

Sherlock, Jr.

Buster Keaton in Sherlock, Jr. *pressed the illusional possibilities of film to their limits. Playing a movie theater projectionist, Keaton used dream sequences, innovative camera tricks, and literally neckbreaking stunts to produce a classic of the silent era. After production on* Sherlock, Jr. *was through, Keaton experienced a series of blinding headaches. Years later, during a physical examination, an x-ray technician asked Keaton when he had broken his neck. It turned out the screen comic had cracked a vertebra which subsequently healed on its own. The fracture, Keaton realized, was probably incurred during a particularly hazardous* Sherlock, Jr. *stunt in which he was blasted by powerful stream of water.*[3]

Monday, June 30, 1924

Buster Keaton's latest release, showing in neighborhood theaters, is a picture in which the leading actor was not only that. He was also the director. Usually it is not pleasant information that a star is directing his own picture. Usually that picture is like some of these Heinegebubler looking glasses that make the short look long and where the thin becomes thick.

Sherlock, Jr. is the name of this film drama. The story has three authors who all worked together, cooperated, collaborated and stitched the pieces of what we have here. Jean Harvez, Joseph Mitchell and Clyde Bruckman are the names of the registered voters who offer this contribution to the history of scenario writing.

They had a lot of fun. No matter what anybody might say about the story, they had fun. They fixed up a plot which is mulligatawny plus. When in doubt about a joke or an idea or a piece of a sketch, they just threw it in.

That is why this *Sherlock, Jr.* is original in many respects. We laugh in spite of what goes before or comes after. But each time we laugh we have a half suspicion maybe we were expected there to come closer to crying.

From the collection of Arnie Bernstein.

A publicity still from Buster Keaton's *Sherlock, Jr.*

The picture is worth seeing just because it has several spots that are original; they had no idea what the public wanted; they put these spots in just to be artists. For novelty and for quirks, and curious, odd scraps of cinema experimentation, go to see Buster Keaton in this *Sherlock, Jr.* He is a projection machine operator in a movie theater while at the same time he is learning to be a detective.

July

He's My Pal

Sandburg's love for cinema in all forms comes through with genuine sincerity in his review of this all-simian two-reeler.

Tuesday, July 1, 1924

For the grimace that haunts, and the slant of the eye that gives us a quizzical feeling in the midriff, we may look at the picture called *He's My Pal*, in which three orangutans march through a strange and baffling monkey work of pantomimic drama.

We do not recall any comedians or tragedians of the screen—with the single exception of Charlie Chaplin—who project such curious and haunting presences from the silversheet as these three jungle animals, ably directed and plotted in this two-reel Fox production.

Of these three musketeer monkeys, two are honest and one is a crook.

A second-story thief sends one of them up into a lady's apartment to steal her jewelry.

He sees her picture on a chiffonier, kisses it, decides to do no stealing there, telephones for help and is then pulled to the ground below by his master.

Help comes. The jewels are saved. The second-story thief is sent to prison.

And the two honest orangutans ride on the back seat of their lady's limousine, out to the prison yard where their third pal is breaking stones in convict clothes with other convicts.

As he breaks stones he looks at his two pals on the back seat of the limousine and pictures what might have been—himself sitting between them and smoking a cigar or licking an all-day sucker as they are doing.

An escape is attempted. He saves the life of a guard and shoots an escaping convict, the second-story thief.

And his reward is that he does at last sit between his two pals and ride proudly away.

This picture may be only a hint of a development to come in the use of animals, properly trained, staged and directed, in photoplays.

Talking Pictures Have Appeared in New York

> *Phonofilms, an early method of recording synchronized soundtracks with the moving picture image, were exhibited at different venues in the early through mid-1920s. Here Sandburg reports on the exhibition of one phonofilm. Chauncey DePew was a nineteenth-century railroad executive, gifted orator, and briefly a United States Senator.*

Thursday, July 10, 1924

Senator DePew's appearance as a Broadway "star," with his name out front in electric lights, has, it is said, created no end of comment along New York's main street. The venerable statesman, diplomat and after-dinner speaker, who will be 90 years old in April, was the first great American to have his words and actions photographed in perfect synchronization, to be handed down to posterity. Dr. Lee DeForest, of radio fame, inventor of the phonofilm as the talking pictures are known, had Mr. DePew talk to the camera on "Memories of Abraham Lincoln." The result is uncanny. Every word, even an occasional cough is perfectly audible, it is said, and in absolute synchronization with the movement of the lips. This is accomplished by the sound being radioed to the camera, where it is photographed on the same strip of film with the action.

Dr. Hugo Risenfeld, managing director of the Rivolo, considers the DeForest talking pictures the dawn of a new and remarkable art. They will be featured at McVicker's Theater next week starting Monday.

Phonofilm Demonstrated at McVicker's Theater

Nine days later, Sandburg reported on the debut of this technological development in Chicago.

Saturday, July 19, 1924

The phonofilm, the Lee DeForest invention showing at McVicker's Theater, is one of those American jokes with an edge to it.

It has the look of the joke of the first horseless carriage, the first wireless communication experiments.

Wheezes and mistakes go along with the operation of it.

It is amusing in the way that a child is learning to walk is amusing.

The human voice is not delivered with clear tones—but the synchronism is surprising.

The lips of the speaker are certainly shaping the words which we occasionally catch, and against prejudice we come to the feeling that the screen is talking, sending sounds to our ears just as it is also sending pictures to our eyes.

They are shrewd in their arrangement of details of the demonstration.

We are shown a dancer dancing without music; the senorita looks like a movie Spaniard; then there is a shift from the silversheet to the phonofilm; and the senorita is dancing to good music, not missing a bar of the p'zzicatta.

A banjo orchestra goes through the motions of playing; they look silly; then from the silversheet we pass to phonofilm; and they are gay.

The steady drive is on to make talking movies.

They will be slow in coming; it would mean adding all the difficulties of vocal art to the art of pantomime.

But—music and dancing will come first.

The saxophone player now showing in this initial phonofilm has an added charm, his playing has an extra vitality for us, because we see him blowing his breath, and executing facial and bodily rhythms going with his music.

Wanderer of the Wasteland

Note Sandburg's mention of the use of the Technicolor process, a growing technology when this Zane Grey Western was made.

Friday, July 11, 1924

Wanderer of the Wasteland sounds like Zane Grey and when we come look it over, as shown at McVicker's Theater this week, it is very Zane Greyish.

In a bizarre setting in a town on the edge of a desert, to which a sidewheeler of a steamboat arrives with passengers and freight, the central character is a young man whom Zane Grey pictures in one desperate situation after another. He escapes hanging for murder and finds himself on the desert fleeing a sheriff's posse. He escapes the posse to find himself near death from lack of water. He famishes for thirst and chases mirages of fresh water, but finally escapes from death by thirst and finds himself with a burro and pack and food. But as he sleeps the burro accidentally sets fire to the food, kicks the water supply over, and again the hero, afoot and without food or water in the desert, narrowly escapes death and finds himself eventually at an oasis with fresh water to drink and game to kill. However, the oasis is small and soon the game is gone and his food supply is lizards, frog, sand, the Gila monster. He is trying to kill a large snake when he is struck down, and friendly Indians arrive—the very next moment after the snakebite. Thus peril and rescue and chance operate, and it is quite Zane Greyish.

The film is in varied colors of the Technicolor process, and demonstrates that lively and effective experimentation is going on with the aim of reproducing on the screen the natural colors of the landscapes and objects in a photoplay.

Jack Holt and Noah Beery have the leading masculine roles, and Kathlyn Williams and Billie Dove, the opposites. Irvin Willat directed.

Manhandled

Among other acts of censorship, Will Hays came out with an official policy against "manhandling" in motion pictures. Working around this ambiguous edict, an executive at Paramount studios suggested the title of Manhandled *to lure in audiences. Writer Frank Tuttle was told to devise some sort of tawdry plot that could live up to this title while not violating the imprecise production rules dictated by the Hays office.[4]*

Friday, July 18, 1924

In *Manhandled*, showing at McVicker's Theater this week, is an artistic and well-worked out opening scene. There are other scenes well worked out, but the opening in *Manhandled* is as good a one as this reviewer has seen in any picture this season.

Feet, hundreds of feet—in shoes—ladies' and misses' shoes—are coming down a stairway.

Sort of queer these feet are—they belong to people—and the people are working girls in a factory, stepping down to punch the clock and quit for the day.

Next the heroine—Gloria Swanson as a working girl—steps out on the street and gets her clothes all splashed by a passing motor car.

Into a New York subway car she steps and is there manhandled, her hat stepped on, her pocketbook and vanity case knocked on the floor of the car.

She gets off and goes home and takes off her shoes.

This is very well done.

The removal of shoes by a young woman who has been in a subway jam requires careful and refined pantomimic art.

And they do it here very humanly and sweetly.

One might almost go back and see *Manhandled* a second time, because of the knack and skill, the refined grace with which Gloria Swanson removes her shoes.

It is as good as the fellow in that O. Henry story who worked in a hat shop, cleaning hats, and each sweltering summer evening went straight home and placed his bare feet against a brick wall and read stories of the sea, the cool, kind ocean.

The husband of the heroine enters. He is an inventor working on a motor car accessory. During two weeks he has refused to go out of an evening with her, because he must work on his invention.

But she has new clothes and is anxious to go stepping.

From there on the developments start.

Tom Moore, Lilyan Tashman, Paul McAllister, Arthur Hausman, Ian Keith and Carrie Scott are members of the cast. It is of Allan Dwan direction. Arthur Stringer wrote the story, from which Frank W. Tuttle did the screen play.

August

Monsieur Beaucaire

Bob Hope starred in the 1946 remake of Monsieur Beaucaire.

Wednesday, August 13, 1924

Well, the boy is back, the tall, handsome paragon of the movie matinee heroes,

Valentino—Rudolfo; the young man with a profile which is a perfect parallel of the face of George Washington as painted by Gilbert Stuart. He is back. He is working in the pictures again. His face and form again shine forth in the silversheet medium.

And the medium or vehicle which they chose for him to come back in is a story written by a young Indiana man just out of college some 20 years ago—a story which is chiefly concerned with portraying the aristocrats of one period in French history and contrasting one of those aristocrats with a barber.

We refer to *Monsieur Beaucaire*, a document in aristocracy, written by the Indiana novelist, Booth Tarkington.

If Tarkington had ever tried to run for the legislature, after this book, he would have lost the barber shop vote, because the story assumes that a French count counts for more as a man than does a barber.

Well, here we see Rudolfo in laces and knickerbockers, in silk stockings, in a powdered wig, with a patch of black on his powdered face, all as befits a nobleman of an old regime of landowners who never worked because they had people working for them who didn't have land.

And Bebe Daniels in wig and skirts bouffant is the vis-à-vis. And we have Lowell Sherman and Lois Wilson and Doris Kenyon for the other offsets and foils.

And it is all sort of dreamy with dressmakers' and tailors' and milliners' creations.

And the audience in the Roosevelt Theater sits in the refrigerated cool of that playhouse and enjoys this play as an imaginative restoration of days and people of an age that is gone.

Direction of the picture was by Sidney Olcott.

DORIS KENYON
Leading Motion Picture Star

From the collection of Arnie Bernstein.

Doris Kenyon of 1924's *Monsieur Beaucaire*, the screen adaptation of the Booth Tarkington novel, which Sandburg jabs as a "document in aristocracy."

Commencement Day

Producer Hal Roach wisely understood that mischievous children made for good comic fodder. His Our Gang *comedies ran from the 1920s through the 1940s, utilizing the talents of numerous child actors. Renamed "The Little Rascals" when the two-reel films were broadcast on television, generations of children have enjoyed the puckish adventures of* Our Gang.

Commencement Day, the latest release of the Hal Roach comedies of *Our Gang* series, collects and presents nearly all the wild tricks that children in school play on each other, on the teacher, and the parents who go to school to see how the young idea is learning to shoot.

As a bunch of mischievous and cantankerous young catamounts, the gang in this film is unbeatable.

The boy with an all day sucker gets red pepper sprinkled on it by another boy, swabs the tongue of a dog with it, and then passes it as a present to another boy, who says it tastes good and licks away at it until he is told that the dog didn't enjoy the taste of it.

The fat boy playing the saxophone solo in the commencement exercises is prevented from continuing his performance by the presence of quantities of red pepper thrust in the end of the horn, and gives an exhibition of sneezing while all the scholars cavort with laughter.

A mule puts his head through the schoolhouse window and contributes his hee-haw. There is a goat who cuts up, a well into which various juvenile characters fall, and a beehive full of live bees is let loose as a climax to empty the school house of pupils, teacher and visiting parents.

Perhaps life is as violent as this comedy, but the spread of the violence is over larger surface.

They put into a two-reel comedy what might happen in a hundred schools in a hundred years.

September

Stereoscopic Films

Another attempt to create three-dimensional films, the stereoscopic technology is a forerunner of what eventually was developed for 1950s filmgoers. Sandburg's prophecy in the last paragraphs of this piece wasn't that far off the mark! There may have been some personal nostalgia in writing this essay; in his younger days, Sandburg worked as a door-to-door salesman of stereoscope viewers and pictures. A popular item in the late nineteenth and early twentieth centuries, the stereoscope viewer created a 3-D effect using photographs shot with a two-lensed camera.

Saturday, September 6, 1924

If you happen to see stereoscopics offered at any theater you may be passing the next few weeks, you will find one or two reels of strange fun mixed with science.

It is showing of binocular or two-eye photography in place of the common single-eye photography of the motion picture.

The camera blinks with two lenses, about as far apart as the two human eyes, and the audience looks at the picture with spectacles furnished by the ushers.

The extra keen vision of two eyes is brought out in a startling way.

Objects and people move out from the screen straight toward the on-looker, so that there is almost an illusion that we could reach out and take hold of what is projected toward us.

This apparatus and what it does is just now a sort of toy or novelty.

We laugh at the newness and peculiarity of it, just as 15 years back we laughed at a motion picture of people walking and running.

But when we consider what toll and experiment there is going on to improve this apparatus, we have the feeling that in five, 10 or 20 years , we may all carry pocket stereoscopes, or receive the glasses at the door, for looking at motion picture plays presented in three dimensions, with the same projection of surfaces in depth, that we have in everyday life.

If to such an apparatus there should then be added the reproduction of sound, the projection of voices in a way perfected and improved over the points now attained, that would be the triple novelty of motion and speech presented in three dimensions.

We would advise all 100 percent movie fans to try and hang on to life 10 or 20 years more.

We'll see what we'll see.

The Family Secret

Peggy Montgomery, better known as "Baby Peggy," was a child star of the 1920s. In the 1930s, as her childish charms diminished with age, she appeared in a few low-budget Westerns. Montgomery later wrote books on Hollywood stuntmen and child stars, as well as her autobiography.

Monday, September 8, 1924

Baby Peggy's latest picture, *The Family Secret*, showing in neighborhood theaters, has its scenario from *The Burglar*, a stage play by Augustus Thomas.

Thus we have in one and the same film the star baby actress of the movies in a plot by the unofficial censor, sometimes termed the czar of the stage world, Augustus Thomas.

And we might say the film goes further than that in its certificates of good character, inasmuch as Gus Thomas took the plot of his play from *Editha's Burglar*, by Frances Hodgson Burnett, the author of *Little Lord Fauntleroy*.

Baby Peggy

From the collection of Arnie Bernstein.

"Baby Peggy" pre-dated Shirley Temple as America's most beloved movie moppet.

And with all this to stand on as a foundation, they made a slovenly photoplay.

As entertainment it is neither rare, medium nor well done.

We are sorry that another year of Baby Peggy Montgomery's life, a year that can never be recaptured, has passed into the limbo of time with no fine artist of the cinema having done justice to her mobile baby face—as Charlie Chaplin did for Jackie Coogan in *The Kid.*

She's a sweetheart whose press agents call her a million dollar baby, and anybody who had a million would gladly pay it over for her delivered in a fluffy silk package.

But she gets no justice in this picture.

She is cast as Peggy Holmes, the child of a rich man's daughter, who married a handsome young poor man, who comes to see his child and is captured and sentenced for burglary to three years in a state's prison. That is, the hard-hearted grandfather has his son-in-law, the father of his grandchild, arrested when he comes to see his child. It's poorly done.

Gladys Hulette and Edward Earle have the supporting roles.

Wine

With the Volstead Act came a new profession: the alcohol bootlegger. Al Capone made a good dollar selling illegal booze, as did a number of other criminal entre-preneurs of the Roaring Twenties. This Prohibition melodrama is typical of many such anti-alcohol films; it is notable, however, for the casting of young Clara Bow as the bootlegger's daughter.

Monday, September 29, 1924

At the outset of the photoplay *Wine*, a Universal production, Carl Laemmle tells the world, "If there is anything in the world I despise it is a bootlegger."

Farthest beneath his contempt in the range of mortals is the illicit peddler of whisky.

And Mr. Laemmle will be satisfied if he can spread this conviction of his through the medium of this photoplay.

Thus his announcement in an extended preliminary statement.

Forrest Stanley, Clara Bow, Myrtle Stedman, Robert Agnew are among the leading players presenting a story of a rich man who was on the brink of bankruptcy.

But in order to save the social position of his family and in response to the pleadings of his wife, he consents to a bargain with a big caliber bootlegger. In exchange for his influence he is to be led on to much money.

Well, we have seen a number of wild scenes in roadhouses, in sumptuous and elaborately fitted up country places for entertainment of the drinking and dancing public of nightlife.

But this picture goes a little farther than any of them, we believe, in depicting the riots of pleasure that it would lead us to imagine are of occasional if not regular occurrence.

The higher-ups among the bootleggers may be of the type here portrayed. And they may not.

For accurate information on bootleggers one might trust newspapers, court records or common gossip and perhaps be possessed of as accurate knowledge as is delivered by this film.

The picture, which is showing in neighborhood theaters, is a snappy, zippy, overdrawn sketch of life as it is lived in the underworld and among the upper classes.

If not taken as information it is cracking good entertainment.

October

Twisted Trails

This is a genuine rarity for Sandburg, a "rotten" review for cowboy star Tom Mix!

The only real rotten picture from Tom Mix that we have ever seen is the latest release called *Twisted Trails.*

As a friend of Tom's we rise to protest.

It is clean enough in one way, and we don't mean to say that it's rotten morally speaking.

Where it's rotten is as art, as Tom Mix art, as a piece of work to compare with the general run of the Mix output.

It's like a cheap novel of the worst kind that the train butchers offer their customers.

Up till this time, Tom Mix has been remarkable for the way he could take a train butcher's wild West story and smooth it out and surprise us with the amount of fun and action and entertaining twists he could put on it.

But in this *Twisted Trails* we have all the stupidity and flaccidity and weak-minded asininity of the trash novel turned out by writers who do two a week at so much per, and feed 'em to the printing presses.

Of course, it seems all the way through that we are comparing a movie with a book.

Which is just what we are doing.

It isn't regular photoplay at all; it wasn't thought up in movie language; when we look at it our mind runs to a trash story of the kind any of us could write with our left hands if we felt a little weak.

Oh, You Tony

While Tom Mix received harsh treatment by Sandburg earlier in October 1924, the cowboy star's equine partner was highly praised in this horse opera.

"A promoter is one who will sell you the ocean provided you will furnish the ships," we are told in a subtitle of *Oh, You Tony,* the latest Tom Mix release from Fox studios.

Mining sharks out looking for shining marks figure in the tale.

Tom Masters, the wealthy ranchman, played by Tom Mix, goes on to Washington to lobby for his home region.

He does well at acting the gawk who isn't up on etiquette.

After dancing with a young lady, whose toes he has stepped on he explains: "I ain't so good on the steps, but I know the holds."

And he greets a now fashionable damsel, whom he used to know in Arizona, with the outburst: "Gosh, Min, I ain't had so good a time since the day you mistook that bee for a blackberry."

But for all his mistakes, he believes and so informs them: "After all is said and done the zebra ain't nothin' but a sport model jackass."

Claire Adams again plays the feminine lead, she being a part owner of the Western ranch which comes near being taken away from Tom by the slickers of Washington.

Tony, the horse, is here seen in some remarkable acting.

We have little doubt that Tony is the most widely known horse to the movie audiences of the world.

Fifty-one pictures now is the number Tom Mix has made for Fox.

We knew the figure was up high, and it seemed to us just about that many.

Ten thousand dollars a week is what we are told Tom Mix is to be paid if he comes through with 10 pictures this year for Fox.

November

The Iron Horse

With The Iron Horse, *director John Ford delivered a Western epic that estab-lished him as a filmmaker to be reckoned with. Though Ford is better known for his sound movies,* The Iron Horse *remains a powerful achievement in his large body of work. John Gutzon de la Mothe Borglum, whom Sandburg refers to, was a sculptor whose 1901 statue of Abraham Lincoln for the United States Capitol Rotunda was the artist's first commissioned work. Borglum also created a bronze bust for Lincoln's tomb in Springfield, Illinois, and—most notably—the four presi-dents of South Dakota's Mt. Rushmore. Along with Sandburg, Borglum was a great Lincoln devotee, even naming his son after the sixteenth President. Sandburg's call on actor George O'Brien was a good one; O'Brien appeared in many films, including* Sunrise *(1927) for F. W. Murnau, and numerous other John Ford pictures, ranging from the silent* Three Bad Men *(1926) to* Cheyenne Autumn *(1964).*

Monday, November 3, 1924

The Iron Horse, a Fox picture which opened its run at the Woods Theater Saturday night, is a story that dwells on the epic of the steam railroad and the locomotive crossing the great plains and connecting the Mississippi Valley with the Pacific coast.

The opening scenes depict Abraham Lincoln about 1842 in Springfield, Ill., bidding farewell to young people heading west. He makes predictions about the railroads to lead westward, and is later shown in the White House in 1862, signing the bill giving government support to the Union Pacific project.

The building of the two railroad lines, one from the west, the other from the east by gangs singing, "Drill, Ye Tarriers, Drill," is the chief historical feature, with a closing scene showing the driving of the golden spike in Utah, where the track layers met.

A love story is woven through these events, the young man, Davy Brandon, having many difficulties in his affairs with Miriam Marsh. George O'Brien, who has this leading role, is well fitted to the part, and will be noted as a comer. There will be plenty of movie goers saying that George O'Brien's work surpasses that of J. Warren Kerrigan in *The Covered Wagon*, while that of Madge Bellamy as Miriam Marsh is better than that of Lois Wilson. Such comparisons are sure to be made.

We would say that as an all-around picture, *The Iron Horse* is as good as *The Covered Wagon*, measures up about equally in historical values, and is as well done.

Both pictures use white-faced Hereford herds of cattle for a period when there were only longhorns roaming the ranges. And each uses an incident from the life of Abraham Lincoln rather obscurely authenticated, so to speak.

But—*The Iron Horse*, for instance, is a far, far better picture than Griffith's *America*, and while not as dramatic is more accurate than *The Birth of a Nation*.

The Indians are rather respectable cigar store Indians, or Indians resembling those in bronze in the public parks, or those in the illustrations in picture books for children.

But the mountains, plains wagons, horses, guns, tracks, rails, locomotives, are all the real thing, and the picture rates high as an achievement in the combination of entertainment and instruction by motion picture art.

Charles Edward Bull, not a regular movie actor at all, but, we are told, a judicial officer residing in Reno, Nev., has the role of Lincoln, and will please all who are pleased with the Borglum sculpture of Lincoln.

Sgt. Slattery and Corporal Casey are played by J. Farrell MacDonald and Francis Powers very capably. Cyril Chadwick, Will Walling, James Marcus, Gladys Huletts, Frances Teague and Fred Koler are members of the cast.

Buffalo Bill is played by George Wagner, Wild Bill Hickok by John Padjam, Gen. Dodge by Tex Driscoll, and Cheyenne Chief by Chief Big Tree.

John Ford directed the production and had his hands full. The story was by Charles Kenyon and John Russell.

Two hours and twenty minutes are required for the film. The recurring theme of the orchestra is "Drill Ye Tarriers, Drill."

A Visit with Josef von Sternberg

In his first paragraph of this piece, Sandburg immediately cast some doubt on Josef von Sternberg's plans to direct Mary Pickford, and for good reason. Von Sternberg's sophisticated approach to storytelling seemed incompatible with Mary Pickford's more naïve fare. Inevitably the director's and star's personalities clashed and their projected plans for a film about a blind woman fell apart. In his autobiography,

Fun in a Chinese Laundry, *von Sternberg wrote, "... My star-to-be asked me to wait ten weeks to accustom herself to the idea while she made a 'normal' film with a 'normal' director."[5] For her part, Pickford referred to von Sternberg as "a complete boiled egg."[6] Though von Sternberg would have more troubles establishing himself in Hollywood, things clicked with* Underworld *(1927) and* The Last Command *(1928). In the early 1930s von Sternberg went to work in Germany where he met Marlene Dietrich. His career was forever linked with hers after their remarkable collaboration on* The Blue Angel *(1930). Apparently von Sternberg and Sandburg developed a mutual admiration; in his autobiography, von Sternberg had little to say of film critics, but singled out "... favorable reviews written by men like Carl Sandburg..."[7]*

Monday, November 10, 1924

Mary Pickford's next two pictures are to be directed, or at least the contracts so read, by Josef von Sternberg, and the natural remark of some people is, "Whoever he is."

Sternberg was in town a day or two ago, and we had a talk with him, or rather we listened, willing to listen, while he talked.

His picture, *Salvation Hunters*, is to go on the screen locally this winter, and it is a pleasure to listen to him talk about how he produced it, how much he spent for settings, and how he believes motion pictures should be made.

In *Salvation Hunters* are only five players, the million dollar settings consisted of the blue sky, the roles portrayed are of people without the price of a ham sandwich.

This with Sternberg himself directing, also doing the film cutting and other mechanical labors, kept the total expense of the picture, to Sternberg, down to $10,000.

And Sternberg talks about this picture as though it were a million dollar film, yet he admits what all Hollywood knows that the overhead and labor outlay came to less than $10,000 cash.

Just to produce a simple little story called *Salvation Hunters*.

Well, not only on the word of Sternberg, but of others, it looks as though Douglas Fairbanks and Mary Pickford saw the picture reeled off, and sort of went up in the air about it.

Fairbanks offered $20,000 for a one-fourth interest in the production, which Sternberg accepted.

And Mary Pickford said, "This is the man who must direct my next two pictures."

We had a long talk with Josef von Sternberg, and he seems to know more about what ought to be done in motion picture art than any one we have met in recent months.

That is, strictly speaking, about motion pictures as a field and medium where the director is not just a manufacturer producing with an eye on what the public will eat up, but producing so that some of the most precious of the personality of the director himself, as an artist, gets into the picture.

Sternberg is not quite 30 years old, and seems to be what in baseball they call a phenom.

He reminded us of Stephen Crane with his talk and his slouch, and the way he would laugh at pain without mocking at it.

And we are glad he is going to direct Mary, for Mary has slipped just a little with *Dorothy Vernon of Haddon Hall* and so on.

She has the stuff that we believe will do fine teamwork with von Sternberg and give us a picture worth seeing twice and then going again.

The Navigator

Using his review of Buster Keaton's The Navigator *as a foundation, Sandburg gives his readers a concise, proletarian study of 1920s comic film techniques as practiced by the major players, Keaton, Charlie Chaplin, and Harold Lloyd.*

Thursday, November 18, 1924

Three men and funny enough to carry comedy through seven reels—and only three so far.

Charlie Chaplin, Harold Lloyd and Buster Keaton.

All the other screen comedians have to content themselves with the two-reelers and be barrel-staved and auto-wrecked for 200 feet.

The three specified rely on specialties: Chaplin on his supreme talent as an actor, Lloyd upon novelty and Keaton upon droll "gags." When you leave a Chaplin picture you remember how great he was, when you leave a Lloyd picture you think how clever the picture was and when you leave a Buster Keaton picture you remember the jokes. In short, Chaplin makes characters, Lloyd makes situations and Keaton makes anecdotes on the screen.

Keaton's *The Navigator* at McVicker's this week, is to the screen what musical comedy is to the stage, a series of vaudeville "gags" strung on the thin line of a story that often breaks and gets lost but which hurts nothing or nobody.

Buster takes his pessimistic mask of a face under the sea in *The Navigator*. He goes down in a diving suit to repair a broken propeller on a liner and wanders off in sober desperate fights with comic swordfishes and fiery octopuses. He wanders on turning his paralyzed countenance upon cannibals who make him god of their isle and embarrass him hideously with their affection, which he fears will turn into hunger at any moment.

Keaton extracts all the humor possible out of the cumbersome, unhuman diving suit and reaches what many steady moviegoers will say is the peak of his career in his new production. Kathryn McGuire, who used to wear a Mack Sennett bathing suit, is his leading lady, the girl for whom he goes on his Robinson Crusoeing on the bottom of the sea.

Death of Thomas H. Ince

The quintessential Hollywood producer, Thomas H. Ince was an astute businessman and ruthless taskmaster possessed with a keen eye for talent. An actor from age six, he joined the movie industry at 28. He quickly developed a reputation as an intelligent writer/director/producer. By the late 1910s he was one of the most powerful men in Hollywood. On November 19, 1924 Ince attended a party thrown by William Randolph Hearst. What happened next has all the makings of a good movie mystery. While aboard Hearst's yacht, Ince lost consciousness and died. Official cause of death, as released to the public, was heart failure following acute indigestion. Stories circulated, however, that Ince had been carrying on with Hearst's mistress, screen star Marion Davies. Gossip bubbled throughout Hollywood, claiming an enraged Hearst shot Ince in the stomach. An official investigation found nothing untoward about Ince's demise, though several key questions about the incident remained unanswered. Considering Hearst's enormous influence as a newspaper magnate (which Orson Welles would brilliantly capture in the dazzling 1941 character study Citizen Kane*), it's no surprise that rumors of a cover-up lingered for many years.*

Saturday, November 22, 1924

The death of Thomas H. Ince removes the most consistent producer of box office success among all the film directors.

Where other producers had their flareups and their dying downs, their good years and bad years, Ince for over a decade went ahead making pictures that made money for himself and for their showmen over America.

Filmland recognized him as its best businessman. He knew what the public wanted. He gave the public exactly that.

Art and subtle deftness of touch were things that he ignored. He knew the value of good casts, he spent lavishly on actors' salaries, he paid directors well, bought high-priced, best-selling novels to film, but the delicacies of the minds of Chaplin, Griffith and von Stroheim he laughed away as non-productive of results. The people did not appreciate fine art, he said. Why force it on them? When the time was ripe, he would make that kind of picture, too.

Force, power, "punch" were his mottoes. His strident figure, his shirt-sleeved histrionics before his casts, firing them to emulate his vigor were common sights in Hollywood. Everything in his pictures built toward some one "walloping punch" in the story, a climax that would "knock 'em into the aisles" as Ince prayed.

The stupendous and exotic settings of DeMille were not for Ince. The extravagant photographic effects of von Stroheim he could not approve. He avoided the melancholy emotionalism of Griffith. Buoyant, strident, red blood drama he liked and that was his output.

Occasionally he dipped into feminism for a theme, largely because one of his stars, Florence Vidor, did not fit into the "punch" dramas, but 90 percent of his pictures went with the rattling whack of an express train going through little towns in the night.

He had a shrewd eye for potential stars. William S. Hart he discovered and with him launched a whole school of Western pictures. Charlie Ray he lifted to the stars and was engaged in lifting Ray again when he died, Charlie having come down disastrously for his own pocketbook in his attempts to star on his own management. Dorothy Dalton he turned from an extra girl into a star. Enid Bennett he brought over from Australia. Louise Glaum he discovered and lifted to a stardom that away from him she did not hold. Bessie Love he starred in the old Triangle days and brought her back after an eclipse in *Those Who Dance*, restoring her to the first rank again. Douglas MacLean was his find. Robert Edeson was introduced to pictures by him, also H. B. Warner and Willard Mack.

The history of motion pictures will never be written without a lot of Tom Ince in it. He is supposed to have taken more profits out of the film business than any other one man.

He knew what would go and he sent it out. It went.

December

The World of Comedies

Two-reel comedies, a staple of 1920s film-going, were cranked out like sausages by Hollywood film factories. Here Sandburg takes a look at the laugh makers beyond the "big three" of Chaplin, Lloyd, and Keaton.

Saturday, December 6, 1924

Under and behind the highly exploited dramatic productions and special "super-productions" is a world of films about which comparatively little is known. Yet it is a busier world than that of the stars and the touted directors, a world that grinds right ahead, year in year out, with no widely press agented occurrences. Its stars go from one picture to another without vacations in New York or temperamental expeditions.

It is the world of comedies.

What a mill it is! What an endless output comes from it!

There is Pathe grinding out 100 a year, two a week from its hoppers, Educational with 70 a year, Fox with 52 a year, and various independents scurrying to bring the grand total of Hollywood's comic output to well over the 800 mark.

This eliminates entirely the Chaplins and Harold Lloyds and Buster Keatons. Their product is of feature length, whereas the comedy world operates on a two-reel basis.

Yet many of these two-reelers represent an investment higher than that which goes into the making of a seven-reel dramatic production. For example Larry Semon's *Kid Speed* packs into 2,000 feet as many settings, actors and as much time for production, as goes into at least half of the program dramas 7,000 feet in length. It can be condensed into 2,000 feet because of the terrific speed with which it is run. Comedies flash across the screen at a tumbling racing rate. Yet they are not made so hastily. Corps of "gag" men, joke-smiths toil on each one, directors strain their minds to make the action funny. Casts are picked, rehearsed, trained and "retakes" are copious. The business of filming a comedy is not the helter-skelter affair it seems when the finished thing dances across the film.

For example, Semon spent three months and close to $100,000 making *Kid Speed*. That is an average expenditure of time and money for a seven-reel program picture with an all-star cast.

Mack Sennett, whose fame is not so great as in the days when he flashed his bathing beauties on the silversheet, nevertheless is as busy as ever. He makes 40 comedies a year and finds ways and means of exhibiting female pulchritude even if the censors have put clothes on his beach women. Dozens of these Sennett productions represent a cost that compares favorably with the longer dramas.

Hal Roach, a prolific comedy-maker, turns out 60 two-reelers a year. Al Christie hands Educational 40 each twelve months.

No shutdowns and reorganizations and expansions for these producers. Their market is stable and eager. The public wants its laughter, its looney guffaws, short, quick and sure.

Little-Known Facts About Lincoln

In December, 1924, Sandburg was nearing completion of the first two volumes in his epic biography of Abraham Lincoln. A revised manuscript of 300,000 words, which would become Abraham Lincoln: The Prairie Years *had been submitted to his publisher, Harcourt Brace. Coincidentally, the film biography* Abraham Lincoln *was released at the same time. Clearly, having immersed himself in Lincoln's life, Sandburg was eager to see the film. In conjunction with the review, Sandburg used the movie column to publish some of the insights he had acquired during his massive research and writing process. These columns represent some of Sandburg's first published work on Lincoln. With the release of* The Prairie Years *in 1926 and the four-volume conclusion* The War Years *in 1939, Sandburg's name would forever be connected with that of America's sixteenth president.*

Little-known facts about the real Abraham Lincoln have been unearthed in profusion by Al and Ray Rockett, the brothers who spent years preparing for and then months in filming the life of the Great Emancipator.

For instance, few people know that Lincoln could never bear to kill animals, indeed shot but one bird or animal in his life, that, a wild turkey, when a pioneer boy. He was tenderhearted to the extreme, but he did not like flowers, saw nothing beautiful in them.

He sold liquor in the log town of New Salem, Illinois, when he was a clerk in Offutt's General Store—yet he did not drink. He sold tobacco and never smoked.

The farseeing exponent of war once it came, a believer in hard relentless fighting as a means of ending the struggle as soon as possible, he is known as perhaps the greatest of war presidents, yet he was of Quaker stock and often referred to his indebtedness to their pacific doctrines.

He seldom corrected his lively little boys, Willie and Tad in their mischief, and was often reproved by his wife for being too lenient with them. His love for them was all-powerful and his despondence after the death of little Willie in 1862 made the nation fear for his reason.

As a boy he was so fond of reading, studying and thinking that his father and some of his early employers despaired of him ever becoming a "good worker" in the frontier life.

Although a consummate politician, he was freer than any office holder in history of the charge of elevating men to office for personal reasons. Not even friendship could lead him to appoint a man to office if there were better-qualified candidates. Often he appointed his severest critics and enemies to high posts when it was evident that they would fill the office well. These characteristics are shown in *Abraham Lincoln*, the wonderful film version of his life, which Al and Ray Rockett produced and which First National is soon to exhibit in Chicago.

When Abraham Lincoln Arrives at Roosevelt Theater

For 60 years America has been puzzled and perplexed over Mrs. Abraham Lincoln. What kind of woman was she? Historians have said too much or too little about her, according to Al Rockett, who with his brother spent three years making their picture, *Abraham Lincoln*, which comes next Monday to the Roosevelt Theater.

She has been alternately called a "scold," a "shrew," a "saint," an abused woman, an abusive woman. Some historians have said she was a tremendous help to Lincoln in his troubles, others have said she increased his troubles. Many historians have indicated that she was a detriment to Lincoln by studiously avoiding all talk about her in their biographies.

"What many historians have left unsaid has been worse for Mrs. Lincoln's reputation than anything they might have said," says Mr. Rockett, "because it has set tongues gossiping.

"Going back to original sources for our production of Lincoln's life, weighing the evidence of people who knew her, we put her into the picture as she really was, a high-tempered, impetuous, intensely loyal wife. If her temper got the best of her occasionally and turned her into a scolding wife, it was because she had much to worry her. Lincoln was loving in the extreme, kind, gentle, soft-spoken, but he was careless around the house, his mind occupied much of the time with the melancholy that rose in his heart, the woes of the world, plans for saving the Union. His mind was too big for him always to observe the niceties of deportment that she thought a president of the United States ought to observe. She was worried by fear for his safety, fear that aristocratic easterners would sniff at his homely manners and absence of formality. Then, too, she was southern. She had brothers in the Confederate army. Men in Washington with silly and excessive patriotism were spying on her on this account. Her two little boys, Willie and Tad, were exceptionally lively and adventurous, and Lincoln out of his overwhelming love for them would rarely restrain or correct them.

"The strain on her was enormous and gossips set going baseless stories about her with the result that the country at one time called her a 'scold.' The facts are that she did now and then lose self-control, but that she was loyal in the extreme, proud beyond all common pride of her great husband, and that she was the very first person in the world to see his great genius and destiny and that she played politics, society, every angle she saw to make him president. She had the ambition of a great love. She had the faults of a great love in an exceedingly high-tempered woman. She as a Kentucky belle, raised in a sort of Ivanhoe-society, wedded to a homely, lanky genius of the common people, a frontier master of men.

"We have tried to show her as she was and to do her justice in the interests of truth."

Lincoln the Man Shown in New Picture at the Roosevelt
Monday, December 29, 1924

"Lincoln the man not Lincoln the myth," was the central idea that animated Al and Ray Rockett when they set out on their three-year job of filming the life of Abraham Lincoln. These brothers had read or knew the contents of almost all of the 5,000 odd books that have been written about Lincoln and were dissatisfied with the attempts of 90 percent of these to make Lincoln into a god-like wraith, something far-off and mystical. They felt that history had been trying to make Lincoln's memory into a statue, towering into the clouds and remote from all human activity.

To make their film *Abraham Lincoln* show the real and human man as he was they spent three years, infinite pains and all their money. How well their picture does this

Chicago Daily News ads for *Abraham Lincoln* (Monday, December 29, 1924—*top*, and Monday, December 22, 1924—*bottom*).

may be guessed by the furor it has caused in New York where it has been shown and may be determined accurately at the Roosevelt Theater.

Abraham Lincoln, the picture, trails with remarkable fidelity Lincoln from birth to death with special emphasis upon his loves, his romance and his married life, all phases which biographies have dealt lightlt with. Al and Ray Rockett show in detail and with fine poetic feeling Lincoln's rustic love affair with Anne Rutledge, his grief at her death, his courtship of the high-spirited Mary Todd, his married life with her, a life so often sensationalized in the gossip of a nation and so minimized in written biographies.

The great incidents in Lincoln's life, his use of humor to steady the nerves of a war-crazed country, his boyhood struggles, his griefs in the presidency, his family life with his two little boys, his quick turn to them for relief from the harassments of political life, his quaint, gentle and profound mental life are all shown with one aim, to tell the truth about this greatest of Americans so that America today will appreciate him as a human being like themselves rather than as the nebulous myth.

Abraham Lincoln

With the writing of Abraham Lincoln: The Prairie Years *nearing completion, it's no accident Sandburg had more than just a critic's interest in a cinematic rendering of the sixteenth president's life. The play*

Sandburg refers to at the end of this review is "Abraham Lincoln" by John Drinkwater, which was originally staged in 1918. See also the accompanying essays on Abraham Lincoln that Sandburg penned in conjunction with this film's release.

Tuesday, December 30, 1924

The photoplay presentation of the life of Abraham Lincoln at the Roosevelt Theater this week is a work based chiefly on the standard biographies of Lincoln.

The stories told by various reels of the picture are familiar ones that have been told often by lecturers, campaign speakers, school readers, and the parents answering questions of children, such as "who was Abraham Lincoln and why do we hear so much about him?"

The part of Lincoln is taken by George Billings. He was a mail carrier in Los Angeles. Early in his life he found out that he looked a good deal like Lincoln. And he studied books about Lincoln. And when he heard that the Rockett brothers in Los Angeles were going to make a Lincoln picture he went to their studio and told them he was the man to play Lincoln. They gave him one quick glance and hired him on the spot.

Of course, being a grown man, six feet four inches tall, he couldn't play the part of the baby Lincoln born in the Kentucky cabin, but he starts in as the young rail-splitter in Indiana and the flatboat man going down the Sangamon and Mississippi Rivers toward New Orleans.

The story of Anne Rutledge and Lincoln is told as that story is usually told. And Anne seems to be the same old-fashioned movie heroine seen in the movies of old-fashioned times.

Mary Todd Lincoln is the best character portrayal in the film. The role of Stephen A. Douglas is so-so, while Gen. Grant is a nervous, fidgety hustler who, in the film, smokes and smokes at his cigars, whereas Grant himself enjoyed chewing the butts as calmly as a horse in green grass.

The picture as history and biography is of the standard of excellence noted in the general run of Lincoln and Civil War books. As drama it is much more truly American, with more competent handling of Lincoln than the Drinkwater stage play.

Abraham Lincoln as a Boy

Wednesday, December 31, 1924

That Abraham Lincoln was a solemnly studious melancholy boy during his youth, a lonely bookish lad, is the popular impression and yet facts to the contrary were discovered by Al and Ray Rockett during their three-year search through original sources for material upon which to make their film *Abraham Lincoln* now at the Roosevelt Theater.

The books that the boy Lincoln had were few and far between and his mind intensely curious about life prompted him to ask questions endlessly of such travelers as came through the Kentucky and Indiana frontiers where he lived. A bright, inquisitive lad, he loosed upon all newcomers such a flood of questions that his father, bluff old Thomas Lincoln, was known to cuff the boy alongside the head with his hat and send him away. Once young Abe said to his cousin Dennis Hanks, with whom he was raised, "There's so many things I want to know and pa won't let me ask about 'em that I don't know how I'm ever goin' to learn anything."

Lincoln's storytelling genius cropped out in his boyhood and he was then, as in later life, the center of an admiring ring wherever he happened to be in the settlements. William Herndon, his law partner in Springfield and the author of what experts agree is the factful life of Lincoln, says: "One who knew the boy says Lincoln would frequently make political speeches to the boys; he was always calm, logical and clear. His jokes and stories were so odd, original and witty all the people in town would gather around him. He would keep them till midnight."

Badly dressed, in winter blue with the cold, in summer half-clad in the heat, the boy was recognized even at that age as a genius. His mind was busy with what it had to work on. His impersonations and imitations of preachers were both comic and admirable, it is reported, and his reproductions of small trials he witnessed before a justice of the peace were sidesplitting.

Altogether a humorous, comical boy with few opportunities to read and with little of the melancholy that developed later.

Abraham Lincoln's Stepmother and Her Influence
Thursday, January 8, 1925

Abraham Lincoln's stepmother, Sarah Bush Lincoln, had a profound practical effect upon the boyhood of the greatest of Americans, yet she had in her a strange strain of mysticism, not an uncommon quality in frontier folk with whom Lincoln was raised. Al and Ray Rockett show this stepmother only in connection with Lincoln's youth in their production, *Abraham Lincoln*, which runs now at the Roosevelt Theater, but they show the profound influence she had upon him and the association between them which was kept up until he bade her farewell to go to Washington to assume the presidency. After his assassination William Herndon, his law partner in Springfield anxious that the truth about Lincoln should be told the world in a time when mythmakers were distorting the martyr's memory into something unreal and misty, went to see the old lady, who was living with her own children in southern Illinois. To him the woman who had so loved Lincoln, boy and man, said: "I didn't want Abe to run for president and I didn't want to see him elected. I was afraid something would happen to him, and when he came down to see me, after he was elected president, I still felt and my heart told me that something would befall him and that I should never see him again."

Lincoln never was permitted time to visit Illinois after he left it in March, 1861, for the inauguration. When he came back it was on the funeral train that wound across the country.

Stolen Sweeties

Saturday, December 27, 1924

Stolen Sweeties is a Fox two-reeler indicated as one of the Monkey Comedy Series.

A wedding is set for two human bipeds on the same day as two simian bipeds or chimpanzees are to have a wedding.

Many troubles occur to stop the double wedding from coming off on time.

These troubles have been planned so as to show what monkeys can do when it comes to screen acting.

The wishes and yearnings written on the faces of these jungle creatures, the careless and simple manner in which they execute their pantomimic roles, comes as a refreshing experience following the general run of photoplays in which men and women move who are thinking so hard and so intensely about how they should play their parts that we sometimes feel sorry for them that they have to live such silversheet lies as they do.

Having that off our chest, we may offer the opinion again that animal actors are going to be seen more and more in the movies.

Screen classics are to be achieved in this field.

The animal comedy recently at the Roosevelt Theater in which monkeys, dogs, rabbits, roosters and hens took their several and diverse roles in a story, was well received.

It may be that what the movies have today is not too much of monkeys but rather not enough.

The Thief of Bagdad

Douglas Fairbanks intended to make The Thief of Bagdad *one of his crowning achievements. William Cameron Menzies, then a rising art director in Hollywood, was hired to create the film's visual design. Working closely with Fairbanks, Menzies created a dream-like setting that gave* Thief *a magical look. As for his own appearance, Fairbanks worked out daily to get his already athletic physique in top condition;* The Thief of Bagdad *would mark the first time Fairbanks appeared in the movies without a shirt, and he wanted a torso to be proud of. Costing a (then) astounding $2 million, the film's set was built on the grounds of what had once been Fairbanks's* Robin Hood *castle. Menzies would go on to become one of Hollywood's most respected art directors, best remembered for his sumptuous work on* Gone With the Wind *(1939) and his own directorial effort* Things to Come *(1936).*

Wednesday, December 31, 1924

The Thief of Bagdad, which is opening its second engagement locally at the Orpheum Theater this week, is what we might call one of the universally acclaimed photoplays.

Probably no one photoplay since the motion picture business and art got going has been greeted so enthusiastically in the circles known as highbrow and lowbrow.

They have a saying in most corners of Hollywood and Long Island that if a picture is made too intelligent and fine, it won't interest and entertain enough people to become a box office success.

In *The Thief of Bagdad*, however, there is both intelligence and fine art quality, and the picture has won large audiences.

Douglas Fairbanks is the producer of it, also the leading player, and it represents the quintessence and distillation of what he has learned about movies since he started in, among the first of the film workers.

"Happiness must be earned" is the opening and closing slogan of the piece, coupled with the apothegm: "On the bedrock of humility thou canst build an enduring structure."

Magic and fantasy of the tales of the Arabian Nights' entertainments are woven through the silversheet story. The telling of the story would be impossible in ordinary theatrical stagecraft. It is precisely the kind of story that the movies can deliver where other media fail. The flying carpet which will, as you sit on it and speak your wish, carry you whither you wish, the crystal ball which obeys as you pass your hand over it and command it to reveal scenes thousands of miles away, besides magic boxes and magic ladders, are devices that are handled best in the cinema. They are its exclusive field, its precious possession, not always employed to advantage, but here seen in shimmering guise.

Therefore, while *The Thief of Bagdad* is in the going and trying to steal into the hearts of Chicagoans, we say it is one of the rare movies worth seeing. This reviewer is going for a third look at it this week.

Monday, April 20, 1925

The Thief of Bagdad, which is showing at the Stratford Theater this week, is a picture we believe has been mentioned three or four times in this corner.

It may be nine or 10 times, possibly 100 that we have made reference to *The Thief of Bagdad*.

However many times it may be, there is no reason for apology or explanation, because the simple fact is that *The Thief of Bagdad* is one of the few pictures that ought to be mentioned over and over.

Old and young enjoy it and derive new health from it.

In the words of the enthusiast about an all-around spring tonic, "It's good for whatever ails you."

This reviewer has gone to see it three times and if he lives will go again that many times more.

A wise and a foolish picture, a persuasive and sweetly reasonable photoplay, yet also wild and impossible.

Before the city aldermen solve the traction problem they will all have to have a look at *The Thief of Bagdad.*

The tax tangles at Washington would all be more easily straightened out if the members of congress could get their throwing arms and their stiff necks loosened up by an evening with Doug Fairbanks' masterpiece.

We trust the Stratford will be packed.

If our burglars, stickup men and safeblowers could all see *The Thief of Bagdad* they might not change their habits, but they might revise their outlooks on life.

A rare, brilliant picture that sort of wakes us up and at the same time makes us a little sleepy—a glad and mysterious picture, this one, *The Thief of Bagdad.*

Lon Chaney's horrifying makeup for *The Phantom of the Opera* remains a powerful and iconic film image.

1925

January

Peter Pan

Peter Pan, *James Barrie's charming tale of childhood fantasy, has been adapted on numerous occasions, including a 1953 Disney animated feature and Steven Spielberg's 1991 reworking* Hook. *Perhaps the best known rendition is the 1960 television* Peter Pan *starring Mary Martin.*

Friday, January 2, 1925

The *Peter Pan* picture having its first run at McVicker's Theater this week is one of those exceptional photoplays where as the reels go by you can tell that those who made it sort of lived with it quite a while before they began working on it, and they kept on loving the picture up to the last flicker.

Yes, they loved this picture before they gave birth to it. They had it alive in their hearts before it took the form it now lives in.

The story they worked with is the same as in James Barrie's stage play, originally produced in this country with Maude Adams in the leading role.

Betty Bronson has the lead in this, and it will be her introduction to a wide audience which will say she has something of birds and sky in her.

Herbert Brenon directed. And some will say this is the first work from him which certifies he has large cinema mastery when he gets down to what interests him.

Never Never Land is shown, where the lost boys live, with the captain Peter Pan, and Wendy, their mother for the time they are lost.

Ernest Torrence plays Captain Hook, the pirate with the skull and crossbones flag at the mast. A fine illusion is achieved in the sword fight between the pirate captain and young Peter Pan. Peter runs his sword into the pirate but no blood comes.

British features of the story are Americanized. When the pirate flag is taken down the new ensign is the star-spangled banner.

Nana, the dog, played by George All, in a droll dog head and dog paws, is a notable feature. The paws have a pantomimic alphabet with which they talk, weep and cavort with glee.

A little bird that has just broken out of its egg, the symbol of joy, is what Peter Pan says he represents. And the spirit of just that is remarkably well presented.

In the end a lady tells him she will take care of him; he shall go to school, then to an office; he shall be president.

And he looks, serious, mournful. He doesn't want to grow up. He must be a boy always. He says good-by and goes back to the woods.

This is one of the exceptional pictures which this reviewer hopes to see two or three times. It is worth more than one view.

Isn't Life Wonderful?

For Isn't Life Wonderful?, *D. W. Griffith took a small cast and crew to the streets of Berlin, capturing a people in the midst of economic crises following Germany's loss in World War I. Lillian Gish later said that the film was ". . . the only picture (Griffith) made after I left him that I thought worthy of him."[1]* Isn't Life Wonderful? *did not fare well at the box office though, and Griffith, financially unable to continue independent production, was forced to return to Hollywood's studio system.*

Tuesday, January 6, 1925

David Wark Griffith's latest production, *Isn't Life Wonderful?*, which is having its first run at McVicker's Theater this week, is a characteristic Griffith piece of goods.

Everybody who has hitherto enjoyed Griffith's pictures should enjoy this one, because he employs the same methods of handling characters and of tinting real life with his own choice of illusory colors, as in his former pictures, with the exception, perhaps, of *Broken Blossoms*.

Romance, very strictly, and as such, is achieved here.

To have turnips and turnips only, to eat, and then to be wildly in love at the same time—to be hungry and underfed while making arrangements for a wedding—there was one place where Griffith could go to find this combination and use it for photodrama.

That place was Germany, during or after the war.

The scenes are located in Germany. But the people are not Germans. They are Polish refugees.

Inga—that's the Polish girl, played by Carol Dempster—goes through many deep miseries after she finds she is in love with Paul, the son of the professor.

Once she stands in line waiting her turn to buy a loaf of bread. And a man comes out every few minutes and marks up the price of bread. And after a while she has to step out of line because she hasn't enough million marks to buy a loaf of bread.

Then there are food scouts, hungry men of skeleton look, who go from the city to the country to take food wherever they may find it.

Desperate men these are that Griffith depicts. They are sort of puppet-like, too. We have the feeling that if Griffith knew Germany and Poland as well as he knows Kentucky, the photoplay would be less romantic and more true to what Ring Lardner, titling a short story, calls "The Facts."

Entertaining film drama that people enjoy. One can listen and hear the audience at McVicker's having a good time.

Some come to cry and get what they want. Other come to laugh and get that. Still others want a little of both and are accommodated.

Bernard Shaw on the Movies

Saturday, January 10, 1925

When Bernard Shaw gets down to naming over the different things that are wrong with the movies, it runs up into quite a list. He says there are too many "hideous makeups, close-ups that an angel's face would not bear."

Shaw, finds too, "overdone and foolishly repeated strokes of expression; hundreds of thousands of dollars spent on spelling effects that I or any other competent producer could secure at a cost of 10 cents; vulgar and silly subtitles; impertinent lists of everybody employed in the firm, from the star actress to the press agent's office boy."

He believes there is a new art in the films. He may be tempted to try his hand at it. Yet having spent a lifetime mastering language and the spoken stage drama, he hesitates about going in for silent screen drama, where the characters can't use words.

"Asking one to write a dumb show is rather like asking Titian to paint portraits in black and white," he flatters himself.

"Still, there is one sort of dumb show that is something more than a play with the words left out, and that is a dream. If ever I do a movie show it will have the quality of a dream."

As to the models of the movies, the famous vegetarian who wrote that great play, *Saint Joan*, has this to say: "The movie play has supplanted the old-fashioned tract and Sunday school prize; it is reeking with morality, but dare not touch virtue. And virtue which is defiant and contemptuous of morality even when it has not practical quarrel with it, is the life blood of high drama."

And he has come to recognize "Movie plays should be invented expressly for the screen by original imaginative visualizers."

Which last is a large order from several points of view, and will not affect the steady output of screen translations of the best selling novels.

HE Who Gets Slapped

A fascinating psychological drama, HE Who Gets Slapped *was the first release of the new movie conglomeration Metro-Goldwyn-Mayer. Lon Chaney's character, a disgraced scientist turned disturbed circus clown, is referred to in both the film's title and subtitles as "HE."*

Monday, January 19, 1925

HE Who Gets Slapped is a triumphant motion picture production. Go see it if you wish, as a specimen of what the motion picture world is rather proud of. It is one of those occasional surprises pointed to with pride by the entire photoplay world because it testifies there is such a thing as motion picture art and cinema artistry.

Plenty of people who saw the stage play by Leonid Andreyev are saying the movie is swifter, is the equal, at least, of the spoken drama in delivering the quizzical and mystical laughter at life that murmured back of Andreyev's acts and scenes.

Lon Chaney playing the clown, "HE," undoubtedly performs in a way that realizes his gifts at their surest. This is one time the role, the story, the director, fitted this player, whose chief note in the gamut has been agony. He now hands his audience agony as before, but a more quiet and strange one.

Norma Shearer in the role of Consuelo shows that she can take a difficult and involved role outside of the respectable societies in which she has hitherto been seen. John Gilbert,

From the collection of Arnie Bernstein.

Norma Shearer's popularity rose in the late 1920s and extended well into the sound era.

Tully Marshall and Marc McDermott, Ford Sterling and Ruth King have their separate parts that build effectively toward a central result.

Victor Seastrom directed the production, helped make the adaptation from the Russian drama and guided it as a photoplay in its decisive lines.

The stage story is somewhat changed. Not in any serious way whatever. The characters are not affected by the changes. The liberties taken with the stage drama are evidently only for the purpose of getting silversheet results. Spoken drama and the silent screen can't say the same things. In a case such as this to have followed the drama as written would have been to end up with one more blundering attempt to give voice to the voiceless.

From beginning to end this picture lights up with the means and devices that are peculiarly those of the motion picture art. If Andreyev had written it in the first place for the screen it would be impossible to translate into the spoken drama.

The showing is at the Chicago Theater.

Monday, February 2, 1925

While *HE Who Gets Slapped* is showing at the Tivoli and Riviera Theaters it would be proper, perhaps, to refer again to this exceptional picture.

It is decidedly not one of those subtle and excellent photoplays which are for grownups only.

More of circus stunts and circus color is brought out than in any picture of the last year. The clowns are the most attractive and loveable clowns we have noticed either in circuses or the movies. Clowning is an art. Only at vaudeville occasionally have we seen clowns that approach these in mummery.

Every once in a while throughout the running of the picture the screen is filled with two moving things. One is a clown figure, whose face is wrinkled and double wrinkled with laughter. The other is a whirling globe, the earth, which he twirls at a dizzy speed.

The clownery of life is the theme. All of us, whether we will or not, must at times by the whimsical play of events take our roles as clowns—that is the idea. And they have set this to a sort of cinema music.

Far back of the players and the play the suggestion is handed us that the slaps of life, the stings and the insolence that arrive to us without wish or explanation ought to be counted on, ought to be expected. If we know how to expect them and if we can learn how to laugh back at them, then we have learned what "HE" learned. "Who are you?" he is asked. And his answer is "I am HE who gets slapped."

February

Broken Laws

Broken Laws is one of the many "problem" pictures made by Dorothy Davenport following the death of her husband, Wallace Reid. Though an attempt to use movies as a force for social good, Davenport's work functioned best as an early form of exploitation film, a staple of carnivals and cheap movie houses from the 1930s through the 1950s.

Thursday, February 12, 1925

Broken Laws is the second of the crusading photoplays issued under the auspices of the widow of Wallace Reid, the deceased star.

Her first one, called *Human Wreckage*, has to do with the dope traffic, and how even children were fed morphine by mothers, while this one tries to tell a parable of the prodigal children who grow up with parents who break laws and as a consequence in their adult years are also lawbreakers.

The film is intended to preach a sermon that will strike deep into the hearts of law-breaking parents so that they will change their ways and bring up the little ones with an understanding of what St. Paul called doing things decently and in order.

The opening reels aim to picture the worst Christmas Eve that ever happened in the houses of well-to-do and supposedly law-abiding people.

The boy tears the gifts off the Christmas tree and says there ain't no Santa Claus.

And the parents go next door to a party, the father with the hope on his lips that a better bootlegger than last time is serving.

The boy, having been locked in his bedroom, uses the bed sheets as a rope and climbs down to the ground in a rainstorm, and enters the house next door where he and a tot of a girl drink punch the boy has stolen from the bowl prepared for the guests.

And so on.

In order to point its moral the film depicts immoral extravaganzas.

Percy Marmont has the leading role, or perhaps shares it with Mrs. Wallace Reid. Other players are Pat Moore and Jane Wray, the child actors; Arthur Ranking, Ramsey Wallace, Virginia Lee Corbin and Jacqueline Saunders. The direction was by R. William Neil, from a story by Adela Rogers St. Johns.

How von Stroheim Made Greed

The story behind Erich von Stroheim's Greed *is, like the film itself, a tragedy of epic proportions. Based on Frank Norris's 1899 novel* McTeague, Greed *tells the story of a crude San Francisco dentist whose life spirals out of control after his wife wins a $5,000 lottery. Von Stroheim faithfully took Norris's book as a blueprint for* Greed, *essentially filming the novel scene for scene. Using a realistic approach, von Stroheim shot on location in San Francisco and in the brutal desert heat of Death Valley.* McTeague *was based on a real murder and von Stroheim insisted on shooting in the home where the actual crime took place.[2] The production, which took nine months, cost $500,000, relatively low considering the length of filming. With more than 200,000 feet of film to edit, von Stroheim turned in a first cut of 42 reels. Twelve people were shown this version, including director Rex Ingram and journalists Idwal Jones and Harry Carr. The decision was unanimous: von Stroheim had created a cinematic masterpiece. The director's original intention was to show the film in two parts, yet at seven hours* Greed *was still too long for most audiences. Working without pay, von Stroheim cut the film down to 24 reels, or four hours. "I could not, to save my soul, cut another foot," he later said.[3] However, von Stroheim's old nemesis, Irving Thalberg, along with studio boss Louis B. Mayer, insisted that* Greed *be edited to a more reasonable length. Hoping he could stave off more trouble, von Stroheim secretly sent a copy of his work to Ingram for further cutting. Ingram obliged, editing* Greed *to 18 reels, then sent von Stroheim a telegram reading: "If you cut down one more foot I shall never speak to you again." Screenwriter June Mathis, who assisted in* Greed's *script, made additional cuts bringing the film to 16,000 feet.[4] Yet Thalberg remained firm that* Greed *would clock in at two hours. Joseph W. Farnum, a studio editor with limited experience (though he later wrote the titles for King Vidor's silent 1928 film classic* The Crowd*), was assigned to reduce* Greed *to just ten reels. Von Stroheim subsequently described Farnum as ". . . a man earning thirty dollars a week, a man who had never read the book nor the script, and on whose mind was nothing but a hat. He ruined the whole of my two years' work."[5] Now running at two hours,* Greed *was unceremoniously dumped into theaters. Some critics, like Sandburg, praised the film as a work of genius; others dismissed it as pretentious and confusing. The material edited out, including deleted subplots and characters, was unceremoniously destroyed. The studio burned the original film negative to extract about 43 cents worth of silver from it.*

The reputation of Greed *among film mavens has grown significantly over the years. Despite the studio-induced butchery, what remains has been acclaimed as one of the greatest films ever made. In 1999, using a combination of production stills and von Stroheim's original shooting script, an approximation of the director's original four-hour cut was put together. Broadcast on the Turner Classic Movies cable channel, this reconstruction gave audiences a glimpse of what* Greed *could have been.*

Von Stroheim disowned the two-hour version of Greed. Years later, when discussing the fiasco, von Stroheim wrote: "If I talked to you . . . for three weeks steadily I could not possibly describe, even to a small degree, the heartache I suffered through the mutilation of my sincere work at the hands of M.G.M. executives."[6]

Friday, February 13, 1925

Erich von Stroheim may worry the life out of his financial backers and drive his players into hysterics with his incessant demand for more realism in their acting, but he does not spare himself. The eccentric, but intensely artistic director proved this when in making *Greed*, he worked for 18 months without a cent of pay, just to make his picture better and better and even better.

When von Stroheim set out to make a motion picture of Frank Norris' great novel *McTeague*, he signed contracts to deliver it to Metro-Goldwyn in six months. He picked a cast after three months of tests and try-outs and began work. In his intense desire to get into his picture the strangely realistic atmosphere of Frank Norris' book, he paid no attention to the flight of time, and before he knew it, his six months were gone, and his picture but half filmed.

He made no appeal to Metro-Goldwyn, but kept on working, taking his actors to San Francisco for some scenes, and then into Death Valley, that weird inferno on the desert, for three months' tortuous filming. Time went on and von Stroheim paid no attention. He was intent on making the literary masterpiece a film masterpiece, and he ordered retakes on most of the scenes so often that his subordinates and actors were worn out. Everybody in the cast wilted, all the cameramen, assistants and carpenters gave out and had to rest up but von Stroheim kept on dreaming, working, cutting and rearranging his story.

At length two years had gone by and von Stroheim was alone with his film. He discharged all actors and helpers and toiled at cutting down his picture. Finally he got it to 24 reels, then to 12, the form in which it will be shown Monday at the Roosevelt Theater.

Tuesday, February 17, 1925

"*Greed*, the picture that is different from any motion picture ever made" is the phrase with which Metro-Goldwyn brings this newest von Stroheim picture to the Roosevelt Theater.

To support this claim the organization advances the following facts: it is the first picture to take two years to make. It is the only picture to cost $2 million without having a single mob scene or "stupendous set" in it. It is completely realistic, telling a simple story of tragedy, comedy, pathos, demanding acting of the type called "heavy," yet it is acted entirely by people who have been slapstick comedians. There is no coincidence, no strange happenings, no lucky or unexpected meetings, no drama of the sort usually seen on the screen and stage. All is drama and acting of a sort totally new to the screen, utterly natural, strangely real as though the onlooker were living in the same house with the characters in a day-by-day existence, seeing into the humor, the pathos, the tragedy, the secret hopes and bitter disappointments of real people.

Erich von Stroheim took two years of laborious, painful work to make *Greed*, keeping his cast reading and re-reading *McTeague*, the Frank Norris novel from which the picture is taken. He kept them moving about the studio in their costumes months without ever letting them dress in any other attire, kept them living as their Norris characters constantly, even when the camera was not grinding and by this method— totally new to the screen—getting from them a brand of acting unbelievably natural, it is said.

Greed is the story of a giant with the heart of a child who married a sweet and ineffectual little woman who became in time obsessed with the idea of thrift, carrying it to the point of madness, substituting love of gold for love of her mate and bringing tragedy into their lives.

Von Stroheim's most startling piece of paradoxy in the picture is the use of players from the two-reel comedies to play both humorous and tragic roles. Gibson Gowland, who gives a powerful and vivid portrait of McTeague, the hero, was on the receiving end of many of the custard pies and kicks launched by Charlie Chaplin, Harold Lloyd and Ben Turpin. Zasu Pitts, playing Trina, his wife, is a graduate of the two-reel

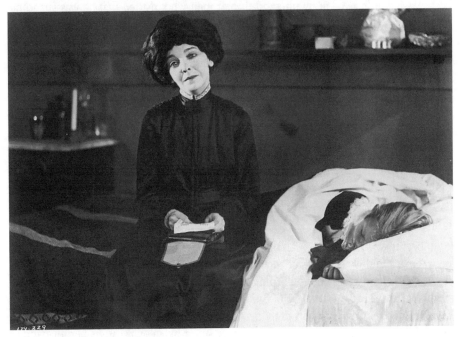

From the collection of Arnie Bernstein.

Zasu Pitts as "Trina" in Erich von Stroheim's butchered masterpiece *Greed*.

comedies, and Chester Conklin, Frank Hayes, Dale Fuller, Sylvia Ashton and Jean Hersholt, who have other important roles, were well-known figures in the comedies.

Another innovation of the picture is that of having some of the action take place in Death Valley, the dread desert into which human beings rarely go even for sight-seeing, so scorchingly hot is it. Von Stroheim took his players into this inferno because Norris' book took them there and the eccentric but talented director kept them there three months until he had obtained the effects he desired.

Greed

Thursday, February 19, 1925

Greed is to be to motion pictures what Theodore Roosevelt or Woodrow Wilson were to politics—either wildly praised or viciously condemned. Only two ways about it. It is the best picture made to date—or the worst.

People whose temperaments are this way will laud it; people whose temperaments are that way will hate it. It is too strong to be judged with the head. No one will be rational about this picture. It will be weighted with the heart and with the emotions, and people will argue over it in the same way they argue over politics and religion.

Rumors of its strangeness, its creeping power, its eccentric composition have been sifting eastward from Hollywood for two years. Its maker, Erich von Stroheim, has been yowled at, clawed at by film and theater men who insisted that he was spending $2 million of their money to make a picture that would be too realistic, too deep for the public.

To which von Stroheim replied that he had a masterpiece to work on in Frank Norris' *McTeague* and that his screen version of it would be as truthful as the story itself. He said that he was working without salary on it, that he was paid for only the first six months and that he had volunteered gladly to toil for nothing during the next 18 months in order to make his picture an epic. He told them that that fact cleared him in his own eyes and furthermore they could all go hang.

Well, it is here. The Roosevelt Theater has it, after all these months of rumors and rampages.

Greed was written by an artist and filmed by a director who in this picture shows he is an artist. It will be remembered.

It begins with a happy marriage, a humorous, extraordinarily human wedding between a hulking, slow-witted dentist and a commonplace and pretty girl of San Francisco. They set up housekeeping, then slowly, insidiously, the yeast of drama begins to rise. The wife wins $5,000 in a raffle, she hides it in her bed. She begins to save on this and save on that, deny her husband carfare when he might be walking, steal dimes from his pocket at night. A former suitor in jealousy causes her husband to lose his dentist's license. The couple slips down hill as greed develops.

A tale told with skilled technique of photography, posing and acting, von Stroheim points his camera from curious angles, intersperses the action with symbolism, varies tenement scenes with mythical, dreaming fantasy.

And he puts actors, story, cameras, settings into a soaring finale, two singed, gasping men-wrecks tottering in the hot-sand inferno of Death Valley.

People will love it or hate it—but they'll be a long time forgetting it either way they go on it.

Monday, February 23, 1925

Among the best pictures which have come to our city within the last year—standing by itself for its low percentage of bunk and hokum—is the photoplay named *Greed*, now in its second week at the Roosevelt Theater.

The novel from which the story and characters are taken is a book by a great writer who came from Chicago, Frank Norris, and the name of the book is *McTeague*.

It is about 25 years since *McTeague* was published; it is still in print and being read; and there are many readers of it who place it among the greatest of American novels.

While Erich von Stroheim, the director of the picture, was working on it the last year, there was plenty of skepticism about whether he could put it over.

But he did.

And he has.

Neither this country nor any other country has produced a long-range story that more ably grips the biblical text, "Money is the root of all evil," and works therefrom a fabric of life, with overtones or implications bordering on the allegorical.

Five thousand dollars of gold falls into the hands of a poor girl unexpectedly.

And from then on that collection of gold pieces is an actor, a sort of living player, in the photodrama.

It is all that is alive in the last flicker, the final fadeout, where two men and a burro are dead in Death Valley.

What we see last of all is the pile of yellow gold pieces spotted with blood drops.

Yes, it gives some of us the shivers to look at this picture; it is as terrible as money is at its worst.

Yet we noticed, through a large part of its showing, that people laughed.

Some scenes and flashes and subtitles are as comic as first-rate two-reel stuff.

The comedy is of the flavor of low life in Shakespeare.

Though the tragic high spots are fierce and relentless, the comic relief is superb.

One of the few grand instances of a movie without hokum, without a happy ending.

The Salvation Hunters

Director Josef von Sternberg's first film earned him instant acclaim. "To me it revealed a spontaneous and admirable film technique, combined with artistic composition and rhythm of presentation," said Charlie Chaplin. "It is a great picture—and different."[7] Chaplin admired the work of von Sternberg's leading lady, Georgia Hale, and hired her to play opposite him in The Gold Rush. *Other powerhouses, including Douglas Fairbanks, Mary Pickford, D. W. Griffith, and Cecil B. DeMille, sang von Sternberg's praises. "With one fell swoop I had become a member of the inner circle," von Sternberg later wrote.[8] Though von Sternberg would face some difficulties before his career solidified,* The Salvation Hunters *was the beginning of a remarkable run.*

Saturday, February 14, 1925

The Salvation Hunters, a picture having its first run in New York this month, has kicked up a good deal more than ordinary interest encountering moviedom.

First of all, it is considered this photoplay must have unusual value because Douglas Fairbanks, having had one view of it, bought a one-fifth interest in it, and because Mary Pickford, having had one view of it, decided that the maker of it must be the man to direct her in her next two pictures. And the contracts were signed.

The director, Joseph von Sternberg, is the author of the story, and on account of his wide practical experience in the mechanical and laboratory ends of the movie industry his hand is seen in various photographic and manufacturing features of the picture.

In the list of names of the staff who worked on the film the title of "laboratory expert" is given to this one. It is recognized that after all the others have put their impress on the film there can be remarkable results achieved by the washing and manipulation of the print that is to go into the projection machines.

The story of *The Salvation Hunters* is simple in its events and subtle in its psychology. Three persons are lost on the path of life, drifters down and out—a young man, a young woman and a child that they have picked up as a mascot. They are living on the wharves and mud scows, close to the slime that a big steam dredge keeps digging out of the harbor bottom.

The big clamshell shovel, moving, closing, opening, is an incessant figure or symbol in the movement of the first two-thirds of the play. It is ruthless, ironic, necessary, hard to get away from. Finally, the three vags do get away—only to face a worse fate than any that threatened in the harbor life.

Proffers and deductions loom before the girl. The boy is a coward, who seems in his weak way to be pushing the girl farther toward misery. Then he wakes up. Lights glimmer in him. Events offer him a chance to fight. And after the fight he is a changed young man.

In photography, in lighting effects, in employment of cheap, everyday materials for surprising and massive scenes, the picture is masterly. We doubt whether sunshine and grass have ever been used more effectively than in these closing scenes, while the moving steam shovel seems to speak with some vast, primitive vocabulary.

In the handling of the tempted drifting girl, a rarely fine series of character portrait is done. One goes away haunted by a dark, elusive struggler.

Whether the picture is destined for a popular success is not known as yet. But that it is an achievement sure to influence motion picture art is a certainty. It lists among the dozen or so of daring accomplishments that have marked headway in motion picture art.

March

Too Many Kisses

Too Many Kisses *is best remembered for the one actor in the cast Sandburg doesn't mention in his review—Harpo Marx. Marx played a childlike character listed in screen credits as "The Village Peter Pan." Appropriately, Marx, who remained a silent comic in the sound era, "spoke" the only line of his career through a subtitle in* Too Many Kisses. *Another co-star, William Powell, went on to become detective Nick Charles in* The Thin Man *film series.*

Friday, March 6, 1925

We do not happen to know who is the hardest working actor in the movies, but it seems to us that probably none of them punches the time clock and reports for duty more regularly and more often than Richard Dix.

All we can say with any certainty is that the McVicker's Theater electric sign has spelled out the name of Richard Dix more often than any other player showing on the screen of that house during the last year.

With him life is one photoplay after another. He has no time in his own life for adventures; what adventuring he does is all on the screen; what he learns about life is learned while knocking around close to a cameraman and a director calling out "Camera."

However, this should not be disappointing to those who enjoy Mr. Dix's work. They may rest happy in the fact that his latest picture, showing at McVicker's, is among the best in which he has appeared. We cannot think of one in which he shows to more advantage.

Too Many Kisses is the title of this one, the implication being that Dix might either be getting kissed too much and too often himself or bestowing too many kisses on

From the collection of Arnie Bernstein.

In his review of *Too Many Kisses*, Sandburg wonders if Richard Dix, a handsome and popular leading man of the 1920s, is either getting or bestowing too many on-screen kisses.

others.

By following the story as told on the screen we are able to find out who it is that is getting too many kisses and why.

In how many lives are there too many kisses?

That was the pointed question the makers of this movie asked as they got ready to name it.

They decided there are few lives across whose years are the imprints of too many kisses.

So they put it on the announcements, the programs, the electric signs: *Too Many Kisses*.

The father of the hero says the latter is getting too many; he is sent to Basque, a province in France, "where no girl dares marry a stranger." There a winsome Spanish girl, played by Frances Howard, is lavish with kisses. The American fights a Basque military officer and wins his woman.

Frank Currier, Albert Tavernier, William Powell, Paul Panzer, Arthur Ludwig and Joe Burke are in the cast. Paul Sloane directed.

Capital Punishment

The turgid melodrama Capital Punishment *was made by producer B. P. Schulberg to cash in on a controversial newspaper crusade against the death penalty. The film was critically bashed, though it did well at the box office.[9] Sandburg's review of the film is clearly a reflection of his stance on capital punishment.*

Monday, March 23, 1925

Capital Punishment, the picture having its first showing at the Castle Theater this week, is one that will surprise those who go to it expecting to see mainly a propaganda film.

While it is a photoplay with a viewpoint it is also very strictly a photoplay with characters and a story.

And the viewpoint isn't concerned with capital punishment, actually so much as with circumstantial evidence and how tricky it can be.

Clara Bow and George Hackathorne work out a love story full of surprises.

And Margaret Livingston is well staged in pieces of action worth seeing; her work is quiet but it is pantomimic art of value.

The opening reel of *Capital Punishment* is a little overdone. A boy who is sentenced to the electric chair goes there and stays there, while the governor of the state fails to make telephonic connections with the man who switches the electric current on.

A wealthy young sociologist is impressed with what has happened and bets his friend Phillips $10,000 that within three weeks he can get an innocent man convicted of murder. The bet is taken by Phillips, who agrees to hide out while his supposed murder is accomplished.

Dan O'Connor, formerly a thief but now going straight, is offered $10,000 to be the supposed murderer. After his conviction on circumstantial evidence the supposed murdered man is to be brought forth well and alive.

This plan seems to be working well. Dan O'Connor is convicted and is the cheerfullest prisoner the warden ever had in the murderers' row of cells.

Then a few things happen and the original plan is knocked galley west. The picture is handled in a masterly way to show the trickiness of circumstantial evidence. The scenario by John Goodrich and particularly the direction by James P. Hogan have produced a film much out of the ordinary.

April

Romola

Romola was shot on location in Florence, Italy. " . . . I never thought the drama matched the splendor of its fifteenth-century backgrounds," star Lillian Gish later said.[10]

Tuesday, April 7, 1925

Again April is here—and Lillian Gish.

They go well together.

A haunting little girl, with fleeting hints of an impossible happiness in the smiles that quiver across her face; a tremulous figure of all youth and every spring is Lillian Gish.

She is all that Tennyson tried to say in "Tears, Idle Tears; Tears, Happy Tears," etc., and something more. She is romance, sentiment, fugitive charm, yet she is alive. She is the statue every sculptor has tried to make of springtime, yet she is quivering with nerves, with fluttering fingers, with eyelash love.

Lillian Gish is Lillian Gish all the more since she lifts each heroine she plays into something "other-worldly." Losing herself in girl after girl of the fictitious screen, she has risen surely to first place among the emotional actresses of the world.

Seeing her in *Romola*, you forget that her sister Dorothy, who is with her, is very humorous and quite desirable; you ignore Ronald Colman and his male fascinations; you may even forget the smashing sea fights, the surging mobs around Savonarola, the beauty of the DeMedici palaces; you are seeing Lillian Gish, child of this world and some other world, too. She has the quality of light in paintings, the sense that rises mysteriously out of words arranged by poets, the mood of music.

To be blunt: Lillian Gish is *Romola*.

Henry King is one of the best directors. He spent $1.5 million of American money in Italy on the picture of George Eliot's novel. He assembled an expensive cast. He introduces probably the loveliest photography yet made. He lavishes on you settings, mobs, backgrounds of historic buildings, battles on the Mediterranean; he delves into the cutthroat intrigues of Florence in its wickedest day, but it all comes to very little in your memory because of Lillian Gish.

Her piteous, captive bird struggles, her whispering lips, her shrieks that you seem actually to hear are what you will get from *Romola*.

The Roosevelt Theater is showing her more than *Romola*.

Seven Chances

Based on a musty comic stage play, Seven Chances *was remade in 1999 as* The Bachelor, *starring Chris O'Donnell. This film's best known sequence, with Keaton running downhill in the midst of an avalanche, was added after* Seven Chances *was completed. Keaton noticed audiences were laughing at a scene where his character, pursued by a throng of scorned women, had to dodge three medium-sized rocks rolling downhill after him. Realizing there was bigger comedy to be had, Keaton re-shot the scene using 1,500 rocks ranging from bowling ball size to enormous boulders.[11] The new scene worked and remains a classic in the Keaton oeuvre.*

Thursday, April 16, 1925

Buster Keaton steps out this week at McVicker's Theater in a film that runs seven reels in length and is the most pretentious offering he has made in the movies.

We have often heard audiences laugh at the productions of this frozen-faced comedian, but in the case of this one the laughter is noisier and more booming.

T. Roy Barnes, Snitz Edwards and Ruth Dwyer are seen in worthy support.

The story is not so new, but they have certainly put new wrinkles, ruffles and curly queues on an old-timer.

It is a case where two young businessmen are hard up for cash to meet outstanding obligations, they must have money or go to the wall.

Along comes a lawyer reading them a will and one of them falls heir to $7 million—provided he shall marry before seven o'clock on the evening of his 27th birthday—that very day, in fact.

Naturally he goes to the Mary Jones with whom he has been keeping company, but, being bashful, to whom he has never proposed.

He tells her in his stumbling way he wants her to marry him that day because some girl must marry him or he will lose $7 million.

She tells him to take his hat and go and she hopes she will never see him again.

It is published in the papers that he must have a bride by seven o'clock or lose the $7 million.

Thousands of prospective brides move to find him, traveling by any and all ways of travel.

And, as expected, not until the final flickers of the final reel do we learn who it is that he actually does marry and whether she is the kind of bride he wished for.

The direction of the picture was mostly by Buster Keaton himself.

Several new sprightly stunts in motion picture narrative are introduced.

It is a Metro-Goldwyn production.

From the collection of Arnie Bernstein.

A contractual "morals clause" in her studio contract forced Gloria Swanson to create a phony cover story about her health.

GLORIA SWANSON

Madame Sans-Gêne

Rarely did Sandburg write about off-screen gossip, but in the case of Gloria Swanson and Madame Sans-Gêne *the temptation was apparently too much. During the course of filming on location in France, Swanson met the man who shortly became the 26-year-old star's third husband, the Marquis Le Bailly de la Falaise de la Coudraye. Their marriage was the talk of movie fans everywhere. Though Sandburg also makes a reference to Swanson's much-publicized appendicitis attack during the production of* Madame Sans-Gêne, *years later Swanson admitted the truth behind this incident. Her divorce from second husband Herbert K. Somborn was not yet completed; however, Swanson had become pregnant by her new paramour. This represented a violation of the morals clause of her studio contract. In an era when the lives of movie stars were routinely scrutinized and destroyed by studio chiefs, tabloid reporters, and the Hays Office, Swanson had little choice. Having a child by another man before her divorce was final would have ended Swanson's career. Though her "illness" was publicized as an appendix removal, Swanson really underwent a secret abortion arranged by French film critic André Daven.[12] Complications ensued, nearly killing the glamorous star. Swanson, already the mother of a daughter and an adopted son, never forgave the Hollywood powers-that-be for forcing her into this situation over their hypocritical "morals clause."*

Wednesday, April 28, 1925

We have often seen Gloria Swanson in psychological pictures where she went through emotions and feelings registering like Cecil De Mille wanted her to.

But now since Cecil De Mille got off the Famous Players lot and made motion pictures like he was going to start his own film corporation and he may yet—

Now we have a chance to see Gloria in history.

And French history at that.

The woman whose character she plays is a woman who says "Me and Napoleon" and it goes.

For Napoleon kisses her hand—and more than respects her.

She is Madame Sans-Gêne, which the French translators for Balaban & Katz tell us is a name that means Madame Devil May Care.

Three queens, one of whom had her careless head cut off, slept in the bedroom used in one of the scenes.

Napoleon used to have his shirts washed by Madame Sans Gêne; she was running a laundry; he didn't pay his bills; but she liked him; so it was all right; more than that she stole a shirt occasionally from customers who had plenty of shirts and passed one on to Napoleon; this because Napoleon was then only a poor lieutenant ready to throw himself into the river.

Then he goes up the ladder of fame, and so does she.

They make a nice story out of it; we might call it a whimsical, entertaining story, whether we believe it or not.

Only the hardhearted would refuse Napoleon having a laundry lady who washed his shirts without pay and even sneaked him an extra shirt.

Yes, they made this picture over in Paris and round about Paris where the scenery is.

Who ever heard of America having a bedroom where three queens slept and one of the queens later had her head cut off?

We have a World's Fair run by women, but no bedroom where three queens have slept.

While she was making this picture Gloria met the marquis of which the world has heard.

While she was making this picture she went to a hospital with appendicitis and thousands of newsboys selling late extras called "Gloria Swanson goes on the table."

If these are not good and sufficient reasons for going to see the latest release at the Roosevelt Theater, what would be an argument?

May

Riders of the Purple Sage

Perhaps Zane Grey's best-known novel, Riders of the Purple Sage *was previously made in 1918. Remakes followed in 1931 and 1941, with a made-for-television version broadcast in 1996. Tom Mix's 1925 version, however, is still considered the best rendition of this Western classic. Mix followed this up a few months later with Grey's sequel* The Rainbow Trail.

Monday, May 4, 1925

We have noticed before this that when Tom Mix comes out in a picture with a story from a Zane Grey novel we don't care for it as much as some others in which Mix plays.

But we notice that William J. Fox and Tom Mix are agreed that the Zane Grey novels are good things for Tom Mix to ride and shoot in on the screen.

And there seems to be no doubt that Zane Grey stories with Tom Mix in the part of the hero have a steady and regular audience that will go to see such a production.

The latest one, *Riders of the Purple Sage*, has Mix playing the hero who drops his real name of Carson and adopts that of Lassiter while he roams the cattle country searching for the dastards who kidnapped his sister and her child.

He has many and various adventures while seeking justice in a world that has handed him so much injustice to start with.

Tom Mix is one of the few men on the screen who can outguess and outwit a gang of outlaws and take them unawares one by one and put them out of the running—and make it half believable.

The Mixian stuff is mixed here as cleverly and persuasively as usual.

He is the one screen actor, who in almost superhuman stunts, in the quality of the mar-vel-ous, is up to the mark of the old timer, Nick Carter.

Mabel Ballin, Warner Oland, Beatrice Burnham, Harold Goodwin, Marian Nixon and Wilfred Lucas are members of the cast. Lynn Reynolds directed.

And we repeat that we would rather see Tom Mix in a Zane Grey novel than to read one.

We believe Tom Mix knows more about the desert, the plains and mountains, the horses and people of the West.

He was born and raised "out thar" while Zane Grey was still studying dentistry and filling cavities in Philadelphia.

The Last Laugh

Considered a cinematic masterpiece, The Last Laugh *is also one of the few silent movies to forego subtitles. The film's only title card comes after the story's tragic conclusion. Intending to parody the "happy ending" prerequisites of Hollywood filmmaking, German director F. W. Murnau had the ultimate creative "last laugh." After the character played by Emil Jannings has been emotionally destroyed, the audience is told that his creator has taken pity on him. The former hotel doorman, reduced to washroom attendant, comes into a huge sum of money. He goes on a wild spending spree, a giddy reverse of the character's previous dire end.*

Tuesday, May 5, 1925

The Last Laugh has arrived and is showing. No picture of the last year seemed to have so many people so interested that they wrote letters asking us, "Is *The Last Laugh* coming or has it been and gone?"

Several original and independent art features connect with this picture, which is having its first run at the Orpheum Theater.

It is a piece of realistic story telling, that is, the people of it cut through and take hold of us like real life, though the action that in real life may take years is here compressed into a swift hour.

In front of a modern skyscraper hotel in Berlin stands the doorman; he calls the taxis and escorts guests in and out.

He is the "front" of the hotel; he wears a long proud coat with shiny big buttons on it.

The coat has become part of him; when the hotel manager notices he is too old and weak to handle the big trunks easily he is shifted to a basement job in charge of the towels and wash bowls of the lavatory.

This happens just as he is due to attend the wedding of his daughter in the tenement where everybody has regarded him as a sort of grandissimo because of his big coat with shiny buttons, which he always wore to his home.

He steals the coat; he has a gay time at the wedding.

But it is found out on him that his job is gone and the coat no longer belongs to him.

The bitterness of the downfall, as told on the screen, touches real life.

Then comes a surprise. A subtitle tells us that in life the story would so end, with the old man a sorry loser in life.

But for purposes of movie drama there is an afterpiece.

And that afterpiece is good; as epilogues go this is a hummer; the audiences enjoy it with chuckles.

Emil Jannings, who played Nero in the *Quo Vadis* picture, is the leading player in this; it was in *The Last Laugh* that he struck reputation.

Monday, June 30, 1925

It is a pleasant commentary that *The Last Laugh*, which had recently a two-week run at the Orpheum Theater, is considered good enough for a further trial on State Street and is running this week at the Randolph Theater.

Those who wish to see a photoplay winning more complete endorsement, perhaps, than any of the past year, for intelligent story, characterization, atmosphere and cinema art, should go to see *The Last Laugh*.

Robert E. Sherwood, the picture play critic of *Life*, told his readers this was one of the best that had ever come along, and his advice was they should go see it.

Some of them went.

And then came such a fusillade of letters reprimanding and abusing Sherwood that he felt called on to write the longest piece he ever wrote for his magazine.

He explained that he had nothing to take back; it is one of the best photoplays ever made; such was his judgment, he recorded that judgment; along with that he had to record his advice that it was worth seeing.

Therefore, if you wish to see a picture play that has kicked up considerable controversy, by all means go and have a cry and a laugh at *The Last Laugh*.

Here is an old man who is the doorman and the taxi starter at a big hotel in Berlin.

And the house manager sees that the old man is too far-gone to handle trunks the way he used to.

His big uniform coat is taken away, the grand coat with the shining buttons, and he is sent to the basement lavatory where he hands guests towels and soap.

When his daughter is to be married at a fine wedding, he steals the coat and makes merry at the wedding.

But it is found out amid the tenements that he is bluffing his way; the coat no longer belongs to him; tragedy as stark as that of "King Lear" follows.

There perhaps, for fidelity to fact of life, the story should end; it is so acknowledged on the screen; but for entertainment there must be an afterpiece.

And at this afterpiece everyone laughs, even those who till then have regarded the piece as too terribly honest and rigorous to put into photodrama.

The Lost World

Years before Steven Spielberg sent computer-generated dinosaurs running amuck in Jurassic Park *(1993) and its sequel* The Lost World: Jurassic Park *(1997), there was* The Lost World. *Based on a science fiction novel by the author of* Sherlock Holmes, The Lost World *thrilled audiences with dinosaur battles and a brontosaurus loose in the streets of London. The movie's dinosaurs were actually rubber models stretched over wooden skeletons, then shot one frame at a time by animator Willis H. O'Brien. Cast members were filmed separately and this footage was combined with the miniature effects. O'Brien later perfected his stop-motion dinosaur techniques in the masterful* King Kong *(1933).*[13]

Monday, May 25, 1925

The Lost World, which is having its first run at the Roosevelt Theater, is a good specimen of the picture that takes its own independent path and makes film history.

Not often do we have a photoplay that is intelligent and exciting, that gives us science and wraps it up in a package of adventure and love.

Out of Conan Doyle's fantastic novel they have created a screen story that runs from a London newspaper office to a plateau in the wilds of the Amazon River and back to London.

Wallace Beery has the best role we have ever seen him in. He is the professor who came back from a South American trip with a story about immense animals of the prehistoric period roaming a certain plateau.

Newspapers and scholars give him the laugh.

An expedition is organized to go and find and explore the region.

Bessie Love plays the role of a daughter of a scientist believed to have lost his life in the region, Glenn Hughes has the part of a newspaper correspondent.

The pterodactyl and the brontosaurus don't sound like much when mentioned as scientific labels for animals of 10 million years gone by.

The still pictures of them in books, the replicas of their forms in museums leave a good deal for the imagination.

But in this movie we see these immense creatures of former times walk and eat and creep and fly and fight so that we really believe there must have been such animals.

Many a child seeing the life portrayed here will have a good deal of the same feeling as on reading of *Robinson Crusoe* or *The Swiss Family Robinson.*

It has some of that identical loneliness and wonder.

We very positively recommend *The Lost World* as among the greatly conceived and greatly worked out motion pictures.

The reels run along an hour and 40 minutes—and it's worth the time.

Saturday, May 30, 1925

The most haunting photoplay production we have seen in a blue moon is this one called *The Lost World.*

Haunting is correct.

The blunt and lovable scientist who comes back to England with a yarn nobody believes about dinosaurs and other colossal prehistoric monsters located in a South American region—he is haunting.

The plateau where the expedition halts and finds these monsters on a high spot disconnected from the rest of the South American continent, the massive brontosaurus, more than 100 feet long, and the fight of this monster with another one—this, too, haunts.

Then the return to London with a captive monster, who falls out of the steel cage in which he has been imprisoned, and who then roams the streets of the capital of the British civilization, toppling over the walls of buildings, sweeping men to death with movements of his tail and dropping through Westminster Bridge into the river—these are scenes that make a curious imprint on the memory, so that they keep coming back afterward.

We have noticed this among young people and grown-ups.

We have heard boys on the street talking about dinosaurs since this picture came.

The Lost World holds us a good deal as Robinson Crusoe.

It is for old and young and a fine specimen of what may be achieved in motion pictures when intelligence, imagination and feeling work together.

Saturday, June 6, 1925

A peculiar picture from several points of view is *The Lost World*, the talk and the sensation of current movies.

While it is a scientific picture in the sense that it shows animals and birds of millions of years ago, animals of species that have disappeared, it is not a strictly scientific presentation because the animals seem to be alive.

They are strange, creepy, terrible animals—the brontosaurus, more than a hundred feet long with a body as bulky as a herd of elephants and a neck as slim and fancy as a giraffe—and the pterodactyl, a bird built so queer that we might think at first it was a new passenger air flivver with camouflage stuck on.

And these animals move, walk, breathe, fight, open their mouths and blink their eyes and wiggle their toes—so cunningly constructed that their movements constantly persuade us they are alive.

They have been reproduced from the bones and fossils of creatures partially reconstructed by scientists, who drew the designs of these animals on the basis of calculations that such animals must have lived on the earth 10 million years ago—or 12 million years ago—what's a million or two in a case like this?

Yet this picture, *The Lost World*, is not so antediluvian and sesquipedalian that it is merely for scholars and those who want to learn science.

It interests the sport page readers because it stages a series of fights and hunts, spectacular conflicts of many sorts.

And it interests those who wish a love story in every movie; this is taken care of.

And one has a mixed feeling of the comic and tragic when the huge brontosaurus escapes from its cage in London, terrorizes the streets of that city, sending crowds of people in frantic flight, wandering into a museum and contemplating the skeleton of one of its ancestors, wandering farther and with its huge weight dropping through

Westminster Bridge into the Thames River. As a novel movie and as something else, *The Lost World* is to be recommended.

June

The Naked Truth

Equal parts education and exploitation, "sex hygiene" films were a cottage industry in the silent era. With titles like Damaged Goods, Whatsoever a Man Soweth, *and* End of the Road, *these films warned audiences about the dangers of venereal diseases that came through "immoral" actions. Yet part of the allure of these films was prurient content, plain and simple. Considering the histrionics and melodrama inherent to the genre, it's no surprise Sandburg looked at films like* The Naked Truth *with a jaundiced eye. Note the sly puns worked into this review!*

Wednesday, June 24, 1925

Speaking of *The Naked Truth*, which is showing at the LaSalle Theater with a posted warning, "Positively adults only admitted over 21 years, by order of Circuit Court," we would say that it sort of straddles its legs into two categories.

On one hand it is an attempt at a scientific presentation of the stern truth that a young man should be taught as a boy to stay away from environments and circumstances in which he is liable to become infected with the germs of what are politely called "social diseases."

And, on the other hand, it is an attempt at the presentation of a melodramatic photoplay showing a set of characters, some of whom tread what is called the straight and narrow way, thereby not acquiring the "social diseases," while others who "take a chance" become the victims of terrible afflictions and enter the care of physicians.

Helene Chadwick and Jack Mulhall, capable and well-known professional screen stars, play the roles of the hero and heroine.

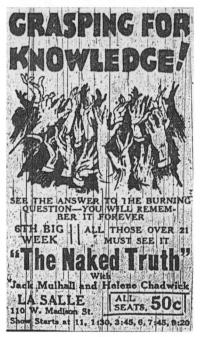

A *Chicago Daily News* ad for *The Naked Truth* promises " . . . the answer to the burning question—you will remember it forever" (Thursday, July 30, 1925).

HELENE CHADWICK
Starring in Goldwyn Pictures

*From the collection of
Arnie Bernstein.*

Helene Chadwick,
the female lead in the
silent exploitation film
The Naked Truth.

As a scientific presentation to grown-up folk of the best methods by which to educate the growing child on the veils and pitfalls of the future sex life, this may or may not be just the way to do it.

A psychologist of keen intuition and sympathy, having had wide experience in the handling of children with particular reference to sex knowledge, would be the most competent critic to pass judgment on *The Naked Truth.*

In a jury of such educational psychologists of experience some of the experts might say it was nowhere near the whole truth and what there is of it isn't anywhere near naked.

As to the photoplay end of it, the pantomimic art of the cinema, we would say we have seen worse pictures, but it was in the earlier days.

As a presentation of "the mysteries of life" it does not have competency and skill that attached to a somewhat similar picture which had its local run two years ago.

July

White Fang

Jack London's tale of canine heroism has been a periodic subject of the movies for many years. Other versions of White Fang *were made in 1936, 1946, 1972, and 1991.*

Tuesday, July 7, 1925

Jack London's dog story, *White Fang*, which was the sequel to his other dog story, *The Call of the Wild*, stands out as a film drama of better than ordinary merit in the picture *White Fang*, with the dog Strongheart in the leading role.

So curious and fleeting a thing is fame that we might almost assume that there are more people who know Strongheart than there are who have heard of Jack London.

To repeat a point we have made previous with reference to the movies, there are millions of people who don't have the book reading habit who for any reason wouldn't care to read the book about White Fang, but who would enjoy keenly the photoplay now showing.

The expressiveness of a dog's face, head and paws in registering what seem to us to be deep emotions on the part of the dog is brought to the front in this film.

Among the high spots is one where the master is leaving the dog and the dog languishes, refuses to eat, looks from the corners of his eyes.

This reaches out with dramatic power, more effectively than most of the human film players.

A good dog at his best is a better pantomimist than the best human players at what is not quite their human best.

Another high spot is where the dog falls on a man, a wrongdoer and kills him.

A rather sudden and wild job of killing it is, and not overdone.

And, as in previous Strongheart pictures, he has a mate and the fadeout shows him and her making signals to each other with their ears.

Theodore von Eltz, Ruth Dwyer and Matthew Betz are among the players supporting Strongheart.

It is a Film Booking Office picture, which was directed by Laurence Trimble and Jane Murfin.

Sally of the Sawdust

Burdened by financial considerations, D. W. Griffith reluctantly left the world of independent production and returned to the studio system for work. After signing up with Paramount, Griffith was assigned to direct the screen version of "Poppy," a popular Broadway show starring comedian W. C. Fields. Retitled Sally of the Sawdust, *the Griffith-Fields pairing seemed an unlikely film combination. Griffith, rooted in Victorian mores, didn't understand the biting humor that Fields built his reputation on. Paramount apparently didn't understand Fields either; they reworked the story to highlight the charms of Carol Dempster over the antics of the star comic. Yet Fields held Griffith in high esteem. "I consider Griffith one of the finest men I ever knew," he told an interviewer. "He is marvelous to work for, most inspiring and encouraging."[14] Fields and Griffith teamed up once more with* That Royle Girl. *In 1936 Fields remade* Sally of the Sawdust *under the production's original name,* Poppy.

Tuesday, July 21, 1925

The new Griffith picture at the Roosevelt Theater, *Sally of the Sawdust*, stands in a class by itself, so far as Griffith himself is concerned.

For years this important originator in photoplay art has been an independent operator, going on his own.

But being artist and manager both was too much work and worry, and he has begun work on a salary for the Famous Players-Lasky corporation.

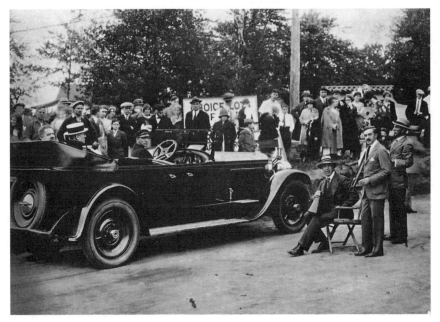

From the collection of Arnie Bernstein.

D. W. Griffith (*seated with megaphone*) directs W. C. Fields
(*back seat of car, far left*) in *Sally of the Sawdust.*

And while making *Sally of the Sawdust*, he remarked something like: "This is the first picture I have made in 10 years where I didn't have a megaphone in one hand and a mortgage in the other."

Well, this Sally picture is good, standing away up among the best of the year.

And some will say it is the best Griffith has done since he made *Broken Blossoms.*

Carol Dempster plays Sally, and this is the most insinuating and implicative work the silversheet has seen of her lithe, swift, straightaway art.

If your heart enjoys that twist of the byway of life where tears and laughter come close to mixing, where pain turns with jokes at itself, and the terms of tragedy and comedy get lost like sunshine and rain during a sunshower, then take a look at Miss Dempster playing Sally, unaccountably merging monkeyshines and majesty.

Sometimes it is an elusive personality and sometimes a deliberate accomplished art of pantomime that stands forth in Miss Dempster's portrayal of Sally, so that she creates great moments—one has to pause and consider whether any recent cinema playing compares with hers.

W. C. Fields as Prof. Eustace McGargle, spieler, faker and three-card man, is also a new development.

In some of the scenes we note that Griffith still keeps his hand; he has superb qualities and maintains his leadership among the entertainers, who achieve something more than entertainment.

Besides circus and carnival people, there are highly respectable persons presented as the story goes.

Besides bootleggers and peanut vendors and acrobats, there are detectives and hypocrites, the goulash of civilization.

Alfred Lunt and Effie Shannon have roles, also Erville Anderson and Glenn Anders, also Charles Hammond and Roy Appleseed.

We recommend *Sally of the Sawdust* as entertainment, a blend of misery and monkeyshines and majesty.

The Lost Battalion

Originally released in 1919, The Lost Battalion *used actual participants of the 77th Division to recreate their World War I exploits in the Argonne Forest, where they held out for six days before relief arrived. The heroic carrier pigeon, Cher Ami, was later awarded a Distinguished Service Cross.*

Wednesday, July 22, 1925

The Lost Battalion, having its first run at the Monroe Theater, is a picture dealing with a part of the 77th division in No Man's Land during the recent Great War.

These made their advance during an offensive in which they lost touch with the French troops on one side and their own division on the other flank.

And they were caught and surrounded in a "pocket."

Without food or water, but with plenty of ammunition, they held off the enemy while they tried to signal airplanes.

Their carrier pigeons were picked off by enemy rifles till at last one flyer, "Cher Ami," got through, losing an eye and a leg.

And they sent out 37 couriers, each of whom failed to get through.

But the 38th man made it—and help arrived—and again there was food and water.

The scenes and actions of the pocketed doughboys are enacted on the film by the same men and officers who were in the actual turmoil in France.

It is a story of adventure, daring, suffering, endurance and heroism—and as such is a photoplay superior to many built entirely of fiction.

Comedian in the Griffith Picture at Roosevelt

Wednesday, July 22, 1925

And now comes the much-ridiculed "brown derby" into its own!

Charlie Chaplin immortalized the black derby; Harry Langdon the flat and funny "lid"; Raymond Griffith the high silk hat; Lloyd Hamilton the checkered cap.

W. C. Fields—who springs to screen comedian fame in D. W. Griffith's *Sally of the Sawdust* at the Roosevelt Theater—has begun to make the "brown derby" famous. Fields has been making the multitude roar for years as chief comic of Ziegfeld "Follies." Now, the camera has caught him and his first big picture proves that his comedy can be put across on the screen even more uproariously than on the stage. His antics with the "brown derby" create laugh after laugh. As the circus juggler, sideshow barker, cardsharper, shell game manipulator, Fields wears the brown derby naturally. His only other means of comedy are a cane (ala Chaplin) and a cigar stump. Undoubtedly Fields had much to do in helping D. W. Griffith make *Sally of the Sawdust* the laugh hit that it is.

The Adventurous Sex

Saturday, July 25, 1925

The Adventurous Sex, showing at neighborhood theaters, might be designated as a novel told on the screen.

It is a narrative of what is sometimes called "the jazz age" and its young people "the children of the jazz age."

A daughter insists she is going to live her life in her own way and rebels against her domineering father.

A grandmother steps in to plead for daughter and to urge that if the home life were of a different order the daughter would be different.

And there is a mother who is somewhat neutral, at a halfway point between the father and the grandmother.

A fast set of tobasco slingers lead the girl on till one night in a semi-nude costume she puts on the gloves and partakes in a pugilistic encounter with another girl.

There arrives at the party in time to witness the contest of the leather pushers the young man to whom she is engaged.

He says he is shocked at what she is wearing and such a costume will not be permitted her in public after they are married.

She retorts she is glad to find out so early that he intends to be a tyrant rather than a husband, so she hands him the engagement ring.

At a later time when she is the victim of a conspiracy and on the face of the evidence seems to have registered at a roadhouse of ill reputation, she finds her former fiancé just the kind of gentleman she would like to have him be.

Clara Bow and Herbert Rawlinson have the leading parts, with able support from Harry T. Morey and Earle Williams.

The continuity by Carl Stearns Claney was from a story by Hamilton Mannon.

It is a Howard Estabrook production.

August

The Street of Forgotten Men

Paul Ash, mentioned in the last paragraph of this review, was a hyperkinetic bandleader who headlined at McVicker's Theater. A typical program at McVicker's would include a comedy short, newsreel, feature film, and Paul Ash's musical antics. Ash's revues, tagged with such Jazz Age names as "Kickin' Kilties" and "Struttin' th' Charleston," were a hit with 1920s movie audiences.

Saturday, August 1, 1925

The blind men with their cups and the cripples with their stumps at the street corners will not like to hear about *The Street of Forgotten Men*.

Beggars stand to lose millions of dollars.

For the picture assumes to take us behind the scenes and show us how street beggars live and work and fake.

Easy Money Charlie is the main character; his left arm is strapped to side; a stump of an arm is fastened from the shoulder; he crooks his back and wins pity, nickels and dimes and quarters.

Percy Marmont plays this role.

He takes care of a girl, who sees him in good clothes, frock coat and silk hat, knowing nothing of his street tricks.

She grows up and the time comes when he either has to leave or she will be the loser.

A fight between a beggar who can see though wearing the sign "I am blind," and a supposedly crippled beggar is the high spot of the picture.

Mary Brian plays the ward of the beggar magnate and Neil Hamilton the young man who wishes to marry her.

The story is an adaptation of a magazine tale by George Kibbe Turner.

Herbert Brenon directed this Paramount picture, which is showing at McVicker's Theater, where it may be the photoplay or it may be the west coast demon, Paul Ash, who is responsible for audiences filling all seats to the top row of the top balcony.

The Ten Commandments

In this atypical review, Sandburg concentrated on budget rather than content. Cecil B. DeMille's epic, originally released in 1923, was a two-part film; the first section dealt with Moses leading the children of Israel out of Egypt, while the second half was a modern tale of sin and redemption. The Ten Commandants *is notable as one of the first films to make artistic use of the new Technicolor photography process. DeMille remade* The Ten Commandments *in 1956, and Sandburg cared little for that version as well. In a letter to a friend, Sandburg stated: "An Associated Press story of some ten days ago quoted me correctly as saying that Ben-Hur is 'A monument of tripe' which could also go for* The Ten Commandments *wrought by Cecil B. DeMille."[15]*

Tuesday, August 4, 1925

While *The Ten Commandments* is showing this week at the Castle and Senate Theaters, it might perhaps be well to take note that this is one of the few pictures that actually ran up and over $1 million in cost.

It is well conceded that by the time the Israelites had crossed the Red Sea and the Egyptians in pursuit were flooded over and destroyed and annihilated and obliterated, the picture was well started on its $1 million expense account.

And there was yet the big fake concrete skyscraper to erect, besides all the time parties, dinners, and clothes, gowns, garbs and apparelings of the sort Cecil De Mille finds necessary for a picture.

In this connection, that of the $1 million cast, we were told by one whom we consider an authority, "When it was finished, *The Ten Commandments* would have to gross over $8 million at the box office in order to pay for its first cost of $1.2 million."

And it was partly in connection with the failure of the picture to approximate this $8 million that Cecil De Mille became involved in differences of opinion at the Famous Players-Lasky headquarters where he had the title of "director general."

And where Cecil De Mille used to be the accredited high man of the directors of Famous Players-Lasky, he is now on the outside of that organization and for six months has been at the head of various producing units from whom month by month pictures have been expected but have not been forthcoming at the offices of the Producers' Distributing corporation.

The Ten Commandments is a strange production from many angles.

It is Cecil De Mille's Masterpiece; he put into it everything he knew about showmanship and what is called hokum; the old homestead and the religious mother with one boy who is good and slow and another boy who is bad and fast; she reads the Bible to them and the panorama of the Red Sea is unfolded; then comes the action wherein the good boy who is slow triumphs over the bad boy who is fast.

We were interested to hear the comment of a member of the general board of the Presbyterian church who teaches the largest Sunday school class in the city of St. Paul. He said, "When I saw the first of this photoplay I said to myself I would like to show it to my Sunday school class. But when I saw the second half I said it wouldn't do."

Leatrice Joy, Rod La Roque and Nita Naldi got their starts to stardom in this picture.

Will Rogers makes the comment that while Jeanie MacPherson is credited with the scenario, the best part of it is from Exodus by a famous ancient author.

The Gold Rush

With his comedy epic The Gold Rush, *Charlie Chaplin set new standards for himself. The inspiration for* The Gold Rush *came to Chaplin while looking at stereoscopes of Alaskan vistas. "In the creation of comedy, it is paradoxical that tragedy stimulates the spirit of ridicule, because ridicule, I suppose, is an attitude of defiance: we must laugh in the face of our helplessness against the forces of nature—or go insane," he wrote in his autobiography.[16] Placing his familiar Tramp within the Alaskan gold rush of the 1890s, Chaplin developed a story filled with both pathos and comic brilliance. The famed scene in which Chaplin and co-star Mack Swain eat a shoe was inspired by tales of the Donner party. An edible piece of footwear was made out of licorice, which Chaplin and Swain dined on like a gourmet feast. Taking three days to shoot, the scene became an enduring image of silent film comedy. On the down side, high concentrations of licorice also work as a laxative, an after-effect that significantly hit both Chaplin and Swain.[17]*

Monday, August 17, 1925

The Gold Rush, the long-awaited Chaplin comedy which has been in the making for almost two years, opened yesterday at the Orpheum Theater, which has housed almost every one of Charlie's feature comedies. In speaking of *The Gold Rush,* Chaplin is quoted as saying: "I want to be remembered by this picture." He has also called it "a symbolic autobiography." But do not be deceived. Charlie Chaplin of the derby, cane, baggy trousers, funny mustache and waddling walk, who has made the whole world laugh more than any other mere comedian that ever lived, has built in *The Gold Rush* a structure of fun and laughter. On the tragedy and misery suffered by the pioneers who first journeyed to the icebound Alaska, and on the drama of the soul-sufferings of the sourdough, who braved mountains, ice, snow and starvation and death in their mad rush for gold, Chaplin has built what some say is the funniest and most hilarious comedy of his career. He has clad himself in the role of a hard-luck sourdough who chases rainbows of the soul and heart in the midst of a mob that chases only one thing, gold. Pathos and suffering are converted into comedy and laughter, there is a laugh in every one of the 8,000 or so feet of *The Gold Rush.*

Friday, August 21, 1925

To see Charlie Chaplin eat his Thanksgiving dinner of boiled "sole" is alone worth the price of admission to *The Gold Rush*, his latest and truthfully heralded "best" photoplay, having its premiere at the Orpheum Theater this week. Mr. Chaplin wrote the play, directed it, and has made it a literal scream by his own inimitable acting.

The Gold Rush deals with the adventures of a lone prospector (Charlie Chaplin) caught by the gold fever of 1898. He fares optimistically forth to conquer the north with the inevitable Chaplin hat and cane, plus a blanket. He is storm swept into the cabin of Black Larsen—desperado. Big Jim Mackay—who has just "staked" a mountain of gold, blows in too, and then the fun begins. It wouldn't be fair to give it all away here. There is, of course, a girl, and such fighting as always occurs in places where "men are men"; but when Charlie, the tramp, suddenly turns multimillionaire, Mr. Chaplin displays real artistry. A final hint—with winter coming on and all that—ambitious moneymakers can profit well by Charlie's lesson in snow shoveling.

Come again, Mr. Chaplin.

Tuesday, August 25, 1925

In *The Gold Rush*, our old college chum Charlie Chaplin has accomplished two things.

He makes use of his old time laugh-making stunts—with a swifter twist to them.

And then he has interwoven serious things not to be found at all in his old time films.

From some angles *The Gold Rush* is an epic in the sense that Frank Norris' novels *McTeague* and *The Octopus* were epic.

Just as a piece of story telling it is immense.

We can name, if required, a printer, a professor, a photographer, a lawyer and a newspaper man who have been to see the picture twice and have viewed it from start to finish three times.

Of all the pictures Chaplin has made this seems to have more of a pull on it to "come see me again" than any other he has made.

A New York friend tells us Charlie had a string of dinner engagements fixed up for him there; he fixed up one or two of them himself.

And then he didn't show up at a single dinner.

They knew, of course, that he wasn't hungry.

And they tried to figure out what happened.

As near as they could spell out the cabalistic signs of the mystic diagram, Charlie eats when he pleases—just as he makes pictures and hands them out to the great hungry public when he pleases.

He is an independent artist 40 ways.

If he arrives today on the Twentieth Century as scheduled he will be looked at a little more hitherto—on account of *The Gold Rush.*

Movies to Be Shown in Air

Thursday, August 27, 1925

America and England may have an unusual preview of *The Phantom of the Opera,* as well as at the openings here and abroad.

But it will be over most people's heads!

Carl Laemmle, president of the Universal Pictures corporation, has offered the Navy department the privilege of showing this spectacular production during the next flight of the dirigibles Shenandoah and Los Angeles. Should this offer be accepted it would mark a step forward in aviation as well as in motion pictures.

The Navy department and Universal realize that amusement will soon be essential during the sometimes monotonous travel between great distances, particularly at night. *The Phantom of the Opera* is Universal's greatest effort, and is a fitting subject to attain the distinction of being the first picture to be shown aboard these giant ships of the air.

Unusual preparations will be necessary for the showing, such as printing the motion picture on special film and other projecting details. Storage batteries would be used to run the machinery for the experiment. Later, when the ships have been equipped to show pictures, the power would be supplied by the ship's generators. Mr. Laemmle, in his offer to the Navy, feels confident that all problems can be overcome and is willing to attempt this to advance the cause of showing pictures in the air.

The Wizard of Oz

Long before Judy Garland went over the rainbow, The Wizard of Oz *was entertaining film fans. L. Frank Baum, the genius behind the original novel, scripted the first version, made at Chicago's Selig Polyscope studios in 1910. Baum later went to California, where he brought many of his Oz tales to screen. This version, probably the best-known after the 1939 MGM classic, featured director Larry Semon as the Scarecrow. Oliver Hardy, in a pre-Laurel and Hardy role, played the Tin Woodsman. Also notable was casting African-American actor Spencer Bell as the Cowardly Lion. Though treated in a stereotypical manner (he is referred to as "Snowball" in the subtitles!), putting a black actor in such a visible role alongside of white players was a genuine rarity for the 1920s. Dorothy Dwan, who played Dorothy, married Semon in October 1925.*

Friday, August 28, 1925

For quite a while Frank Baum's book *The Wizard of Oz*, later made into an excellent musical stage production, has lain untouched.

And nobody made a movie of it.

Then somebody around Larry Semon got the notion he could do it.

And we are told it is "knutty knock-out."

Which it isn't at all.

It is three ordinary or below-par two reelers wrapped up into a six-reeler which we are told to take as a regular feature picture.

If those who made this picture had lived with it and cared for it and cared about it as the group did who made *Peter Pan*, we might have had a glorious photoplay comparable to *Peter Pan*, but American in spirit whereas *Peter Pan* is British.

The Wizard of Oz, as produced, is not a fair match and a just equivalent on the screen for that odd and strange children's book Frank Baum wrote.

LARRY SEMON.

From the collection of Arnie Bernstein.

Comic Larry Semon co-wrote, starred in, and directed the 1925 version of *The Wizard of Oz.*

Co-starring with Larry Semon are Dorothy Dwan and Mary Carr, also Bryant Washburn and Joseph Swickard, also Charlie Murray and Oliver N. Hardy.

There were players in plenty.

But they didn't know what they were trying to do.

It is the only poor picture we have seen Larry Semon showing in.

September

The Merry Widow

After the fiasco of Greed, *Erich von Stroheim was assigned to turn Franz Lehár's operetta* The Merry Widow *into a silent movie. Though von Stroheim initially objected, he ended up taking the job. The resulting film was so long that once again studio chiefs were forced to cut von Stroheim's work. For European release, the film was distributed in two parts,* The Merry Widow *and* Honeymoon.

Monday, October 19, 1925

Erich von Stroheim has driven whole schools of picture producers crazy. The Austrian director with his expensive ideas of production, his insistence on making what he wants and how he wants it, irrespective of what the public wants, has been a costly experiment in Hollywood.

But in *The Merry Widow* he has made a picture that probably satisfies his producers, himself and the public. Certainly it is his first production to make vast sums of money. All across America today, *The Merry Widow* is making money roll in.

In it, as viewed this week at the Roosevelt Theater, von Stroheim has been as artistic as he pleased. His old mastery in situation is here again, but in continuity, where he was always weak, he is now strong.

Quite a personality, quite an independent artist, this von Stroheim. It is true he quarreled with Mae Murray, the star, all through the making of the picture, but Mae should thank her lucky stars for von Stroheim. He has stopped her disconcerning pouts and St. Vitus technique, tamed her down and taught her to take her time. The result is that Mae Murray is part of her picture now.

She makes a real personage out of the American chorus girl whose wedding to a European prince is prevented by stern kings and who, to get revenge, marries an aged and noble millionaire just in time to wear widow's weeds at his funeral and to spend his fortune in Parisian frivolities.

With John Gilbert as Prince Danilo, the hero, with Tully Marshall as the senile and crippled millionaire, with George Fawcett and Josephine Crowell as the king and queen, and with a newcomer, Roy D'Arcy, as the villainous crown prince, *The Merry Widow* has a cast of genuine distinction to support Miss Murray.

The waltz scene, the climax of *The Merry Widow* when it was Lehar's operetta, most famous of all musical comedies, is retained brilliantly, but *The Merry Widow* in films is infinitely stronger of story, richer of production, than when on the stage.

November

The Dark Angel

Known as "The Hungarian Rhapsody," Vilma Banky was a European film star who made her Hollywood debut with The Dark Angel. *She developed quite a reputation as a romantic lead in the late 1920s, then retired from the movies with the advent of sound.*

Thursday, November 12, 1925

The new movie star, the lady from Budapest, Miss Vilma Banky, is a screen performer of no mean parts, if we may so speak.

In *The Dark Angel*, where she plays the feminine opposite of Ronald Colman, who is now understood generally to outrank Rudolph Valentino, she is to be seen at the Chicago Theater in the first run of that photoplay this week.

The director, George Fitzmaurice, should be credited with achieving a certain well-lighted lyric quality in the opening scenes of this picture.

There is love making with an element of restraint and understanding not common to the movies as made these days.

The story is about Kitty Vane and Capt. Alan Trent, she being the daughter of Sir Robert Vane and he being an officer whose leave of absence is cancelled.

So they don't marry, it is too late for a license.

But they have six memorable hours before he must go.

A fortuneteller who reads fate in a crystal ball sees the captain killed, as a dark angel wings upward.

And three candles fall from the hands of Kitty Vane and she is in darkness and a dark angel moves by her—at the moment the captain falls on the battle line.

The war ends, and Capt. Gerald Shannon, played by Wyndham Standing, marries Kitty Vane, though she can never be wholly his.

What then?

Capt. Alan Trent is found to be alive, he didn't die in the war.

And of course, to pursue this plot further here would not be fair to those who are to see the picture.

But they have worked it out very nicely, a smooth piece of storytelling.

As we said before George Fitzmaurice should be credited for touches of lyric quality.

Helen Jerome Eddy, Frank Elliott and Florence Turner have roles.

Metro-Goldwyn produced the picture.

The Man on the Box

The "Oceana Roll" Sandburg refers to is Charlie Chaplin's "Dance of the Rolls" from The Gold Rush *(1925).*

Tuesday, November 17, 1925

In *The Man on the Box* we may look at the best picture Warner Brothers have as yet brought into their new playhouse, the Orpheum Theater.

Syd Chaplin is seen in the cleverest film work that has been noticed from him.

Harold MacGrath's novel and stage play of the same title is the basis of the story.

And some parts of it are wrought out in a way that surpasses the novel.

Foolish, sometimes bordering on the silly, occasionally completely silly, it gets by with its audiences because on these points it is often original.

The imitation of Theodore Roosevelt comes with a quick surprise and a deft touch that have a quality of Charlie's "Oceana Roll" dance.

The audience laughs in a sudden, gustatory manner that indicates something different from ordinary slapstick comedy is in the going on the screen.

Harold MacGrath might blink his eyes about the humpty dumpty treatment of some of his chapters and situations.

Yet Warner Brothers have probably improved on MacGrath rather than diminished his story and character values.

The story has to do with a young society man who becomes a livery groom in order to be near a girl he admires.

Still later he puts on another disguise, this time wearing petticoats, flesh-colored silk stockings.

As a screen play it cannot be recommended as one that all the way through is of just the sort for the entire family to go to.

But among adults it can be cited as a better-than-ordinary farce.

Charles "Buck" Reisner directed and also acted a role. Alice Calhoun and David Butler are seen in support.

Little Annie Rooney

Though she played a 12-year-old girl in Little Annie Rooney, *Mary Pickford was actually a 32-year-old grown woman (and powerful movie producer) when this film was released.*

Friday, November 20, 1925

A few days ago we mentioned a picture as being pretty good for the grown up people but not exactly the kind of a movie to take the whole family to.

And today we sort of hold the balance even by mentioning *Little Annie Rooney* with Mary Pickford in the main role as being a movie that the whole family can take their seats in a movie house and enjoy.

And the kids will like it a little better than the big folks.

Annabelle Rooney, known as Annie for short, is the daughter of Officer Rooney, a policeman who is sure to make all the young people think better of policemen in general.

They live where the flats and tenements have crowded New York streets in front and lively back alleys behind.

There is much fighting among children to begin with in this film.

The girl, Annie Rooney, does a little more fighting than anybody else.

A new song is being whistled and sung about how Annie Rooney has a sweetheart and she fights a freckle-faced boy that she doesn't care to have singing the song at her.

Nine or 10 different nationalities figure in the fighting, also a white horse named Carlbaldui, who belongs to an Italian fruit peddler.

Five dollars worth of fruit was spilled around through kid tricks.

And they try to earn the five dollars with a show in an alley.

Well, it's a clean picture and better than ordinary.

It may not prove Mary Pickford is a great actress but it will interest children.

William Haines, Walter James, Gordon Griffith, Carlo Schipa and Spec O'Donnell are in the cast.

Hugh Bay plays Spider and Joe Butterworth plays Mickey.

United Artists put their imprint on it, and William Beaudine directed.

The first run is on at the Roosevelt Theater.

That Royle Girl

The second effort of D. W. Griffith and W. C. Fields was That Royle Girl. *Known in Hollywood as a film no one wanted, the project had already been passed on by several directors. Griffith understood their reasons; he dubbed the property "a lame idea." [18] Despite his protests, Griffith was told by his employers to make* That Royle Girl. *Though Sandburg gave the film a favorable review,* That Royle Girl *took a critical bashing. Today no copy of this motion picture is known to exist; the American Film Institute lists* That Royle Girl *as one of their "Ten Most Wanted" missing films.*

The film was shot on location in Chicago, which explains some of Sandburg's references in his review. The Wilson Avenue district was notorious for vice and drug crime. Chicago is located in Cook County; DuPage County is west of the city.

Saturday, November 21, 1925

D. W. Griffith seems to have given us two photoplays inside of the last six months and that is making 'em faster than he ever has in previous years.

The second of these is *That Royle Girl*, having its first run at the Chicago Theater this week.

It is a Paramount picture and produced under some sort of a contract that Griffith has now to make film for the Famous Players or Adolph Zukor or nobody else.

The time was when Griffith was doing his own producing, picking the stories for his pictures and taking a year or a year and a half to finish just one movie.

These explanations for the benefit of those who know the Griffith who did the main work back of *Intolerance* and *Broken Blossoms.*

The release this week of *That Royle Girl* is aimed first of all at getting the interest of the audience, holding the moviegoers in their seats, giving them laughter, suspense, shocks, thrills or melodrama.

The story is an adaptation from a novel by the Chicago fiction writer, Edwin Balmer, who offers us a portrayal of life as it is lived sometimes in the Wilson Avenue district.

Carol Dempster has the role of the young woman whose father is a hard drinker and whose mother is a drug addict.

Out of a sodden environment of vice and luxury and graft this girl rises as a lily from the mud, if we may use the conventional and the accepted cliché that gets by with the general run of fiction writers.

W. C. Fields is the father, James Kirkwood is our own Cook County state's attorney, and as the chief prosecutor representing the people of Cook, from the DuPage County line extending to the lake, we might say he is a humdinger.

Harrison Ford is the boy who almost goes to the gallows; the almost goes for him as surely in the movie as it generally does in real life.

An entertaining movie that, so far as we could note in the audience at the Chicago Theater, held onlookers with the suspense of interest, the laughter and the thrills that they seek entering the portals of that Babylonian interior of Balaban & Katz.

December

The Phantom of the Opera

If there is one role Lon Chaney is remembered for, it is his lead in The Phantom of the Opera. *Chaney's skull-like makeup became one of the cinema's most enduring images. Reportedly, Chaney had many production arguments with director Rupert Julian, so Edward Sedgwick was brought in to finish production. Chaney also directed many of his own scenes.*[19] *Universal built a large studio to hold the interior set, backstage area, and grand staircase of the Paris Opera House. This was the first steel-and-concrete stage built for a Hollywood production. The structure, known as Stage 28, still stands on the Universal lot, one of the few remnants in modern Hollywood of the silent era.*[20] *Appropriately, Stage 28 was used in the Chaney film biography* Man of a Thousand Faces *(1957), starring James Cagney.*

Monday, December 7, 1925

The Phantom of the Opera gives a new meaning to the word "sensational."

Universal's new production seeks for the chilling thrill, the scene that scares you, which is yet so new, so fascinating that your pleasure surpasses your scare. Its climax creeps upon you by compelling degrees; you shrink from it, yet you would not miss it.

Reel after reel speeds by and you sit on your chair edge waiting, waiting for the climax, which is to be the unmasking of the strange "phantom." Through crowds, lonely streets, tunnels, spooky corridors and gala throngs this "phantom" stalks. Detectives follow him, walls open to him, he is here, there, and then neither here nor there, always with his mask. A girl worships him, a hero hates him, mobs hunt him, still he hides behind a bland, smooth, horrible, vacant false face. Sometime he is going to toss it off and show you just what it is he's hiding—and you wait for that "sometime"—terribly fascinated, aching with suspense.

He sits at an organ, this "phantom" deep down in the subterranean caverns beneath the Opera House of Paris, looking through his bland and innocent and mysterious mask at the keys over which his fingers run. Behind him on a deep divan, swathed in silks, is the girl he has taught to sing so well that she has conquered all Paris. Behind her, still further, is the magnificent room where the phantom sleeps—in a coffin. Above, the hunt for them goes on. A frantic love, a dogged detective, and a mob of outraged stagehands from the Opera are hunting the phantom who has made the girl opera star and stolen her after terrorizing the audience, with switching lights off and

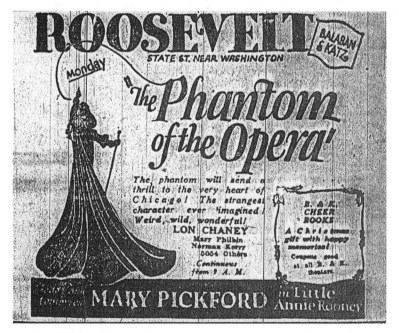

A *Chicago Daily News* ad announcing Lon Chaney in *The Phantom of the Opera* at Balaban & Katz's Roosevelt Theater (Saturday, December 5, 1925).

on, with terrible threats and acts.

The great moment is at hand. The girl can stand the suspense no longer. Neither can you. She has been warned never to lift the mask. But now when he is intent on his music, she comes closer, closer, her fingers steal toward the ribbon that fastens the mask. Her fingers give one final twitch—and there you are!

You may squeak out loud with excitement, but you'll stay in the theater, for with that the action grows swifter and carries you on with it. But you'll never forget that one indescribable moment when your eyes are creeping, creeping toward the ribbon that fastens on the mask, creeping with the frightened fingers of the girl.

The Phantom of the Opera gives Lon Chaney another fantastic makeup—one that resembles Chaney not at all, resembles nothing you ever saw or will see again. This is a tribute to his makeup and the versatility of his acting. A genuine artist, Mr. Chaney.

Mary Philbin and Norman Kerry are the lovers. Arthur Carew the mysterious detective. The mobs are led stridently, splendidly by Gibson Gowland and the scenery is mountainous, its settings partly in color. Rupert Julian directed the picture and its current release is at the Roosevelt Theater.

Apparently Sandburg had second thoughts about his review of The Phantom of the Opera. *A few weeks later he wrote the following:*

Monday, January 11, 1926

Sometimes when we don't know what else to say about a production we remark, "It's a novelty, anyhow."

And *The Phantom of the Opera*, having its run at the Castle Theater this week, is strictly among the novelties of the season.

The moviegoers who have a good time telling each other through the opening reels just how the story is going to come out in the last reels can't have their customary satisfaction. An old fashioned terror and mystery story of the French school, and by a French writer, is done here in a clever manner worth the study of psychologists of public taste.

The aim is to send cold shivers registering down the spines of the members of the audience.

But these cold shivers must not be too cold, must not go so far as they did in *The Cabinet of Dr. Caligari.*

Nor as they did in Erich von Stroheim's *Greed*, which picturized Frank Norris' novel *McTeague.*

The latter two movies were not very strict box office successes; they were too fierce.

In making *The Phantom of the Opera* they figured on scaring the audience—but not too much, not too fierce.

The phantom public wants its phantoms on the screen, but these phantoms mustn't be too phantasmagoric.

Lon Chaney's best acting, with his hands, is to be seen in this picture. He wears a grisly mask most of the time and therefore the talking must be done with his hands, or the shoulders or feet.

And he does very well with hands and shoulders.

And wisely leaves Charlie Chaplin as the unchallenged champion of speech with the feet.

Go West

Buster Keaton's co-star in Go West *was a cow billed as "Brown Eyes." In order to achieve comic chemistry between human and animal, Keaton personally trained the bovine performer.[21] During the shooting of* Go West, *production ground to a halt for two weeks when Brown Eyes went into heat.[22]*

Thursday, December 17, 1925

It seems rather silly to say that any screen comedy will leave unforgettable impressions on you—but that seems exactly what Buster Keaton's *Go West* is likely to do at McVicker's Theater this week. Although the theater at times is explosive with hearty guffaws, *Go West* may not be the funniest thing that sour-faced Buster has ever done, but it is by far the most enjoyable bit of humor this writer has seen from the Keaton fun factory. This comedian comes close to the Chaplinesque in his serious comedy. Buster is one of the few comedians of the screen at whom you can laugh without feeling a bit ridiculous yourself. *Go West* is a burlesque or parody or some kind of a takeoff on the melodrama of the "wide open spaces." Buster hit upon a stroke of originality that comes near to robbing him of the picture's starring honors. The "stroke" is Brown Eyes, a cow! Who would think of cow-starring with a bovine leading lady—except Buster?

If you are burdened down with the pre-holiday shopping worries, if you haven't yet got into the traditional Christmas spirit, amble over to McVicker's and let Buster jolly you into the proper mood.

And what Buster fails to do, Paul Ash's gang, guided by George Givot, will accomplish for you with their lively musical program.

The Big Parade

With The Big Parade *director King Vidor wanted to make a new kind of war story. "It would be the story of the average guy in whose hands does not lie the power to* create *the situations in which he finds himself but who nevertheless feels them emotionally," Vidor later wrote.[23] Writer Laurence Stallings, a Marine Corps veteran who had lost a leg at Belleau Wood during World War I, brought a unique sense of realism to the screenplay.* The Big Parade *made a star of John Gilbert, who showed a remarkable dramatic range with his gritty performance.*

Tuesday, December 29, 1925

Since the world war came to an end seven years ago many kinds of war pictures have come along.

And *The Big Parade* tells more about the war than any one picture, and probably more than all other war pictures put together.

The run of this photoplay, starting at the Garrick Theater this week, deserves to be a long one.

It's a story, and it's history and it's tragedy and comedy.

It would be terrible and heart breaking if it were not for the funny high spots and the sublime depths of it.

And what is it particularly about?

Well, the story is old; the big war breaks; lovers part; three doughboys, a structural iron worker, a bartender and a hitherto good-for-nothing boy become close buddies; they are billeted back of the big parade and Jim or James Apperson (John Gilbert) meets a French girl, Melisande (Rene Adoree); the troops move up.

And oh! It's something to talk about—the last half of this picture—and something to sit speechless and think about.

The screen, the cinema, the photoplay is terrific when it comes to telling of certain massive panoramic human shows.

Laurence Stallings, who wrote the story of *The Big Parade*, is a newspaperman who wrote a novel, *Plumes*, collaborated on *What Price Glory*, and then turned his hand to a movie—and he has outdone all but two or three of the good workers in the movie achievement.

King Vidor, who directed, caught the big idea in general, and is now to be remembered as the director who directed *The Big Parade*.

Hobart Bosworth, Claire McDowell, Claire Adams, Robert Ober, Tom O'Brien and Karl Dane are in the cast.

It takes two hours and more for the picture to run, and it is swift, gripping, has a fine aftermath of things to think about and feel and wonder on.

This reviewer is going again once or twice; it is one of those pictures worth seeing more than once.

Monday, July 25, 1927

On a second view of *The Big Parade* one has time to think. No such opportunity is ever given any one during a first look at this achievement in emotionalism. Certainly not since *The Birth of a Nation* has a picture so stormed the emotions of its spectators. One must laugh, weep or fall into love or hate with these characters which Stallings put on paper and King Vidor transferred to the screen.

However, on a second visit there comes a chance to consider things. For instance, those machine guns of the enemy, which mow down the doughboys as they march through the woods. Who has ever seen a human to equal them in hatefulness? Slowly they climb to a pitch of villainy to which no screen actor ever attained. It is not the men who point the guns that we hate, it is the inanimate little rod that spits death.

King Vidor shows it to you in flashes, cutting back to the doughboys who are coming on, marching slowly, marching steadily, with something of the inexorable rise of a thunderstorm—and with something, too, of the terrible solemnity of death march music. They go down here, there in casual topplings. Not one of them gesticulates heroically in the mock agonies of actors. They simply drop and the death walk goes on.

Will the machine guns reach the three doughboys about whom you care? It is a moment of aching suspense, and although it is a short scene, it seems hours long to spectators. Probably films never approached this suspense before or since; accomplished because it seems impossible that all three of the soldiers, John Gilbert, Karl Dane and Tom O'Brien, can, by any chance, escape the villain.

Vidor interrupts the suspense but once, and that when Karl Dane with great satisfaction and elaborate nonchalance shoots down from a tree the sniper who has been killing doughboys. Saintly old ladies, highly aesthetic customers, patrons of refinement now in McVicker's Theater, peal into laughter and delight as the gaunt Dane spurts derisive tobacco juice at his malicious foe.

But Vidor snatches the scene back into that terrifying suspense again a second later and the death walk goes on.

Many there are who insist that *The Big Parade* is the greatest of all pictures, but there are more who say, "Well, anyway, that march through the woods is the greatest scene motion pictures ever had."

Tumbleweeds

Tumbleweeds is the last film of William S. Hart. Despite good reviews, the picture did poorly at the box office. Convinced his work had been deliberately mishandled by the distributor, Hart sued United Artists. He won the legal battle, but victory marked the end of Hart's movie career. In 1939 Hart re-released Tumbleweeds, *adding music and sound effects as well as a spoken prologue to the film.*

Wednesday, December 30, 1925

Bill Hart, the first and foremost of riding and shooting men in the early days of the movies, is showing in *Tumbleweeds* in a first run at the Castle Theater this week.

We incline to think this is the best picture Bill Hart has come along in for several years.

Not that his work as a screen player will particularly please his friends as having more strife and action; his own work is about the same as it used to be.

But the story of the picture is out of the ordinary, having to do with a Western land rush, and as history goes it registers passing well or better.

Thousands of buggies, horsemen, covered wagons, democrat wagons and one old style high bicycle line up for the cannon shot that is to send them racing over the line—"empire builders," says a subtitle, "in the maddest stampede known in American history."

While we may not believe that as a stampede it equals the battle of Bull Run, still and all as stampedes go it has its points.

While the land rushers are rarin' to go, waiting for the signal, Don Carver (Bill Hart) is a prisoner in a stockade, charged with being a "sooner," having been on forbidden ground sooner than he should.

There is a lady of his heart who refuses to believe him guilty, though the evidence is against him.

Saloons, dance halls, spielers and street fakers, land boom town scenery, is rather intelligently handled.

Barbara Bedford is the leading woman; others in the cast are Lucien Littlefield, J. Gordon Russell, Richard R. Nell, Jack Murphy, Lillian Leighton, Monte Collins.

The story, by Hal G. Evarts, was adapted for the screen by C. Gardner Sullivan and directed by King Baggot.

Greta Garbo radiated with elusive beauty.

1926

January

The Eagle

If Rudolph Valentino has lost any of his popularity with the fair sex since he made his most successful pictures he is going to regain all his lost ground and then some with *The Eagle*, his newest production which burst plushingly upon Chicago today.

This statement is based upon the remarks of those who sat near the writer at the Roosevelt Theater during the very first performance. How those young ladies did thrill to Rudolph's romantic heroism! Undoubtedly, *The Eagle* is going to be rated Valentino's best in a long time—perhaps the best thing he has done since *The Four Horsemen*.

It must not have been difficult for Valentino to do his romantic best with the beautiful, blond Vilma Banky as his inspiration. This Hungarian star is likely to give American favorites a close race for top honors some of these early days.

The Eagle has the advantage of a rapid-fire plot, full of motion and romance, with a background of beautiful and interesting settings. *The Eagle* is the name given to a mysterious, masked Robin Hood who roams the Russian forests. You soon learn that "the Eagle" is Rudolph; exiled Cossack lieutenant, out to get revenge for a wrong done to a kinsman. Rudolph flees the Russian army when he fails to respond to the unblushing overtures of his empress, the naughty Catherine the Great, who would number him among her numerous amours and make him "another general." Louise Dresser, as the flirtatious empress, does a splendid bit of pantomime, not too subtle, yet not so broad as to be offensive. As the masked "Eagle," Rudolph is a regular Doug Fairbanks for action. He recalls to mind *Don Q*. This part of the picture—with its spirit of adventure—will please the male portion of the audiences. It may surprise some men, too—they didn't know it was in Rudolph. Then there is much excitement as Valentino gains admittance to his enemy's home as a French teacher for the beautiful daughter (Vilma). His wooing of Miss Banky puts "the sheik" back on his pedestal.

If you enjoy romantic adventure, with a handsome sheik hero and darlingly blond heroine, in a story spiced piquantly here and there, you should be one of those flocking to the Roosevelt.

February

Death of Barbara La Marr

Billed as "The Girl Who is Too Beautiful," Barbara La Marr was another victim of Hollywood's drug culture. Though the studio claimed "excessive dieting" caused her death, in reality La Marr succumbed to a narcotics overdose. A few years later an Austrian immigrant to Hollywood adopted the name "Hedy Lamarr" in tribute to her predecessor. Cardinal Désiré Joseph Mercier, whom Sandburg refers to in the last paragraph, was known as the "Voice of Belgium" for his opposition to the World War I German invasion.

Saturday, February 6, 1926

The art of the silent silversheet and that of the spoken stage production have one wide difference.

If Al Jolson and Eddie Cantor are feeling not so good they close up their shows, the house goes dark and there is nothing doing.

But when Barbara La Marr is stricken and passes out from the land of the living it may happen—as it is now the case—that immense audi-

Barbara La Marr (right), "The Girl Who Is Too Beautiful" was another victim of the 1920s underground drug culture that permeated Hollywood. This still is from the 1921 production *The Prisoner of Zenda.* La Marr and co-star Ramon Novarro (center) are pictured with director Rex Ingram (left).

From the collection of Arnie Bernstein.

ences are viewing the last performance in which she engaged.

In *The Girl from Montmartre*, Miss La Marr is a leading player in the photoplay having its first run at McVicker's Theater this week.

And there was something dreamy and illusory for this reviewer in watching her lithe, swift form, her gamut of elusive facial expressions on the McVicker's screen in Chicago on the day of her burial on the West Coast.

The screen is a strange register.

We thought so again as we saw the public revival of a meeting and greeting of the living faces of Woodrow Wilson and Cardinal Mercier.

Von Sternberg to Work with Chaplin

A Woman of the Sea *was the only time Chaplin hired an outside director to work for his studio. Von Sternberg's original story, first called* The Sea Gull *and then* A Woman of the Sea, *was intended as a comeback vehicle for Chaplin's former leading lady, Edna Purviance. Upon seeing the completed work, Chaplin felt the film was unreleasable. While von Sternberg brought a sense of visual beauty to the project, the film story was confusing and dull. Critic and documentary filmmaker John Grierson, one of the few people ever to see* A Woman of the Sea, *later said: "The final version satisfied neither Chaplin nor Sternberg. It was still extraordinarily beautiful—but empty—possibly the most beautiful film I have ever seen."* [1] *No copy of* A Woman of the Sea *is known to exist.*

Saturday, February 6, 1926

The news is good news that Josef von Sternberg is working in the Chaplin studios, directing a picture written expressly for Edna Purviance.

Whatever it is that Charlie and von Sternberg are framing on Charlie's longtime leading lady our guess is that it will be good.

Chaplin's independence and originality are shown in his taking on von Sternberg, whose *Salvation Hunters*, while no box office success, was a grand effort at new style in storytelling and character portrayal and atmosphere in photoplays.

Ben-Hur, A Tale of the Christ

The story of the making of Ben-Hur, *an epic behind-the-scenes tale of adventure, diligence, tragedy, and unintended comedy, is brilliantly detailed in film historian Kevin Brownlow's homage to silent cinema,* The Parade's Gone By . . . . Ben-Hur *was remade in 1959 with Charlton Heston in the lead and William Wyler as director. The second version won a record 11 Academy Awards; for Sandburg's decidedly*

different point of view of the Ben-Hur *remake, see the commentary for his review of*
The Ten Commandments, *Tuesday, August 4, 1925.*

Monday, February 8, 1926

The picturization of *Ben-Hur, A Tale of the Christ* by Gen. Lew Wallace will occupy
the stage of the Woods Theater beginning this evening, and twice daily hereafter. New
York, Boston, Chicago and Philadelphia are the only cities which will see the epic this
season. First, a word of history to the younger generation. *Ben-Hur* was put forth by
Gen. Lew Wallace in 1880, and for 45 years the book enjoyed a circulation second
only to Holy Writ.

A *Chicago Daily News* ad for *Ben-Hur,* "the
mightiest picture in all the history of the screen"
(Friday, November 11, 1927).

It is a tale that weaves intimately
the founding of Christianity into
the environment and lives of the
characters, the young Ben-Hur being pictured as a contemporary of
the Savior.

A beautiful romance links the
Jewish prince and Esther, the
daughter of his steward Simon-
ides.

The story begins in Bethlehem
with the star and the adoration of
the wise men, then deals with the
oppression of Judea and the ruin
of the Hur family by Roman edict.
The hero is successively a slave in
the galleys, then by turn of fortune, a Roman duumvir's adopted
son the richest subject in Asia, winner of the Antioch chariot race and then animated
by the Jewish ideal of a temporal messiah he raises a legion to take up arms for Jesus of
Nazareth. But the Prince of Peace comes not into a worldly kingdom. Ben-Hur is
bidden to put up his sword, becoming a humble follower of the Master. His long-lost
mother and sister are restored to him and are cured of sickness by divine healing.

For nearly a quarter of a century, from Nov. 29, 1899, the stage play of *Ben-Hur,*
founded on the above story, was the most popular stage attraction in America. This has
been succeeded in turn by the Metro-Goldwyn-Mayer motion picture, which was
begun in 1923 and completed December 1925. Abraham L. Erlanger has seen to it that
the new *Ben-Hur* is a faithful picturization of book and play, but with the immensely
grander resources of the motion picture art, especially in the sea fight and the chariot
race. Ramon Novarro heads the cast of 150,000 players. Metro-Goldwyn-Mayer have
expended $4 million on the picture.

Wednesday, February 10, 1926

Ben-Hur, the long-awaited picture has arrived and taken up its stand in the Woods Theater for a run.

Of all the so-called sacred pictures which we have viewed on the screen, this one has a truer and more reverential tone than any we have seen.

The figure of Christ appears on a number of occasions, but there is never a revelation of the face, the effect being conveyed by the apparition of merely the hand or the two arms or the shoulder.

Two scenes in this photoplay stand out dominating it.

One shows the galleys of the Roman navy sailing the sea, and in the hold the galley slaves, long rows of them, "chained to the galleys" as the saying goes.

The orchestra carries on a crude drumming rhythm that synchronizes with the unending monotony of the slave life.

The other dominant scene is the chariot race.

It would be expected that a movie of Gen. Lew Wallace's widely read masterpiece would have a chariot or two and horses and dust.

Fred Niblo, the director, Cedric Gibbons, the art director, and the Metro-Goldwyn organization in general rose to the challenge that they must make this chariot race stand out.

Horses, horse heads, horse feet and a champing and a hullabaloo, and an immense sporting event, are effectively portrayed.

The run of the picture is nearly two hours and a half.

Though the first half-hour or so is not convincing, it begins to get hold of its audience—or vividence—from there on—and the bursts of applause come frequently.

Ramon Novarro plays the Jew who becomes a galley slave and later a Roman citizen, while Francis X. Bushman is a fierce Roman soldier.

Betty Bronson has the role of the Madonna.

May McAvoy, Claire McDowell, Kathleen Key and Carmel Meyers carry the important roles.

The American Venus

One of the contestants in The American Venus'*s beauty pageant is Louise Brooks. Already a veteran of Broadway stages, Brooks made an undistinguished film debut in* The Street of Forgotten Men *(1925). Though she played numerous flapper roles in the Colleen Moore vein, Brooks became a legend after working in Germany with director G. W. Pabst. She made two classic films with Pabst,* Pandora's Box *and* Diary of a Lost Girl *(both 1929). Upon her return to Hollywood, Brooks found that cult status in European art films meant nothing to the studio powers-that-be.*

She appeared in a few films, including a two-reel comedy directed by Roscoe "Fatty" Arbuckle and a small part in the gangster classic The Public Enemy *(1931) with James Cagney. After her final picture,* Overland Stage Raiders *(1938), a B-Western featuring John Wayne, Brooks moved to New York and wound up working as a sales clerk. Late in life she was rediscovered by a new generation of film lovers. In 1982 Brooks published a memoir,* Lulu in Hollywood.

Tuesday, February 9, 1926

One of our most American institutions is the beauty contest.

First is the announcement of the hanging up of the prize, the conditions of the award and the names of the judges.

Then we hear of the award of the judges, look the winner over and say whether we think she ought to have won.

After which there is nothing much to do till the next contest.

And now the Chicago Theater is showing a picture, called *The American Venus*, which is a smart takeoff on our national custom.

Though Louise Brooks became a cult figure for her work with German director G. W. Pabst, she appeared in several Hollywood flapper roles during the 1920s, including one as a beauty pageant contestant in *The American Venus*.

From the collection of Arnie Bernstein.

The plot begins in Centerville, N. J., for the sketch does have a plot.

And our heroine gallivants on to Atlantic City to represent Jersey among the states of the union which have each a little lady in a float of her own passing before the judges' stand.

Incidentally, and for good measure, a fashion show is thrown in.

The tricks of the magician, who produces an amazing array of gowns worn by picked mannequins, employs the motion picture technique at what it can do most skillfully.

Meanwhile schemers and plotters and conspirators go merrily along framing the works for their own candidates to win.

Esther Ralston and Fay Lanphier are the feminine talent, also Edna Oliver and Louise Brooks.

Ford Sterling, Lawrence Gray and Ernest Torrence, too, are in the cast.

The clever direction was by Frank Tuttle, while Townsend Martin did the story.

The Sea Beast

This was the first cinematic rendition of Herman Melville's novel Moby Dick. *Remakes, all using Melville's original title, followed in 1930 and 1956, as well as a 1998 cable television version.*

Monday, February 15, 1926

The Sea Beast, having its first run at the Orpheum Theater this week, is a remarkable and an exceptional picture in several respects.

John Barrymore, the spoken stage player, has in this movie done a stretch of acting on the silent screen that some of his friends will rate as better than anything in his stage work.

It is a photoplay sure to be named among those few photoplays that have a sea tang.

That is, the moviegoers who enjoyed *Down to the Sea in Ships* are sure to take a liking to this one.

Millard Webb, the director, should come in for credit.

A *Chicago Daily News* ad for John Barrymore in *Sea Beast* (Tuesday, February 9, 1926).

And, furthermore, a man, dead now these many years should also be named as most important of all.

We refer to Herman Melville, the author of *Moby Dick*, one of the American classics among books, a story of the sea and an almost magical whale, a whale with personality and power and character.

The story is changed somewhat from the way Melville's book has it, or perhaps not changed so much as added to.

Melville could boast that he had done a book, a bully, long, swaggering tale of the sea, with heroes galore and gory, but no women, no woman.

This being a movie for the great American public, it was considered necessary to add to the screen story a love tale.

Dolores Costello plays the lady who inspires the fiercest chase of all, who sought to capture the mystery whale, Moby Dick.

The most loveable wooden legged man in all plays or storybooks, some people will say of this role of John Barrymore.

We wish this production luck and recommend it as among the better of the photoplays.

Stars in Unfamiliar Makeup

Saturday, February 27, 1926

It's becoming the fashion for the idols of moviedom to assume unfamiliar makeup in the early reels of their productions and to sacrifice their vanity upon the altar of "better acting." Norma Shearer disguises her beauty under homely garb, spectacles and wearing weazened expressions in *His Secretary*, which exhibits her as a cocoon and then as a butterfly at the Chicago Theater this week.

From Hollywood comes the news that Marion Davies has clipped her hair to boyish cuts and donned man's garb for *Beverly of Graustark*, and also that Gertrude Olmstead is an ultra-plain, dismal and most unattractive young lady in her makeup for *Monte Carlo*, which approaches.

So much for the ladies.

Ben Lyon, whose strides toward Wallace Reid's former place in moviedom are growing longer and stronger with every picture, is to exhibit himself next week at the Chicago Theater as a stuttering, near-sighted, frowsy, dull little bank clerk in a small town. Fired from his job because he mixes his accounts with dreams of marriage to Mary Kelly, a waitress, he wanders, growing a full beard and becoming uglier and uglier with each reel. However, his travels head to Hollywood where he is seized as a type and becomes in spite of his wishes, a "sheik," being rechristened by astute press agents "Don Juan Hartes." His managers publicize him as the modern "Bluebeard" and marry him to seven different women, so that in spite of his willingness to make concessions to art, Mr. Lyon finds himself handsome before the picture is over.

Certainly this new movement among the players bodes well for the movies. It means that the posing, strutting, preening days have gone and that the stars are willing to play roles instead of play themselves.

We are escaping the juvenile days when movies dealt wholly with superficial aspects, such as mere pulchritude and personal popularity. The actors are digging in nowadays, trying for reality and definite characterization.

March

The Vanishing American

Though an attempt to consider the West from a Native American point of view, The Vanishing American *starred white actor Richard Dix wearing dark makeup in his Indian role.*

Monday, March 1, 1926

Out between Arizona and Utah lies a country that Zane Grey says is practically unexplored by man. Near it are the reservations of the Navajos and the Pintos, and across one span of it, in fantastic, primeval engineering, stretches the Rainbow Bridge.

Here the deserts and mountains fight. Here the Indian gods had a terrific wrestle one time when the world was congealing out of the mists and putties of chaos. Jagged ramparts gesture upward and the deserts pull and wear at them, torture them, century in, century out, to drag the rocks down to dust.

This is the setting for Paramount's latest "epic," *The Vanishing American*, and it is the setting that outdoes every human action in the picture. It outdoes even a majestic story, a pathetic story told on a scale that dwarfs even *The Covered Wagon*. No actors, no filmmakers can hope to dominate that scenery. The mountains and deserts are "camera hogs" that whip any actor ever seen or to be seen.

The Vanishing American is an attempt, a bizarre attempt, at setting down on gelatin the story of the American red man in broad strokes, pointed up with a modern romance of a heroic copper-skinned chief and a white girl school teacher on the reservation.

The first Americans, matted of hair, club swinging, cave-dwelling, rise over a horizon. After them come the cliff dwellers, and after these the savage war-makers, direct ancestors of the modern Apaches. Tremendous battles range through the cliffhouses—and then silence. Come, too, the Spanish conquistadors, cowing the red men with gunpowder.

Then the blue-clad troopers of Gen. Crook, the weather-beaten scouts of Kit

Carson. Cannons boom and the red man quits the warpath.

The modern world comes. Indians on reservations, white men through crooked Indian agents cheating the red men of their lands, their horses.

The world war comes. To it goes Nophanie, wise and stalwart young idol of the tribe, leading the first Americans, hundreds of them, to fight in Flanders.

Back from war they come, some crippled, some shell-shocked, to find that the white looters have robbed them of their lands, ravaged their women, taken their homes for stables.

Border war comes again. They take to the warpath and the whites scurry for cover. Nophanie pleads for peace, gives his life for it, while the white girl weeps across his bronze chest.

The Vanishing American achieves a mood, a distinct feeling in its passionate sentiment for the red man. It is partisan, exaggerated, pleading. Nothing is spared to make it impressive. Costuming, mobs, scenery are lavishly provided. The cast is large and good. Richard Dix, Lois Wilson, Noah Beery, Malcolm MacGregor, Bert Woodruff, Shannon Day, some exceptional Indian actors, including a rare little boy actor, son of Man Hammer.

George Seitz directed it. Zane Grey wrote it. The Roosevelt Theater shows it.

Miss Brewster's Millions

BEBE DANIELS, as Satan Synne, in "The Affairs of Anatol." A Para. Picture.

From the collection of Arnie Bernstein.

Comic flapper Bebe Daniels, the star of *Miss Brewster's Millions.*

See also Brewster's Millions, *Monday, February 7, 1921.*

Wednesday, March 10, 1926

This Bebe Daniels party won't last long giving us such photoplays as *Miss Brewster's Millions,* having its first run at McVicker's Theater this week.

It is one of those roaming, lackadaisical movies where nobody cared much about anything.

That is, the production is so-so, neither here nor there, neither fish, fowl nor good red herring, as sea captains remark previous to spitting on the deck and telling the crew, "I want silence and damn little of that."

The last time we saw George Barr McCutcheon's novel *Brewster's Millions* in a film, the leading part was taken by "Fatty" Arbuckle.

And now, instead of a male heir spending Brewster's millions, we have a female heir.

A year or two and maybe an ostrich or a baboon will be

throwing Brewster's dollars at the moon.

Who knows?

The audience laughs, the picture classifies as entertainment; probably no one has any right to kick about it.

Ford Sterling and Warner Baxter do their stuff, and Clarence Badger directs, and when it is all over we have seen another movie, an hour has passed and we are ready for Paul Ash, than whom none is whoomer in his particular field.

But what is Paul Ash's particular field?

We refuse to answer; that is his secret; his job is to make things sizzle in concatenated jazz; he knows his crowd and they get theirs.

Pleasures of the Rich

Friday, March 12, 1926

Pleasures of the Rich was the name they chose for the picture having its first run at the State-Lake Theater this week.

The rich are not so awful rich, as here seen.

We have seen more splendiferously rich, more lavish and splashy rich people in several Cecil De Mille blowouts.

Nor are the pleasures very strictly pleasures, as such.

But a title is a title.

Having made a picture they got to call it something, don't they?

Now this one is a little better than the general run of pictures and we have no hard words about it.

We only got to thinking about what a fierce job it would be sometimes to have to give names to one picture after another the way they turn them out in the Hollywood factories where the time sheets say this and that photoplay must be ready for the exhibitors on such and such a date.

Now here our old friends Helene Chadwick, Mary Carr, and Jack Mulhall are to be seen.

And the story is about our heroine whose father runs a string of grocery stores and falls out with his wife and gets into trouble with a younger woman till a scandal is whispered around.

And the heroine has everything her heart can wish for except the young man of her choice and her heart's desire, as sometimes happens.

Time passes by and circumstances work against her and she believes she has lost forever the one of her dreams.

In her room in her elegant home she sets up the photograph of her best one, and alongside it a note which can mean nothing else than that she has decided to jump in a lake and end all.

Such is the plot up to five minutes before the final fade out.

We leave any regular filmgoer to say how it can be brought to a successful finish, so as to keep the good will of the audience—or as some of the wise crackers have it—the vividence.

The Torrent

While on a 1924 talent hunt in Europe, movie mogul Louis B. Mayer hired Mauritz Stiller, one of Sweden's top directors, to work in Hollywood. Stiller agreed on one condition: that MGM hire his favorite discovery, a talented screen performer named Greta Garbo. Though initially unhappy with the offer, Mayer agreed to Stiller's terms. It proved to be a consequential move. With her American debut in The Torrent *(also known as* Ibáñez' Torrent*) Garbo proved herself to be the very essence of a Hollywood star. A hit with American audiences from the start, Garbo's career in silent and sound films became the stuff of legend.*

Wednesday, March 17, 1926

The Torrent, opening its run at the Roosevelt Theater this week, is considerable of a film play.

Ibáñez, the Spanish novelist who wrote *The Four Horsemen of the Apocalypse*, is the author of the book from which the story is taken.

Ricardo Cortez steps forth in character work that has class, that shows he can enter into fine shadings and gradations of portrayal work.

And Greta Garbo, we might say many things of her, picking words of praise to tell about her.

The story begins with the once humble girl who returns to her province home in Spain.

And she is now a prima donna.

The young man close to her heart, though they have drifted apart somewhat, has just been elected a deputy to the national parliament.

They toy with one another's hearts.

"Love comes once in a life and then passes by."

He marries another girl, allowing his mother to push him into the marriage.

The new husband and his former love have a night together—and the mother of his new wife starts trouble.

This singer goes to America, years pass, she returns to Spain.

And the former lover sends her orange blossoms again.

They meet—and what does she see?

A man on whom flesh and age have put their marks, while "It is the business of a prima donna to keep young."

The finish is neither sweet nor bitter but bittersweet.

Dangerously close to what some people will call a sad, unhappy ending for a movie.

But a nice, independent change from what we have been used to.

The Torrent is decidedly among recommended pictures.

May

Movies and Children

Monday, May 17, 1926

A mother has her boy at her side watching a two-reel comedy where a little man is strapped to a chair while a big man is at a battery turning on electric current.

"Is it really going into him?" the boys asks his mother.

"No, no: it's just make believe," says the mother.

"Oh," says the boy, all alive, and going ahead later and asking more questions. "Is it really, is it really?" And the mother replying each time, "No, no: it's just make believe."

What is there to this talk that the movies bring up children faster than they should be brought up?

Is there anything or something to that the movies age a child too quick?

Isn't it a terrible job the movie makers are up against in trying to provide pictures that interest young and old in the same moment?

A while ago we sat in a private audience and watched the filming of an old-time Chaplin picture for several children whom we have known since they were babies.

And where the grownups laughed and were having a good time the little ones were silent and at times shuddering.

If that could happen with a Chaplin picture that they love for the quality of its humor and its fine human elements, then what of many pictures lacking the fine Chaplin stuff?

The mother referred to above has more than ordinary wisdom.

At one point as *The Lucky Lady* was being reeled off, the boy asked, "What is she? Is she a bad girl?"

"No," said the mother, "she's just full of life."

That was how we knew she was a mother with a heart of understanding.

June

Paris

Playing one of her many 1920s flapper roles, Joan Crawford nearly stole the show in Paris. After sound came to the movies, she developed into a powerful dramatic talent, becoming a Hollywood legend in the process.

Tuesday, June 8, 1926

Some clever people figured out just what Charlie Ray would be best in if it wasn't going to be an egg crate wallop or a country ball player.

It's named *Paris*, and it is a mighty smart movie with one of those plots that goes this way and that and lures us on fools us up to the last flicker.

The plot, in other words, fills a long-felt want.

Joan Crawford in all her sizzling flapper glory.

From the collection of Arnie Bernstein.

'Tis the Oriental Theater picture for this week of which we speak; long after the Paul Ash stuff for this particular week is forgotten there may be recollection of the trickery of this story and some of its scenes and characters. It is Charlie Ray's best.

He is ably and wonderfully assisted by Joan Crawford; in fact, we are inclined to think it is Joan Crawford rather than Charlie Ray that gives the picture its main swing.

The story shows us an American loaded with cash and mazuma, in Paris where he picks up with the idol of his life in the shape of a woman.

She tells him it is no 50-50 arrangement; that he is to give her everything and she is to give him nothing.

She goes to her apache lover who is in jail, shows him earrings, bracelets, jewels galore, letting him know that when he gets out they won't have to steal any more; they'll have plenty to live on.

He gets jealous and right there in a stir yanks a jeweled earring off her ear.

And soon we are led up to places where the average movie audience is sure how the plot is going to work out; but it doesn't work out that way; a pleasant surprise and a big trick laugh is at the finish; and there is plenty of healthy laughter.

This is one of the few times when we have seen the picture take hold of the audience and carry it away from Paul Ash.

July

La Bohème

In creating the dying Mimi of La Bohème, *Lillian Gish avoided liquids for three days and kept cotton pads in her mouth to absorb saliva. "The movies," said director King Vidor, "have never known a more dedicated artist than Lillian Gish."* [2]

Thursday, July 8, 1926

And now we have *La Bohème* at the Roosevelt Theater with Lillian Gish playing the girl who had a hard time and John Gilbert playing the man who didn't understand at first and in the end is seen weeping and filled with remorse.

The settings are Parisian, aiming at the atmosphere of bohemia.

The sweet child, as played by Miss Gish, aims to help the pure and aspiring young man, as played by Mr. Gilbert.

There is much happiness, but one night when she comes home he is furious as he asks where she has been; her explanations convince him; he hugs her and kisses her and then happens to see what she has on her feet; by way of shoes he believes she is not what she should be; he beats her; he slugs her mouth with his fist; she is picked up bleeding; then comes sorrow for her, a successful drama for him and on the night of the celebration of his success there is a terrible reconciliation.

Somehow as we view this production from the directorial hand of King Vidor it seems to us just a passable puppet play employing figures that don't at all lift into the breath of life.

Perhaps if we hadn't seen Miss Gish in *The Birth of a Nation*, in *Broken Blossoms* and in *Way Down East*, playing much the same sort of a role, plumbing much the same depths of human sorrow, we might have been more easily convinced. In these others she runs the same gamut of feeling and shade of expression and was handled by one who knew better how to bring her out.

But maybe this is a personal whim.

From the collection of Arnie Bernstein.

Lillian Gish, perhaps the finest screen performer of the silent era.

Mantrap

Wednesday, July 21, 1926

Mantrap, the picture made from Sinclair Lewis' latest novel, is easily among the bigger and better pictures.

The smartest and swiftest work as yet seen from Miss Clara Bow is here in this.

Ernest Torrence and Percy Marmont come through, too, with pretty nice work.

The story isn't so much; but the director and the players all had an interest in it and collaborated so as to produce an up and coming movie. It is on this week at the Oriental Theater.

A couple of New York men start for western Canada for a vacation; arriving, they find a manicure girl from Minneapolis, married and keeping house for a storekeeper—though her housekeeping is not so strict but that she lets him peel the potatoes occasionally.

The two vacationers quarrel and separate; the Minneapolis girl leaves her man and maneuvers so that she is running away, heading back to civilization with the New York (divorce) lawyer.

The screen yarn ends happily, whereas the novel closes vaguely and leaves things up in the air, foggy, like life.

Lots of smart subtitles in this about the smartest this summer.

Of course, if James Oliver Curwood and such are your heroes and if you want life in "the great open spaces" all cheerio maybe you won't care about *Mantrap*.

Even at that you may decide Alverna, as played by Clara Bow, is more of a heroine than we have as yet had from Curwood and his kind.

We put *Mantrap* among the recommended pictures.

Son of the Sheik

After a series of so-so pictures, Rudolph Valentino came back with a vengeance in Son of the Sheik. *Self-parodying his famous "sheik" image, Valentino gave the best performance of his career. The set design by William Cameron Menzies gave* Son of the Sheik *the right mixture of dreamy exoticism. The film, sadly, was Valentino's last. See Sandburg's essay "Girl's Idea of Prince Was Rudolph Valentino," Saturday, August 28, 1926.*

Friday, July 30, 1926

The comeback of Rudolph Valentino in the *Son of the Sheik* is all that can be asked for by those who were accustomed at one time to rank him highest, those who first gave him that nickname of "the great lover."

It was *The Four Horsemen* and *The Sheik* that put him on the map.

And now in the *Son of the Sheik* he does everything that he did in *The Sheik* only with more restraint and decency.

But in this latest film he plays two parts, that of a sheik and the son of a sheik.

It is having its first run at the Roosevelt Theater this week and seems to be giving pleasure to the patrons thereof.

Vilma Banky is the leading lady, playing a dancing girl who wins the son of the sheik, against the wishes of his iron-willed father.

Then she loses her sheik.

But wins him again.

'Tis a movie.

Miss Banky is excellent as the dancing girl who loves, hates and loves.

Mr. Valentino is excellent as sufferer, as rescuer, as rider, as the handsome male of the desert sands who will brook no disturbance of his peace of soul.

Karl Dane is excellent, not quite so excellent as when he excelled as Slim in *The Big Parade*, but considering his Arabian clothes, the rags around his head and so on, pretty good at that.

George Fawcett, Bull Montana, Montague Love are other stars of a starry cast.

George Fitzmaurice directed and must have had his megaphone filled with the sands of the desert along the pacific coast dunes several times.

August

It's the Old Army Game

> *The Ziegfeld Follies was a Broadway revue that showcased dancers, musicians, and such varied comic talents as Bert Williams, Will Rogers, and W. C. Fields.* It's the Old Army Game *used some of the sketches Fields had developed on the Follies' stage. Co-star Louise Brooks was a former Follies player. Brooks's then-husband, Edward Sutherland, was the film's director; it was the first of five pictures Sutherland would helm for Fields.*

Monday, August 2, 1926

It's the Old Army Game, showing at neighborhood theaters, is the first of a series of pictures in which W. C. Fields is to star.

Mr. Fields is an actor who came up from the burlesque circuits into the Ziegfeld "Follies" and was first seen in the films under the direction of D. W. Griffith in *Sally of the Sawdust*.

Now he is seen in a picture whose story was done by J. P. McEvoy, author of *The Potters*, formerly of Chicago but now being in New York and being also what is known as an "émigré" from hereabout.

Mr. McEvoy wrote a piece for the stage billed *The Comic Supplement*, which made a very good show, according to all reports, but Flo Ziegfeld, who financed it, suddenly withdrew his support and the show quit in Washington, D. C. of all places.

It was as if they could tell their troubles to Congress or the President.

However, it was out of *The Comic Supplement* that Mr. Ziegfeld lifted three scenes which he inserted into the "Follies," and they were generally understood to be the backbone and sinew of the "Follies," the chorus girls and the costumes being the ephemera and the cuticle.

Now what we are getting at is that these three scenes which were the sinew and backbone of the "Follies," taking the place of Will Rogers, who was planning a trip to Europe for conferences with H. G. Wells and Mussolini—these three scenes are the meat and bone of this picture, *It's the Old Army Game*.

So if you decide to go see *It's the Old Army Game*, don't blame us for not having informed you fully and completely as to the history of the incidents which make up the story.

The New Yorker who sells New York lots to people down in Florida is handsome.

And the picnic scene tells us part of what is wrong with the country, though it does not go so far as to tell us what to do about it.

A Hero of the Big Snows

Rin-Tin-Tin, the dog who is a movie star, seems to be a friend of the children.

The audiences at the State-Lake Theater greeting him in his latest, *A Hero of the Big Snows*, have a larger than usual number of children.

At the first appearance of Rin-Tin-Tin, the children chortle glee and clap their hands, indicating they know him and like him.

The grownups who come along with the children seem to share in the fun.

The plot in this picture is about a bad man who was mean to his dog.

But there was a good man who saw the dog in trouble.

And the good man tried to fight the bad man but got the worst of it and would have suffered with sore feelings, indeed, had it not been for the dog, who, out of gratitude for his new-found friend, leaped to the rescue.

Later appears a lady dog for whom Rin-Tin-Tin has affection.

And the lady dog belongs to a lady who becomes the special friend of the man who owns Rin-Tin-Tin.

They have many troubles, of course, before they all finally end up in a happy home, while in the dwellings of the wicked there is wailing because they have been defeated.

Alice Calhoun, Don Alvarado, Leon Willis and Mary Jane Miliken are the principal human players, though of course they count for less than the canine players.

Battling Butler

In his review of Battling Butler, *Sandburg refers to Tom Wilson, a white actor who specialized in African-American roles early in his career. His best-known part in this capacity was as Austin Stoneman's black servant in* The Birth of a Nation *(1915). In the sound era Wilson largely played character and supporting roles.*

Buster Keaton comes to bat again, this time not only as the director of a picture.

Battling Butler, showing at the Oriental Theater, is a hot sketch, we might say.

It starts with a lively story with a novel plot, and we should say it is a pretty good handling the plot and the players get.

The hero, Alfred Butler, becomes engaged to a young lady and marries her, on the point that he is a manly man, expert in the manly art of self-defense, and not only that, but he sets forth that he is a champion lightweight.

When a fight is arranged between "The Alabama Murderer" and Battling Butler, the new wife of Alfred Butler insists on watching her husband train; also she insists on going to the knockout match where her husband, as she believes, is to be a principal.

Though her husband tries to stop her, she comes on and is fooled up till shortly before the fight, when she is captured and imprisoned in a room near the fighters' quarters, but barred from a view of the ring.

At about the time her husband is disgraced before her, as a quitter and a bluffer, things begin to happen that are a pleasant surprise, if not a thrill to the audience.

A well-directed picture, this is because it took close figuring to decided how long one fighter can give punishment to another before the other becomes a turning worm.

Sally O'Neill, Snitz Edwards, Francis McDonald, Mary O'Brien and Tom Wilson are members of a cast that valiantly supports the frozen-faced star.

Tom Wilson, who is probably the best known player of Negro roles, is seen here for the first time in a new role that shows he can do competently a different order of work than hitherto seen from him.

Fig Leaves

Fig Leaves *was the second film for Howard Hawks. Hawks would develop into one of Hollywood's most versatile and idiosyncratic directors, with films like* Scarface *(1932),* Bringing Up Baby *(1938),* His Girl Friday *(1940),* To Have and Have Not *(1944), and* Gentlemen Prefer Blondes *(1953) to his name.*

Thursday, August 12, 1926

Fig Leaves, the first important production to be released locally in recent weeks, is this week's feature at the Castle Theater.

It is an elaborate production and we can understand the Fox organization being enthusiastic about it.

The elaboration finds its place chiefly in and about the shop of a Fifth Avenue costumer.

His car runs down a young woman, who falls to the pavement, is wet by a street sprinkler, and is badly messed up.

She is taken then to his shop to be outfitted; he will do that much for her though his phrasing is that she "was loitering in front of my car."

Divested of the garments the street sprinkler has soaked and garbed in new devices of the highly modish establishment she looks different; M. Josef Andre takes a shine to her; he apparels her in many new conceptions.

But he discovers that she has a husband, and she discovers that her husband does not care to have her in the costuming business, while she believes she discovers her husband in undue familiarities with the lady across the way; out of this mix-up the plot travels a winding pathway.

Andre Beranger plays the costumer, George O'Brien the husband, Olive Borden the wife, and Phyllis Haver the lady across the way.

Howard Hawks directs the picture.

September

Three Bad Men

In 1948 John Ford remade Three Bad Men *as* The Three Godfathers *starring John Wayne.*

Monday, September 6, 1926

Three Bad Men is the latest young stalwart from the studios and factories and laboratories of William K. Fox. The picture is having its first run at the Monroe Theater and in neighborhood playhouses. When we refer to it as stalwart we mean it is up and coming, stands on its own feet, and if not outstanding it is upstanding.

It is about three dirty two-gun men who are in the Dakota land rush of 1877. They are wanted hither and yon over the map by sheriffs, police chiefs and state's attorneys. They have robbed banks, trains and livery sables, but never were caught red-handed.

And they find an assassin, a homeless, fatherless child; they adopt her; she travels with them and runs the gang. These three men are played by J. F. MacDonald, Thomas Santschi and Frank Campeau, while the heroine, for 'tis she, is played by Olive Berden.

Comes then young Dan O'Malley, as played by George O'Brien. He joins up with the outfit, having proved himself a "fittener fightin' man." The characters take part in melodramatic action before the final scenes, where justice is done. Among the players are Otis Harlan, Alec B. Francis, Phyllis Haver and Lou Tellegen.

John Ford, the director who made *The Iron Horse*, is the sponsor for this one.

Variety

German director E. A. Dupont's Variety, *a powerful tale of carnival denizens, was a huge hit with American audiences. Sandburg was among its many fans.*

Tuesday, September 14, 1926

And now in our midst we have *Variety*, the long-awaited *Variety*, the much-praised *Variety*.

The electric sign talents of Balaban & Katz are spelling the name *Variety* in dusky red lights in front of the Roosevelt Theater.

For an original photoplay there should be an original electric sign.

It is time to say we are pleased that *Variety* has come into our midst, that it was worth waiting for and at least seeing, that it has not been praised too much.

Emil Jannings, the male star, does the best all-around work we have seen from his prolific and changeful face, while Lya De Putti, the new female star, is far out of the ordinary and will be discussed freely among 10 or 20 million moviegoers in this country during the coming year.

The story is one of the oldest known in the annals of the human family; a man leaves one woman for another and the second woman double-crosses him for a handsomer man; there is murder and retribution.

And the old story is handled skillfully, is made the string on which many lanterns of themes, exploits and expressions are set forth in shadows, glimmer and blaze.

The characters are show people, and the atmosphere is that of the show world; we see marvelous vaudeville and superb trapeze feats.

In making this picture they realized there was vast opportunity for play of light, for contrasts and looming shadowgraphs in the realms of trapeze performance where there are double and triple somersaults, and an actor swings blindfolded in midair.

Variety is one of the few sure masterpieces of film art.

Those who want novelty, a change from the usual, may find it here; those who want storytelling, character, atmosphere, along with a wizardry of photography, direction and stage management, will make no mistake about seeing *Variety*.

Friday, October 1, 1926

That remarkable photoplay *Variety* is in its closing three days; it is to be shown in a limited run at neighborhood theaters; its run of two weeks at the Roosevelt Theater is a short one; that the crowds have not been larger may indicate one thing or another; we leave the psychologists who think they know public taste to figure it out.

Variety is a masterly piece of film drama from several points of view, whether of story, of characters, of general atmosphere, of photographic art, sets, lighting, or of direction.

This reviewer has seen *Variety* three times, and will slip into the Roosevelt for one more view, if occasion offers. It is a varied box of tricks, a swift and shifting lot of facts and illusions with which this picture deals. The events as told, and the characters as developed, have a little of the mystery of life itself; the disclosure is by a high order of art, intelligence and technical skill.

Understand—*Variety* isn't what some people might call a highbrow picture. Not by a long shot. It would interest any child interested in circuses, trapeze acting with triple somersaults, acrobats and juggling—and then besides its gayety it tells a story at moments wayward and brutal, but no more so than some of the books of Charles Dickens, for instance.

We have heard several persons who saw *The Miracle* last winter, and who have been to see *Variety*, make their declarations that as a work of art they would give *Variety* a higher rating. Of course, their opinions are personal.

Monday, October 11, 1926

Variety, the European masterpiece of film drama, which has brought much comment that more productions of this type should be brought to this country and put on exhibition as pacemakers to some of our American directors, is the feature at the Castle Theater this week.

One important player in the cast of this picture is the Berlin Wintergarten audience that watches the trapeze act. The faces of rows of spectators are shown, the eyes and nostrils of individual onlookers upturned in curiosity, expectation as to what is happening or what turn of luck might happen high in the dome of the building where the performers are executing double and triple somersaults.

The motion picture can do this thing, and does it regularly, in a way that the legitimate drama cannot. Audiences as part of the stage drama must be limited to the size of the stage. But in a motion picture play an audience may be enormous, and the circling, panoramic camera gathers it all and passes it to the projection machine, which throws it on the little screen, where the little human eye gathers it as if it were reality.

The crowd may be in the Wintergarten in Berlin, it may be at a big league or World Series ballgame, it may be in the Yale bowl seeing football or at the Hollywood Bowl in song service or at pontifical mass of the Eucharist congress in the stadium of Soldiers' Field. We have seen all these crowds employed with dramatic effect on the screen.

In *Variety* there is exceptional skill in the portrayal of the crowd of spectators of the trapeze act.

Vitaphone Demonstrated

The Vitaphone was a revolutionary device in the development of motion picture sound. In what proved to be a painstaking process, action would be recorded on film with microphones simultaneously recording sound to a disc. A motion picture projector synchronized with a record player was used to show the final product. Warner Brothers' studios, which owned 70 percent of the Vitaphone Corporation, put together a program of musical shorts and premiered them as part of a double bill with Don Juan. *This John Barrymore adventure had some synchronized sound effects as well, including swords clanging and bells ringing. Warners released some 100 Vitaphone shorts in 1926, a figure doubled in 1927.[3] Talking movies were clearly on the horizon.*

Thursday, September 16, 1926

The first presentation locally of a motion picture play with a mechanically synchronized orchestral accompaniment took place last night at McVicker's Theater when Warner Brothers put on their Vitaphone show.

The picture play was *Don Juan* with John Barrymore starring, with Willard Louis as the male comic, Mary Astor as the leading lady, and Estelle Taylor, wife of Jack Dempsey, in the role of Lucrezia Borgia.

Preceding the movie there was a demonstration of what the vitaphone can do in presenting concert numbers by famous artists; the audience sees the performer in a close-up view with the advantage that those in the rear of the theater get a clearer impression than if the performer were there in life; the music created reaches the audience sometimes as vivid as if it were the real thing.

Will H. Hays, director general of organized motion pictures, made a speech, via motion picture and vitaphone, in which he said, "The future of motion pictures is as far-flung as all the tomorrows." He congratulated those who have produced the synchronization of picture and sound and indicated that the movies of the future are to be bound up with mechanical devices for bringing music to as widespread audiences as those of the motion picture world.

During the reeling of the photoplay, *Don Juan*, the audience heard a running accompaniment by the New York Philharmonic Orchestra. The illusion of an actual orchestra creating this music was often complete.

The character of Don Juan is a dual role for Barrymore. First he is a Spanish grandee tricked by his wife; his son to believe in no woman. The son, played by Barrymore, is a philanderer of proportions and excess; the tale moves through many dark affairs with Rome for a background and the time of the Borgias as the period.

A house filled with representative first nighters from the triple fields of motion pictures, music and drama, greeted the performance. Also, there was a sprinkling of those highly developed persons who are interested in the new discoveries and inventions of that two-legged creature man; they came representing civilization with hoping eyes on the future.

The Campus Flirt

Tuesday, September 21, 1926

Bebe Daniels in *The Campus Flirt*, showing at the Chicago Theater, does Harold Lloyd's stuff with reverse English. She comes to Colton College bound to make the school jump at her word, being a daughter of the particularly cultured Somebodies of Michigan. Colton College has other ideas, and the story develops out of the school's effort to make the daughter of the particular Somebodies of Michigan conform.

For they are a democratic bunch at Colton, and apparently quite as virtuous as they ought to be—except for a dark young man with a Rolls-Royce and a motorboat, who is balanced by a fair young man with a curious flair for holding the stop watch on the female track team of the school.

Well, the daughter of the particular Somebodies of Michigan gets snagged up with him of the Rolls-Royce, accidentally gets drunk, and the usual complications ensure when they pair up for a motorboat ride.

The thrilling drama comes in when the dark-haired youth knocks out the fair one of the stopwatch, against whom he nurses an evil grudge, and hides him away. For this happens the day before the great track meet, and who will there be to hold the ticker?

How she gets him out and how she wins the track meeting give a final flourish to a good movie.

This one has the additional feature of having Charlie Paddock, holder of more track titles than he can count, play the part of the girl's coach. He shows a little speed himself in the picture.

The Flaming Frontier

1926 was the fiftieth anniversary of General George Armstrong Custer's famed "Last Stand" at Montana's Little Big Horn River. To honor the event, Universal put together an epic recreation. The film utilized hundreds of extras for the battle sequences, with an 1885 graduate of West Point serving as technical advisor. Critics had great praise for The Flaming Frontier. *It was a big hit with audiences as well, yet we may never know how good the movie really was. Though some of the battle footage was recycled in a 1930 movie serial* The Indians are Coming, *there is no known print of* The Flaming Frontier.[4]

Wednesday, September 22, 1926

Gen. George A. Custer of "Custer's Last Battle" fame, and President Ulysses S. Grant are not the least of the characters portrayed in *The Flaming Frontier*, this week's release at the Randolph Theater. For we may also see portrayals of Sitting Bull, Rain-in-the-Face and others.

A cleanly done story that in some of its flow of narrative, its atmosphere and American color reminds us of certain tales that ran in the old *Youth's Companion*.

Hoot Gibson plays the main hero, but there are subsidiary heroes, such as Gen. Custer, played by Dustin Farnum; and even the Indians in this picture have a touch of the heroic, for the people of Sitting Bull and Rain-in-the-Face are shown as having

318 "The Movies Are"

wrongs "almost too great to be endured" thrust upon them by the whites.

The hero has been a daring young plainsman on the frontier, and for bravery and toil is awarded a West Point cadetship. At the military academy he gets in bad, taking the blame for something another fellow did. The other fellow happens to be the brother of his sweetheart, which is a situation not unheard of in literature and drama before today. However, it is nicely worked out and it may be predicted that this picture will please a wide audience.

Anne Cornwall is the leading lady and others in the cast are Ward Crane, Kathleen Key, George Fawcett, Noble Johnson and Joe Bonomo. It is a Universal production and was directed by Edward Sedgewick.

October

One Minute to Play

Harold "Red" Grange, a football star at the University of Illinois, turned pro in 1924. His popularity on the field translated into lucrative endorsement contracts and—inevitably—a shot at the movies. In 1926 he was paid a phenomenal $300,000 for One Minute to Play. *Grange did have certain conditions, however: "I don't want to play a sheik part," Grange stated publicly. "This business of lollygagging around with a girl most of the time, as movie actors usually do in all the pictures I've seen, is not in my line."[5]*

Thursday, October 7, 1926

We have heard this chatter about Red Grange being a movie actor, now that the picture, *One Minute to Play*, is showing at the Rialto Theater.

Just because *One Minute to Play* is an interesting movie, better than ordinary, and because well-handled football is dramatic and Red Grange in running with the ball is fascinating doesn't say he is next going into character parts and compete with Richard Dix, Jack Mulhall, Tommy Meighan, or that there would be any wisdom in trying to have him fill the vast, vacant void left by the passing of Valentino.

Red Grange is a crackerjack of a football player, a mighty clean specimen of male manhood to look at, with a ghostly cunning and sagacity about fooling the fellows that try to block him when he runs with the pigskin.

That is, if we are going to classify our DuPage County iceman in the field of cinema art, the comparison must be with Strongheart or Rin-Tin-Tin rather than the general run of pretty boys who do the starring.

A nice, snappy story, of the kind run in the snappy story magazines, of the kind written by Oliver Optic, is what we find in *One Minute to Play*.

And the direction is capable and the photography unusually good. The scrimmages and the rough stuff of the game of football are done in mass confusions and swift, blurry effects that tell the story. Red runs in line with his nickname of the Galloping Ghost.

Sam Wood, as director, did well. The cast includes Mary McAllister, Charles Ogle, Lee Shumway, George Wilson, Ben Hendricks, Jr., Lincoln Stedman and Jay Hunt. The characters of a college president and a crotchety, prospective donor of an endowment, are excellently done by Charles Ogle and Jay Hunt.

Private Izzy Murphy

George Jessel, a product of New York's Yiddish theater, was well known, thanks to his success in the stage show "The Jazz Singer." Though Al Jolson starred in the film version of The Jazz Singer, *Jessel's popularity with audiences was assured.* Private Izzy Murphy *was typical of 1920s ethnic stereotype humor on both stage and screen.*

Friday, October 15, 1926

Private Izzy Murphy, which is now running at the Orpheum Theater, has in its leading player George Jessel, who is synchronously appearing in "The Jazz Singer," a stage play, at the Harris Theater, thus achieving the feat of being a movie actor and a perfectly legitimate dramatic player in the same town in the same week.

Those who see the movie at the Orpheum for 50 cents may, if they doubt the star is the one inimitable and indubitable George Jessel, walk across the Loop to the Harris Theater and for two dollars get up close to the stage and identify him.

The character he essays in the picture is that of I. Patrick Murphy, which is not his right name, but which may win more business where his delicatessen is located. When the World War has the United States entering he goes and by a series of mistakes is enlisted as I. Patrick Murphy, and by reason of his first name Isadore comes to be known as Private Izzy.

The Irish and the Jews are set forth in contrasts of various sorts, much the same as in "Abie's Irish Rose." Patsy Ruth Miller plays the rose.

The story is packed with a good deal of plain human interest, well handled by the director, Lloyd Bacon.

Vera Gordon plays the mother of "Private Izzy" and Philip Lonergan the father. This is a better-than-ordinary picture and a Warner Brothers production.

Kid Boots

Eddie Cantor, along with George Jessel, had been a part of the New York Jewish theatrical tradition of the early twentieth century. In the mid-1920s, as the fortunes of Cantor and Jessel were rising, they joined fellow actors within the Yiddish theater to form the first Yiddish-English theater guild.[6] Cantor enjoyed Broadway success with the show "Kid Boots" and quickly leaped into the film version. Though popular with silent audiences, Cantor's movie career really took off with the advent of sound.

Monday, October 18, 1926

And now we have the widely known Yiddish playboy, Eddie Cantor, as a movie star in a picturization of *Kid Boots*. And it is surprising what a smart piece of film drama can be worked out from a musical stage show.

We also learn that a comedian whose reputation has been built partly around his singing of songs can get along very nicely in the silent medium of the silversheet, where nobody uses the voice, not even John Barrymore in the vitaphone, as yet.

Clara Bow, Billie Dove and Lawrence Gary are the capable support for Mr. Cantor in a story that travels fast. It takes the lowly hero in a lowly hand-me-down clothes shop, connects him with a crisp heroine, who says she doesn't care about the looks of a man, but he must be "reliable." The accent is on "reliable." A subsidiary hero is breaking from his faithless wife, whose lawyers are scheming to have them "together, alone," so that the final decree of divorce cannot be entered. The lowly and homely hero assists his pal so that "together, alone" is not possible.

Florenz Ziegfeld, who produced the stage show, gave this picture his personal supervision and it has a certain characteristic Ziegfeld skill and crisp know-how. Frank Tuttle directed and the results measure up fully to *The American Venus*, *The Palm Beach Girl* and other Tuttle affairs. Tom Gibson did the scenario. The length is nine reels, and as we noted, it travels fast and with few regrets.

How One Marx Brother Reacted to Pictures

In the early 1900s, Groucho Marx and his brothers Harpo, Chico, Zeppo, and Gummo, along with their mother/manager Minnie, lived in Chicago. At the time, Chicago was a good central location for vaudevillians touring national theater circuits. The literary-minded Groucho spent off-hours nosing around the Covici-Mc-Gee Bookstore on Washington Boulevard. A popular gathering place for writers, it was here Marx first rubbed elbows with Sandburg.[7] In 1920, like many vaudeville acts, the Marx Brothers took a stab at filmmaking. The result was a spoof of the movie business called Humorisk. *By all accounts,* Humorisk *was an amateur production. Embarrassed by this effort, the brothers had the only print destroyed.[8]*

The negative for Humorisk *was later mislaid, and probably tossed out by an errant movie projectionist.*[9] *Harpo later appeared in* Too Many Kisses *with Richard Dix (see review, Friday, March 6, 1925). Though mocking of the film industry in this interview, Groucho and his brothers would soon be movie stars themselves. "The Cocoanuts," a Broadway show in 1926, was turned into a successful talking picture in 1929. The rest is history.*

Saturday, October 30, 1926

The Four Marx Brothers playing in "The Cocoanuts" at the Erlanger Theater are old-time friends of Charlie Chaplin. They remember when they traveled on the same circuit, playing the same vaudeville theaters as Charlie Chaplin, in the days when the nickelodeon was a promise of the film industry to come. And now when the Marx Brothers get to Los Angeles Charlie Chaplin always has a box at their show and they throw a line of jokes aimed at Charlie. And when he visits New York and the Marx Brothers are playing there he goes to the Long Island home of Julius (Groucho) Marx, goes yachting and clam digging with Groucho, suggests names for any new Grouchos that may have arrived and examines the fresh additions to the collections of Japanese prints and masks of savage south sea tribesmen on which Groucho discourses. So far, so good. What we started to say was that Groucho doesn't care much about the movies. While the other arts have progressed the last 10 years the movies have stood still, says he, in these words "In Chicago, as in New York, Baltimore and elsewhere, have sprung up the ice-cooled, in-closed stadiums, symphony orchestras, super-super features, generals and admirals ushering patrons to plush-covered seats, velvet drapes, lobbies filled with oil paintings and foliage, long, searching articles in the *Nation* and the *New Republic* on the significance and importance of the photofilm and the Hollywood movie to Germany.

"And what of it? I ask: what of it? I planked down 65 cents at the Lyric, one of Baltimore's new movie art palaces, and went in and saw a show that was the same in general design as the one I used to see in the old days for a dime. What I expected was the new highbrow cinema entertainment I had been reading about. What did I see? A two-reeler where the comedians throw grapefruit at each other and wind up throwing a policeman out of the window. Then came a super six-reeler, *The Sea Wolf,* climaxed with what was obviously a cardboard ship on fire sinking on what was unquestionably a papier-mâché ocean. Then came an announcement of the best places in Baltimore to shop and the proud boast that the projection machine is operated by a union operator."

Now, we could understand how some people would guess that the Baltimoreans saw Groucho Marx coming. The screen advertising and the union operator announcement must have been put on for his special benefit; they have not been seen locally in years. And the ocean in *The Sea Wolf* must have been a special papier-mâché one that they slipped over on Groucho. When this reviewer saw the ocean in *The Sea Wolf* it looked like the Pacific Ocean near Hollywood, the same one into which Balboa took a header off a cliff.

In the case of these Marx Brothers we can't be sure of anything, except that they kid each other and they kid the public. One of them, Harpo the Redhead, says never a word throughout the performance of "The Cocoanuts," yet renders a superbly fantastic pantomimic character portrayal. He creates a droll animated dummy, the loveable clumsy one that figures in folk tales, the one that has wisdom and grace in spite of all his mistakes. We would not be surprised to see Harpo Marx seized one of these days, transported to Hollywood, and set forth triumphantly in a fantasy tentatively titled *Beautiful Though Speechless*.

November

The Black Pirate

Though Douglas Fairbanks had dabbled with color tinting and early Technicolor sequences in previous efforts, The Black Pirate *was his first effort to be filmed entirely in color. "Really, I don't know what it's all about," Fairbanks said of the color process. "None of us does. That's why it is all so confoundedly interesting."* [10]

Thursday, November 4, 1926

It seems that Douglas Fairbanks said to himself he would make a pirate picture book that would be a world-beater, with pirates bloody, pirates gleesome, pirates galore all over the place, living and scuffling pirates, dead and gory pirates.

This he has done in *The Black Pirate*, starting its run this week at the Roosevelt Theater.

To make sure it would be a picture book photoplay, Mr. Fairbanks, the producer and businessman, who is the same as the Mr. Fairbanks who is a movie player and acts in the pictures, presented this film in colors.

We can tell one pirate from another by his red, blue or yellow bandanna tied around the head.

It is hard to tell which is the ugliest of the pirates, however. Personal tastes are different. Each moviegoer is entitled to his own free guess and opinion as to which has the fiercest mug in this particular outfit.

Doug himself plays the Black Pirate, in southern seas which a pirate ship has been making unsafe for merchantmen carrying honest cargoes. Ships are looted and blown up. There is a treasure island where the gold and jewels are hidden. And the Black Pirate arrives to become chief of this crew which, of course, is the motliest of motley crews. The intention was to have the picture very motley with bad men, and full of motley atmosphere.

Billie Dove plays the princess who is stolen and for whom men defy death and the elements. Anders Randolf has the role of a pirate chief. The cast includes Donald Crisp, Sam De Grasse, John Wallace, Fred Becker, Charles Belcher and Charles Stevens.

The production is United Artists and Albert Parker directed. While as a Fairbanks picture, it isn't up to the quality of *The Thief of Bagdad*, it has the punch and picturesqueness of *Robin Hood*.

The Temptress

> *Mauritz Stiller, Greta Garbo's mentor, was the original director on* The Temptress. *MGM had him removed after disagreements over Stiller's un-orthodox shooting methods; some studio heads feared that Garbo would follow him.[11] Fred Niblo was brought in to direct, yet Garbo stayed and* The Temptress *was a popular and critical hit.*

Wednesday, November 24, 1926

It is not the way of Greta Garbo to eat rose leaves in order to show filmgoers that she is an idle, destructive female. Vampires used always to do this. Some of them yet register wantonness by consuming a big bowl of deep red roses while they roll their eyes at some helpless he-man who is being sent simply off his nut by the sight of so much beauty.

Greta Garbo tempts in her own way, very cool of manner, very easy and very, very sure. Where Lya De Putti is all fire and flesh, Greta Garbo is half-myth, the spirit of unmoral, not immoral, love, wavering and trailing through the picture, *The Temptress*, like the essence of all siren hearts over time.

In *The Temptress* she may be seen to take a nominal husband to protect her vampiring raids among the fatuous bankers of Paris, also she may be seen to lead one banker to dramatic and howling suicide. And, moreover, for six whole reels she sets an engineering camp in the Argentine so mad with desire that a mammoth dam is destroyed by jealous rivals, friends saber each other to death and two men duel viciously with wicked blacksnake whips.

For all the deaths she occasions, reputations she wrecks and lifeworks she ruins this heroine of Blasco Ibáñez somehow is urged upon you as blameless, as sinned against rather than sinning, as the traditional female whose mere beauty causes sin to flourish.

Greta Garbo, slim, pale, like willows turning yellow in autumn, is the one actress, sure enough, to put into this role if it is to be made plausible. Gowned to kill, directed in such a manner that her face is full into the camera most of the time, she scores a downright triumph.

Antonio Moreno, Roy D'Arcy, Lionel Barrymore, Marc MacDermott, Robert Andersen—all good people for their roles—have a lot to do in this long special from

Metro-Goldwyn-Mayer's workshops. Fred Niblo, who made *Ben-Hur*, worked on this and shows again his talents for arresting, vivid scenes and his inabilities to humanize plot.

Presentation is at the Roosevelt Theater, where Greta Garbo may be recommended as something indeed for all adults to look upon.

The Winning of Barbara Worth

Though directed by Henry King and written by Frances Marion and an uncredited Lenore J. Coffee, with titles by Rupert Hughes, Sandburg devotes much of this review to his former Daily News *colleague, Ben Hecht. Hecht, a former Chicago journalist, as well as novelist, playwright, and screenwriter, apparently was in town the day that Sandburg saw* The Winning of Barbara Worth. *With his trademark edgy humor and rough characters, Hecht was a polar opposite to the more saccharine writer Harold Bell Wright, author of the novel* The Winning of Barbara Worth. *The Cook County hangings Sandburg mentions later became the inspiration for one of Hecht's finest efforts, the play* The Front Page *(co-written with Charles MacArthur). Wallace Smith was another Chicago journalist turned screenwriter. Schlog's was a downtown hangout favored by Chicago newspaper writers of the 1910s and 1920s.*

Tuesday, November 30, 1926

Just why *The Winning of Barbara Worth*, a film production based on the widely sold novel of the same title, by Harold Bell Wright, should be offered to the screen public and opened for its run at the Orpheum Theater on the same day that Ben Hecht, author of *Humpty Dumpty, Count Bruga* and *Broken Necks*, arrives in the city and greets his former associates at Schlog's, is a matter for conjecture or a riddle to which the answer is anybody's guess and the devil take the hindmost.

Now, for those who wish a bang-up Western picture with the kind of a love story we have all heard of before, with first-rate shooting and riding, with first-rate desert scenery, cactus and cacti that are guaranteed to be the real thing, *The Winning of Barbara Worth* is a picture worth seeing.

Ronald Colman, who is always in the argument when successors to Valentino as a heartbreaker are being discussed, plays the leading role, that of Willard Holmes. And Vilma Banky plays Barbara Worth and is what some might call svelte and others would say is swell. Charles Lane plays Jefferson Worth and Paul McAllister is the seer.

With Ben Hecht now half-way to Hollywood, under contract to write scenarios, furnish ideas and tell them what he knows about a photoplay that would win public patronage sufficient to pay for production and yield a measure of profit for the producers, while at the same time advancing the cause of cinema art, we are not sure of what is happening in the screen realm, except that the producers seem to be trying all things, like the Apostle Paul, and holding fast to that which is good.

The customers of the movie theaters include many shades of belief and opinion. That Harold Bell Wright and Ben Hecht are gathered together under the Hollywood tent is significant of we do not know just what.

It was our privilege to report to Ben that in Hollywood he would meet his old friend and associate, Wallace Smith, author of *The Little Tigress* and other books. Ben and Wallie sat side by side and reported for their respective newspapers 11 hangings in Cook County and one in DuPage County. They have cultivated cool behavior and will not be buffaloed by anything they meet in Hollywood—that is one of the certainties of the situation.

December

Sparrows

Sparrows is considered Mary Pickford's finest effort. The alligator sequence Sandburg alludes to was very real. For this scene Pickford had to carry a baby through a swamp of hungry alligators. Though understandably apprehensive about being just jaws' length away from live alligators, Pickford gamely agreed to director William Beaudine's insistence that the shot could not be faked. Reportedly, Pickford's then-husband Douglas Fairbanks happened to visit the Sparrows *set and flew into a rage when he saw what was going on. Despite Fairbanks's demands that the sequence be created through special effects, Pickford did the scene on Beaudine's terms.[12]*

Tuesday, December 7, 1926

Mary Pickford's best picture is this *Sparrows*, opening its run this week at the Roosevelt Theater. If there was anything to the films of years back that won her the title of America's sweetheart or the pigtail queen that title is better supported by this production than anything hitherto. Of course, there was one called *Suds* that had its points. But we believe many will say *Sparrows* is the goods, the topnotcher, the grand prix.

Just a story of a baby farm—kept by a man as real and terrible as the Bill Sikes of Dickens—and there is a kidnapping—and there is an escape and a capture. The old-time melodramas are beaten and backed off the boards, considering some of the tricks, suspensions and solutions to be seen here. The calculation is mathematical and gets down to fine points once in a while as when the kids have escaped from their barn prison and are crossing a swamp where fearsome alligators linger and yawn in the muddy, boggy waters. Will the limb of a tree break as the children, one by one clutch and crawl along it with the open-mouthed alligators waiting below?

Mary Pickford,
"America's
Sweetheart" on
screen, was a
perceptive and
powerful film
industry figure
behind the scenes.

Yet, while this is melodrama it happens that once in a while the picture achieves fantasy. It's a real world and it isn't. Of course, such sweet, tough kiddoes and kiddees are not seen in actual life. And the ending scenes are not dragged too far. Yet it rises and holds one with elemental power of story telling and of character portrayal. We would say this is strictly among the recommended photoplays of the current output.

William Beaudine directed it and it surely is about his best. Gustav von Seyffertitz plays the terrible baby farm man, Grimes, and Roy Stewart and Mary Louise Miller play interesting roles. The production is handled by United Artists.

While London Sleeps

While it may be upsetting to art film aficionados, Sandburg makes a convincing argument in his comparison here of a Rin-Tin-Tin picture to the German Expressionist classic The Cabinet of Dr. Caligari*!*

Tuesday, December 14, 1926

For a wild running melodrama of a detective story, a dog story and a love story all in one three-time thriller we would recommend *While London Sleeps*, this week's offering at the State-Lake Theater.

What would you? Here is the Hawk, the terror of the Limehouse district. Against the Hawk and his gang is Inspector Burke of Scotland Yard. Right onto the front doorknob of the police inspector the Hawk sent his challenge, "Come down to the Limehouse tonight, if you dare." And says the inspector, "We must! The honor of Scotland Yard is at stake."

So they go. They take the dog, Rin-Tin-Tin, along. Yet even as they leave the inspector's home we see the Hawk prowling about the lawn, shrubbery and trees with an Ape Man.

By and by the Ape Man has climbed through a window and carried away the inspector's daughter. And by and by the inspector has returned home, led by the unerring scent of the dog, Rin-Tin-Tin. His scent on a manhunt is as keen in the streets of the metropolis of London as in the trackless wilds roamed by the Northwest Mounted Police.

In the end the dog gets his man, saves the daughter of the Scotland Yard inspector from a fate less awful than death, if you know what we mean, and of course saves the honor of Scotland Yard.

Rin-Tin-Tin is the star of the piece. Helene Costello and DeWitt Jennings carry the roles of daughter and father ably. George Katsmarof is the Ape Man and with the surrounding scenery at times reminds one of spots in *The Cabinet of Dr. Caligari.* As detective and dog stories go we rate this among the current topnotchers. It was directed by Walter Morosco and is a Warner Brothers production.

Will Rogers, Our Unofficial Ambassador Abroad

Here Sandburg reviews a series of Will Rogers' two-reelers that were released throughout 1927. Despite Sandburg's comment that "Men nearest him (Rogers) say that he is done forever with acting roles and parts in movies and stage productions," Rogers continued doing film and theater until his untimely death in a 1935 plane crash with aviator Wiley Post.

Thursday, December 23, 1926

Yesterday, in Chicago, representatives of the large film distributing companies and theatrical chains set themselves down to look at Will Rogers' latest adventure in independent artistry. They had the first view of Rogers' individually made and personally produced travel pictures, a series of one-reel tours of European nations.

Nothing of Hollywood, nothing with the stamp of film convention is in these pictures. They speak subtly, but tellingly, of the change in Rogers himself. For Will Rogers has outgrown the lariat. Men nearest him say that he is done forever with acting roles and parts in movies and stage productions. He doesn't want even to pretend he's somebody other than he is. He feels that in magazine articles, radio talks and lecture tours he can be himself more than he used to be when performing his comic parts in "The Follies" and in the motion pictures he once played for Sam Goldwyn.

Rogers took a motion picture camera along on his last European tour and came back with a picture original in every respect. In the first two of the series, shown privately yesterday, Rogers with his hat on the back of his head is shown as a philosopher and guide of the typical moviegoer through Europe. He moves in and out of the scenes, presenting the president of the Irish republic, jaunting car drivers, Celtic faces, landscapes, streets, important buildings and interjecting whimsical, salty comment with that homely, human smile of his.

His is a magnificent independence, when, arms locked with President Cosgrave of Ireland, he jerks a thumb at Cosgrave's leading minister alongside, and laughs into the camera, "This is a pretty cold bird."

His is an irresistible impudence and charm when he pokes a fat Dutch peasant lady and asks her why she doesn't reduce. She roars with mirth and informs him that it is mostly petticoat, not avoirdupois. Whereupon Rogers obtains and proudly displays to the camera Dutch fashions in voluminous petticoats. "Noting could be a stranger sight to American women," he observes.

The subtitles are all his own.

What Price Glory?

Despite the restrictions of the Hays Office, audiences could clearly lip-read the curse words flying out the mouths of Victor McLaglen and Edmund Lowe in this realistic war drama. In 1952 director John Ford remade What Price Glory? *with James Cagney.*

Monday, December 27, 1926

One moment you're in the busy whirl of traffic in Randolph Street, the next you're away off in France living again the war as vividly, as dramatically, as real as you'll ever be able to live it eight or one hundred years after it's over.

That's the Aladdin transformation which awaits one who steps into the Garrick Theater to see the screen version of *What Price Glory?* William Fox, with Raoul Walsh directing and the help of a lot of men who have had a friendly speaking acquaintance with the late party over there, have taken this graphic tale of the great conflict and turned out a masterpiece that's hard to tell from the original.

It is the story of the comedy, the drama, the tragedy, the harshness, the cruelty and the futility of the war as it was lived by the men—and the women—who fought it. It isn't overplayed and it isn't theatrical. It is the war in stark reality—except, perhaps, in that melodramatic ending, which, let's hope, they put in more as a theoretical "kick" rather than to be swallowed as an actuality.

Strangely enough, comedy forms the greater part of this masterful yarn of the war, rich, uproarish, screaming comedy. But the drama and tragedy is there, drama that thrills and tragedy that grips. The battle scenes, of which there are many, tell the grim story of war as no tongue or pen will ever tell it. They are some of the greatest at which a camera has ever clicked, either in the real or make-believe. That "big push," the streaming over the top, the confusion, the terror, the spitting machine guns, the roaring, tearing, thundering barrages, are enough to make any ex-participant want to dive for the nearest shell hole.

The story, of course, revolves around those two hard-boiled, swearin' leathernecks, Capt. Flagg and Sergt. Quirt, and their eternal clash over the feminine spoils of war. Victor McLaglen is the batter-nosed, foul-mouthed, hardened captain and Edmund Lowe is the tough sergeant. They are everything Laurence Stallings and Maxwell Anderson must have had in mind when they wrote the story. Dolores Del Rio is the charming, chic, delectable Charmaine who reminds you so much of the girl you left behind—over there.

The cussin' in the stage play that shocked pious souls is there, too. Not in subtitles, but it's there—if, like the preacher's son, you know all the words and can read lip movements.

Maybe you missed the big show and wished you hadn't. Maybe you didn't miss it and wished you had. Either way you'll be sorry if you miss *What Price Glory?* It's war as real as you'll ever see it, and withal it's a sermon on peace, for in it you'll find, as nearly as you'll ever find, the answer to that question—what price glory, anyway?

Saturday, January 15, 1927

Here is a strange matter.

Here is a motion picture with homely ruffians for heroes, with a faithless flirt for heroine, with an unorthodox ending and with blasphemy and profanity and suggestion coursing through it—here is a picture rich with all the taboos, achieving the unquestioned triumph of the season.

What Price Glory? violates every maxim in the screen director's guidebook and literally bowls over the very people for whom these guidebooks were prepared.

Housewives, grandmothers, orthodox matrons in hundreds sit thrilling and weeping and shaking with laughter most strangely and inexplicably in the Garrick Theater these days. They have never done anything but flee from such factors in real life. They have never loved drunken, carnal screen characters before. Probably they never will again. But they do these days in the Garrick.

The thing is sheer magic, sheer necromancy in its heroizing of two battered, foul-tongued professional soldiers. Capt. Flagg and Sergt. Quirk come to the screen as stronger, better rounded characters than to the stage. Laurence Stallings and Maxwell Anderson made them famous. Raoul Walsh and William Fox made them immortal. It is the camera that must receive the credit. It is the camera that erects, in its shots of Flagg's head, such a statue to the ancient professional soldier as Phidias could never have done.

Here is the secret for the incredible popular triumph of *What Price Glory?* on the screen. It rises above the appeals of patriotism, sentiment, humor, and romance—although it has all those things—to shake the whole emotional structure of spectators with an epic portrait of two fascinating and violent men. It rises to the heights of doing the professional soldier as he has waited 5,000 years to be done, without gloves, without patronage and with sure, certain truthfulness.

The professional soldier swears, he wastes his leisure on scarlet women, he drinks, he carouses, he is vulgar and brutal.

Well, he was so in the camps of Caesar, Alexander, Napoleon and Frederick the Great.

The hard-boiled fighting man violates every canon of the respectable civilian. Well, it was so in the legions of Gustavus Adolphus, of Cyrus the Great and William Tecumseh Sherman.

The man who fights as a trade, rather than for any flag or slippered burgher, has his kindly moments, his codes of honor, his manliness in odd moments in battle lulls.

This was true in the ranks of Hannibal and Marshal Ney.

What Price Glory? soars above all rules and canons of picture making because it holds to these truths. The broken-nosed head of Flagg as it comes through the smoke, cool, bitter, deadly, while young marines drop, drop, drop behind him and Germans shoot, run and fall before him, is the head of Caesar.

The face Flagg turns to the light of love Charmaine as he comes out of the trenches on leave is the face all professional warriors have turned to the crimson vivandiers since war was war.

Becoming the tale of two age-old characters, romance, adventure, humor all become merely obligators to a saga, a hero-song.

From the moment *What Price Glory?* begins until it ends it can do nothing, say nothing that is not in the epic mold. Victor McLaglen may be a good actor but he is something finer than that here. He is Capt. Flagg; he is Caesar. Edmund Lowe may be close to him in artistry but he is almost as completely Sergt. Quirk, Alexander the Great kissing Persian camp-followers after the day's red work is done. Dolores Del Rio suddenly seems to be a great actress. She is nothing of the kind. She is merely the perfect sweetheart of those laughing, faithless men who seldom marry because they are too busy defending whole populations of women whom they never see, nor care to see.

A Little Journey

Specializing in comic smart alecks and peppy college lad roles, William Haines was a popular romantic lead with 1920s filmgoers. A former Wall Street office boy, Haines's career began after he won a 1922 "New Faces" competition. This eventually led Haines to Hollywood and stardom. Ultimately Haines's screen days ended due to Hollywood's homophobia. One of the first openly gay actors in the film community (a fact carefully avoided by studio publicity), Haines was ultimately fired for his off-screen lifestyle by MGM mogul Louis B. Mayer. It didn't matter; Haines was already building a second career as an interior decorator. He became well respected in this field, creating living spaces for Joan Crawford, Carole Lombard, Lionel Barrymore, Claudette Colbert, Jack Warner, and Walter Annenberg. In 1969 Haines designed his masterpiece in the residence of Anneberg, America's ambassador to Great Britain.

Thursday, December 30, 1926

William Haines is the smartest of the smart-alec impersonators. In fact he has made the business of playing wise-cracking show-offs particularly his own. In *Memory Lane* he began his experiments with juvenile adventures in conceit. The picture lifted him out of the leading man class and elevated him close to stardom. *Brown of Harvard* shot him higher. And now in *A Little Journey* at the Oriental Theater he is dealing with the same idea.

His idea is that brash, forward, irrepressible young Americans between 18 and 22 are funny and admirable and pathetic, usually all at the same time. He has a definite and unerring feeling for smart-alecs, an ability to sketch their ridiculous excesses of vitality and wild, young tenderness. Any spirited young man trying to cover up his wonderment and timidity with hard-boiled boldness is Mr. Haines' own private dish.

A Little Journey is the story of such a youth meeting a nice girl on a train. For all that the boy is fresh and gauche there is something about his undertone of sentiment that wins the girl. But, she tells him, she is on her way to meet another man and marry him. The other man is rich and kind but older. So the boy takes his grief to the smoking car where sits a happy man in his middle years, bursting with conversation. It is the other man who has come to meet his bride-to-be on the train in the morning some hours before she expects him.

The plot is worked out in simple human ways, close-ups of faces working with natural emotions, little strokes of humor that rise out of sympathy. Everything is done in simple realism, refreshingly low conversational tones. Claire Windsor is the girl and Harry Carey, off his horse for once, the other man. Carey hasn't quite enough facial expressions to do his role as it should be done, but Haines is ideal. Watch him! He's going still further.

From the collection of Arnie Bernstein.

Clara Bow personified bold sexuality as the Jazz Age "It" Girl.

1927

January

Bardelys the Magnificent

Rafael Sabatini wrote the novel that Bardelys the Magnificent *is based on. The female lead, Eleanor Boardman, was director King Vidor's second wife; she also starred in his 1928 masterpiece* The Crowd. *Though Vidor downplayed the qualities of this film, he agreed with Sandburg on the shot of John Gilbert and Boardman floating downstream. "I have often been asked," Vidor later wrote, " 'What was that picture you directed in which two lovers drift in a boat through leaves and willow branches?' They have forgotten the title, the actors, the author, even the melodramatic plot, but the magic of the camera made its indelible impression."* [1]

Tuesday, January 4, 1927

Rumors of Mark Twain's death continue to be exaggerated. He is alive in the minds of men. Witness the superb manner in which his books keep on selling in the republic. Witness how his spirit of defiance to bunk, to solemnity, to inhumanity lives again in the younger humorists of our national literature.

It lives again, subtly it is true but unmistakably in the work King Vidor has lavished upon *Bardelys the Magnificent* at the Chicago Theater this week. Without the trail blazing of *A Connecticut Yankee at King Arthur's Court* long ago, King Vidor would scarcely have handled the theme of chivalry, knighthood and braggart-heroes in the American manner which characterizes *Bardelys*.

Bardelys is another Sabatini tale, written like *Scaramouche* and *The Sea Hawk*, about the rascally, lovable, daredevils of chivalry. Sabatini writes such things with a straight face and a racing heart. King Vidor couldn't quite film it in the same state of illusion. He makes his hero rather an American in spirit, doomed to enjoy himself quite satirically with the pomp and pretense of Bourbon codes of honor. Nothing like

334 "The Movies Are"

this is admitted on the face of the film. John Gilbert is *Bardelys* and he wears the penciled goatee, the rapier, the plumed hat, the daring laughter of the traditional heroes of chivalry. He boasts that he will win a maiden whose fame as the "unkissed" has spread over France. He risks life and reputation (both hers and his), and he climbs ivy-laced walls, hides behind beds, fights duels and does all the Sabatini tricks. But none of them quite seriously. Vidor has court favorites trip on their trains and fall uproariously now and then. He has popinjay courtiers essay duels with Gilbert and be worsted by Gilbert's walking stick in lieu of a sword. There is a gay attitude of kidding the courtiers and the whole Sir Walter Scott notion of romance throughout the action.

There is in *Bardelys*, too, a faint note of satire leveled at Douglas Fairbanks as well as at "the age of chivalry." Gilbert does everything in the way of strenuous action that Doug has done, only he does it preposterously. For instance, amid all the running and surprising escapes of a pursuit about the castle walls, Gilbert suddenly seizes the four corners of a tablecloth and, using it incredibly as a parachute, descends some 80 feet to alight in the carriage of the king, who saves him. He does impossible acrobatics in escaping from the gallows by using enemy spears as a toboggan. All of it is great fun, gasping surprises, even if the tongue of the director and star reside in their cheeks.

One moment is, however, genuine. That is when Vidor stages a lyric love scene between Bardelys and Roxalanne (Eleanor Boardman). The camera follows the pair as they float downstream with willow leaves and willow shade playing on their faces. An ecstatic, wheel-headed bit of loveliness and one of the reasons that King Vidor roosts near the top of the coop.

Bardelys is big, very big. New York paid $2 admission for it. And, at it, you are comfortable either way you take it, either as a gorgeous romance or as a sly and thrilling satire on romance.

The General

Buster Keaton's The General *is one of the few genuine masterpieces in all cinema. Consistently cited by critics, scholars, and film buffs worldwide for its sleek storytelling and epic qualities,* The General *was also Keaton's personal favorite among all his films. Yet in its time* The General *received mixed reviews and performed poorly at the box office. Ironically, Keaton's greatest artistic achievement led in part to his downfall as a leader in the motion picture industry. In 1956, shortly before Keaton's renewed popularity of the 1960s,* The General *was remade by Disney as* The Great Locomotive Chase *with studio stalwart Fess Parker.*

Tuesday, January 18, 1927

If they'll put Buster Keaton at the head of the armies next time there's a war his maneuvers will bring that war to a pleasant, painless and prompt conclusion, because the belligerents will simply die laughing.

At least that is the impression one gets viewing him in *The General*, a Joseph M. Schenck production, directed by Buster Keaton and Clyde Bruckman, the star's first feature for United Artists, and now having its first Chicago showing at the Orpheum Theater.

The General, we are told, is based upon historical fact and treats in a lighter vein an incident during the Civil War known as "the Andrews railroad raid," which occurred in the spring of 1862 when a band of Union soldiers invaded Confederate territory and captured "The General," one of the south's crack railroad engines.

Buster plays the part of Johnnie Gray, the young railroad engineer who piloted "The General," and Marion Mack is Annabelle Lee, his sweetheart, upon whom Johnnie is calling when war is proclaimed. Annabelle's father and brother hasten to enlist, but because his sweetheart expects it of him Johnnie gets there first in true Keatonesque style.

Rejected because authorities consider him of greater value in the engine cab than in the ranks, Johnnie finds himself scorned by sweetheart and friends as a slacker until the northerners take it into their heads to steal "The General" and cut off the Confederate army from its source of supplies.

Annabelle Lee happens to be in the baggage car when the raid takes place and is carried off into the enemy country—Johnnie in hot pursuit—neither of glory nor his sweetheart, but of his beloved engine. How this pursuit covers him with honor; jumps him into the rank of commissioned officer and throws him into the arms of his adored one must be seen to be appreciated.

The play is chockfull of hilarity, pathos and thrills, such as when Johnnie chases himself with a loaded cannon; attempts to burn down a bridge and gets on the wrong side of the fire; shoots a cannon into the air and with fool's luck hits the dam that floods the river and puts the enemy to rout. And if any young "modern" thinks short skirts and knickers an attribute to agility, let her behold the acrobatics of Marion Mack in hoopskirt and lace beruffled pantalets.

Others in the cast are Glen Cavender as Capt. Anderson; Jim Farley, Gen. Thatcher; Frederick Vroom, a southern general; Charles Smith and Frank Barnes as Annabelle's father and brother; Joe Keaton, Mike Donlin and Tom Nawn as three Union officers, plus thousands of extras.

If you want a good laugh, don't miss *The General.*

The Kid Brother

Like Buster Keaton's The General, *Harold Lloyd's* The Kid Brother *is considered to be the pinnacle in Lloyd's career. Yet critical opinion was diverse, and audiences remained indifferent to the film. Lloyd would make one more silent, the 1928* Speedy. *His sound career, while steady, never matched the quality of Lloyd's 1920s achievements.*

Monday, January 24, 1927

Harold Lloyd is the king of them all when it comes to pleasing American audiences. Who cares whether his income is big or little, whether he hires "gag" men or thinks up his own predicaments and their solution—the fun is there. It is clean, it is direct and it is American.

The Kid Brother is the latest exemplification of these facts.

Beginning as a gawky, bashful country boy, the character he plays passes from one comic and picturesque situation into another, from sideshow mishaps to embarrassed love affairs. The piece mounts in tempo to a furious fight and chase at the finale that brings volleys of yelps from little boys and big ones and the girls, too, in the dusk of McVicker's Theater.

No pies thrown, no uncouth actions, no dirt, nothing to sicken one as has been the case with the comedies of some who are lauded as greater artists than the home-grown hickory Harold.

The Kid Brother is generally regarded as the best of the Harold Lloyd pictures. Others try to improve their work as they go on, but Lloyd does it.

Faust

To achieve the amazing visual effects in Faust, *director F. W. Murnau and cinematographer Karl Freund built an elaborate set inside the German UFA studio. A customized rollercoaster, outfitted to hold a movie camera, was then installed within this set to film the flight of Mephistopheles.* [2]

Thursday, January 27, 1927

The allies of the devil, war, plague and famine riding the world; the archfiend in satanic arrogance climbing to the very gates of heaven; the challenging angel, contending that evil must fail so long as one good man remains; the wager over the soul of Faust—"Faust the scholar, Faust the good man using his knowledge to better the lot of mankind"—so begins the unfoldment of the film version of Goethe's immortal tragedy. *Faust* is another masterpiece added to UFA's already long list of screen achievements.

It was in 1774 that the German poet Goethe began his dramatization of the eternal struggle between good and evil, influenced by the traditions surrounding the almost legendary figure of Dr. John Faust, a 16th century necromancer who lived in the province of Suabia.

In the poetic drama Faust is a scholar who aspires to penetrate the essence of things;

a student whose unremitting application has given him mastery of the accumulated knowledge of generations, who yet seeks deeper to fathom the mysteries of life.

In the picture Faust is first shown striving for a cure to rid the world of plague. His townspeople are dying like flies about him and finally, in despair, he turns to black magic for succor. He barters his soul for the power to heal, but the devil's power is nullified by the power of the cross and Faust is branded as one possessed.

In utter hopelessness the aged alchemist is about to kill himself when the devil bargains anew for his soul, this time in exchange for "youth and life." Faust signs the bargain in blood and the two ride forth on the devil's cloak (Faust a young man again) to taste the pleasures of the world.

After a time of riotous living comes Marguerite, the one pure element in the life of Faust; her betrayal, her sorrow, her death and the power of her love that in the end redeems the bartered soul.

In producing the picture a great and successful effort has been made to retain the 16th century atmosphere. In the earlier parts the illusions age, sorrow and sickness are beautifully set in the somber tones of a Rembrandt, while the very breath of spring is felt in the scenes when Faust meets Marguerite and happiness is in the air; then the blinding snows at the last that drive well into the beholder's consciousness the bitterness of woman's disillusion.

The picture was produced under the direction of F. W. Murnau, whose name stands high among directors, with Emil Jannings as "the evil spirit called Mephisto," and Mr. Jannings plays the devil with sleek and unsurpassed insidiousness. Gosta Ekman, heralded as Sweden's greatest (and he must be the handsomest, too) actor, plays Faust; Camilla Horn, "a screen find," is Marguerite, and Yvette Guilbert, one time famous French diseuse, makes a delectable Martha, and every soldier, every citizen, every child—though unknown and unsung—is an artist.

The picture is having its first Chicago run at the Randolph Theater, where it opened last Saturday. If you want to see a masterpiece don't miss it.

Thursday, February 17, 1927

Faust, now finishing its engagement at the Randolph Theater, is one of the most beautiful of all works of the moving picture. It should be in the library of every art school and museum of America. Before the artistic composition, which dominates every single scene, the players and the plot become insignificant. Even Emil Jannings cannot steal this picture from the art director. For once this vivid personality of the screen is shadowed, snowed under by the cameraman.

In the first reels it seems that he may "run off" with the honors as he had done in every photoplay he touched. At the *Faust* opening Jannings is the squat, toad-like satanic primitive Teutonic mythology, a soiled and awful creature, something finely imagined and electrically conceived in Jannings' sensitive brain. Here he is one with the eerie and mystic scenic effects which Murnau, the director, has conceived. He belongs to the wild moors, the dead trees that gesture madly against the bare night sky, the infernal rings of fire that squirm at Satan's victims.

So long as Jannings sticks to his conception of Satan as a fat and squalid old man with a reptile's mind, he is the Jannings of *Passion*, *The Last Laugh* and *Variety*. But when Mephistopheles, in the adaptation of the Goethe version, leads the rejuvenated Faust into fleshly romance Jannings adopts the conventional costume of grand opera tradition. He tries to make himself wickedly handsome. Black silk, a rapier, a tail, and lipstick adorn him—and all at once he is nothing but a grand opera basso, artificial, skilled but spiritless.

Into the highly impressionistic, profoundly beautiful settings Gosta Ekman and Camilla Horn as Faust and Marguerite fit like Grecian god-statues into the Parthenon. Indeed, for all the strenuous action of the story, Ekman as the youthful Faust and Miss Horn as the melting Gretchen never lose that peculiar sculptural perfection which the German picture makers first displayed in certain shots of *Variety*'s characters.

Any good Hollywood cast would have done better by the story, but no one in America would have dared so absolute and uncompromising a piece of devotion to scenic beauty. No one in Hollywood has yet freed his imagination to attempt the toilsome, idealistic search for perfection that is shown in *Faust* backgrounds, brackens at midnight, trees that Holensai would weep over, strange and terrible birds of hell flailing the sky with their wings, and gardens filled with the very ache of springtime.

The Potters

With The Potters, *W. C. Fields continued refining his character of a harried family man, a role he would play numerous times during the sound era. Unfortunately,* The Potters *is believed to be lost.*

Friday, January 28, 1927

When Pa Potter, goat of his family and butt of high-pressure stock salesmen, suddenly finds that the oil shares he has foolishly purchased are worth a fortune, he puts on one of the funniest three minutes that the screen has ever carried.

He does it as only W. C. Fields can do this sort of thing. Fields, the screen's leading expert at doing fumbling, foolish characters, celebrates Pa Potter's one big moment in a drab career by tearing the dull, prim living room to shreds; he whoops, he bounds, he kicks pillows, he tosses 200 pieces of sheet music into the air and bucks around the little apartment like nothing so much as a Clydesdale mare with a horsefly fast to the middle of its back.

In the corners his family cowers. Fields is free; he is doing the sort of thing he does best, light-headed, trivial-minded chaos. And he does it so that no one will ever dare do it again.

W. C. Fields plays J. P. McEvoy's *The Potters* for all he is worth, which is considerable, and for all it is worth, which is somewhat less. The slight story, by rights, should be told in a two-reel comedy, but thanks to the genius of Fields it fills out seven spools with a high average of laughter.

In Fields' hands, *Pa Potter* becomes far more of a character than in either McEvoy's humorous articles or stage comedy. Fields makes him the blunderer supreme, the eternal butt and goat with figments of cuteness coming and going in his stupid head, and with just enough humanity and realism in his art to keep Potter safe in your affections. Fields' supporting cast here is inconsequential. Paramount made it and the Oriental Theater displays it as a companion attraction to Paul Ash.

February

Tell It to the Marines

This is one of the few roles Lon Chaney had which didn't require elaborate makeup. Tell It to the Marines *is also the first Hollywood feature to receive full cooperation and consultation from the United States Marine Corps.*

Monday, February 7, 1927

Big guns have boomed across the silver curtains of Chicago cinema theaters for weeks now—and they do again in *Tell It to the Marines* at McVicker's Theater, which starts its three weeks engagement of Lon Chaney's new starring vehicle today.

However, *Tell It to the Marines* is not a drama of the world war. It's a story of fighting men who fight to love, who love to fight—and they do both in all quarters of the globe. It's an epic story of that strange organization called "leathernecks" by Americans and "devil-dogs" by the ex-kaiser.

In it we find Lon Chaney, sans any makeup whatever except the uniform and "hash-marks" of continuous service of a hardboiled veteran sergeant of the crops. And Eleanor Boardman is a pretty nurse in the medical corps. And William Haines is a callow youth with an urge for romance—which he finds aplenty during his period of enlistment.

There are many thrilling moments in *Tell It to the Marines*. Those of us in Chicago who have watched the daily papers reporting the progress of the marines as they guard Uncle Sam's mails from attack by metropolitan bandits will get a real kick out of these smiling boys as they walk irresistibly through cordons of Chinese bandits or "mop up" a revolution in some of Uncle Sam's tropical isles. Through all their adventures the "hardening process" of American youth is a constantly encouraging sight, interrupted only by great roars of laughter or moments of thrilling suspense.

Tell It to the Marines is something you must see. It's so good they're still charging $2 to see it in New York, although McVicker's clings to its popular prices.

It

The Flapper Era reached its pinnacle with Clara Bow and It, *a film loosely based on one of Elinor Glyn's libidinous tales. " 'It' is an indefinable sort of sex appeal," Glyn stated. "There are few people in the world who possess it. The only ones in Hollywood who do are Rex, the wild stallion; actor Tony Morenp; the Ambassador Hotel doorman; and Clara Bow." [3] ("I was awfully confused about the horse," Bow later said, "but if she thought he had 'It,' then I figured he mustbe quite an animal." [4]) There was no coincidence in Moreno and Bow making Glyn's list; Paramount studio moguls paid the popular and influential author $50,000 for the endorsement. [5] The film was a critical and popular success, ensuring Bow's legendary status as "The 'It' Girl." In 1960, five years before her death, Bow told Hollywood columnist Hedda Hopper that only Marilyn Monroe possessed the same qualities that embodied "It." [6]*

Friday, February 11, 1927

Some one pretty sensible handled *It.*

Always, before, Elinor Glyn's stories made producers, directors, continuity writers howl and bellow when filming time came. It used to be a hard job to make her characters human and genuinely romantic when filmed.

But when they came to film *It*, which madame had written to expound her new theory of what attracts people of opposing sexes, they tossed madame's story to the cruel waves that roar on the Pacific Rocks. They kept the name *It* and made Mme. Glyn reel good by leading her in, like a queen to be photographed as herself explaining what *It* is to Antonio Moreno.

But the story which runs in a current magazine is not at all like the film, not like it in any respect, not even the names of the characters.

The screen *It* is smart, funny and real. It makes a full-sized star of Clara Bow and it lifts William Austin out of the minor class into the upper crust of screen comedians.

Miss Bow is a warm-hearted, smart alec, bewitching little shop girl. She stands behind the lingerie counter looking impudently and longingly at the handsome owner of the great department store. As she does so her employer's "silly-ass" friend, Mr. Austin, comes through the store looking for people with "It." He had read Elinor Glyn's declaration that some people have "It" and some do not; that "It" is a strange quality and you recognize it immediately. Luckily Mr. Austin looks at Clara Bow and calls out, "She has 'It.' "

He is right.

The plot is Clara's conquest of her employer. The interest of the picture is the bright stimulation of looking at Clara, of laughing at the subtitles, which are funny, and looking at Clara again. She's most likely another Swanson.

Flesh and the Devil

The *"earnest . . . exchange of kisses" between* Flesh and the Devil *stars John Gilbert and Greta Garbo that Sandburg writes of were very real; the actors had fallen in love during the making of this film.*

Monday, February 28, 1927

If there was ever, in screendom, as earnest an exchange of kisses as that between John Gilbert and Greta Garbo in *Flesh and the Devil* let him who knows of it speak now or forever hold his peace. John and Greta play the lovemaking roles of this Sudermann drama with a sincerity and realism that saves it from being pure sensationalism.

So high-keyed is this story, so rapturous and never-ending are the embraces of its hero and heroine that it might readily have toppled, in the filming, into mawkish sentimentalism.

But John and Greta, under the fine, sane direction of Clarence Brown, make the lovers so real that *Flesh and the Devil* becomes a screen triumph. In its showing at McVicker's Theater so far there has not been uttered from the audience a single one of those satirical "smacks" with which embarrassed adolescents are fond of greeting lengthy kissing on the screen.

Fervent *Flesh and the Devil* is, but never unhuman, nor over romantic.

Sudermann told a tale of extravagant emotions, of a girl unable to be true and of the two boyhood friends whom she came between. One of these youths is Gilbert and one Lars Hanson. The one played by Gilbert is cajoled and captivated by this enigmatic, ardent girl and entangled in her wiles before he discovers her husband. A duel. The husband dies. The lovers are to marry after a decent interval. The army sends him away for a year and when he returns he finds the girl wedded to his bosom friend. Even that is not enough to kill love in him, and when the girl, helpless before her own wantonness, is eager to elope with him, he agrees in sobbing torment. The denouement is unexpected, but inescapable and of a superior sort of happiness.

Miss Garbo is hereafter a star to be reckoned with, so perfectly does she create a character for the heroine, lovely, pitiful, thrilling Felicitas, who drifts downward without ever realizing that the world holds such things as morals.

March

The Taxi Dancer

Joan Crawford graduated from minor flapper parts to meatier roles with The Taxi Dancer. *Sandburg's assessment of her was on the money. Nora Bayes was a stage actor who also appeared in a few films. Gertrude Ederle was a young American who had made history on August 6, 1926, as the first woman to swim the English Channel. She subsequently made a few vaudeville and film appearances.*

Monday, March 7, 1927

The Taxi Dancer dances furiously at the Chicago Theater this week, throwing her flitting shadow across the lives of four men of the screen, but she is handicapped. Whenever *The Taxi Dancer* is on the screen the crowds in that show place are either waiting for Nora Bayes or whispering about how Nora sang this or that song.

This is the fate pictures sometimes meet. Stage stars come along and overshadow film production mercilessly. Paul Whiteman, Van and Schenck, Gertrude Ederle and now Nora Bayes have done this. The flame that is Miss Bayes tossing off flakes of laughter to the distant balcony crowds, as flambeaux toss off sheets of fire, burns brightly in this program. Generous with her encores, as of old, expansive and infectious with her incomparable smile, Nora is enough to put woe into the celluloid hearts of film characters.

Still, *The Taxi Dancer* serves. Starting as a comedy of the "upstage" variety, human and humorous in its slants on life in Broadway rooming houses, it may wind off into the mazes of melodrama, but it does keep your eye on a new star, Joan Crawford. For over a year Joan has been learning how to act. Metro-Goldwyn-Mayer officials who picked her off the Winter Garden stage have been letting her little by little in minor roles. At first Joan had only one thing to recommend her, the most nearly perfect figure in filmdom. Now, by the dint of hard work, Joan can act.

As a southern girl from a sleepy town, who comes to New York and is forced to do "taxi dancing" to earn her living, she is human, very human, without, however, erring seriously. Taxi dancing is the nickname for dancing that the girl employees must do with male patrons in public ballrooms where the fee per dance is 10 cents, half going to the house and half to the girl.

Out of this life Joan is lifted by a lighthearted young gambler, Owen Moore, and by various scheming millionaires of the nightlife variety. Melodrama runs riot in the last reels and comes to earth only when the grinning, heartwarming face of Owen Moore flashes into it.

The Scarlet Letter

In the 1920s, Nathaniel Hawthorne's novel The Scarlet Letter *was under scrutiny by various self-appointed watchdog groups overseeing Hollywood. Apparently Hawthorne's tale of adultery and moral hypocrisy among religious leaders was too volatile a subject at the time for film adaptation. Appealing to these organizations, Lillian Gish personally wrote letters on behalf of a proposed* Scarlet Letter *movie. ". . . They agreed to lift the ban if I would be personally responsible for this film," Gish later recounted.[7] Gish brought in prolific screenwriter Frances Marion to write the script and hired Victor Seastrom as director. The result was one of Gish's best films.* The Scarlet Letter *was previously made in 1911, 1913, and 1917. Other versions followed, including a 1934 adaptation with Colleen Moore, a 1972 German telling by director Wim Wenders, and a 1995 revisionist* Scarlet Letter *featuring Demi Moore and a non-Hawthorne, happy Hollywood ending.*

Monday, March 21, 1927

Lillian Gish has been in a good many terrible fixes in her screen career, but none more pitiable than when, in *The Scarlet Letter*, she is manacled down to the stocks on Boston Commons and made a shameful object lesson to the young Puritans for having skipped and run on the Sabbath.

Those little white hands of Lillian's hang in resignation, her meek face, minus hate, droops and there she sits, under the placard of shame, waiting for the Puritan fathers to come clumping back to lift her sentence.

All Hester Prynne had done, up to that time, had been to chase her canary through the woods on Sunday morning and, in the course of the pursuit, to have skipped once and patted her hands together twice. Such an infernal display of happiness and joy outraged the Puritans, on their way to church, and they had Hester thrown into the stocks.

The Puritans catch thunder all through Victor Seastrom's film version of Hawthorne's novel, *The Scarlet Letter*. They are depicted as fanatical, cruel, pathological in their love of inflicting pain. They sew a scarlet letter "A" on Hester's bosom to brand her with shame for not having told what man was the father of her child. They spy on merrymakers, listening for gossip, snoop up and down the aisles of churches thumping on the head men who fall asleep. They fuss with little children about beliefs and souls and devils. They enjoy persecuting and being persecuted.

And when they summon poor, delicate, beautiful Lillian Gish up to the pillory to be branded with "The Scarlet Letter" you will wish for nothing so much as a horde of red Indians to be coming over the stockades and through the town, massacring the Puritan fathers even at the sacrifice of Thanksgiving dinners.

The Scarlet Letter is Hawthorne's classic, filmed in fine honesty to the spirit of the

A *Chicago Daily News* ad for Lillian Gish in *The Scarlet Letter* (Thursday, March 24, 1927).

story and with sufficient closeness to the letter to escape the censors. To it Lillian Gish gives one of her unrivaled performances, spiritual and human both, exaltedly imaginative and artistic.

But the picture is more than a starring vehicle for Miss Gish. It is quite a show on its own hook, big, magnificently historical, powerfully dramatic. Hawthorne wrote a daring story. Seastrom turned it into a picture that dares to be poignant and poetic in the midst of sensational happenings such as brandings, desertions, seductions, public confessions of sin and moral accusations.

Its local debut is at the Chicago Theater this week.

Sorrows of Satan

Sandburg's comparison of D. W. Griffith to Walt Whitman was no small praise; Whitman's poetry had enormous influence on Sandburg's own literary achievements. Showing a more expressionistic visual style than his previous films, Griffith made some strides towards another comeback with Sorrows of Satan. *Yet the once-great director's return to former glory was not to be. Adolph Zukor, the head of Paramount, disliked Griffith's work on* Sorrows of Satan *and demanded changes in the film. The result was a disappointment to Griffith, artistically, personally, and financially.*

Wednesday, March 23, 1927

D. W. Griffith remains the creative artist.

Born in Kentucky, where the talk every evening in the lamplight was of pioneers, he is still the pioneer of motion pictures, still exploring new horizons, opening up new fields, hacking ahead, traveling alone in spirit, at least.

Like Daniel Boone, who won the Dark and Bloody Ground, but who neglected to file it under his own name, Griffith has neglected to put a fortune aside for himself. Pioneers have frequently been of such admirable folly. Nowadays Griffith works for the big producers who came along after his first pioneerings and filed on the land he cleared. This confuses him a little. But it does not keep him from striking out after new ideas now and then.

He hits on what may be developed into a new screen technique in parts of his *Sorrows of Satan*, now at McVicker's Theater. The melting of shadows into other shadows, the criss-crossing of shadows to converge eventually into the sardonic, polished face of Adolphe Menjou, a mocking and modern Satan, is as interesting a coinage of Griffith's mind as was the "close-up," the "mist portraits" and a dozen other inventions of his in other days. Also the myth scenes which introduce *Sorrows of Satan*, those eerie moments when Jehovah's angels, under Michael, cast forth from paradise the rebellious hordes of Satan, are Griffith at his most inventive and dramatic best.

Sorrows of Satan has the sense of vastness, chaos, originality and sudden interludes of unimagined beauty that make Griffith so much akin in his present stage, to Walt Whitman, the poet. There was a time when Griffith was a Charles Dickens and Walt Whitman in one. Lately the Whitman mood predominates. He no longer tells stories as directly and absorbingly as once he did.

Marie Corelli was no author for Griffith to attempt to follow in screening. Her novel, *Sorrows of Satan*, is flimsy, sensational, hectic. In trying to justify it for his own use Griffith evidently suffered, for the story his picture tells is neither Corelli nor Griffith.

Still, everything Griffith does is worth any one's time. *Sorrows of Satan* is not enough to enhance Griffith's reputation, but it would make his reputation if he had been heretofore unknown. The old magic of his touch burns in scenes wherein two starving writers, a boy and a girl, blend their sufferings and ideals, in frigid garrets. It lives again in the orgies of London bohemias where Satan, in evening clothes, takes the boy to wean him from his love and his ideals. The picture is rich in emotion, in gripping episodes, in momentary moods, which will absorb any onlooker who does not have the misfortune to be always looking, through filmdom, for another *Broken Blossoms* or *Intolerance*.

The cast is competent. Menjou, Ricardo Cortez, Carol Dempster and Lya De Putti have the star roles.

April

Children of Divorce

Sandburg singles out a pair of up-and-coming actors in Children of Divorce. *Einar Hanson, best remembered for director G. W. Pabst's* The Joyless Street *(1925, Germany), died in a 1927 car wreck. His co-star, Gary Cooper, became a respected acting talent, winning Best Actor Oscars for* Sergeant York *(1941) and* High Noon *(1952). Cooper and Clara Bow fell in love on the set of* Children of Divorce, *though their affair didn't last long.*

Monday, April 4, 1927

Paramount's two best beauties—Clara Bow, petite and vivacious, and Esther Ralston, tall and gracious—costar in *Children of Divorce*, now at McVicker's Theater. Clara the fickle, and Esther the steadfast, are here put to work to live the serious dramatic roles of Owen Johnson's story, "The Enemy Sex." And the male stars come and go through the story, one of them a strapping youngster, Gary Cooper, whom Paramount expects to be the next great Western star, another Einar Hanson, handsome and artistic, but no one can take spectators' eyes off these two girls, especially in their never-ending wardrobes of elegance.

Frank Lloyd, who did *The Sea Hawk*, has his go at modern society drama in *Children of Divorce*, and he goes a long way, keeping in his picture unusual sumptuousness but subordinating it justly to the absorbing story of the two girls who grew up parentless and who struggled through the maze of society's shams and pretenses to find love which might prove true.

Children of Divorce is an indictment of divorce and of parents who separate without thought of what wreckage may devolve upon the children. It is weighty drama, but relieved by the flash and beauty, the verve and life of the girl stars, and in the final moments when they solve the problems their own mistaken marriages have brought down as a heritage from their fathers, they strike a realization of tenderness and power that is tremulous with tears.

Norman Trevor, Hedda Hopper, Edward Martindel and Julia Swayne Gordon are also in the production.

Long Pants

After Charlie Chaplin, Buster Keaton, and Harold Lloyd, there was Harry Lang-don. Langdon was one of the most idiosyncratic screen stars of the 1920s. His unusually youthful features, coupled with his child-like costumes, gave Langdon the appearance of a naïve creature caught in a warp between pre-pubescence and adulthood. After a series of successful two-reelers, Langdon teamed up with direc-tor Harry Edwards and the up-and-coming talent Frank Capra. The trio made two successful films, Tramp, Tramp, Tramp *and* The Strong Man *(both 1926). Capra directed both* The Strong Man *and* Long Pants, *using his own comic touch to bring out the best Langdon had to offer. Yet Langdon envisioned himself as another Chaplin and demanded complete artistic control of his work after* The Strong Man. *While a good comic actor, Langdon lacked a basic sense of film production, let alone any business knowledge. By 1931 the baby-faced clown was bankrupt. Though he appeared in a few films until his death in 1944, Langdon remained on the fringes of Hollywood for the rest of his life.*

Wednesday, April 13, 1927

The third of Harry Langdon's full-length pictures is *Long Pants.* The other two were *Tramp, Tramp, Tramp* and *The Strong Man. Long Pants* does for the screen what "Seventeen" did for the state—presents the joys and sorrows of boyhood. It is a story of eternal youth; it is tragedy told with laughs.

Harry is an adolescent who, in day dreams, pictures himself as a real man of the world. However, he feels that before he can impress this fact upon the public he must persuade his mother to let him change from knee breeches to long trousers. When at last this battle is won he bicycles down the street to give the neighbors a chance to view this turning point in his career.

He rides by a stalled car in which sits Alma Bennett, a crook known to the police and the press as "the Princess." He feels that this is the woman whose love would bring out the great soul that is in him. Amused, she plays up to him, but his mother is calling and when he returns his "princess" is gone. Meanwhile preparations for his marriage to Priscilla, the neighbor's daughter, progress according to his parents' plans. Harry balks at the altar when he sees a newspaper story that his unknown charmer is in jail. He goes to her rescue only to land in jail himself.

Later he repents his rashness and thoughts of Priscilla and his mother come to him and he marries the simple and gentle Priscilla.

Color photography has been introduced into the picture and the scenes are beautiful. It is showing this week at the Diversey Theater and Belmont Theater.

May

Chang

Merian C. Cooper and Ernest B. Schoedsack, the team behind Chang, *went on to create the 1933 classic* King Kong.

Chang is the title of the new feature film at the Roosevelt Theater. It is a picture of jungle life brought here from the dense jungles of northern Siam by Merian C. Cooper and Ernest B. Schoedsack, two adventurous youths who a few years ago gave the screen *Grass.*

Chang, let it be told without further delay, means elephant—a beast greatly feared by the native tribes on account of its enormous strength. The picture shows what a destructive force a herd of chang can be, stalking through the native villages and razing the frail habitations as a man kicks over a child's house of cards.

Chang serves as well as any other word to identify the picture, which is a realistic presentation of the brave and resourceful fight a primitive family of the Lao race puts up against hunger and the jungle beasts. The philosophic person could easily draw an analogy between the jungle enemies and the evil forces civilized man has to combat. Are there not beasts of prey, he might ask, as dangerous in centers of civilization as anything the tribesman encounters? What about the snakes and tigers of the human family? Is it not true that civilized man is as helpless in the face of floods and fires and earthquakes as the family of Kau in the pathway of lions and tigers and the dreaded chang itself?

In the picture a pioneer of the jungle is show at his daily tasks. His wife tends the children and grinds the grain, weaves the baskets and looks after the home built on stilts and reached by a ladder. Bimbo, a white gibbon, and gibbon or monkey is another word not in the vocabulary of the average moviegoer, is the companion of the children and living testimony to the truth of the theory of evolution.

Stealthy panthers and tigers seek out the few domestic animals that are the property of the jungle family. After a raid of this kind the natives band together to trap them. The various devices created and set to catch the enemies are extremely interesting and the thrill one gets at the sight of a beast caught is no different from the joy he feels when Tom Santschi or Lon Chaney or a Beery brother falls into the trap set by the hero for the villain.

There are human traits in the animals as, for instance, the bear mother's care of her cub, the elephant's rescue of her young, the gibbon's devotion to the children and all this appeals to the emotions of the beholder.

Cooper and Schoedsack were 18 months in the jungle making the film record of primitive man and terrorizing beast. Where they secreted themselves with their grinding motion picture camera is a mystery for there are many scenes taken when it must have been dangerous to be around. It is said they carry only camera, film and rifle and must wait until their return to civilization to know what they have really obtained.

Whatever you do, go, if you are at all interested in wild animals or adventure, go to see *Chang.* It is probably the apotheosis of the travelogue.

Thursday, June 23, 1927

Although *Chang* has been duly reviewed and praised in these columns as one of the most interesting and unusual pictures ever made, it deserves the second showing and more; just as it deserves the seeing several times. New wonders present themselves at each visit. It stays on at the Roosevelt Theater and saves one a trip to Siam.

In pictorial form it tells the happenings in the life of a primitive family living on a little clearing close to the jungle. There are father, mother and three children, the youngest an infant. Their home is a thatched hut, set on stilts, with a stairway which may be drawn up, and is every night after the family and the household pets are safely housed.

The garden is plowed and tilled by primitive methods and a rice crop brought to the ripening; only to be trodden down by the chief villain of the story—Chang.

This Chang is a young one, and when it is captured and tethered to one of the supporting pillars of the house it acts as a magnet for Mother Chang, who rescues it, and in so doing turns over the human habitation. The escape of the family and Bimbo, a white ape or gibbon, is as exciting as any "case" in the movies.

Preparations for trapping and killing the enemies—lions, tigers and other jungle beasts—are a part of the fight for existence depicted. There are scenes of fishing for food among others.

The destruction of the native village by elephants on the rampage is the big dramatic moment, followed by another when the herd of wild elephants is corralled.

The Red Kimona

Dorothy Davenport (Mrs. Wallace Reid) continued her crusade against vice with The Red Kimona *(aka:* The Red Kimono*). Part of her "Sins of the World" series,* The Red Kimona *was ostensibly a denunciation of prostitution. Despite Sandburg's positive review, however, most critics dismissed* The Red Kimona *as tripe. Davenport based this film on the true story of Gabrielle Darley, a former prostitute who turned her life around. Yet Darley was never told about the production. Upon seeing her story portrayed on film, Darley hired a lawyer, sued Davenport, and won.[8] Though Adela Rogers St. Johns is credited as* The Red Kimona's *writer, editor, and future director, Dorothy Arzner adapted St. Johns' story for the screen.*

Monday, June 13, 1927

Mrs. Wallace Reid is seldom heard from except at such times as she brings a preachment of some kind before the public. Her present appearance on the screen is as a storyteller and advocate for kindness toward women who have "erred."

The Red Kimona is the title of the picture she presents, with Priscilla Bonner as the principal character and wearer of the red kimona. Adela Rogers St. Johns is named as the writer of the story and Walter Lang as the director.

The subject is treated with due regard to the conventions and there is nothing any one can take exception to in the presentation.

Gabrielle is first seen as a young village maiden of school age. She is the product of a sordid and unhappy home, with a father whose chief concern is to rid himself of her care. The beguiling words of a stranger, who tells her he loves her, are music to her ears and she is persuaded to go with him to the city where they are to be married—and never are. He introduces her to the underworld and leaves her there. Later she learns that he is to be married and she follows and, in desperation, shoots him. Acquitted of murder she tries to regain her place among respectable people, but her "past" is forever bobbing up and she finds it impossible to keep a job.

More consideration for those who are struggling upward in Mrs. Reid's plea. Priscilla Bonner makes the heroine gentle and appealing and the cast, which includes Mary Carr, Tyrone Power, Sheldon Lewis and Theodore von Eltz, is a capable one.

July

Running Wild

In 1935 W. C. Fields remade Running Wild *as* The Man on the Flying Trapeze. *Mary Brian, who played Fields's daughter here, reprised her role in the remake as well. Fields was well known throughout vaudeville and on Broadway stages as an accomplished juggler, which Sandburg refers to in his opening sentence.*

Thursday, July 14, 1927

W. C. Fields, even without the tennis balls he used to juggle in "The Follies," is a great comedian. Nobody better than he, not even Chaplin, knows the gestures, the alert movements, the quick jumps that light the fuse of laughter and nobody can be more abject and pitiful than he in his moments of dejection. The fact that he is getting on, that he is a man of experience, that he has, in Huxley's words, "warmed both hands at the fire of life," gives him a mellowness that the younger screen comedians lack. It is not slapstick humor that makes W. C. Fields amusing, it is fidelity to human nature at its weakest and funniest.

In *Running Wild*, the picture which divides time with Paul Ash's show at the Oriental Theater this week, Fields plays the part of a poor worm which eventually turns.

Elmer Finch is the second husband of a shrewish wife and stepfather to her spoiled son. Finch has a daughter of his own, who tries to help him be a man, but finds the job almost beyond her. So much for his position at home. In business it is much the same.

He has worked 20 years as bookkeeper without ever having had an increase in pay and nothing in his work has ever warranted his employer in giving him one. He does, however, make an effort to increase his usefulness, but with disastrous results to himself and to the firm.

Finally he falls into the hands of a professional hypnotist who gives him a courage he had hitherto woefully lacked. He then sets out to do all the things he had wanted to do, but had not known how to accomplish. His "furors transitoris," as the brain specialists have it, lasts long enough for him to subdue all who have opposed him and in the end he is respected and happy, and the pretty and much put-upon daughter comes into her own happiness when the young man of her choice wins his father over.

Mary Brian is the girl, Claude Buchanan the young man, Marie Shotwell plays an ungrateful part in the disagreeable stepmother, and Barney Raskle, as Junior, in the meanest, hatefulest cub of a boy that one could imagine. The cast is not a long one, but it is well chosen.

Running Wild is not an epoch-making picture, but it does give the star an opportunity for excellent character work.

Metropolis

Easily one of the most influential and important films of the silent era, Fritz Lang's Metropolis *broke new ground in both visual design and the political impact of popular film. During the early days of World War II, Lang told an interviewer about a meeting he had with Joseph Goebbels, Adolph Hitler's propaganda minister, shortly after the Nazi rise to power in Germany. "[Goebbels] told me that, many years before, he and the Führer had seen my picture* Metropolis *in a small town, and Hitler had said at that time that he wanted me to make Nazi pictures."[9] In 1934 Goebbels extended an offer to Lang on behalf of Hitler to direct and produce Nazi propaganda. That same night Lang fled Germany. He eventually re-established himself as one of Hollywood's most idiosyncratic directors. Thea von Harbou, Lang's ex-wife, who co-scripted* Metropolis, *became a leading screenwriter in the Nazi film industry.*

Monday, July 18, 1927

The complaint of the motion picture theater men in the past has been that while everybody praises German movies when they are shown on this continent, nobody goes to see them.

Americans whoop and carry on about what wonderful pictures *Passion, The Golem, Dr. Caligari, Variety* and *Faust* were and write big letters to the newspapers demanding to know why the public doesn't get more pictures like those. But when those pictures were running the American people were not at all worried about showing the theater man that he was a benefactor of art because he presented great pictures.

It may be that *Metropolis*, now at the Roosevelt Theater, will break this spell or hoodoo, whatever you want to call it.

Metropolis has a sensational idea understandable to anybody and capable of being enjoyed by any one who likes to speculate on the future. It has scientists who, in a mammoth laboratory, create a mechanical woman, utilizing electricity in a way that is expected to be common in 2900 A.D. This woman is beautiful, but without any morals or conscience. For night clubs in this city of a thousand years from now she does a skirtless dance that is contrary to all but Moslem laws, and for the millions of workers in their depths she preaches revolution, destruction, general hades. She is beautiful, seductive, ruinous and is played with a serpentine, pagan skill by Brigitte Helm, the alluring German actress.

Any one who had a good time at *The Lost World* will have a better time at *Metropolis*, for it carries the spectator into the world of a thousand years hence. No such settings have ever been attempted before on the screen, not even in *Intolerance*. Buildings rise like mountains in the air. Thousand of feet up are curving causeways for automobiles, others for pedestrians, at other heights are airways for behemoth airplanes. Down under the city in subterranean caverns are the monstrous machines by which the city is operated. There, too, are the workers, dumb, cattle-like hordes, who lockstep with beaten spirit, thousands and thousands of them, to the huge elevators which carry them in 12-hour shifts to their duties.

The entire city is controlled by one man, John Masterman, financial overlord and industrial Napoleon. It is the workings of the plot that bring him down at last when the mechanical woman, the creature of his laboratories, spurs his slaves to revolt and wrecks the mountainous machines about his ears.

Metropolis is photographed by Karl Freund, who did *Variety*, and for its photography alone, should not be missed. It is easily the most interesting thing in our theaters today.

August

The Unknown

In 1932 director Tod Browning reworked the story of The Unknown *for his dark masterwork* Freaks.

Monday, August 1, 1927

Lon Chaney returns to the sideshows of circus life and their connections with the underworld for his latest melodrama, *The Unknown*, at the Chicago Theater this week. Chaney was directed by Tod Browning, who made *The Unholy Three*, *The Blackbird* and *The Road to Mandalay*, and together they are said to achieve suspense that is extremely acute in the new story of intrigue.

Norman Kerry who has often appeared with Chaney in big productions such as *The Hunchback of Notre Dame* and Joan Crawford, the most beautifully formed actress in Hollywood, according to that city's decision, are his chief supports, while art photography of a new kind is used in the many romantic scenes of the drama.

Chaney has the role of knife-thrower extraordinary in the circus that travels across modern Spain. He throws the knives, with his feet, having given out, before joining the circus, that he has lost his arms. Alonzo, the armless, he is nicknamed and his skill with his pedal extremities rivals that of any two-handed rival. Estrellita, dancer and bare-limbed poseur against the board wherein Alonzo sinks his knives is beloved by Malabar, the strong man, and the plot thickens, since Alonzo, too, loves her.

The story gives Chaney, perhaps his major opportunity to be alternately vicious, sympathetic, terrible and pathetic, a blend of emotions which Chaney can so admirably achieve.

Madame Pompadour

Tuesday, August 16, 1927

Dorothy Gish, in powdered wig and heavy brocades, is a Pompadour calculated to turn the head of any "sweet papa," let alone the impressionable monarch, Louis XV.

Her Madame Pompadour is a lovely creature forced into the role of king's mistress by fate and an ambitious mother, according to the screen version of that shady chapter in France's history.

The Gish piquancy makes plausible the incident of her excursion into romance along byways not trod by kingly feet. It shows her looking for adventure in the haunts of the common people who rail against "the Pompadour" for her extravagances which tax the people to starvation. The most rabid of these is a poet, Laval, who first attracts her attention by an outburst against her as her carriage passes in the Paris streets. She leads him later to believe she is a seamstress from the palace and when their meetings are discovered by the king's spies, she easily lies out of it by saying she has been tracking down her enemies and proves it by having Laval and his friends arrested, only to have them released later. Laval she promises a place as soldier in her bodyguard and so in love with him is she that she plans to flee with him from Paris.

Enemies discover her intrigue and try to poison the king's mind against her, but by pretty wiles she overcomes his doubts and, realizing that her love can bring nothing but harm to Laval, she dismisses him once and for all.

The story is consistently handled, the settings are magnificent as behooves the locale, and the actors are admirably fitted to their roles.

Antonio Moreno might have been give more to do as the young man of Madame Pompadour's choice, his handsome face and fiery eyes being used mostly as a foil for

Dorothy's delicacy. He is not even given a chance to draw his sword.

Henri Bose makes a good-looking Louis, and Gibbs McLaughlin, resembling the pictures of Robespierre, is a stupid but industrious spy upon the actions of Madame Pompadour.

The picture, now showing at the Oriental Theater, along with Paul Ash's "College of Jazz," is likely to be a popular one.

September

Camille

Here Sandburg notes "time and the taste of film fans must decide" on the future of Camille *co-star Gilbert Roland. Beginning as an uncredited extra in* The Lost World *(1925), Roland ultimately enjoyed a lengthy screen (and television) career, taking lead and supporting roles well into the 1980s. See also Sandburg's review of the Nazimova* Camille, *Monday, September 19, 1921.*

Wednesday, September 7, 1927

Camille has resumed its place on the Roosevelt Theater screen and is again attracting admirers of Norma Talmadge, other fans who are curious to see the new lover of the screen, Gilbert Roland, and still others who remember the play is one of the greatest love stories of literature and wish to see it again, even though it be a modern version and savors little of the illustrious past.

It is beautifully costumed, exquisitely set and well photographed. More luxurious and tasteful mountings can scarcely be imagined. Certainly the surroundings of the famous actresses who played the Lady of the Camellias on the stage were never so costly. Fancy Clara Morris or even Sarah Bernhardt as handsomely arrayed, but then—neither were the lilies of the field.

Gilbert Roland is a handsome and fiery Armand and may be the longed-for successor to Rudolph Valentino or at least a worthy rival to John Gilbert. Time and the taste of film fans must decide.

It is not likely that a more beautiful Camille or a sweeter one will love than Norma Talmadge. That she is not the Camille of the Dumas story is generally agreed; not the wanton, ardent, self-forgetting, gay and irresistible Camille. But she is a charming actress and the picture is worth seeing.

The Way of All Flesh

In 1927 the first awards given by the Academy of Motion Picture Arts and Sciences—honors which are better known as the "Oscars"—were handed out to recognize the best the film industry had to offer. Emil Jannings became the first "Best Actor" for his performance in The Last Command, *though he was also nominated for his work in* The Way of All Flesh.

Thursday, September 15, 1927

They say that when Emil Jannings is working on a screen role his loving wife leaves him for the time, remaining away until such time as the picture is done and Emil his own amiable self again.

Night and day, the story goes, he lives his role, brooding, thinking, holding his mind to the limits of his dramatic character. He wears the kind of clothes the character would wear, talks like him, eats like him, thinks like him, goes to the studio in his

Popular with European and American audiences, native German Emil Jannings was the first screen star to win an Academy Award for "Best Actor."

From the collection of Arnie Bernstein.

costume ready for work.

The story seems plausible enough when Jannings' pictures reach town, for no artist, unless it be Charlie Chaplin, can achieve one-quarter of Jannings' reality in a role. No one ever came to the screen with such utter disappearance of self. To this day the moviegoers of the country have no definite and clear mental picture of what Jannings' own face looks like. It has changed so utterly from one picture to another as to make the man himself misty and far away. Which is another way of saying that Jannings is incomparably the greatest of all screen actors, unless it be that the aforesaid Charles Spencer Chaplin can tie him.

The debut of Jannings in his first American picture does much to explode the theory that Germans are greater than Americans in making pictures. This and that German director or cameraman has been hailed as a surpassing genius as the result of some German picture that reached America. But nine-tenths of these German masterpieces have had Emil Jannings as chief player and now that his first American picture, *The Way of All Flesh*, is seen to be another unquestionable masterpiece, it becomes evident that most of the genius of UFA's Berlin-made pictures has been nothing more or less than Jannings.

Any picture in which he plays looks superior, exceptional, packed with genius. His amazing ability to make audiences think and feel with him makes also directors, cameraman and other actors look superior. He lends naturalness to the whole picture, realism to every action.

In *The Way of All Flesh*, now at McVicker's Theater, he is every bit as marvelous in depicting character and character-change, just as amazing in his capture of the minor bits of naturalism or of the thundering emotional climaxes, as he was in his series of German pictures from *Passion* to *Variety*.

His role is that of a Milwaukee banker, upstanding, domestic, good, who loses his name and reputation as the result of one fatal spree with the ruinous Phyllis Haver in a Chicago underworld honky-tonk.

As the aged derelict, Jannings achieves an aching intensity of sympathy, a poignancy such as the screen never saw before and which is almost too near to heartbreak to be understood in any manner.

An incredibly good, mysteriously powerful performance.

Three's a Crowd

Thursday, September 22, 1927

Harry Langdon's new comedy, *Three's a Crowd*, is a slow-moving, rather sad affair which has little in it to stir a crowd to laughter. The story has too much of heartbreak for the poor, lonely fellow to make one wish to laugh at him.

Something of Chaplin's genius lies in his thoughtful moments and the artistic way he handles situations and undoubtedly he can move his audiences to tears and to laughter also, given half a chance, but when the story has as little of humor and as much of tragedy as *Three's a Crowd*, the laugh stops in the throat.

You see, it is this way. Harry plays an odd sort of person who works for a rough wagon mover and lives alone, except for a doll, in an attic at the side of a big warehouse. He climbs an endless number of outside stairs to reach his home and, the time being winter, the steps are covered with snow. They are as much out of plumb as the funny stairs in *Caligari* and Harry is the only one who can negotiate them readily, but this he does frequently with a funny, bow-legged gait.

To this eyrie he brings a wretched girl whom he picks up in the snow—a girl he had watched through his telescope and loved silently, even though she had married someone else and seemed lost to him forever. Poverty and illness had overtaken her, the discouraged husband deserted her and there was nobody to help except Harry. He does some quick and funny acting when he finds out the nature of her illness and it results in organizing a crowd of tenement women who run at the sound of "storks" as fire horses do at the clang of the fire bell. Doctors come, too, but stop at the foot of the stairs. Harry grabs their satchels and runs ahead and they are compelled to follow.

Harry's delight in the baby is pathetic. The action halts monotonously at that point, though the audience at the State-Lake Theater the other night found much amusement in the pie that was made out of a necessary piece of baby's wearing apparel and the bed he made for himself out of a table.

A palmist had read for him a happy future and so, when the husband returns and takes back his own, Harry has no redress except to smash the palmist's windows.

Swim, Girl, Swim

Here Sandburg points out the popularity of the University of Southern California with late 1920s filmmakers, noting "one wonders why the film companies don't move their studios up to this university campus." His words were prophetic. In 1929 USC, in conjunction with the Academy of Motion Picture Arts and Sciences, became the first university in the country to offer a Bachelor of Arts degree in film. The school continues to maintain close ties with Hollywood, with graduates working at all levels of the movie industry.

Friday, September 30, 1927

Bebe Daniels was very much pleased with the success of her picture *The Campus Flirt*, in which she introduced college atmosphere and Charlie Paddock, the track athlete. So she has made herself another thing of the kind, *Swim, Girl, Swim*, involving collegiate surroundings and Gertrude Ederle, the channel swimmer.

"Trudy" is more aquatic than collegiate, but the University of Southern California makes up for this. Incidentally one wonders why the film companies don't move their studios up to this university campus. There must be a producing company each week on the educational grounds. Bebe uses their students and swimming suits in *Swim, Girl, Swim* and Richard Barthelmess is coming along in *The Drop Kick*, wherein he used their football squads.

It is all part of the rage for college pictures that is on the public now. A little while and this craze will pass, having done the cause of education no particular good.

Bebe plays a bookworm who through farcical circumstances is made to appear a superswimmer. In fact, she can't swim at all. However, she plunges in, gets separated from the field, picked up in a motor boat, shipped across the course, thrown out in an accident and blunders and puffs to shore, where she is acclaimed as the winner.

An old formula, carried out smoothly and acted fetchingly by Bebe in a bathing suit. James Hall, as usual, is Bebe's leading man and handsomely fills the "young love" requirements of the story. "Trudy" Ederle is present, displaying her famous ability better than she ever did in films before.

October

College

After the financial disaster of The General, *studio moguls no longer admired Buster Keaton's cinematic ideas. Facing trouble in his marriage, along with a growing alcohol problem, Keaton followed up his best film with one of his weakest,* College. *A pale imitation of Harold Lloyd's successful* The Freshman, College *lacked the energy and inventiveness of Keaton's best work.*

Friday, October 7, 1927

Again the campus and athletic fields of the University of Southern California furnish the setting for professional movies and again it must be urged upon the film industry that it face the situation frankly and move itself bodily from Hollywood onto the university grounds. Judging from the films that the studios are putting out, Hollywood is done and the University of California has taken its place. How the professors at the university can conduct classes with Richard Barthelmess kissing coeds in the hallways, Bebe Daniels in a bathing suit kicking the president soundly and Buster Keaton bounding through the classroom windows with Snitz Edwards in comic pursuit is something to be imagined.

This same Keaton is now on the Oriental Theater's screen with a string of gags and burlesque incidents from collegiate life, labeling the whole thing *College.* In it he has scores of real college athletes, the baseball team of the University of Southern California, rowing stars from Syracuse, Yale, et cetera, fraternity houses, track meets, practically everything packed into seven slapstick reels.

Film producers, noting the immense popularity of colleges, how all educational institutions are crowded, how collegiate styles in clothing, in slang, in hairdress are copied by youth everywhere, are feeding the public collegiate romances, both serious and comic, in innumerable reels. Many people will take *College* as a satire on college romance pictures more than as a satire on education institutions.

College is in the familiar Keaton vein and while it may be scarcely as funny as *The General* or his recent pictures, in the sympathetic atmosphere of the Oriental Theater, where Paul Ash's personality has warmed and stirred patrons to a mood for enjoying whatever comes along, *College* is being hailed with a fury of whoops and guffaws.

Annie Laurie

"Fans always wrote asking why I didn't smile more in films," Lillian Gish said in her autobiography. "I did in Annie Laurie, *but I can't recall that it helped much."* [10]

Thursday, October 13, 1927

Lillian Gish has been through some pretty tough situations in movies. But she never went through the war and blood, hell fire and damnation that surrounds her in *Annie Laurie*.

Annie, in the old song, had a voice that was sweet and low, but in the picture she had to have a voice that was loud and shrill to be heard over the oaths, bellows, screams and clashes of arms that filled bonnie Scotland at the time her beauty was at its fairest.

Annie, daughter of Sir Robert Laurie of the clan Campbell, gets entangled in the goriest feud of Scotch history, that between the Macdonalds and the Campbells. She enters at the moment in which the Macdonalds are crowded back into the hills, cutting and slashing away at the Campbells, who, after the manner of Campbells, keep coming and coming after them. She is beloved by the biggest and fiercest of the Macdonalds (Norman Kerry) and by the slyest and foxiest of the Campbells (Creighton Hale) and the story is so flashed on the screen that sweet old ladies in the Roosevelt Theater these days cry aloud with delight when Norman takes Creighton up in his arms, at the finale, and throws Creighton from the battlement walls to a smashing death.

Annie Laurie is like no other of Lillian Gish's pictures. It has few or none of those fluttering, Victorian interludes of sentiment in which Lillian kisses doves or wild flowers or, as in *The Birth of a Nation*, bedposts. It is all action and fighting and gusty challenges. Lillian herself climbs a mountain and lights the fiery beacon which summons the Macdonald clans to rescue their kinsmen from treacherous death. She is in and out of the Glencoe massacre, up and down battlement walls, is praised and cursed, and has altogether a livelier time than she ever had since Griffith pointed the first camera at her many years ago.

Wings

The first movie to win the Academy Award for "Best Picture," Wings *brought together a great cast with exciting aerial stunts. William Wellman, nicknamed "Wild Bill," was assigned to helm the project. One of the few directors in Hollywood who'd actually flown in combat during World War I, Wellman combined* Wings' *human story with thrilling choreography of airplanes in battle. Wellman used in-plane cameras to give audience members a pilot's eye view of bombing raids and high-flying dogfights. The timing of* Wings' *release couldn't have been better. On May 20, 1927, Charles A. Lindburgh became the first man to fly solo from New York to Paris. In the wake of this historic feat, the public was hungry for anything related to airplanes.* Wings *satisfied that desire and then some.*

Monday, October 31, 1927

Nearly 10 years after the end of the world war the story of the war from the air is told in a stupendous picture called *Wings*, which opened at the Erlanger Theater last evening.

The 10 years have brought some realistic stories of the conflict, notably *The Big Parade* and *What Price Glory*, not to mention the humorous *Better 'Ole*, but *Wings*, it would seem is bound to hold a place all its own and way above the others as actual achievement, regardless of heart interest.

Because of the enormous difficulty of making the air shots and the almost prohibitive cost, the air story of the war has not been told until now. The picture was two years in the making and taxed the resources of the Paramount studios. Even then it could not have been done without the cooperation of the war department and the help of the navy planes. Aces of the world war were called upon to assist and altogether the production was something over which to marvel. It is announced as a Lucien Hubbard production directed by William A. Wellman.

Full recognition of all the obstacles comes when one sees the picture, and no other film which can be called to mind is capable of giving quite the same number of thrills. Partly is this so because of the romance, the mystery, the glamour of flying. Here are a dozen Lindberghs, it seems, all courageous, all skillful and all engaged in a serious duty.

The love story running through it is a dignified one—just the kind that happened in every one of our neighborhoods. Two young chaps going away to war, both of them in love with the same girl, and one of them loved by another girl, and the stay-at-homes all sorrowing. The idealistic friendship between the two men is preserved as faithfully here as it was in *Beau Geste*, and the small part a sweet girl at home plays in their lives is delicately traced. Jobyna Ralston is this girl. To Clara Bow falls the role of an American girl in war service in France. Her vivacity is kept within bounds and she is a relief from the somber scenes of war. With all this, care is taken that the feminine element is made negligible. It is man's work that is being pictured and men are the heroes. Richard Arlen, a veteran of the world war, having served with the Royal Flying Corps of Canada, is one of the youthful leads and Charles Rogers is the other. Richard Tucker is seen as the air commander, and a glimpse is given of Gary Cooper as Cadet White. Henry B. Walthall is an invalid father of one of the flyers and the rest of the cast is made up of well-known names.

November

Seventh Heaven

In 1927, at the inaugural Academy Awards ceremony, Oscars were handed out for both Dramatic and Comedy Direction. Seventh Heaven *earned Frank Borzage the first win in the Dramatic category. In 1937 James Stewart and Simone Simon starred in director Henry King's* Seventh Heaven *remake.*

Monday, November 7, 1927

Seventh Heaven, by Austin Strong, has been a play, a vaudeville sketch and a movie, and the movie is the greatest of them all. It was directed by Frank Borzage and shows much that in the play was left to the imagination. The war scenes, for instance, are equal to anything in *What Price Glory* or *The Big Parade*, although they are briefer, being only a small part of what is, at that, a very long picture. The mobilization of the taxicabs and the part they played in saving Paris is another of the elaborations. Scenes in subterranean Paris, where Chico, the hero, worked until he dragged himself from the sewer to the eminence of hoseman, a street cleaner, are revealed to the eye as no stage could show them. Even the significance of the title is made clear when the seven flights of winding stairs are climbed to reach the "heaven" at the top of the house in the old Latin Quarter, to which Chico takes Diane. Realistic to a degree, all of it.

The story of *Seventh Heaven* became so well known when the John Golden stage production was going the rounds of the theaters that most moviegoers know it, but for the sake of those who do not it may be told that it is a story of Diane, a beaten and miserable girl of the Paris gutters, and Chico, a "very remarkable fellow," as he himself avers. Chico, working in his sewer, rescues Diane from an absinthe-crazed older sister and, to protect her from the police, announces that she is his wife. He takes her home to prevent being found out—but only to stay until the police have satisfied themselves. Diane makes a heaven of his garret and when the time comes for her to go he will not let her. He makes her his wife in truth, or would have had not his regiment been ordered to the front immediately with only time for a hurried wedding which they, he and Diane, perform.

Then comes Chico's fighting days and Diane's "carrying on" at home, and how it ends may not be told—for that is a surprise. Janet Gaynor is the Diane and Charles Farrell the Chico, the best the play has had.

The Monroe Theater is the first theater in Chicago to show this Fox masterpiece. In New York and Lost Angeles, where it was released earlier, the price of seats was much higher than the Monroe asks and Chicago moviegoers are lucky to be able to see such an unusual film at so modest a tax.

Movietone accompaniment adds materially to the value of the picture. Synchronization of sound and action is almost perfect.

No Place to Go

Mervyn LeRoy, who made his directorial debut with No Place to Go, *ultimately became one of Hollywood's most versatile filmmakers. Among the many works he directed are such renowned pictures as* Little Caesar *(1931),* I Am a Fugitive from a Chain Gang *(1932),* The Gold Diggers of 1933 *(1933),* Waterloo Bridge *(1940), and* The Bad Seed *(1956). He also produced the 1939 classic* The Wizard of Oz.

Wednesday, November 9, 1927

In *No Place to Go* photoplay at State-Lake Theater, the young lovers, cruising the south seas, leave the comparative safety of the cannibal islands to embark on the uncharted seas of matrimony only to find the going so hazardous that for a time their craft is in danger, but movie art and a director's skill lead them into safe harbor.

To be less nautical, but more intelligible, the story, by Richard Connell, entitled *Isles of Romance,* has been scenarized to good effect by Adelaide Heilbron and made into a movie by First National, directed by Mervyn LeRoy. And by the way, it is LeRoy's first picture and he is one of the youngest directors in the business. No one observing the technique would ever suppose the director had had so little experience. It is a peppy picture, different from most, and meant for persons like yourself—intelligent and appreciative.

Mary Astor, lately bobbed, plays the daughter of wealth, Sally Montgomery, and Lloyd Hughes, always admirable, plays Hayden Eaton, a personable young man from her father's bank. They are seen first in a roof cabaret enjoying the jungle atmosphere. Sally is romantic and wants to be wooed at the altar of the great outdoors. A trip to the south sea islands on the family yacht seems to offer the desired opportunity for adventure. Under the Southern Cross Sally's desire for romance grows. She persuades her devoted admirer (of course, he is on the yacht) to go with her in a small boat at night to visit a nearby island. They take a supply of canned goods, but forget a can opener. Each blames the other. Sally sulks and Hayden amuses himself with his golf sticks. Then the cannibals appear. They expect to be made into a cannibal feast. Russ Powell is a scream as a comic cannibal chieftain.

In the meantime, consternation on the yacht. A search of the islands and Sally and her disillusioned companion are rescued. Back in New York convention decrees that they marry, but temper and disposition have not improved and they pull at the knot until they finally establish a separating line which neither will cross.

A vivid dream about a cannibal chief terrifies Sally and she flies to Hayden for protection. Guess the rest. You'll love the kidding and the novelty of the setting.

Underworld

In 1920, while Sandburg began work as the Daily News's *film columnist, Alphonse "Al" Capone came to Chicago from his native Brooklyn at the behest of a former associate, Johnny Torrio. In a few short years Capone—whose knife-marred mug earned him the nickname "Scarface"—had become the most powerful and feared man in the Windy City. Capone's criminal influence stretched from the inner circles of City Hall to the outer reaches of Chicago's suburbs. Chicago and Capone's violent reign became synonymous; decades after Scarface passed away, his name still conjures up images of an era filled with crooked politicians, booze-filled speakeasies, and the sneering blasts of Tommy guns. Ben Hecht, Sandburg's former* Daily News *colleague, made his screenwriting debut with* Underworld, *penning a work loosely based on the exploits of his hometown's most notorious citizen. The script was developed from an 18-page story treatment Hecht had written. Interestingly, this initial treatment was labeled as "moody Sandburgian."[11] For his work on* Underworld *Hecht won the first-ever screenwriting Oscar for "Original Story." In 1932, Hecht and* Underworld *producer Howard Hawks re-worked their original film into the gangster classic* Scarface. *Sandburg's opening paragraphs in this review contain some of his best film writing, accurately capturing the raw emotions of 1927's crime-weary Chicagoans.*

Monday, November 14, 1927

The scene is yesterday at noon. The doors of the Roosevelt Theater swing open and crowds wander out. A "spill" has come, a "spill" being the departure of large groups of customers at the end of the picture.

Those faces look exhausted, eyes turn up and down State Street as in a daze. *Underworld* has left them limp, these Chicagoans who have come to see the gunmen and gangsters of their city brought at last to the screen.

Within the theater packed rows of faces are staring as the picture starts again on its endlessly circling path of savagery. Faces have been rapt and nerves have dangled in suspense here before, but never like this. Good reason. *Underworld* has more suspense

A *Chicago Daily News* ad for *Underworld* quotes Sandburg's review: "Nothing ever approached it for sheer excitement and intensity" (Tuesday, November 15, 1927).

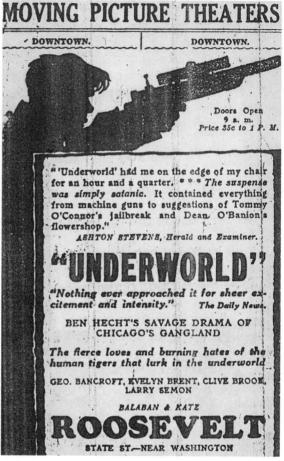

than almost any picture ever made before. Films there have been more realistic—*The Last Laugh*, for instance, films there have been more achingly poignant—*Broken Blossoms* for one, but no work for the screen ever approached this for sheer excitement, for intensity.

Ben Hecht, the Chicago reporter and novelist, wrote it as his maiden scenario. Josef von Sternberg, all artist, directed it. The business office inserted sentiment here and there in the work of these two exotic geniuses, Hecht and von Sternberg, but the story is theirs, between them and to their score goes one of the great ones in screen history.

Over and above them, however, towers a new American actor, George Bancroft. Bancroft, ever more than his author or his director, is microscopically honest with his job. He plays "Bull" Weed, gangster-terror of the underworld with complete conviction. He is like Wallace Beery, only better; he is, at times, evenup in power with the greatest of them all, Emil Jannings. Indeed, in the swift, irresistible rush of *Underworld's* first two reels, Bancroft reaches out from the screen to seize his spectators and make them his as completely as Jannings ever did.

"Bull" Weed is king of the Chicago jungle, "Attila at the gates of Rome," a laughing king who rescues bums from the gutter and when they ask him what they can do for him, gasps: "nobody helps me. I help other people," and then breaks into jaguar guffaws. "Bull" is good to "Feathers," his "moll." He sticks up a jewel shop on Michigan Avenue to get a diamond necklace "Feathers" craves, privately deeming the ornament vulgar, though he does.

"Bull" Weed stops little boys stealing apples, advises them not to rob, gives them big bills and boots their little posteriors while he bellows in merriment.

But when "Bull" Weed must hang for having killed "Buck" Mulligan in the latter's flower shop, then Bancroft rises to tragic majesty. How he accomplishes it without sacrificing his roughness, his toughness, his winning smile, only he can tell. But he does it. Jail breaks, smashing machine-gun battle with the police, vicious thumbs in the white throat of a woman, jungle blood burning up, all are used by him to tighten emotions almost to the breaking point. No mock heroics, no posturing, no theatricalism in Bancroft. He is "Bull" Weed and a magnificent animal, many magnificent animals all in one, leonine, tigerish, rogue-elephantine, but animals with the sublime gift of being able to grin.

Underworld does for the sophisticated adult what football does for the college boy. And Bancroft achieves something of the herculean glory of a gory fullback, with von Sternberg as his general, showing him the openings, guiding his raging course. Von Sternberg achieves impressionistic settings without the use of fancy photography. At a gangster ball "Bull" Weed wades knee-deep through paper ribbons to rescue his girl from his enemy, and the confetti and the ribbons are like the sea, moving elementally all the while. Von Sternberg's genius lies in his ability to use for dramatic effect shadows, lines, movement that naturally belong in the picture.

For support, Bancroft has two who catch the mood of *Underworld* and who never slip therefrom, Clive Brook, gentleman-pal of "Bull," and Evelyn Brent, feline mate of the jungle rogue. Both are better than they ever were before—or may be again.

The Jazz Singer

History tells us that The Jazz Singer *was the first "talking picture." In reality the soundtrack contained several synchronized musical numbers heard on Vitaphone technology, something movie audiences were accustomed to by late 1927. Though the majority of the "talking" in* The Jazz Singer *was done through subtitles, there was a little bit of synchronized dialogue—most notably Al Jolson's famous line, "You ain't heard nothin' yet!" Considering the revolution that* The Jazz Singer *would ignite in the film industry, Sandburg's reaction to the first "talking picture" seems surprisingly blasé.*

Wednesday, November 30, 1927

Heart throbs, tears, religion, "Mammy," love and syncopation—these made up *The Jazz Singer* as Al Jolson and the vitaphone put over the vocal picture, and the Warner Brothers' capital entertainment at the Garrick Theater last evening.

Not a dry eye in the house when the jazz singer stood in the cantor's place in the synagogue and intoned the sacred hymns of his people, while his aged father within earshot lay dying, happy in the thought that his son, the fifth Rabinowitz, had not failed in his duty to the Lord.

It was all gripping and tender and religious—just as was the play of the same title which ran here a year or so ago at the Harris Theater, with still another gifted Jewish boy, George Jessel, playing the title role.

There is, of course, but one Jolson and he made the Jakie Rabinowitz who ran away from his orthodox father's house and became a cabaret singer, a very real young man, the choice between duty and a career a difficult matter. The vitaphone did a great deal to help, reproducing the songs and some of the other sounds in the course of the action.

Aside from the wonderful Jolson there are other fine actors in the cast. Warner Oland as the Cantor Rabinowitz gives a notable characterization, as he usually does. Not enough has been said about the acting of this really cultured player. Oland has been an instructor of drama at Williams College and during that period translated the works of August Strindberg. His work in pictures has earned him a high place.

Eugenie Besserer gives one of her inimitable mother impersonations, and May McAvoy is charming as always as the girl who takes an interest in the jazz singer and helps him along in his career.

The Garrick was crowded last night. It is likely to be throughout the engagement with two performances daily.

December

Love

This was the second collaboration between Greta Garbo and her then real-life love interest, John Gilbert. Though the intensity of their passion gradually faded, the duo made three more films together: A Woman of Affairs *(1928),* A Man's Man *(1929), and* Queen Christina *(1933). In 1935 Greta Garbo remade* Love *as* Anna Karenina, *the original title of Leo Tolstoy's novel.*

Wednesday, December 28, 1927

Love is the Hollywood translation of that well-known Russian word, "annakarenina."

At least Hollywood has put out Count Leo Tolstoy's novel, *Anna Karenina* under that short and simple title. *Love* is the best of all titles to give any picture in which John Gilbert and Greta Garbo meet, and in *Love* John and Greta are staging their first annual reunion today at the Roosevelt Theater.

About a year ago John and Greta were co-starred in *Flesh and the Devil* and the result was the most swimmy-headed succession of kisses and clasps that the screen ever presented. Now, a year later, we find John and Greta rushing at each other with open arms and lips all puckered up for some more of those caresses which made the heart of the world act like a broncho bucking in a box stall.

The two are capable of getting further lost in dreams of love, capable of kissing more convincingly, hugging more earnestly than any two other co-stars in the career of the screen. So intense and personal are their vows and embraces that an innocent bystander is apt to feel embarrassed at thus intruding upon the emotions of others.

John and Greta play with what is really fine sincerity and abandon. They look their best in their roles and know it, which means that they act with confidence and power. Their roles are powerful roles, too, as translated into action, roles rich in character and emotion. Greta is Anna Karenina, young and smartly gowned wife of an elderly, haughty statesman of Petrograd. She is trapped by a snowstorm in a rural hostelry where also comes, rubbing his nipped ears, a young cavalry nobleman, who attempts to win her then and there.

Anna, being a good wife and a young mother, repulses him and, meeting him again in Petrograd where they discover themselves in the same aristocratic strata, forgives him reluctantly. They try to kill their love, hold to duty heroically, but wilt eventually and in stormy rapture rush away to the Riviera, figuring the world well lost.

They handle skillfully, artistically, the inexorable call of home, Greta's yearning for her deserted baby, John's attempts to hold her in spite of his twinges of conscience as he thinks of his regiment.

George Fawcett, Emily Fitzroy, Brandon Hurst and a pretentious cast support the co-stars and support them well. *Love* lives up to its name and the fame of the Gilbert-Garbo combination.

From the collection of Arnie Bernstein.

Lon Chaney in a scene from *London After Midnight*, the "holy grail" of missing silent films.

1928

January

London After Midnight

For his vampire role in London After Midnight, *Lon Chaney created one of his most fiendish makeup designs. Chaney's eyes bulged from the sockets, while his teeth were sharp and animal-like. This film later became the center of a real-life London murder. One viewer, claiming to be deeply disturbed by Chaney's perfor-mance, stated in court that he suffered hallucinations and a subsequent epileptic seizure after seeing* London After Midnight. *In the midst of his seizure, the defen-dant insisted, he had killed a young woman. The British court found him not guilty by reason of insanity.[1] Though on the American Film Institute's "10 Most Wanted" missing films list, rumors have persisted over the years that copies of* London After Midnight *exist. One story has it that an eccentric film collector refuses to let go of the only existing print until he is paid an exorbitant ransom.[2] Other tales claim that badly damaged copies have been shown at various screenings. In reality these and other reports have proven to be nothing more than urban legends for cinemaphiles.* London After Midnight *is often referred to as the "holy grail" of missing films. In 1935 director Tod Browning remade the story as* Mark of the Vampire. *Lionel Barrymore played the police inspector and Bela Lugosi was the vampire—roles Chaney had played in a dual performance for* London After Midnight.

Ravinia, which Sandburg refers to in the last paragraph, is a long-running summer music showcase held in Chicago's north suburbs.

Monday, January 9, 1928

When Inspector Burke comes on the screen in *London After Midnight* there is a vast buzzing in the Chicago Theater. Everybody in the audience is asking everybody else, "What actor is that?"

No wonder. Inspector Burke is played by Lon Chaney with little or no makeup. The world has forgotten what Lon Chaney's real face looks like and when he lets his own countenance shine forth he is disguised most of all.

In *London After Midnight* Chaney has all his legs and ears, all the normal features of mankind, and it is an interesting study to look upon him and wonder where those eyes and arms have been all these years.

Chaney only put on black-tailed nose glasses and a little pair of gray sideburns for his role of Inspector Burke, the hypnotic detective of Scotland Yard. For the major portion of this new Tod Browning story Lon is the mysterious man hunter and crime solver, but along about the middle of the picture he takes on another role, a minor one, but a part that outdoes for sheer terror anything even he ever saw in a looking glass. This secondary role is that of a squat and batlike little man in a high hat and an awful face who hangs around a haunted house. Wherever he goes through the cobwebbed mansion of fear there goes also a weird lady in white clothes and with mournful eyes and they move so spookily that the neighbors in this old English town are rapidly going nuts.

The story of how Inspector Burke solves the mystery is one of the most diverting and suspenseful in all the long association of Chaney, the actor, and Tod Browning, the director. Conrad Nagel, Marceline Day and H. B. Walthall have parts, but do not have them seriously enough to interfere with Mr. Chaney and his performance.

To soothe the jumpy nerves of patrons after this ghost-detective tale the Chicago Theater has Jesse Crawford back again at the organ from which he extracts such fine Irish tenor melodies. It has further such singers as Margery Maxwell, the Ravinia soprano, in an elaborate orchestral production by the inventive and musical Mr. Spitalny.

Appendix

Following are useful Internet resources on both Carl Sandburg and silent movies.

Carl Sandburg

The Carl Sandburg Historic Site Association (http://www.galesburg.net/~heasly/)

The Carl Sandburg Historic Site, Galesburg, IL (http://www.misslink.net/sandburg/)

The Carl Sandburg Page (http://alexia.lis.uiuc.edu/~rmrober/sandburg/home.htm)

Connemara: Sandburg Home National Historic Site, Flatrock, NC (http://www.nps.gov/carl)

Sandburg, Carl. 1916. *Chicago Poems* (http://www.bartleby.com/165/index.html)
A free, on-line edition of the book.

Sandburg, Carl. 1918. *Cornhuskers* (http://www.bartleby.com/134/index.html)
A free, on-line edition of the book.

Silent Film

The Internet Movie Database (http://www.imdb.com)

National Film Preservation Board of the Library of Congress (http://lcweb.loc.gov/film/)

National Film Preservation Foundation (http://www.filmpreservation.com)

The Silent Circle (http://welcome.to/thesilentcircle)

Silent Movies (http://www.cs.monash.edu.au/~pringle/silent/)

Silent-Movies.Com (http://www.silent-movies.com/)

Silents are Golden (http://www.silentsaregolden.com/)

The Silents Majority (http://www.mdle.com/ClassicFilms/)

The Silents Majority Taylorology (http://www.silent-movies.com/Taylorology/)

Notes

Sandburg and Movies

1. Robert Andrews, *Columbia Dictionary of Quotations* (New York: Columbia University Press, 1993), 197.

2. Frederick Lewis Allen, *Only Yesterday: An Informal History of the Nineteen-Twenties.* (New York: Bantam Books, 1946), 121-2.

1920

1. Paul Sann. *The Lawless Decade: A Pictorial History of a Great American Transition: From the World War I Armistice and Prohibition to Repeal and the New Deal* (Greenwich, Connecticut: Fawcett Publications, Inc., 1971), 80.

2. Ibid., 83.

3. Mack Sennett as told to Cameron Shipp, *King of Comedy* (New York: Pinnacle Books, 1975), 67.

4. Lillian Gish with Ann Pinchot, *The Movies, Mr. Griffith and Me* (San Francisco, California: Mercury House, 1988), 230.

5. Gary Carey, *Doug & Mary: A Biography of Douglas Fairbanks and Mary Pickford* (New York: E. P. Dutton, 1977), 113-4.

6. Mary Pickford, *Sunshine and Shadow* (Garden City, New York: Doubleday & Company, Inc., 1968), 133.

7. Charles Chaplin, *My Autobiography* (New York: Pocket Books, 1966), 198.

1921

1. Gish, 235.

2. Carl Sandburg, *Abraham Lincoln: The Prairie Years and the War Years* (New York: Harcourt, Brace and Company, 1954), 709-10.

3. Herbert Mitgang, *Dangerous Dossiers: Exposing the Secret War Against America's Greatest Authors* (New York: Ballantine Books, 1989), 65.

4. Gish, 222.

5. David Stewart Hull, *Film in the Third Reich* (New York: A Touchstone Book published by Simon and Schuster, 1973), 268.

6. Herman G. Weinberg, *Stroheim: A Pictorial Record of His Nine Films* (New York: Dover Publications, Inc., 1975), 35.

7. Ibid.

8. Ibid.

9. Pickford, 150.

10. Carey, 111.

11. Pickford, 150.

12. Penelope Niven, *Carl Sandburg, A Biography* (New York: Charles Scribner's Sons, 1991), 198.

13. Tony Crnkovich, "*Molly O'* : Lost Film Found" (*Classic Images*, Vol.250, April 1996, www.ClassicImages.com).

14. Richard Schickel, *D. W. Griffith: An American Life* (New York: Simon and Schuster, 1984), 454.

1922

   1. Sennett, 12.

2. Gish, 245.

3. Tom Dardis, *Harold Lloyd: The Man on the Clock* (New York: Penguin Books, 1984), 112.

4. Chaplin, 213.

5. Kevin Brownlow, *The Parade's Gone By . . .* (New York: Alfred A. Knopf, 1969), 255.

6. Niven, 275.

7. Michael F. Blake, *Lon Chaney: The Man Behind the Thousand Faces* (New York: The Vestal Press, Ltd., 1993), 92.

1923

1. Sennett, 252.

2. North Callahan, *Carl Sandburg: His Life and Works* (University Park, Pennsylvania and London, England: The Pennsylvania State University Press, 1987), 77.

3. Gloria Swanson, *Swanson on Swanson* (New York: Random House, 1980), 196.

4. Colleen Moore, *Silent Star* (Garden City, New York: Doubleday & Company, Inc., 1968), 129.

5. Pickford, 153.

6. Rudi Blesh, *Keaton* (New York: Collier Books, 1971), 220.

7. Brownlow, *The Parade's Gone By . . .* , 110.

8. Sennett, 269.

1924

1. Chaplin, 321.

2. Gish, 150.

3. Blesh, 242.

4. Swanson, 203.

5. Josef von Sternberg, *Fun in a Chinese Laundry* (London: Columbus Books, 1987), 207.

6. Eileen Whitfield, *Pickford: The Woman Who Made Hollywood* (Lexington, Kentucky: The University Press of Kentucky, 1997), 242.

7. Sternberg, 207.

1925

1. Gish, 262.

2. Erich von Stroheim, edited by Joel W. Finler, *Greed* (New York: Simon and Schuster, 1972), 16.

3. Ibid.,, 28.

4. Weinberg, *Stroheim: A Pictorial Record of His Nine Films*, 97.

5. Stroheim, 28.

6. Stroheim, 30.

7. Herman G. Weinberg, *Josef von Sternberg* (New York: E. P. Dutton & Co., Inc., 1967), 22.

8. Sternberg, 160.

9. David Stenn. *Clara Bow: Runnin' Wild* (New York: Doubleday, 1988), 46.

10. Gish, 264.

11. Tom Dardis, *Keaton: The Man Who Wouldn't Lie Down* (New York: Penguin Books, 1980), 124-5.

12. Swanson, 232-3.

13. Carlos Clarens, *An Illustrated History of the Horror Film* (New York: Capricorn Books, 1968), 52-3.

14. Schickel, *D. W. Griffith: An American Life*, 511.

15. Herbert Mitgang, editor, *The Letters of Carl Sandburg* (New York: Harcourt Brace Javanovich, 1988), 527.

16. Chaplin, 327.

17. David Robinson, *Chaplin: His Life and Art* (New York: McGraw-Hill, 1985), 339.

18. Schickel, *D. W. Griffith: An American Life*, 514.

19. Clarens, 48.

20. Blake, 134.

21. Blesh, 261.

22. Dardis, *Keaton: The Man Who Wouldn't Lie Down*, 132.

23. King Vidor, *A Tree is a Tree* (New York: Harcourt, Brace and Company, 1953), 111.

1926

1. Weinberg, *Josef von Sternberg*, 30.

2. Vidor, 132-3.

3. Clive Hirschhorn, *The Warner Bros. Story* (New York: Crown Publishers, Inc., 1979), 30-3.

376 Notes to Pages 317-369

4. Frank Thompson, *Lost Films: Important Movies that Disappeared* (New York: The Citadel Press, 1996), 135-43.

5. Sann, 135.

6. Nahma Sandrow, *Vagabond Stars: A World History of Yiddish Theater* (New York: Harper & Row, 1977), 292.

7. Hector Arce, *Groucho* (New York: Perigee, 1980), 74-75.

8. Ibid., 107-8.

9. Ibid., 131.

10. Richard Schickel, *His Picture in the Papers: A Speculation on Celebrity in America, Based on the Life of Douglas Fairbanks, Sr.* (New York: Charterhouse, 1974), 112.

11. Karen Swenson, *Greta Garbo: A Life Apart* (New York: Scribner, 1997), 113.

12. Carey, 165.

1927

1. Vidor, 106

2. Siegfried Kracauer, *From Caligari to Hitler: A Psychological History of the German Film* (Princeton, New Jersey: Princeton University Press, 1974), 148.

3. Sann, 176.

4. Stenn, 82.

5. Ibid., 81.

6. Sann., 178.

7. Gish, 285-6.

8. Kevin Brownlow, *Behind the Mask of Innocence* (Berkeley and Los Angeles, California: University of California Press, 1992), 93.

9. Kracauer, 164.

10. Gish, 292.

11. William MacAdams, *Ben Hecht* (New York: Barricade Books, Inc., 1990), 101.

1928

1. Blake, 206.

2. Thompson, xv.

Bibliography

Acker, Ally. *Reel Women: Pioneers of the Cinema, 1896 to the Present.* New York: Continuum, 1993.

Allen, Frederick Lewis. *Only Yesterday: An Informal History of the Nineteen-Twenties.* New York: Bantam Books, 1946.

Anger, Kenneth. *Hollywood Babylon.* San Francisco, California: Straight Arrow Books, 1975.

———. *Hollywood Babylon II.* New York: New American Library, 1985.

Arce, Hector. *Groucho.* New York: Perigee, 1980.

Barnouw, Erik. *Documentary: A History of the Non-Fiction Film.* New York: Oxford University Press, 1980.

Bergeen, Laurence. *Capone: The Man and the Era.* New York: Touchstone, 1996.

Blake, Michael F. *Lon Chaney: The Man Behind the Thousand Faces.* Vestal, New York: The Vestal Press, Ltd., 1993.

Blesh, Rudi. *Keaton.* New York: Collier Books, 1971.

Brooks, Louise. *Lulu in Hollywood.* New York: Alfred A. Knopf, 1982.

Brownlow, Kevin. *Behind the Mask of Innocence.* Berkeley and Los Angeles, California: University of California Press, 1992.

———. *The Parade's Gone By . . . .* New York: Alfred A. Knopf, 1969.

——— and John Kobal. *Hollywood: The Pioneers.* New York: Alfred A. Knopf, 1979.

Callahan, North. *Carl Sandburg: His Life and Works.* University Park, Pennsylvania, and London, England: The Pennsylvania State University Press, 1987.

Card, James. *Seductive Cinema: The Art of the Silent Film.* New York: Alfred A. Knopf, 1994.

Carey, Gary. *Doug & Mary: A Biography of Douglas Fairbanks and Mary Pickford.* New York: E. P. Dutton, 1977.

Chaplin, Charles. *My Autobiography.* New York: Pocket Books, 1966.

Clarens, Carlos. *An Illustrated History of the Horror Film.* New York: Capricorn Books, 1968.

Crafton, Donal. *Before Mickey: The Animated Film, 1898-1928.* Cambridge, Massachusetts: The MIT Press, 1984.

Dardis, Tom. *Keaton: The Man Who Wouldn't Lie Down.* New York: Penguin Books, 1980.

———. *Harold Lloyd: The Man on the Clock.* New York: Penguin Books, 1984.

de Mille, Agnes. *Dance to the Piper & And Promenade Home: A Two-Part Autobiography.* New York: De Capo Press, Inc., 1980.

DeMille, Cecil B., *The Autobiography of Cecil B. DeMille.* Edited by Donald Hayne. Englewood Cliffs, New Jersey: Prentice-Hall, Inc., 1959.

Durnell, Hazell B., M. A., Litt. D. *The America of Carl Sandburg.* Washington, D. C.: The University Press of Washington, D. C., 1965.

Edmonds, Andy. *Frame-Up! The Untold Story of Roscoe "Fatty" Arbuckle.* New York: William Morrow and Company, Inc., 1991.

Eisner, Lotte H. *The Haunted Screen.* Translated by Roger Greaves. Berkeley and Los Angeles, California: University of California Press, 1973.

Endres, Stacey and Robert Cushman. *Hollywood's Chinese Theatre*. Los Angeles, California: Pomegranate Press, Ltd., 1992.

Everson, William K. *American Silent Film*. New York: Oxford University Press, 1978.

———. *The Art of W. C. Fields*. New York: Bonanza Books, 1967.

Eyman, Scott. *The Speed of Sound: Hollywood and the Talkie Revolution, 1926-1930*. Baltimore, Maryland: The John Hopkins University Press, 1997.

Fenin, George N. and William K. Everson. *The Western, From Silents to the Seventies*. New York: Penguin Books, 1977.

Franklin, Joe. *Classics of the Silent Screen*. New York: The Citadel Press, 1959.

Fussell, Betty Harper. *Mabel, Hollywood's First I-Don't-Care Girl*. New Haven, Connecticut and New York: Ticknor & Fields, 1982.

Gabler, Neal. *An Empire of Their Own: How the Jews Invented Hollywood*. New York: Anchor Books, 1989.

Gebert, Michael. *The Encyclopedia of Movie Awards*. New York: St. Martin's Paperbacks, 1996.

Geduld, Harry M. *Focus on D. W. Griffith*. Englewood Cliffs, New Jersey: Prentice-Hall, Inc., 1971.

Gish, Lillian with Ann Pinchot. *The Movies, Mr. Griffith and Me*. San Francisco, California: Mercury House, 1988.

Golden, Harry. *Carl Sandburg*. Greenwich, Connecticut: Fawcett Publications, Inc., 1962.

Gomery, Douglas. *Shared Pleasures: A History of Movie Presentation in the United States*. Madison, Wisconsin: University of Wisconsin Press, 1992.

Hayner, Don and Tom McNamee. *Chicago Sun-Times Metro Chicago Almanac*. Chicago: Bonus Books, Inc., 1991.

Hirschhorn, Clive. *The Warner Bros. Story*. New York: Crown Publishers, Inc., 1979.

Hull, David Stewart. *Film in the Third Reich*. New York: A Touchstone Book published by Simon and Schuster, 1973.

Jackson, Carlton. *Zane Grey*. Revised Edition. Boston, Massachusetts: Twayne Publishers, 1989.

Katz, Ephraim. *The Film Encyclopedia*. New York: Harper-Perennial, 1994.

Kerr, Walter. *The Silent Clowns*. New York: Alfred A. Knopf, 1975.

Kirkpatrick, Sidney D. *A Cast of Killers*. New York: E. P. Dutton, 1986.

Koszarski, Richard. *An Evening's Entertainment: The Age of the Silent Feature Picture 1915-1928*. Berkeley and Los Angeles: University of California Press, 1994.

Kracauer, Siegfried. *From Caligari to Hitler: A Psychological History of the German Film*. Princeton, New Jersey: Princeton University Press, 1974.

Lambert, Gavin. *Nazimova, A Biography*. New York: Alfred A. Knopf, 1997.

Leyda, Jay. *Kino: A History of the Russian and Soviet Film*. London, England: George Allen & Unwin Ltd., 1973.

MacAdams, William. *Ben Hecht*. New York: Barricade Books, Inc., 1990.

Maltin, Leonard. *Of Mice and Magic: A History of American Animated Cartoons*. New York: New American Library, 1980.

McDonald, Gerald, Michael Conway, and Mark Ricci. *The Films of Charlie Chaplin*. Seacaucus, New Jersey: The Citadel Press, 1973.

Medved, Harry and Michael Medved. *The Hollywood Hall of Shame: The Most Expensive Flops in Movie History.* New York: Perigee Books, 1984.

Mitgang, Herbert. *Dangerous Dossiers: Exposing the Secret War Against America's Greatest Authors.* New York: Ballentine Books, 1989.

Moore, Colleen. *Silent Star.* Garden City, New York: Doubleday & Company, Inc., 1968.

Niven, Penelope. *Carl Sandburg, A Biography.* New York: Charles Scribner's Sons, 1991.

Perry, Lilla S. *My Friend Carl Sandburg.* Edited by E. Caswell Perry. Metuchen, New Jersey and London, England: The Scarecrow Press, Inc., 1981.

Pickford, Mary. *Sunshine and Shadow.* Garden City, New York: Doubleday & Company, Inc., 1955.

Ramsaye, Terry. *A Million and One Nights: A History of the Motion Picture Through 1925.* New York: Touchstone, 1986.

Robertson, Patrick. *The Guinness Book of Movie Facts & Feats.* New York: Abbeville Press, 1994.

Robinson, David. *Chaplin: His Life and Art.* New York: McGraw-Hill, 1985.

———. *Hollywood in the Twenties.* Cranbury, New Jersey: A. S. Barnes and Co., Inc., 1968.

Sandburg, Carl. *Abraham Lincoln: The Prairie Years and the War Years One-Volume Edition.* New York: Harcourt, Brace and Company, 1954.

———. *Always the Young Strangers.* New York: Harcourt, Brace and Company, 1953.

———. *Chicago Poems.* New York: Dover Publications, Inc., 1994.

———. *Ever the Winds of Chance.* Urbana and Chicago, Illinois: University of Illinois Press, 1983.

———. *Poems for the People.* Edited by George and Willene Hendrick. Chicago: Ivan R. Dee, 1999.

———. *Remembrance Rock.* New York: Harcourt, Brace and Company, Inc., 1948.

———. *The American Songbook.* New York: Harcourt, Brace & Company, 1927.

———. *The Complete Poems of Carl Sandburg: Revised and Expanded Edition.* New York: Harcourt Brace & Company, 1991.

———. *The Letters of Carl Sandburg.* Edited by Herbert Mitgang. New York: Harcourt Brace Javanovich, 1988.

Sandburg, Margaret, editor. *The Poet and the Dream Girl: The Love Letters of Lilian Steichen & Carl Sandburg.* Urbana and Chicago, Illinois: University of Illinois Press, 1987.

Sandrow, Nahma. *Vagabond Stars: A World History of Yiddish Theater.* New York: Harper & Row, 1977.

Sann, Paul. *The Lawless Decade: A Pictorial History of a Great American Transition: From the World War I Armistice and Prohibition to Repeal and the New Deal.* Greenwich, Connecticut: Fawcett Publications, Inc., 1971.

Schickel, Richard. *D. W. Griffith: An American Life.* New York: Simon and Schuster, 1984.

———. *His Picture in the Papers: A Speculation on Celebrity in America, Based on the Life of Douglas Fairbanks, Sr.* New York: Charterhouse, 1974.

Sennett, Mack. *King of Comedy.* As told to Cameron Shipp. New York: Pinnacle Books, 1975.

Stenn, David. *Clara Bow: Runnin' Wild.* New York: Doubleday, 1988.

Sterling, Bryan B. and Frances N. Sterling. *Will Rogers in Hollywood.* New York: Crown Publishers, Inc., 1984.

Sternberg, Josef von. *Fun in a Chinese Laundry.* London: Columbus Books, 1987.

Stroheim, Erich von. *Greed.* Edited by Joel W. Finler. New York: Simon and Schuster, 1972.

Swanson, Gloria. *Swanson on Swanson.* New York: Random House, 1980.

Swenson, Karen. *Greta Garbo: A Life Apart.* New York: Scribner, 1997.

Thompson, Frank. *Lost Films: Important Movies that Disappeared.* New York: The Citadel Press, 1996.

Usai, Paolo Cherchi. *Burning Passions: An Introduction to the Study of Silent Cinema.* Translated by Emma Sansone Rittle. London, England: British Film Institute Publishing, 1994.

Vidor, King. *A Tree is a Tree.* New York: Harcourt, Brace and Company, 1953.

Walker, Alexander. *The Shattered Silents: How the Talkies Came to Stay.* New York: William Morrow and Company, Inc., 1979.

Weinberg, Herman G. *Josef von Sternberg.* New York: E. P. Dutton & Co., Inc., 1967.

———. *Stroheim: A Pictorial Record of His Nine Films.* New York: Dover Publications, Inc., 1975.

Whitfield, Eileen. *Pickford: The Woman Who Made Hollywood.* Lexington, Kentucky: The University Press of Kentucky, 1997.

Yannella, Philip R. *The Other Carl Sandburg.* Jackson, Mississippi: University Press of Mississippi, 1996.

Index

Aasen, John, 194, 195
Abraham Lincoln, 235-241
"Abraham Lincoln as a Boy", 239-240
"Abraham Lincoln's Stepmother and Her Influence", 240-241
Abraham Lincoln: The Prairie Years, 10, 58, 235, 238
Abraham Lincoln: The War Years, 58, 235
Abramson, Ivan, 145
Acker, Jean, 121
Adams, Claire, 143, 229, 289
Adams, Franklin P., 158, 159
Adams, Maude, 245
Adams Theater, 75
Ade, George, 165
Admirable Crichton, The, 180
Adoree, Rene, 289
"Adventurous Life of a Reel News Reporter, The", 35
Adventurous Sex, The, 284-285
Affairs of Anatol, The, 47, 48, 49
"Against Censorship in Massachusetts", 149
"Age Limit of a Film, The", 120
Agnew, Robert, 227
"Ain't Nature Wonderful in New Science Films", 16
Alcatraze, 143
Alcazar Theater, 57, 70, 193
Alden, Mary, 28
Alice Adams, 181-182
All, George, 246
Allen, Dina, 31
Alvarado, Don, 311
Always Audacious, 25
Always the Young Strangers, 47
America, 213-214, 230
American Film Institute, 284, 369
American Songbag, The, 10
American Venus, The, 297-299, 320
Anders, Glenn, 273
Andersen, Robert, 323
Anderson, Erville, 273
Anderson, Maxwell, 329, 330
Anderson, Sherwood, 165
Andreyev, Leonid, 248
Anna Karenina, 366

Annenberg, Walter, 331
Annie Laurie, 359-360
"Another Myth Goes Down", 58
Arbuckle, Roscoe "Fatty," 4, 5, 33, 34, 56, 114, 129, 176, 298, 302
Art of the Film, The, ix
Arzner, Dorothy, 349
Ash, Paul, 275, 288, 303, 307, 339, 350, 354, 359
Ashton, Sylvia, 254
Astor, Gertrude, 175
Astor, Mary, 30, 175, 316, 362
Atherton, Gertrude, 68
Austin, William, 340
Ayres, Agnes, 152, 175

Babbitt, 144
Baby Peggy, 175, 225, 226
Bachelor, The, 261
Bacon, Lloyd, 319
Badger, Clarence, 54, 303
Bad Seed, The, 362
Baggot, King, 291
Balaban & Katz, x, 127, 285, 286, 314
Ballin, Hugo, 170
Ballin, Mabel, 170, 171, 264
Balmer, Edwin, 285
Bancroft, George, 364
Band Box Theater, 74, 78
Banky, Vilma, 281, 293, 294, 309, 324
Bara, Theda, 4, 23, 24, 95, 133
Barbee's Loop Theater, 28, 36, 54, 83, 93, 94, 128, 145, 157, 158, 164
Bardelys the Magnificent, 333-334
Barnes, Frank, 335
Barnes, T. Roy, 170, 171, 175, 261
Barnyard, The, 174
Barrett, James Lee, 10
Barrie, James, 245
Barry, Leon, 215
Barrymore, John, 103, 120, 121, 134, 135, 136, 299-300, 316, 320
Barrymore, Lionel, 323, 331, 369
Barthelmess, Richard, 36, 38, 78, 101, 102, 214, 358
Battling Butler, 311-312

Baum, L. Frank, 279, 280
Baxter, Warner, 303
Bay, Hugh, 284
Bayes, Nora, 342
Be Reasonable, 118-118
Beach, Rex, 106
Beaudine, William, 284, 325, 326
Beau Geste, 360
Beautiful Though Speechless, 322
Beban, George, 105
Bedford, Barbara, 170, 291
Beebe, Ford, 20
Beery, Noah, 175, 221, 302, 348
Beery, Wallace, 147, 182, 190, 191, 267, 248, 364
Belasco, David, 93, 94
Belcher, Charles, 323
Bell, Spencer, 279
Bella Donna, 160-161
Bellamy, Madge, 230
Belmont, Theater, 347
Belmore, Lionel, 148
Ben-Hur, A Tale of the Christ, 295-297, 324
Bennett, Enid, 147, 234
Beranger, Andre, 313
Berggren, P. John, 45
Bergman, Ingmar, 203
"Bernard Shaw on the Movies", 247
Bernhardt, Sarah, 86, 354
Berquist, Rudolph J., 86
Besserer, Eugenie, 366
Best Years of Our Lives, The, 123
Better 'Ole, 360
Betty Boop, 135
Betz, Matthew, 271
Beverly of Graustark, 300
Beyond the Rainbow, 177
Big House, The, 55
Big Parade, The, 288-290, 309, 360, 361
Big Punch, The, 57-58
Bijou Dream Theater, 68
Billings, George, 239
Birth Control, 128
Birth of a Nation, The, 9, 29, 36, 37, 78, 127, 204-206, 230, 290, 208, 311, 359
Black Pirate, The, 322-323
Black Roses, 74-75
Blackbird, The, 352
Blackstone, Jack, 208

Blackstone Hotel, 78, 79
Blinn, Holbrook, 189
Blood and Sand, 136, 149
Blot, The, 82-83
Blythe, Betty, 95, 96, 97
Boardman, Eleanor, 171, 333, 334, 339
Boat, The, 110-111
Bogart, Humphrey, 29
Boganovich, Peter, xii
Bonner, Priscilla, 349, 350
Bonomo, Joe, 318
Booth, John Wilkes, 58
Borden, Olive, 313
Borzage, Frank, 316
Bose, Henri, 354
Boston Theater, 23, 26
Bosworth, Hobart, 171, 289
Bow, Clara, 4, 177, 227, 259, 275, 308, 309, 320, 332, 340, 341, 346, 361
Bowers, John, 119
Boyd, William, 175
Brabin, Charles, 184, 185
Brand, Max, 143
Breamer, Sylvia, 197
Brenon, Herbert, 245, 175
Brewster's Millions, 56
Brian, Mary, 275, 350, 351
Bridge on the River Kwai, The, 74
Bringing Up Baby, 312
British Board of Film Censors, 150
Broadway, 20, 72, 73, 88, 93, 95, 106, 197, 219, 271, 297, 310, 320, 321, 342, 350
Broken Blossoms, 9, 77-78, 89, 186, 246, 272, 285, 308, 345, 364
Broken Laws, 250
Bronson, Betty, 245, 297
Brooks, Louise, 4, 297-299, 310
Broun, Heywood, 178
Brown, Clarence, 341
Browning, Tod, 12, 113, 352, 269
Brown of Harvard, 331
Bruckman, Clyde, 217, 335
Bubbles, 135
Bull, Charles Edward, 230
Burdette, Gladys, 102
Burke, Joe, 259
Burnett, Frances Hodgson, 225
Burnham, Beatrice, 264
Burnham, Julia, 19

Burning Daylight, 18
Burton, Clarence, 175
Busch, Mae, 203
Bushman, Francis X., 297
Butler, David, 283
Butterworth, Joe, 284

Cabinet of Dr. Caligari, The, 4, 66-69, 81, 89,
    118, 148, 201, 285, 287, 326, 327, 351, 357
Cagney, James, 298, 328
Cain, Robert, 175
Calhoun, Alice, 283, 311
Call of the Wild, The, 140, 206-207
Camille (1921), 85-86
Camille (1927), 354
Campeau, Frank, 313
Campus Flirt, The, 316-317, 357
Cantor, Eddie, 294, 320
Capital Punishment, 259
Capone, Al, 226, 363
Capra, Frank, 347
Carew, Arthur, 287
Carey, Harry, 331
Carpentier, Georges, 73, 74, 93-95
Carr, Harry, 251
Carr, Mary, 280, 303, 350
Carrigan, Thomas, 17, 18
Carter, Leslie, 183
Carter, Nick, 264
Caruso, Enrico, 62, 63
Castle Theater, 259, 276, 287, 291, 312, 315
Cast of Killers, A, 114
Cavender, Glen, 335
Chadwick, Cyril, 158, 230
Chadwick, Helene, 269, 270, 303
Champ, The, 55
Chaney, Lon, xi, 9, 12, 42, 124, 125, 148, 187,
    188, 244, 248, 285-288, 339, 348, 352, 353,
    368-370
Chang, 347-349
Chaplin, Alice, 211
Chaplin, Charlie, xi, 2, 3, 4, 8, 9, 40, 50, 51,
    52, 54, 61, 62, 63, 66, 67, 69, 70, 76, 77, 78,
    89, 91-93, 114, 117, 118, 120, 126, 131,
    137, 146, 147, 148, 165, 170, 171, 175, 178,
    179, 195, 196, 197, 201, 202, 219, 226, 232,
    233, 234, 235, 253, 256, 274, 277, 278, 282,
    283, 288, 295, 305, 321, 346, 350, 356
Chaplin, Sydney, 195, 196, 282

"Chaplin at Close Range", 61
Chaplin's Dramatic Creed, 202
Chapman, Edythe, 175
"Charlie Chaplin's New One", 76
Cher Ami, 273
Cherryman, Rex, 86
Cheyenne Autumn, 229
Chicago Poems, 3, 24
Chicago Rothacker studio, 133
Chicago Theater, 98, 102, 104, 105, 109, 117,
    120, 127, 148, 158, 159, 170, 184, 203, 204,
    249, 282, 284, 285, 298, 300, 316, 333, 342,
    344, 352, 369, 370
Chief Big Tree, 230
Children of Divorce, 346
Christie, Al, 235
Citizen Kane, 233
"Claims Movies are Rest Cure", 143
Claney, Carl Stearns, 275
Clansman, The, 127
Clarence, 151, 152
Clark, Walcott D., 173
Clifton, Elmer, 177
Coan, Blair, 45
Cocoanut Grove fire, 57
Cocoanuts, The, 321, 322
Cody, Lew, 114, 171, 197
Coffee, Lenore J., 324
Cohan, George M., 204, 215
Cohan's Grand Theater, 146
Colbert, Claudette, 331
Coleman, Ronald, 191
Collected Poems, x
College, 358-359
Collier, William, Jr., 20
Collins, Jackie, 184
Collins, Monte, 291
Colman, Ronald, 260, 282, 324
"Color Technology", 34
"Colossal Effort Devoted to Picture Production",
    137
"Comedian in the Griffith Picture at Roosevelt",
    274
"Comic Supplement, The", 310
Commencement Day, 223-224
Compson, Betty, 175
Conklin, Chester, 170, 254
Connecticut Yankee, A, 106

Connecticut Yankee in King Arthur's Court, A, 106, 333
Connell, Richard, 362
Convict 13, 19
Coogan, Jackie, 2, 52, 53, 76, 120, 148, 226
Coolidge, Jake, 35
Cooper, Gary, 346, 361
Cooper, Merian C., 347, 348
Corbin, Virgina Lee, 250
Cornwall, Anne, 318
Cortez, Ricardo, 175, 304, 345
Costello, Dolores, 300
Costello, Helene, 327
Coutts, John E., 131
Covered Wagon, The, 166-169, 178, 230, 301
Craig, Nell, 97
Crandall, Harry M., 19
Crane, Stephen, 232
Crane, Ward, 318
Crane, William H., 170
Crawford, F. Marion, 191
Crawford, Jesse, 105, 158, 159, 370
Crawford, Joan, 4, 306, 307, 331, 342, 353
Crisp, Donald, 78, 323
Crowd, The, 251, 333
Crowell, Josephine, 281
Cruze, James, 25, 158, 166, 169, 175, 176, 178
Cummings, Irving, 153
Currier, Frank, 259
Curwood, James Oliver, 153

Dalton, Dorothy, 24, 234
Damaged Goods, 269
Dana, Viola, 175
Dane, Karl, 289, 290, 309
Dangerous Age, The, 151
Dangerous Business, 48
Daniels, Bebe, 56, 175, 302, 316, 357, 358
Daniels, Richard, 215
D'Arcy, Roy, 281, 323
Dark Angel, The, 281-282
"Darkest Hollywood in Short Travesty", 122
Daudet, Alphonse, 91
Daven, André, 262
Davenport, Dorothy (Florence Reid), 109, 110, 159, 160, 250, 349, 350
Davies, Marion, 233, 300
Davis, Mildred, 115, 116, 173
Daw, Marjorie, 204

Day, Marceline, 370
Day, Shannon, 302
Day Dreams, 174-175
"Death of Barbara La Marr", 294-295
"Death of Thomas H. Ince", 233-234
Debs, Eugene, 93, 94
DeForest, Lee, 219-220
De Grasse, Sam, 323
De Grey, Sidnery, 215
de Mille, Agnes, 46
DeMille, Cecil B., xi, 9, 46, 126, 131, 162, 175, 176, 180, 211, 234, 256, 262, 276, 303
de Mille, William C., xi, 9, 46, 47, 151, 152, 175, 176, 210-212
Dempsey, Jack, xi, 73, 74, 93-95, 180, 193, 194, 316
"Dempsey-Carpentier Fight", 93-95
"Dempsey-Firpo Fight", xi, 193-194
"Dempsey-Gibbons Fight Pictures", 180-181
Dempster, Carol, 186, 214, 247, 272, 272, 285, 345
De Putti, Lya, 314, 323
De Quincey, Thomas, 66
Denker, Henry, 10
De Roche, Charles, 175
Desert of Wheat, The, 100
Desert Sheik, The, 123
Dexter, Elliott, 112, 170, 173, 187
Diary of a Lost Girl, 297
Dickens, Charles, 147, 148, 345
Dictator, The, 133
Dietrich, Marlene, 231
Dill Picklers, 165, 166
"Distinction Made Between Photoplay and Merely a Picture", 150
Diversey Theater, 347
Dix, Richard, 171, 211, 257, 258, 301, 318, 321
Dixon, Thomas, 127
Dr. Jekyll and Mr. Hyde, 120-121
Dr. Jekyll and Mr. Zip, 120
Dog's Life, A, 42, 93
Don Juan, 316
Don Q, Son of Zorro, 39, 293
Donlin, Mike, 335
Don't Nag Your Wife, 68
Dorothy Vernon of Haddon Hall, 232
Doubles for Romeo, 61

Douglas Fairbanks in Robin Hood, 137, 138, 146
Douglas Fairbanks Picture Corporation, 85, 241, 323
Dove, Billie, 221, 320, 323
Down to the Sea in Ships, 177, 178, 299
Doyle, Arthur Conan, 266, 267
Dracula, 113
Dream Street, 58
Dresser, Louise, 293
Dreyer, Theodor, 9
Drinkwater, John, 239
Driscoll, Tex, 230
Drop Kick, The, 358
Dubois, Helen, 211
Dunbar, Helen, 175
Dupont, E. A., 313
Durant, Harry, 30
Dwan, Allan, 41, 147, 222
Dwan, Dorothy, 279, 280
Dwyer, Ruth, 261, 271

Eagle, The, 293-294
Earle, Edward, 226
Ebert, Roger, ix-xii, 11
Eddy, Helen Jerome, 41, 282
Ederle, Gertrude "Trudy", 342, 357, 358
Edeson, Arthur, 147
Edeson, Robert, 234
Educational, 235
Edwards, Blake, 95
Edwards, Harry, 347
Edwards, J. Gordon, 95, 96, 97
Edwards, Snitz, 175, 189, 261, 312, 358
Einstein, Albert, 173, 174
"Einstein's Theory of Relativity", 173-174
Ekman, Gosta, 337, 338
Eliot George, 128, 260
Elliott, Frank, 282
End of the Road, 269
"Enemy Sex, The", 346
Ercole, George, 35
Erlanger Theater, 321, 360
Essanay Film Company, 45, 46, 77
Estabrook, Howard, 275
Evarts, Hal G., 291
Everybody's Sweetheart, 20
Extra Girl, The, 197-198
Eyes Wide Shut, 47

Fable of the Sheik, The, 123
Face at Your Window, The, 31
Fairbanks, Douglas, xii, 4, 39, 55, 60, 84, 120, 138, 146, 147, 175, 200, 201, 231, 241-243, 256, 293, 322, 323, 325, 334
Family Secret, The, 225-226
Famous Players-Lasky, 30, 48, 49, 70, 98, 169, 212, 266, 271, 276
Farley, Jim, 35
Farnum, Dustin, 71, 317
Farnum, Joseph W., 251
Farrar, John, 178
Faust, 336-338, 351
Fawcett, George, 175, 281, 309, 318, 367
Faye, Julia, 175
Federal Bureau of Investigation (FBI), 61
Felix the Cat Shatters the Sheik, 123
Ferguson, W. J., 58
Fields, W. C., 194, 271, 272, 284, 285, 338, 339, 350
Fig Leaves, 312-313
"Fighters in Action in Motion Pictures", 73
Film Booking Office, 271
"Filmless Movies: How They Are Made, The", 158
Film Row, 72
Finlayson, James, 175
Fireman, Save My Child, 87
Firpo, Luis, 193, 194
First Circus, The, 87
First National Pictures, 49, 65, 102, 146, 187
Fish Films, 192
Fitzmaurice, George, 282, 309
Fitzroy, Emily, 367
Five Kisses, 48
Flaming Frontier, The, 317-318
Flaming Youth, 186-187
Fleischer, Max, 135
Flesh and the Devil, 341, 366
Floorwalker, The, 40
Flying Pat, 32
"Follies, The". *See* Ziegfield Follies
"Fooled the Camels", 97
Foolish Wives, 88, 89, 150
Fool There Was, A, 133
Forbidden Thing, The, 41-42
Ford, Harrison, 285
Ford, John "Jack", 163, 165, 229, 230, 313, 328

Ford Photoplay, 24
For the Land's Sake, 8
Foundling, The, 55
Four Horsemen of the Apocalypse, The, 63, 136, 293, 304, 309
Four Marx Brothers, The. *See* Marx Brothers
Fox, William, 31, 95, 133, 264, 313, 328, 330
Fox Film Corporation, 17, 26, 31, 70, 73, 96, 97, 106, 124, 133, 163, 228, 229, 230, 235, 242, 312, 362
France, Anatole, 112
Francis, Alec B., 175, 313
Freaks, 113, 352
Free Air, 144
French, Charles, 202
Freshman, The, 358
Freund, Karl, 336, 352
Frost, Robert, 126, 211
Fuller, Dale, 254
Fun In a Chinese Laundry, 231

Gable, Clark, 206
"Galleries are Again Holding Their Own", 111
Garbo, Greta, 38, 85, 292, 304, 323, 324, 341, 366, 367
Gardner, Jack, 175
Garland, Judy, 279
Garrick Theater, 289, 328, 329, 365, 366
Gay and Devilish, 125-126
General, The, 334, 335, 358, 359
Gentlemen Prefer Blondes, 312
Geraghty, Tom, 25
Gerrard, Charles, 197
Ghost Breaker, The, 148, 149
Gibbons, Cedric, 297
Gibbons, Tom, 180
Giblyn, Charles, 17
Gibson, Edmund "Hoot", 19, 20, 212, 216, 217, 317
Gibson, Tom, 320
Gilbert, John, 138, 186, 248, 281, 289, 290, 307, 333, 334, 341, 366, 367
Gillingwater, Claude, 170, 171, 181
Girl from Montmarte, The, 295
Girl Shy, 214-215
Girl Who Ran Wild, The, 146
Gish, Dorothy, 32, 127, 128, 260, 353-354

Gish, Lillian, xi, 4, 32, 36, 37, 38, 53, 78, 127, 128, 191, 205, 246, 260, 307, 308, 343-344, 359-360
Glendon, J. Frank, 156
Glyn, Elinor, 184, 185, 340
Goddard, Jean-Luc, 8
Godowsky, Dagmar, 170
Goebbels, Joseph, 351
Goethe, 336, 338
Going Up, 204
Goldberg, Rube, 40, 66, 69
Gold Diggers of 1933, The, 362
Gold Rush, The, 256, 277-279, 282
Goldwyn, Sam, 328
Goldwyn-Cosmopolitan, 185
Goldwyn Pictures Corporation, 28, 36, 54, 55, 61, 98, 112, 170, 202, 203
Goldwyn-Bray Pictograph, 16
Golem, The, 81, 82, 89, 201, 351
Gone With the Wind, 9, 241
Good, Will B., 33
Goodrich, John, 259
Goodrich, William, 33
Goodwin, Harold, 264
Gordon, Julia Swayne, 346
Gordon, Vera, 319
Gosfilmofond, 98
Go West, 288
Gowland, Gibson, 253, 287
Grand Larceny, 112, 113
Grandma's Boy, 131-132
Grange, Harold "Red", 318
Grauman, Sid, 176
Graves, Ralph, 166, 198
Gravina, Cesare, 183
Gray, Lawrence, 299, 320
Greatest Love of All, The, 105
Greatest Story Ever Told, The, 10
Great Locomotive Chase, The, 334
Great Moment, The, 185
Great Northern Theater, 161, 191
Greed, 251-255, 280, 287
Green, Alfred E., 175
Greer, Horace, 197
Grey, Lita, 51
Grey, Zane, 70, 71, 100, 221, 263, 264, 301, 302
Grierson, John, 295
Griffin, Carlton, 215

Griffith, D. W. (David Wark), 9, 10, 29, 32, 36, 37, 41, 58, 67, 77, 78, 87, 88, 89, 101, 102, 127, 128, 178, 185, 190, 191, 201, 203, 204-206, 213-214, 230, 233, 234, 246, 247, 256, 271, 272, 274, 284, 285, 310, 344, 345, 359
Griffith, Gordon, 284
Griffith, Raymond, 170, 274
Guest, Edgar, 41
Guilbert, Yvette, 337
Guile of Women, 54-55

Hackathorne, George, 183, 259
Hail! A Coming Star, 30
Hail a Woman, 100
Hail the Woman, 100
Haines, William, 4, 284, 331, 339
Hale, Alan, 124, 167, 175
Hale, Creighton, 359
Hale, Georgia, 256
Hamilton, Clayton, 157
Hamilton, Cosmo, 47
Hamilton, Lloyd, 175, 274
Hamilton, Neil, 213-214
Hammer, Man, 302
Hammerstein, Elaine, 170
Hammond, Charles, 273
Hammond, Norman, 113
Hampton, Benjamin B., 47, 48, 49
Hampton, Hope, 116, 175
Hanson, Lars, 341
Harcourt, Alfred, 144
Hardy, Oliver, 77, 194, 206279, 280
Harlan, Otis, 126, 313
Harmeyer, R. E., 86
Harris, Mildred, 51
Harris Theater, 319, 366
Hart, William S. "Bill", 8, 20, 21, 22, 26, 57, 100, 101, 175, 198, 212, 213, 234, 290, 291
Harte, Bret, 22, 146
Hartigan, Pat, 215
Harvez, Jean, 217
Haskell, Jean, 170
Hausman, Arthur, 222
Haver, Phyllis, 213, 313
Hawks, Howard, 312, 313, 363
Hawley, Wanda, 158
Hawthorne, Nathaniel, 343
Hayakawa, Sessue, 74, 75

Hayes, Frank, 254
Hays, Will, 5, 111, 114, 122, 125, 126, 132, 133, 150, 213, 221, 262, 316, 328
Hayworth, Rita, 136
Headin' Home, 79-81
Headless Horseman, The, 151
Hearst, William Randolph, 233
Hecht, Ben, 3, 10, 66, 69, 99, 165, 324, 325, 363, 364
Helm, Brigitte, 352
Henabery, Joseph, 57
Hendricks, Ben, Jr., 319
Henry, Gale, 175
Hepburn, Katherine, 181
Hergesheimer, Joseph, 101, 103
Hernandez, Anna, 198
Hero of the Big Snows, A, 311
Hersholt, Jean, 254
Her Temporary Husband, 196
He's My Pal, 218-219
Heston, Charlton, 206, 295
HE Who Gets Slapped, 248-249
Hiers, Walter, 149, 175
Higgin, Howard, 110
High Noon, 346
High Sierra, 29
Hill, Wycliffe A., 76, 79
His Girl Friday, 312
His Secretary, 300
Hitchin' Posts, 3, 15
Hogan, James P., 259
Hollywood, 175-176
Hollywood Follies, 123
"Hollywood's Sympathies are with Wallace Reid's Widow", 159
Holmes, Stuart, 175
Holmquist, Sigrid, 175
Holt, Jack, 175, 221
Honest Hutch, 28, 54, 55
Honeymoon, 280
Honor First, 138
Hook, 245
Hoover, J. Edgar, 62
Hope, Bob, 222
Hopkins, Anthony, 187
Hopper, Hedda, 340, 346
Hopwood, Avery, 106
Horn, Camilla, 337, 338
Horton, Clara, 49

Howard, Frances, 258

"How Censors Differ in Thought and Deed", 78

"How Many Pies Make a Hit in the Movies?", 31

"How One Marx Brother Reacted to Pictures", 320

"How von Stroheim Made Greed", 251-252

Hubbard, Lucien, 360

Hughes, Glenn, 267

Hughes, Lloyd, 362

Hughes, Rupert, 165, 170, 324

Hugo, Victor, 187, 188

Hulce, Thomas, 187

Hulette, Gladys, 226, 230

Hull, E. F., 97

Human Wreckage, 250

Humorisk, 320-321

Hunchback of Notre Dame, The, xi, 187-188, 353

Hunt, Jay, 319

Hurst, Brandon, 367

I Am a Fugitive from a Chain Gang, 362

Ibáñez, Vincente Blasco, 64, 136, 304, 323

Ibsen, Henrik, 112, 113

Icebound, 210-212

Idle Class, The, 91-93

Ince, Thomas H., 100, 233, 234

"Indian Supers on 'Strike' ", 22

Ingram, Rex, 63, 64, 251, 294

Inspiration Pictures, 100

International Workers of the World (IWW), 100

Intolerance, 9, 36, 37, 88, 190, 285, 345, 352

"Inventor in Chicago at Work on Motion Pictures for the Blind", 133

Iron Horse, The, 229-230, 313

Iron Trail, The, 106

Irving, Washington, 151

Isles of Romance, 362

"Is 'Love Interest' End and Aim of All?", 132

Isn't Life Wonderful?, 246-247

It, 332, 340-341

It's the Old Army Game, 310-311

James, Walter, 284

Jannings, Emil, 264, 265, 314, 355, 356, 337, 338, 365

Jazz Singer, The, xii, 319, 365-366

Jennings, DeWitt, 327

Jessel, George, 319, 320, 366

Johnson, Noble, 318

Johnson, Owen, 346

Jolson, Al, 294, 319, 365, 366

Jones, Buck, 4, 57, 58, 212, 216, 217

Jones, F. Richard, 198

Jones, Idwal, 251

Jones, Jack, 28, 166

Joy, Leatrice, 175, 277

Joyce, Peggy Hopkins, 201

Julian, Rupert, 285, 287

Jurassic Park, 266

Just Tony, 143

Katsmarof, George, 327

Keaton, Buster, xi, 4, 9, 18, 33, 38, 50, 110, 111, 126, 174, 175, 190, 191, 207, 208, 217, 218, 232, 234, 235, 261, 288, 311, 334, 335, 346, 358, 359

Keaton, Joe, 207, 335

Keene, Laura, 58

Keith, Ian, 222

Kenyon, Charles, 230

Kerrigan, J. Warren, 167, 169, 175, 230

Kerry, Norman, 183, 287, 353, 359

Key, Kathleen, 297, 318

Keystone Film Company, 30, 36, 40, 119

Kid Boots, 320

Kid Brother, The, 335-336

Kid, The, 2, 51, 53, 54, 59, 89, 93, 98, 120, 148, 197, 226

Kid Speed, 235

King, Claude, 185

King, Henry, 101, 191, 260, 324, 361

King, Ruth, 249

King Kong, 266, 347

King of Comedy, 30, 118

Kipling, Rudyard, 141

Kirkwood, James, 285

Knott, Lydia, 202

Koko, 135

Kosloff, Theodore, 175

Koter, Fred, 230

Kubrick, Stanley, 47

La Bohème, 307-308

Laemmle, Carl, 78, 82, 87, 227, 279

Lake, Alice, 170

La Marr, Barbara, 5, 171, 294-295
Land of Lafayette, The, 19
Landis, Cullen, 126
Lane, Charles, 335
Lang, Fritz, 351
Lang, Walter, 350
Langdon, Harry, 274, 346, 356
Lanphier, Fay, 299
La Roque, Rod, 277
LaSalle Theater, 63, 269
Lasky, Jesse, 25, 166
Last Command, The, 231, 355
Last Laugh, The, 264-266, 338, 364
Laughton, Charles, 187
Laurel, Stan, 77, 194, 206
Lawson, Victor E., 3
Lean, David, 74
Le Bailly de la Falaise de la Condraye, Marquis, 262
Lee, Lila, 46, 110, 136, 149, 175
Lee, Ronald C., 182
Legend of Sleepy Hollow, The, 151
Lehár, Franz, 280
Leighton, Lillian, 175, 291
LeRoy, Mervyn, 166, 362
Lesser, Irving, 153
Lewis, Sheldon, 120, 350
Lewis, Sinclair, 308
Levin, Meyer, 3
Lieber, Fritz, 96
Life of the Party, The, 33
Limelight, 76
Lincoln, Abraham, ix, 10, 58, 106, 122, 219, 229, 235-241
Lincoln, Mary Todd, 236, 237, 238, 239
"Lincoln the Man Shown in New Picture at the Roosevelt", 237-238
Lindburgh, Charles, 360
Lindsay, Vachel, 10
Little Annie Rooney, 283-284
Little Caesar, 362
Little Tigress, The, 325
Littlefield, Lucien, 291
Little Journey, A, 331
"Little-Known Facts About Lincoln", 235-236
Little Lord Fauntleroy, 89-90
Livingston, Margaret, 259
Lloyd, Frank, 346

Lloyd, Harold, x, 4, 115, 131, 132, 171, 172, 194, 195, 206, 214, 232, 234, 235, 253, 316, 335, 336, 346, 358
Lloyd, Lewis, 158, 159
Logan, Jacqueline, 175
Lombard, Carole, 331
London, Jack, 18, 99, 141, 206, 207, 270
London After Midnight, 12, 113, 368-370
Long Pants, 346-347
Lost Battalion, The, 273
Lost World, The, 266-269, 352, 354
Lotus Eaters, The, 103-104
Louis, Willard, 316
Love, 366-367
Love, Bessie, 170, 171, 234, 267
Love, Montague, 309
Love Light, The, 48, 55, 64, 65
Loves of Ricardo, 105
Lowe, Edmund, 328, 329, 330
Lubitsch, Ernst, 65, 189
Lucas, Wilfred, 263
Lucky Lady, The, 305
Lugosi, Bela, 113, 369
Lulu in Hollywood, 298
Lunergan, Philip, 319
Lunt, Alfred, 273
Luring Lips, 85
Lying Lips, 48, 85
Lyon, Ben, 300, 301

MacArthur, Charles, 165, 324
MacDermott, Marc, 249, 323
MacDonald, Francis, 204, 312
MacDonald, J. Farrell, 230, 313
MacFarlane, Peter Clark, 54
MacGrath, Harold, 283
MacGregor, Malcolm, 302
Mack, Marion, 335
Mack, Willard, 234
MacLean, Douglas, 234
MacMurray, Fred, 181
MacPherson, Jeanie, 175, 277
Madame DuBarry, 65
Madame Peacock, 23-24
Madame Pompadour, 253-254
Madame Sans-Gêne, 262-263
Madison Street Theater, 40
Main Street, 144
"Making of Pictures is Industry, Not Art", 69

Male and Female, 180
Maltese Falcon, The, 30
Man from Hell's River, The, 153
Manhandled, 221-222
Mann, Hank, 175
Mannon, Hamilton, 275
Man of a Thousand Faces, 285
Man on the Box, The, 282-283
Man on the Flying Trapeze, The, 350
Man's Man, A, 366
Mantrap, 308-309
March of the Vampire, 369
Marcin, Max, 31
Marcus, James, 230
Marion, Frances, 55, 324, 343
Mark of Zorro, The, 39
Marmont, Percy, 250, 275, 308
Marsh, Mae, 186
Marshall, Tully, 188, 197, 249, 281
Martin, Mary, 245
Martin, Townsend 299,
Martindel, Edward, 346
Marx, Chico, 320
Marx, Groucho, x, 320, 321
Marx, Gummo, 320
Marx, Harpo, 257, 320, 321, 322
Marx, Minnie, x, 320
Marx, Zeppo, 320
Marx Brothers, x, 320-322
Mathis, June, 86, 137, 170, 251
Maxwell, Margery, 370
May, Doris, 125
Mayall, Herschel, 158
Mayer, Louis B., 251, 304, 331
Mayflower Photoplay Corporation, 30, 35, 42
Mayo, Frank, 3, 15, 171, 185
McAllister, Mary, 319
McAllister, Paul, 222, 324
McAvoy, May, 152, 175, 297, 366
McCutcheon, George Barr, 56, 302
McDowell, Claire, 289, 297
McEvoy, J. P., 310, 339
McGrail, Walter, 187
McGuire, Kathryn, 119, 158, 233
McKay, John W., 35
McKim, Robert, 175
McLaglen, Victor, 328, 329, 330
McLaughlin, Gibbs, 354
McLean, Douglas, 204

McTeague, 126, 251-255, 278, 287
McVicker's Theater, 77, 117, 149, 152, 160, 166, 173, 174, 183, 190, 210, 220, 221, 232, 245, 246, 247, 257, 261, 275, 288, 290, 295, 302, 316, 335, 339, 340, 341, 345, 346, 356
McWade, Margaret, 181
Meighan, Thomas, 175, 318
Melford, George, 98, 124
Melville, Herman, 299, 300
Menjou, Adolphe, 202, 345
Menzies, William Cameron, 241, 309
Merry Go Round, 182-183
Merry Widow, The, 280-281
Metro-Goldwyn-Mayer (MGM), 10, 248, 252, 261, 282, 296, 297, 304, 323, 324, 342, 331
Metro Pictures, 18, 19, 86, 182, 207
Metropolis, 351-352
Meyers, Carmel, 297
Mickey, 12, 108, 113-114, 119, 165
Midsummer Madness, 46
"Mighty Cameraman, The", 61
Miliken, Mary Jane, 311
Miller, Carl, 202
Miller, Mary Louise, 326
Miller, Patsy Ruth, 170, 188, 319
Minter, Mary Miles, 114, 136, 302-303
Miracle, The, 315
Miracle Man, The, 42-43, 89, 148
Miss Brewster's Millions, 56
Mitchell, Joseph, 217
Mix, Tom, xi, 8, 9, 26, 27, 28, 57, 70, 72, 73, 95, 96, 124, 143, 163, 165, 186, 198, 199, 212, 216, 217, 227, 228, 229, 264
Moby Dick, 299, 300
Molly O', 98-99, 119, 165
Monkey Comedy Series, 241
Monroe, Marilyn, 340
Monroe Theater, 208, 313, 362
Monsieur Beaucaire, 222-223
Montana, Bull, 175, 309
Monte Carlo, 300
Montgomery, Peggy. *See* Baby Peggy
Moore, Colleen, 4, 103, 186, 187, 297, 343
Moore, Demi, 343
Moore, Owen, 175, 196, 197, 342
Moore, Pat, 250
Moore, Tom, 222
Moran, Clark, 119
Moreno, Antonio "Tony", 323, 340, 353

Morey, Harry T., 275
Morgan, Byron, 41
Morris, Clara, 354
Morosco, Walter, 327
Moscow Art Theater, 102, 161, 165
"Movie Location Shortage", 29
"Movies and Children", 305
"Movies are Getting Decidedly Better, The", 178
"Movie Stars Differ About the Subtitles", 165
"Movies to Be Shown in Air", 279
Mulhall, Jack, 269, 303, 318
Murfin, Jane, 271
Murnau, F. W., 229, 264, 336, 337
Murphy, Edna, 215
Murphy, Jack, 291
Murray, Charlie, 280
Murray, Mae, 281
"Musical Score for Covered Wagon Includes
   Classical Airs", 169
Mutual Film Corporation, 40
My Wife's Relations, xi, 126-127
Myers, Harry, 106

Nagel, Conrad, 46, 370
Naked Truth, The, 269-270
Naldi, Nita, 136, 177, 277
Name the Man, 203
Nanook, 140, 142
Nanook of the North, 11, 139-142, 169
Navigator, The, 232-233
Nawn, Tom, 335
Nazimova, Alla, 23, 24, 85, 86
Negri, Pola, 65, 66, 160, 161, 175
Neighbors, 50
Neil, Hamilton, 275
Neil, R. William, 250
Neilan, Marshall, 103, 170, 171
Nell, Richard R., 291
"New Color Process", 116
Newmeyer, Fred, 173, 215
Niblo, Fred, 85, 137, 170, 171, 297, 323, 324
Nichols, George, 198
Night Life in Hollywood, 155
Nilsson, Anna Q., 103, 170, 171, 175
Nineteen and Phyllis, 49
Ninotchka, 65
Nixon, Marian, 264
Noblesse Oblige, 68
No Place to Go, 362-363

Normand, Mabel, 4, 9, 12, 30, 36, 98-99, 108,
   114, 115, 119, 164, 165, 197, 198
Norris, Frank, 99, 126, 251-255, 278, 287
"Nothing 'Stuck Up' About Ben", 77
Novak, Eva, 153
Novarro, Ramon, 294, 296, 297
Novello, Ivor, 186
Nyla, 140, 142

Ober, Robert, 289
O'Brien, George, 229, 230, 313
O'Brien, Mary, 312
O'Brien, Tom, 289, 290
O'Brien, Willis H., 266
O'Connor, T.P., 150
Octopus, The, 278
O'Donnell, Chris, 261
O'Donnell, Spec, 284
Oglamond, William, 86
Ogle, Charles, 158, 175, 319
O. Henry, 91, 113
"Ohio Censor Board Sets Up Standards", 129
Oh, You Tony, 228-229
Oland, Warner, 264, 366
Old Nest, The, 85
Oliver, Edna May, 211, 299
Oliver, Guy, 175
Oliver Twist, 147-148
Olmstead, Gertrude, 300
One Day, 185
O'Neill, Sally, 312
One Law for All, 19, 20
One Minute to Play, 318-319
Only 38, 173
"On Sydney Chaplin", 195-197
Optic, Oliver, 318
Orchestra Hall, 65, 81, 139, 141, 171
Oriental Theater, 307, 311, 331, 339, 350, 354,
   358
"Origin of the Custard Pie", 30
Orphans of the Storm, xi, 127-128
Orpheum Theater, 33, 176, 185, 190, 197, 201,
   202, 214, 265, 277, 278, 282, 299, 319, 324,
   335
"Our Gang", 206, 223, 224
Our Hospitality, 207-208
Oursler, Fulton, 10
Out of Luck, 178
Out of the Dust, 133

Out of the Inkwell, 135
Out of the Snows, 133
Overland Stage Raiders, 298
Over the Hill, 85, 88

Pabst, G. W., 297, 298
Paddock, Charlie, 317, 357
Padjam, John, 230
Palm Beach Girl, The, 320
Palmer, Attorney General Mitchell A., 100
Palmer House Hotel, 69
Pandora's Box, 297
Panthea, 38-39
Pantheon Theater, 104
Panzer, Paul, 259
Paramount Pictures Corporation, 25, 82, 124,
   149, 221, 271, 275, 284, 301, 339, 340, 344,
   346
Paris, 306-307
Parker, Albert, 323
Parker, Fess, 334
Parker, Lonnie Blair, 37, 127
Parrot, Charles, 215
Parsons, Louella, 30
Pasha, Kalla, 175
Passion, 65, 338, 351, 356
Passion of Joan of Arc, The, 9
Pastime Theater, 163
Pathe, 35, 215, 235
Patinkin, Mandy, 187
Pay Day, 117-118
Penalty, The, 42
Penrod and Sam, 178
The People, Yes, 13
Percy, Eileen, 175
Perfect Flapper, The, 216
Perils of Pauline, The, 17
Peter Pan, 245-246, 280
Phantom of the Opera, The, 244, 279, 285-288
Philbin, Mary, 183, 287
Phillips, Carmen, 158, 175
"Phonofilm Demonstrated at McVicker's
   Theater", 220
Photodramatist's League, 76
Pickford, Jack, 20, 175
Pickford, Mary, 4, 20, 24, 39, 48, 55, 56, 64,
   65, 84, 89, 90, 91, 93, 120, 146, 175, 189,
   190, 201, 230, 231, 256, 283, 284, 325, 326
"Pictures that Show World War are a Risk", 63

Pilgrim, The, 165, 179, 196, 201
Pitts, Zasu, 170, 175, 253
Player, The, 154, 170
Pleasures of the Rich, 303-304
Plumes, 289
Poe, Edgar Allen, 66, 69
Popeye, 135
Poppy, 271
Post, Wiley, 327
Potters, The, 310, 338-339
Pouf Pouf, 76
Pound, Ezra, 126
Powder River, 208-210
Powell, Russ, 363
Powell, William, 257, 259
Power, Tyrone, 136, 350
Powers, Francis, 230
Prairie Years, The. See Abraham Lincoln: The
   Prairie Years
Prisoner of Zenda, 294
Private Izzy Murphy, 319
Prodigal Daughters, 165-166
"Producers Too Scared?", 134
Pryor, Richard, 56
Public Enemy, The, 298
Purviance, Edna, 53, 91, 197, 201, 202, 295

Queen Christina, 366
Queen of Sheba, The, 95-97
"Questionnaire, A", 179-180
Quinn, Anthony, 187
Quotation Walk, 7
Quo Vadis, 265

Radio-Keith-Orpheum (RKO), x
Rainbow Trail, The, 264
Ralston, Esther, 299, 346
Ralston, Jobyna, 215, 361
Rambova, Natacha, 86, 121
Randolf, Anders, 323
Randolph Theater, 25, 46, 51, 52, 53, 54, 71,
   90, 208, 265, 337
Ranking, Arthur, 250
Rappe, Virginia, 5, 33, 176
Raskle, Barney, 351
Ravinia, 369, 370
Rawlinson, Herbert, 275
Ray, Charles, 4, 49, 50, 120, 143, 234, 306, 307
"Reason that Rogers is Leaving Pictures", 106

Red Kimona, The, 349-350
Reeves, Alice, 31
Reid, Florence. *See* Davenport, Dorothy
Reid, Wallace, 5, 25, 26, 71, 106, 107, 109, 110, 114, 148, 149, 152, 155, 157, 160, 250, 300
Reilly, Gina, 31
Reinhardt, Max, 65
Reisner, Charles "Buck", 175, 197, 283
Remembrance Rock, 6, 7
Remembrance Rock, 10
Rent Free, 109
"Report Calls Picture a Record Breaker in Amount of Film", 87
Revillon Freres Corporation, 142
Rex—King of the Wild Horses, 215
Reynold, Vera, 211
Reynolds, Lynn, 143, 264
Rialto Theater, 77, 117, 318
Rich, Irene, 189
Rickard, Tex, 93, 94, 194
" 'Ride 'Em Cowboy' Always Goes", 216-217
Riders of the Purple Sage, 70, 263-264
Ridgeway, Fritzi, 175
Riegel, Vernon, 130
Riesner, Dean, 175
Rin-Tin-Tin, 4, 9, 153, 311, 318, 326-327
Riviera Theater, 127, 249
Roach, Hal, 197, 206, 207, 223, 224, 235
Road to Mandalay, The, 353
Roaring Twenties, The, 29
Roberts, Theodore, 71, 166
Robin Hood. See Douglas Fairbanks in Robin Hood
Robinson Crusoe, 267
Rockett, Al and Ray, 236, 237, 238, 240
Rodenbach, Clark, 12
Rodwsky, Dagmar, 124
Rogers, Will, 14, 28, 29, 54, 55, 61, 106, 121, 151, 175, 198, 199, 277, 310, 327, 328
Roland, Gilbert, 354
Romeo and Juliet, 183
Romola, 260
Roosevelt Theater, 42, 98, 112, 121, 127, 132, 135, 137, 177, 236, 239, 240, 252, 254, 260, 263, 267, 271, 274, 281, 284, 286, 287, 293, 294, 302, 304, 307, 309, 314, 322, 324, 325, 348, 349, 352, 354, 363, 366
Rootabaga Pigeons, 10

Ropin' Fool, The, 121
Rosenthal, Boris, 31
Rose Theater, 19, 31, 49, 104, 138, 143, 180
Rosher, Charles, 89
Rosita, 189-190
Rothacker, Watterson R., 120
Running Wild, 350-351
Russell, George, 213
Russell, J. Gordon, 291
Russell, John, 230
Ruth, "Babe" (George Herman), 79, 80, 81, 156
Rutledge, Anne, 238, 239

Sabatini, Rafael, 333
Safety Last, 171-173
Sailor-Made Man, A, 115, 131
Saint Joan, 247
St. John, Al "Fuzzy", 129
St. Johns, Adela Rogers, 250, 349
Sally of the Sawdust, 271-273, 310
Salomy Jane, 178
Salvation Hunters, The, 231, 256-257, 295
Sandburg, Lilian Steichen, ix, 2, 6, 8, 16
Sandburg birthplace, 6
Sanger, Margaret, 128
Santschi, Tom, 313, 348
Sarg, Tony, 87
Saunders, Jacqueline, 250
Sawing a Woman in Half, 131
"Says *Foolish Wives* Cost a lot of Money", 87
Scarface (1932), 312, 363
Scarlet Letter, The, 343-344
Schenck, Joseph, 110, 111, 335, 342
Schildkraut, Joseph, 128
Schipa, Carlo, 284
Schnitzler, Arthur, 47, 48
Schoedsack, Ernest B., 347, 348
Schulberg, B. P., 259
Scoffer, The, 42, 43
Scott, Carrie, 222
Sea Beast, The, 299-300
Sea Gull, The, 295
Sea Hawk, The, 346
Seastrom (Sjöström), Victor, 202, 203, 249, 343
Sea Wolf, The, 321
Sedgewick, Edward, 285, 318
Seigmen, George, 182, 183
Seitz, George, 302
Select, 20

Selig Polyscope Company, 26, 279
Semon, Larry, 174, 235, 279, 280
Senate Theater, 104, 276
Sennett, Mack, 30, 36, 40, 77, 98-99, 114, 118, 119, 158, 164, 197, 198, 233, 235
Sergeant York, 346
Seven Chances, 261
Seventh Heaven, 361-362
Shannon, Effie, 273
Shannon, Frank, 211
Shaw, George Bernard, 106, 247
Shearer, Norma, 248, 300
Sheik, The, xi, 44, 97-98, 124, 152, 160
Sheik's Wife, The, 124
"Sheiks as They Ride Through the Movies", 123
Shepherd of the Hills, 41
Sherlock Holmes, 266
Sherlock, Jr., 217-218
Sherman, Lowell, 38, 112
Sherry, J. Barney, 191
Sherwood, Robert E., 122, 123, 266
She's a Sheik, 123
Short, Gertrude, 110
Shotwell, Marie, 351
Shoulder Arms, 52, 93, 196,
Shriek of Araby, The, 123, 124, 158
Shumway, Lee, 319
Sign of the Rose, The, 105
Silent Call, The, 119-120, 143
Sills, Milton, 171, 187
Silvers, Louis, 37
Simon, Simone, 361
"Sinclair Lewis and Film", 144
Singer Jim McKee, 212-213
"Sins of the World" series, 349
Siskel, Gene, 11
Six Days, 184-185
Sjöström, Victor. *See* Seastrom, Victor
Slabs of the Sunburnt West, 10, 59
Sloman, Edward, 18
Smalley, Phillippe, 187
Smallwood, Ray, 86
Smith, Al, 150
Smith, Charles, 335
Smith, Clifford S., 213
Smith, Gladys. *See* Pickford, Mary
Smith, Wallace, 324, 325
Smythe, Addison, 19
Socialist Party, 93, 100

Society Sensation, A, 208
Somborn, Herbert K., 262
Son of the Sheik, 123, 309-310
Sorrows of Satan, 344-345
Souls for Sale, 154, 170
South of Suva, 134, 135-136
Spanish Lancer, The, 190
Sparrows, 325-326
Speedy, 3351
Spielberg, Steven, 245, 266
Spoilers, The, 178
Spoor, George K., 45
Sprotte, Bett, 189
Stage 28, 285
Staking His Life, 20-22
Stallings, Laurence, 289, 329, 330
"Stanislavsky Tells About Motion Pictures and Their Faults", 161
Stanislavsky, Constantin, xi, 161, 162
Stanton, Richard, 31
Starr, Frances, 93, 94
"Stars in Unfamiliar Makeup", 300-301
State-Lake Theater, 146, 303, 311, 327, 329, 330
Stedman, Lincoln, 319
Stedman, Myrtle, 185, 187, 227
Steichen, Lilian. *See* Sandburg, Lilian Steichen
Stereoscopic Films, 224-225
Sterling, Ford, 175, 249, 299, 303
Stevens, Charles, 323
Stevens, George, 10
Stevenson, Robert Louis, 120-121, 167
Steward, Roy, 326
Stewart, Anita, 176
Stewart, George, 176
Stewart, James, 361
Stiller, Mauritz, 304, 323
Stockdale, Carl, 198
Stolen Sweeties, 241
Stone, Sharon, 136
" 'Story's the Thing' Says One in the Work", 156
Stowe, Harriet Beecher, 206
Standing, Wyndham, 282
Strangers Beware, 19
Stratford Theater, 242, 243
Street of Forgotten Men, The, 275, 297
Strong, Austin, 361
Strongheart, 9, 119, 270, 318
Strong Man, The, 347

Strothers, Bill, 173
Studio, 129
Suds, 90, 325
Sullivan, C. Gardner, 291
Sunrise, 229
Sunset Blvd., 154, 170
Sutherland, Edward, 310
Suzanna, 164, 165
Swain, Mack, 277
Swanson, Gloria, 4, 166, 173, 176, 183, 184, 222, 262, 263, 341
Sweet, Blanche, 170, 171
Swickard, Joseph, 280
Swim, Girl, Swim, 357-358
Swiss Family Robinson, The, 267

"Talking Pictures Have Appeared in New York", 219-220
Talmadge, Constance, 48, 110, 120
Talmadge, Natalie, 110, 111, 120, 126
Talmadge, Norma, 24, 38, 85, 110, 111, 120, 207, 354
Tashman, Lilyan, 222
Tavernier, Albert, 259
Taxi Dancer, The, 342
Taylor, Estelle, 176, 316
Taylor, Robert, 85
Taylor, Sam, 173, 215
Taylor, William Desmond, 108, 113, 114, 164, 197
Teague, Frances, 230
Tearle, Conway, 186
Tellegen, Lou, 313
Tell It to the Marines, 339-340
Tell Me Why, 128
Temple, Shirley, 226
Temptress, The, 323-324
Ten Commandments, The, 276-277
Terhune, Albert Payson, 103
Texans, The, 26
Thalberg, Irving, 182, 251
That Royle Girl, 272, 284-285
"There's an Art in Choosing a Pie", 31
Thibault, Jacques Anatole, 112
Thief of Bagdad, The, xii, 29, 200, 241-243, 323
Things to Come, 241
Thin Man, The, 257
Thirty Days, 157
This Land of Opportunity, 19

Thomas, A. E., 157, 225
Thomas, Elton. *See* Fairbanks, Douglas
Thomas, Olive, 20
Thornby, Robert 125
Those Who Dance, 234
Three Ages, The, 190-191
Three Bad Men, 229, 313
"Three Dimensional Photography", 45
Three Godfathers, The, 312
Three Jumps Ahead, 163
Three Musketeers, The, 84, 91
Three Weeks, 185
Three's a Crowd, 356-357
Through Darkest Hollywood with Gun and Camera, 123
Tiger's Cub, 17, 18
Tilbury, Zeffie, 86
Tivoli Theater, 127, 249
To Have and Have Not, 312
Tol'able David, 101-102, 191
Tolstoy, Leo, xi, 366
"Tom Mix Passes Through Chicago", 72
Tonight or Never, 166
Tony, xi, 26, 36, 143, 228-229
"Tony Sarg's Aims and Efforts", 87
Too Many Kisses, 257-259, 321
"Too Much Sex Stuff in the Movies", 47-49
Too Much Speed, 71
Torrence, Ernest, 245, 299, 308
Torrent, The, 304-305
"To Test a Picture's Worth", 99
Totheroh, Roland E., 117
Tramp, Tramp, Tramp, 347
Trap, The, 124
Traumnovelle, 47
Trevor, Norman, 346
Trimble, Laurence, 271
Trouble in Paradise, 65
Trowbridge, J. T., 211
Truffaut, Francois, 8
Tucker, George Loane, 42, 43, 89
Tumbleweeds, 290-291
Turner, Florence, 282
Turner, George Kibbe, 275
Turpin, Ben, 30, 77, 123, 158, 176, 253
Tuttle, Frank, 221-222, 299, 320
Twain, Mark, xi, 28, 67, 106, 122, 333
Twisted Trails, 227-228
"Two Anti-Red Films", 19-20

"Two Current Films Up for Comparison", 145
"Two Orphans, The", 127

UFA, 336, 356
"Uncensored Movies", 198-199
Uncle Tom's Cabin, 205, 206
Underworld, 174, 231, 363-365
Uneasy Enemy, An, 32
Unholy Three, The, 113, 352
United Artists, 90, 201, 284, 290, 323, 326, 335,
Universal Film Manufacturing, 78, 79, 88
Universal Pictures Corporation, 82, 87, 182, 208, 279, 286, 317, 318
University of Chicago, 21, 74
University of Southern California, 357
Unknown, The, 352-353
Urson, Frank, 71

"Vagaries of Censorship", 150
Valentino, Rudolph, 4, 23, 44, 63, 64, 85, 86, 97-98, 112, 113, 121, 136, 138, 149, 151, 186, 198, 208, 282, 293, 294, 309, 318, 324
"Vamp of the Movies Replaced by Mothers", 85
Vanishing American, The, 301-302
Variety, 313-315, 338, 351, 356
"Victor Seastrom in Hollywood", 202-203
Vidor, Florence, 170, 181, 234
Vidor, King, 114, 170, 181, 251, 288, 289, 290, 307, 308, 333, 334
"Visit with Chaplin", 58
"Visit with Josef von Sternberg, A", 230-232
Vitaphone, 315-316, 365
"Vitaphone Demonstrated", 315, 316
von Eltz, Theodore, 271, 350
von Harbou, Thea, 351
von Seyffertitz, Gustav, 326
"Von Sternberg to Work with Chaplin", 295
von Sternberg, Josef, 9, 174, 230-232, 256, 295, 364, 365
von Stroheim, Erich, 3, 87, 88, 89, 170, 182, 233, 251-255, 280, 281, 287
Vroom, Frederick, 335

W.M. Productions, 22
Wagner, George, 230
Walker, Johnnie, 170, 171
Wallace, Gen. Lew, 296, 297
Wallace, John, 323

Wallace, Ramsey, 250
Walsh, George, 170, 189
Walsh, Raoul, 29, 328, 330
Walthall, Henry B., 361, 370
Walton, Gladys, 113, 146
Wanderer of the Wasteland, 221
Ward, Artemus, 106
Warner, H. B., 183, 224
Warner, Jack, 331
Warner Brothers Pictures, 33, 282, 283, 315, 316, 319, 327, 365
War Years, The. See Abrham Lincoln: The War Years
Washburn, Bryant, 176, 280
Washington Park, 95
Waterloo Bridge, 362
Watson, Thomas, 127
Way Down East, 36, 37, 41, 88, 101, 127, 308
Wayne, John, 298, 313
Wayne, Maude, 176
Way of All Flesh, The, 355-356
Webb, Millard, 299
Weber, Lois, 82, 83, 104
Wegener, Paul, 86
Welles, Orson, 233
Wellesley, Charles,
Wellman, William, 360
Wenders, Wim, 343
West, Claire, 176
What Do Men Want?, 104
Whatever Happened to Baby Jane?, 154, 170
What Happened to Rosa, 36
What Price Glory?, 289, 328-330, 360, 361
Whatsoever a Man Soweth, 269
What the Ocean Hides, 24
Wheat, Larry, 176
"When Abraham Lincoln Arrives at Roosevelt Theater", 236-237
While London Sleeps, 326-327
White, Pearl, 17
White Fang, 270-271
Whiteman, Paul, 342
White Oak, 100-101
White Rose, The, 185-186
White Sheik, The, 123
White Sister, The, 191
Whitman, Walt, 344, 345
Who's Loony Now?, 68, 69
"Why Scenarios Go Wrong", 76

Why Worry?, 194-195
Wildness of Youth, The, 145, 146
Wild Oats, 128
Wild Strawberries, 203
Williams, Ben Ames, 25
Williams, Bert, 104, 310
Williams, Earle, 275
Williams, Kathlyn, 152, 170, 171
Willis, Leon, 311
"Will Rogers Lassos Motion Picture Fans", 121
"Will Rogers, Our Unofficial Ambassador
  Abroad", 327-328
Wilson, George, 319
Wilson, Lois, 46, 167, 169, 176, 211, 230, 302
Wilson, Tom, 311, 312
Windsor, Claire, 104, 112, 170, 171, 331
Wine, 226-227,
Wings, 360-361
Winning of Barbara Worth, The, 41, 324-325
Wise Kid, The, 113
Without Benefit of Clergy, 141
"Without the Cane and Derby", 58
"With Will Rogers", 60
Wizard of Oz, The (1925), 279-280
Wizard of Oz, The (1939), 362
Woman of Affairs, A, 366
Woman of Paris, A, 201-202
Woman of the Sea, A, 295
Wonder Man, A, 74
Wood, Sam, 319
Woodruff, Bert, 302
Woods, Walter, 57
Woods Theater, 37, 95, 167, 169, 229, 296,
  297
"World of Comedies, The", 234-235
Worsley, Wallace, 188
Wray, Jane, 250
Wright, Harold Bell, xi, 41, 324, 325
Wyler, William, 295

Young Rajah, The, 151

Zallner, Arthur, 19
Zaza, 183-184
Ziegfeld Follies, The, 104, 106, 274, 310, 328,
  350
Ziegfeld, Florenz, 310, 320
Ziegfeld Theater, 67, 68, 86
Zukor, Adolph, 344

Carl Sandburg (1878-1967) was born in Galesburg, Illinois. An accomplished and distinctly American writer, Sandburg published more than 40 books including volumes of poetry, children's books, and a six-volume biography of Abraham Lincoln. *The War Years*, Sandburg's last four volumes of his Lincoln biography, won the Pulitzer Prize in 1940 for history; a second Pulitzer came in 1951 for the collection *Complete Poems*. His other poetry books include *Chicago Poems* (1916), *The People, Yes* (1936), and *Harvest Poems, 1910-1960* (1960). Through his love for folk music, Sandburg traveled the country and personally collected numerous indigenous ballads and songs, which he published in the volume *The American Songbag* (1927). Sandburg also wrote children's tales, including *Rootabaga Stories* (1922). His non-fiction includes *The Chicago Race Riots* (1919), *Mary Lincoln, Wife and Widow* (1932, with P.M. Angle), and an autobiography, *Always the Young Strangers* (1953). Sandburg's only novel, *Remembrance Rock*, was published in 1948.

Arnie Bernstein, editor of this volume, is the author of *Hollywood on Lake Michigan: 100 Years of Chicago and the Movies*, which won a 1st place American Regional History Publishing Award for the Midwest region. A film historian and writer of articles, fiction, comedy, CD-ROMs, and television scripts, Bernstein is a long-time admirer of Sandburg and silent movies. He lives and writes in Chicago.

Photo by Holly Pluard. The 1973 charcoal sketch of Carl Sandburg by Ed Weiss hangs in the Chicago Authors Room of the Chicago Public Library's Harold Washington Library in downtown Chicago.

Also by Arnie Bernstein

Winner of an American Regional History Publishing Award
1st Place—Midwest!

Hollywood on Lake Michigan:
100 Years of Chicago and the Movies

by Arnie Bernstein

with foreword by *Soul Food* writer/director George Tillman, Jr.

This engaging history and street guide finally gives Chicago and Chicagoans due credit for their prominent role in moviemaking history, from the silent era to the present. With trivia, special articles, historic and contemporary photos, film profiles, anecdotes, and exclusive interviews with dozens of personalities, including Studs Terkel, Roger Ebert, Gene Siskel, Dennis Franz, Harold Ramis, Joe Mantegna, Bill Kurtis, Irma Hall, and Tim Kazurinsky.

0-9642426-2-1, December 1998, softcover, 364 pages, 80 photos, $15

From the back cover:

From the earliest film studios, when one out of every five movies was made in Chicago, to today's thriving independent film scene, the Windy City has been at the forefront of American moviemaking.

Blues Brothers. Within Our Gates. Hoop Dreams. The Gore-Gore Girls. My Best Friend's Wedding. Call Northside 777. His New Job. Henry: Portrait of a Serial Killer. They are all pieces in Chicago's rich film history.

Join writer/film historian Arnie Bernstein as he honors Chicago and Chicagoans for their active role in a century of filmmaking. Exclusive interviews with current directors, actors, writers, and other film professionals; visits to movie locations and historical sites; and fascinating tales from the silent era are all a part of this spirited and definitive look at our "Hollywood on Lake Michigan."

From alleyways to the lakefront, from the 'L' tracks to suburban streets, Chicago is a sprawling backlot of cinematic creativity and stories. See the Windy City like you've never seen it before—both on screen and on the set—in the first book ever to chronicle the engaging history of Chicago and the movies.

Ghosts and Graveyards

Chicago Haunts: Ghostlore of the Windy City
by Ursula Bielski
From ruthless gangsters to restless mail order kings, from the Fort Dearborn Massacre to the St. Valentine's Day Massacre, the phantom remains of the passionate people and volatile events of Chicago history have made the Second City second to none in the annals of American ghostlore. Bielski captures over 160 years of this haunted history with her unique blend of lively storytelling, in-depth historical research, exclusive interviews, and insights from parapsychology. Called "a masterpiece of the genre," "a must-read," and "an absolutely first-rate-book" by reviewers, *Chicago Haunts* continues to earn the praise of critics and readers alike.
0-9642426-7-2, October 1998, softcover, 277 pages, 29 photos, $15

New!
More Chicago Haunts: Scenes from Myth and Memory
by Ursula Bielski
More spooky glimpses into a city and its people haunted by their history in more ways than one . . .
1-893121-04-6, October 2000, softcover, photos, $15

New!
Haunted Michigan: Recent Encounters with Active Spirits
by Reverend Gerald S. Hunter
"True ghost stories" you've never heard before, from Hunter's personal investigations.
1-893121-10-0, October 2000, softcover, photos, $14

Graveyards of Chicago:
The People, History, Art, and Lore of Cook County Cemeteries
by Matt Hucke and Ursula Bielski
Ever wonder where Al Capone is buried? How about Clarence Darrow? Muddy Waters? Harry Caray? Or maybe Brady Bunch patriarch Robert Reed? And what really lies beneath home plate at Wrigley Field? *Graveyards of Chicago* answers these and other cryptic questions as it charts the lore and lure of Chicago's ubiquitous burial grounds. Like the livelier neighborhoods that surround them, Chicago's cemeteries are often crowded, sometimes weary, ever-sophisticated, and full of secrets. They are home not only to thousands of individuals who fashioned the city's singular culture and character, but also to impressive displays of art and architecture, landscaping and limestone, egoism and ethnic pride, and the constant reminder that although physical life must end for us all, personal note—and notoriety—last forever. Grab a shovel and tag along as Ursula Bielski and Matt Hucke unearth the legends and legacies that mark Chicago's silent citizens— from larger-than-lifers and local heroes, to clerics and comedians, machine mayors and machine-gunners.
0-9642426-4-8, November, 1999, softcover, 228 pages, 168 photos, $15

Regional Favorites

Used and abused. Straightened and channelized. Reversed and revered. But *never* ignored...
An Intimate Biography of the Heroic Creek that Chicago Made

New!

The Chicago River: A Natural and Unnatural History
by Libby Hill

When French explorers Jolliet and Marquette used the Chicago portage on their return trip from the Mississippi River, the Chicago River was but a humble, even sluggish, stream in the right place at the right time. That's the story of the making of Chicago. This is the *other* story—the story of the making and perpetual re-making of a river by everything from pre-glacial forces to the interventions of an emerging and mighty city. Author Libby Hill brings together years of original research and the contributions of dozens of experts to tell the Chicago River's epic tale from its conception in prehistoric glaciers to the glorious rejuvenation it's undergoing today, and every exciting episode in between.
1-893121-02-X, August 2000, softcover, photos, $16.95

> "Imagine reading a biography of your spouse or best friend, and being surprised and delighted at the biographer's fresh take on somebody you thought you knew pretty well. Libby Hill has done that with this book, reintroducing me to a body of water I thought I knew, surprising me with new facts, and delighting me with new ways of thinking about the facts I thought I had mastered."
> —*David Jones, Community Planner, Friends of the Chicago River*

> "Libby Hill's book is a valuable resource for students and history buffs. It is a "must read" for anyone who wants to know how or why the course of the Chicago River was reversed. I highly recommend it."
> —*Peggy Bradley, Metropolitan Water Reclamation District of Greater Chicago*

> "It may not be much of a river, as rivers go, but what a history! From prehistoric glaciers to contemporary Deep Tunnel, Libby tells the whole fascinating story of the Chicago River with great enthusiasm, eloquence, and factual accuracy. Anyone who reads this book will never again take our hometown stream for granted. It's a must read for all Chicago buffs."
> —*Bill Hinchliff, veteran docent for the Chicago Architecture Foundation*

A Native's Guide to Chicago, 3rd Edition
by Sharon Woodhouse,
with expanded South Side coverage by Mary McNulty

Venture into the nooks and crannies of everyday Chicago with this unique, comprehensive budget guide. Over 400 pages of free, inexpensive, and unusual things to do in the Windy City make this the perfect resource for tourists, business travelers, visiting suburbanites, and resident Chicagoans. Called the "best guidebook for locals" in New City newspaper's 1999 "Best of Chicago" issue!
0-9642426-0-5, January 1999, softcover, 438 pages, photos, maps, $12.95

Order Form

The Movies Are: Carl Sandburg's Film _____ @ $17.95 = _____
Hollywood on Lake Michigan _____ @ $15.00 = _____
Chicago Haunts: Ghostlore of the Windy City _____ @ $15.00 = _____
More Chicago Haunts _____ @ $15.00 = _____
Haunted Michigan _____ @ $14.00 = _____
Graveyards of Chicago _____ @ $15.00 = _____
The Chicago River _____ @ $16.95 = _____
A Native's Guide To Chicago _____ @ $12.95 = _____

Subtotal: _____
Less Discount: _____
New Subtotal: _____
8.75% tax for Illinois Residents: _____
Shipping: _____
TOTAL: _____

Discounts when you order multiple copies!
2 books—10% off total, 3-4 books —20% off, 5-9 books—25% off, 10+ books—40% off

Low shipping fees
$2 for the first book and $.50 for each additional book, with a maximum charge of $5.

Order by mail, phone, fax, or e-mail.
All of our books have a no-hassle, 100% money back guarantee.

Name_____

Address_____

City_____**State**_____**Zip**_____

Please enclose check, money order, or credit card information.

Visa/Mastercard#_____**Exp.** _____

Signature_____

4650 North Rockwell Street
Chicago, Illinois 60625
773/583-7800
773/583-7877 (fax)
order@lakeclaremont.com
www.lakeclaremont.com

Lake Claremont Press Books in Print

The Chicago River: A Natural and Unnatural History
by Libby Hill

Graveyards of Chicago:
The People, History, Art, and Lore of Cook County Cemeteries
by Matt Hucke and Ursula Bielski

Chicago Haunts: Ghostlore of the Windy City, Revised Edition
by Ursula Bielski

Hollywood on Lake Michigan: 100 Years of Chicago and the Movies
by Arnie Bernstein, with foreword by writer/director of *Soul Food*, George Tillman, Jr.,

A Native's Guide to Chicago, 3rd Edition
by Sharon Woodhouse, with South Side coverage by Mary McNulty

A Native's Guide to Chicago's South Suburbs
by Christina Bultinck and Christy Johnston-Czarnecki

A Native's Guide to Chicago's Western Suburbs
by Laura Mazzuca Toops and John W. Toops, Jr.

A Native's Guide to Chicago's Northwest Suburbs
by Martin A. Bartels

A Native's Guide to Chicago's Northern Suburbs
by Jason Fargo

New and Forthcoming Titles

More Chicago Haunts: Scenes from Myth and Memory
by Ursula Bielski (October 2000)

Haunted Michigan: Recent Encounters with Active Spirits
by Reverend Gerald Hunter (October 2000)

Ticket to Everywhere: The Best of *Detours* Travel Column
by Dave Hoekstra, with foreword by Studs Terkel (October 2000)

Literary Chicago: A Book Lover's Tour of the Windy City
by Gregory Holden (October 2000)

A Native's Guide to Northwest Indiana
by Mark Skertic (Spring 2001)

Great Chicago Fires
by David Cowan (Spring 2001)